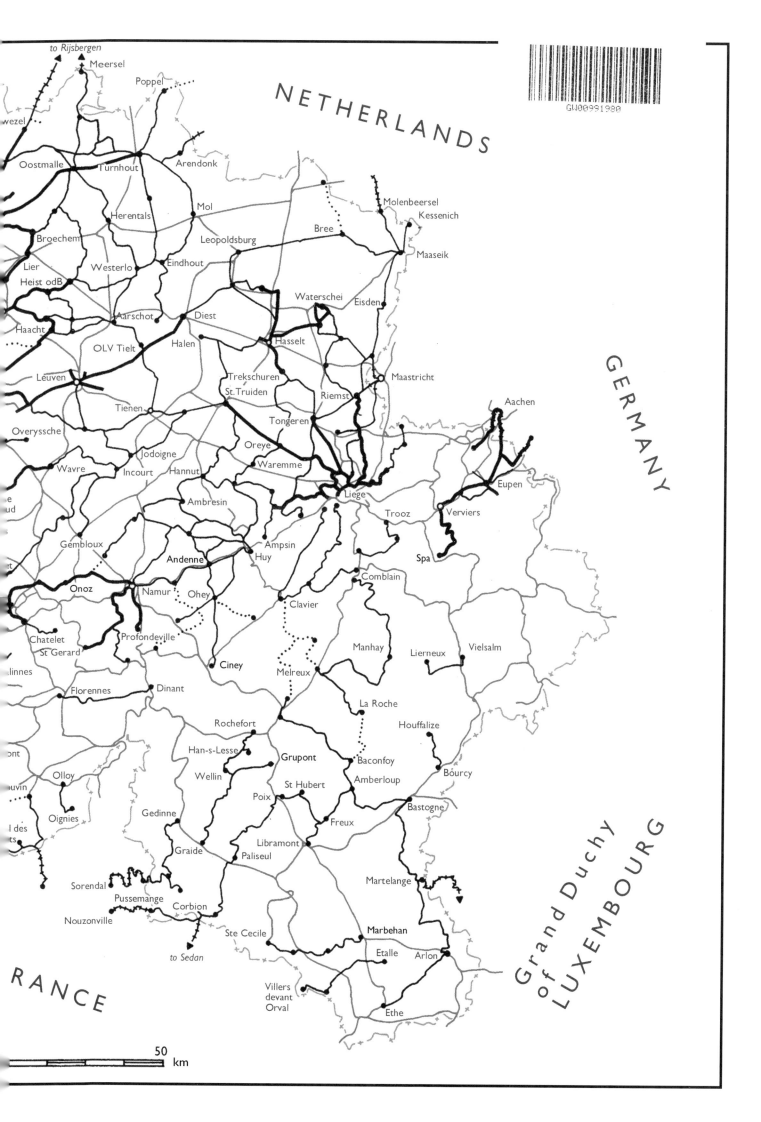

NETHERLANDS

GERMANY

Grand Duchy of LUXEMBOURG

FRANCE

to Rijsbergen
Meersel
Poppel
wezel
Oostmalle
Turnhout
Arendonk
Molenbeersel
Kessenich
Herentals
Mol
Bree
Broechem
Leopoldsburg
Maaseik
Lier
Westerlo
Eindhout
Heist odB
Waterschei
Eisden
Haacht
Aarschot
Diest
Hasselt
OLV Tielt
Halen
Maastricht
Leuven
Trekschuren
St.Truiden
Riemst
Tienen
Tongeren
Overyssche
Oreye
Jodoigne
Waremme
Wavre
Incourt
Hannut
Aachen
Ambresin
Liege
Eupen
Gembloux
Ampsin
Huy
Trooz
Verviers
Andenne
Spa
Onoz
Namur
Ohey
Comblain
Chatelet
Profondeville
Clavier
St Gerard
Ciney
Manhay
Lierneux
Vielsalm
linnes
Florennes
Dinant
Melreux
La Roche
Houffalize
Rochefort
Han-s-Lesse
Grupont
Baconfoy
Olloy
Wellin
St Hubert
Amberloup
Bourcy
Poix
Bastogne
Oignies
Gedinne
Freux
des
Graide
Libramont
ts
Paliseul
Martelange
Sorendal
Pussemange
Corbion
Marbehan
Nouzonville
Ste Cecile
Etalle
Arlon
to Sedan
Villers
devant
Orval
Ethe

50 km

The Vicinal Story
Light Railways in Belgium 1885 - 1991

by

W.J.K. Davies

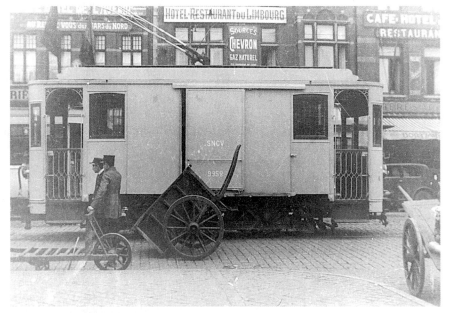

ABOVE The postman cometh - or useth theSNCV anyway. An unusual shot of a motor luggage van on postal duties outside Oostende (the late K E Hartley)

PREVIOUS PAGE Unique to Limburg were the two Type 23 Garratt locomotives for the coal traffic. Here one is seen at Riemst on a goods train during the war. (collection P Roovers)

Cover Picure
The village of Roux is one of the more attractive settlements in the Charleroi area and showed some typical trackwork for the Vicinal network in the area. In September 1976 SM 9133 (ex-S 10075) was on route 41 heading for Charleroi. (M. R. Taplin)

LRTA

Published by Light Rail Transit Association
9 Hinderwell Road, Scarborough, YO12 4BD

ISBN 0-948106-32-8

Designed by Just My Type, Gloucester GL4 4AE
Printed by Delmar Press Ltd, Nantwich, Cheshire CW5 5LS

The SNCV in its glory. An express train on the Enghien line just before the First World War: Type 18 locomotive and some of the, then new, vestibuled 4-wheeled coaches. (SNCV)

CONTENTS

Preface to the 2nd Edition

It is now over 20 years since the first edition of this history was published and since that time many changes have taken place. Most importantly, the Societé Nationale des Chemins de Fer Vicinaux (SNCV) has been wound up, for political reasons and it therefore seems sensible to terminate its story at that point.

Much new and amended information also has come to light, particularly with regard to the minutiae of equipment and the urban tram networks, and it seems desirable to take these into account where possible - but only where possible. Chronicling such a disparate organisation as the SNCV will always provide problems because of the sheer size of its network and the variety of enthusiast interests that are involved....electric trams and their features; rural light railways; bus routes; social and political factors which often overlay the technical ones more common to enthusiast study. The Societé was unique in Europe in the breadth of its original concept and operation, so a general history can only skim the surface. If you want to find out details of urban trackage in Gent and the minutiae of route numberings and indicator boards in Bruxelles; or the layout of stations on the Houfallize - Bourcy line in the Ardennes; or the detailed history of a particular variety of 4-wheeled electric tramcar.... then you will have to look to the increasing number of specialist publications appearing in both French and Flemish. Fortunately the LRTA is prepared to sponsor a more detailed study of the equipment, which is of general interest, and so we have separated that into a volume of its own; Dirk Eveleens Maarse has made a particular study of SNCV stock and I am happy to leave that aspect entirely to him and his collaborators.

This volume will cover the overall history and geography with just enough general background on the equipment so that it can be placed in historical context and can be broadly identified in photographs. The original notes are thus still relevant. The SNCV is such a vast subject that anyone trying to sort out even its rail operations will inevitably run into a host of problems; for an organisation which, at its peak, ran some 6000 km of track, owned about 3000 units of motive power and survived two world wars, it can hardly be otherwise. Four problems arise at once, one general and three concerned with details:

(1) Firstly the Belgian term, "Capital" though fundamental to the concept of the SNCV, may well be unfamiliar in Britain. Briefly, the SNCV, when it planned a line, was effectively applying to be able to spend a previously agreed sum of money (the Capital) to be contributed by state, provinces and local communes in specified proportions. This Capital in turn underwrote the authorising documents and was listed under a unique number in the Societé's register. Within it, extra sections of line, modifications, additions to stock, etc, could be authorised from time to time and subsumed within the Capital by adjusting the amount subscribed - in practice inevitably increasing it. The SNCV normally used the term "authorised' when referring to the success of its own applications. The term "concession" was usually employed to mean the granting to a private company of permission to operate one or more Capitaux,

or parts thereof, for a fixed period of time. Because all SNCV lines were traced throughout their life by their appropriate Capital number, I have used this as the major identification symbol. A consolidated list of capitaux appears in Appendix 1

(2) Quoted distances differ widely with the source and the date because lines were modified, extended or cut back, and because often the authorised length did not agree with the real thing. One has to decide on some ruling. I have taken the authorised distances as quoted by the SNCV just prior to World War 1 and, for subsequent lines, the authorised length at or soon after original completion of the appropriate Capital. Where this differs from an operational length, it is usually because the line concerned ran for some distance over tracks common to another Capital already in existence, and where this is known it is given. Intermediate distances, where given, are "real" ones, normally as set out in closure information in SNCV reports.

(3) Dates are a perennial hazard and even to quote them on such a lavish scale ensures that there will always be some incorrect ones. Closure dates are comparatively easy, although even the SNCV is not consistent in indicating whether the date quoted is that of the last day of service or the following day; however, the difference is minimal in the case of passenger services, and "official" closure dates for goods traffic are notional in any case! There is also some chance of confusion since it is easy to assume that, where a bus service over a former tramway route started on a certain date, the rail service necessarily finished the previous working day. This was not always so; sometimes there was a lapse of years. Opening dates, unless otherwise indicated, are those recorded officially by the SNCV - but sections of line were, in practice, often in use before their official opening, while occasionally there was a gap between official and "real" opening; where local historians indicate these they have been included but not guaranteed! As regards dates of authorisation, these are even more confusing at times since three different ones are often quoted (and often without indication as to which of the three they refer to): date agreed by the government, date signed by royal decree (Arreté Royal) and date of publication in the 'Moniteur Belge'. In the majority of cases I have quoted the Arreté Royal which was that preferred by the SNCV; very occasionally the 'Moniteur Belge' date has had to be used; there was usually about a week's difference.

(4) As to place-names, with many having names (some similar and some very different) in two languages, not to mention spellings which have changed over the years and other versions which are traditionally used by many British people, the historian's task is very hard. As a general rule, I have tried to use the name in common use within its area, and the LRTA, who are the publishers of this book, have asked that this be taken to its logical conclusion, including modern spellings, so that the story can be related to modern maps and railway timetables, for example. And so, while I would have preferred the more familiar East

Flanders, West Flanders and Antwerp, the book will refer to Oostvlaanderen, Westvlaanderen and Antwerpen. Readers will therefore find Flemish names paramount in Vlaanderen, Antwerpen and Limburg, and French names emphasised in Hainaut, Namur, Liége and Luxembourg. As for Brabant, caught squarely in the middle, I have tried to give both names wherever possible on their first or sometimes second occurrence. At this point it needs to be pointed out that dual versions of a name are written as A/B while the format A (B) implies that B is a location within A. As for Bruxelles, to duplicate every location name, including street names, would use up much precious space, and I have decided that use of the French form alone is generally adequate, especially since they are probably more familiar to British visitors. For the rest of Brabant, strongly Flemish areas are given Flemish names, but the French forms are probably used more often. Although company names are left in their original form, the modern spellings are the norm in the text. I cannot guarantee 100 per cent consistency.

It is also convenient to mention here that, while strict adherence to language conventions would have required all Flemish references to the SNCV to be given as Naamloze Maatschappi van Buurtspoorwegan (NMVB) (and German ones as Nationale Kleinbahn Gesellschaft (NKG), this would impose an unreasonable burden on the reader. Therefore, wherever we are in Belgium, the text will refer to the SNCV, or the Vicinal or the Société , and the name of the modern main-line railway undertaking will appear as SNCB, and never as NMBS. There are two further points to note. I have refrained from quoting Capital costs on two grounds: firstly, that they are irrelevant after this lapse of time, and secondly that they changed very frequently for even the smaller lines as modifications were made or equipment changed. The second point is that to provide a comprehensive index would have been an enormous task. I have, instead, provided a sectional list at the head of each chapter and a tabulated summary of concessions to include major references, while in a later volume Dirk will deal with rolling stock, etc, in numerical sequence.

Acknowledgements

The first edition of this book, while I took responsibility for any errors and omissions, was really a collaborative work - and, happily, could not have been written without help not only from British sources but from both the Flemish and Walloon cultures (in strict alphabetical sequence of course!). That gratitude is reiterated here since, while any "first' history has mistakes, it is pleasing to see how much of the original information has survived intact. Six people in particular, two from each "area", provided help, support and encouragement over a long period. In Belgium I must acknowledge above all the help and kindness of Edmond de Backer, a longtime friend and correspondent and an indefatigable sorter-out of problems and of his brother Paul an acknowledged expert on all aspects of the SNCV. From the Flemish side the late Inspecteur Van de Eede of the SNCV provided many official documents and the late Engineer Debot, well-known to many Belgian enthusiasts, carried on a voluminous correspondence for many years and provided me with many drafts of his unpublished memoirs; I am only sorry that all the anecdotes therein could not see the light of day. In England, without the late John Price and his invaluable field notebooks, much of the modern material would have been lost. Three others helped very substantially; in Belgium, the then commandant Pierre Roovers sorted out many errors and provided new information to fill in gaps and has done so again; in Britain the late Geoff Baddeley did the same while the late Jack Wyse took on the overall editing task. Others were very helpful and even this revised addition reflects their valuable contributions: Monseigneur Cammaerts, Mm van Campenhoudt, Mativa, Hausmann, the late Mm Delmotte of Nangis and Desbarax of Bruxelles, Inspecteur Watelet of the SNCV; in Britain, B Y Williams and J W Smith. The current edition adds Dirk Eveleens Maarse and through him the work of D DeVolder, and in England Mike Taplin to the list while Roger Smith has markedly improved on my amateur mapwork and Janet Taplin has undertaken the thankless job of production editor. Others like John Laker and Geoffery Skelsey offered excellent modern photographs and had there been room would have been gratefully received but there are plenty of modern publications but few really historic views. Lastly, although it is officially extinct, those items provided provided by the former SNCV are still acknowledged to it as (one hopes) a fitting memorial.

W J K Davies, Wheathampstead 2006.

General Key to Monochrome Map Symbols

PROVINCIAL & NATIONAL MAPS	DETAILED MONOCHROME MAPS
SNCV electric	SNCV new electric
SNCV non-electric	SNCV electric ex steam
SNCV not built	SNCV non-electric
main line railways	track shared with other operator
national borders	SNCV standard gauge
provincial borders	SNCV authorised but not built
	closed lines (non-electric/electric)
	connecting light railway or tramway
	main line railway
	national borders
	provincial borders

Introduction: The Real SNCV

There is a problem in trying to write a history of a large and disparate organisation such as the SNCV with a hundred years of development and change behind it. In all the dates and the lists and the route numbers, the reality tends to get lost - and there was a reality. If the current enthusiast's general picture of Belgium is one of rather dreary if efficient standardisation, of cream bogie tramcars grinding endlessly down long straight roads or grinding up narrow industrial streets, then that is true; but it is only part of the truth. Even if you had to be a tram fanatic to jump for joy as the umpty-fifth "Standard" bogie car or type "S" car hove into view or departed from a big city tram station, well, those had their own charm, and the charm was often of the landscape and the light railway ambience. For, except in the big cities, the SNCV lines were light railways first and foremost and, in their great years, they felt like light railways the world over. Why, as late as 1965, you could ride an Edwardian brake-third behind a snorting steam- hauled train as it wound its way beside the road up to Sprimont quarries - and if that was fun, what must it have been like in the old days when you could traverse the length and breadth of the country by such trains.

Certainly even then the stock you rode in was likely to be "standard", to the extent that meeting an odd "unskirted" engine at Hannesche or a Garratt nosing its way across the Limburg plain might have seemed a new discovery. Yet the lines were not standard; with their fifty or so different operating companies, each with its own foibles, and with the wide variations in lineside furniture, they couldn't be. In the Ardennes you could travel for miles through the hills and woods and not see a railway building; the "stations" were two-dimensional skeletons, complete arrays of loops and sidings laid out in the grass with the tallest structures being point levers and a sloping "tram halte" sign beside a rutted cart track. Yet elsewhere there were tall substantial station-houses which put many standard-gauge ones to shame, with spreading yards and workshops which thought nothing of building vehicles in quantity.

Even the "standard" trains with their 0-6-0 tram engines and dark green four-wheelers took on a special ambience as they slid quietly along the verges of dusty country lanes or ground noisily up into the squares of sleepy rural towns while their passengers straggled from the local bar. For, just as in other countries, the thrice-daily arrival of "the tram" was a real event for country folk, something to be savoured every time it happened. The electrics, too, had their moments: the massive "Titanic" cars pulling real mixed trains into Bruxelles, the long gaggles of four-wheeled trailers rocking and rolling along the sand dunes behind an Ostende - Blankenberghe two-axle motor, the "panoramic" cars of Spa, more usually and rudely known as the "boats" because of their pitching and rolling; they all provided a variety which can easily get lost in the serious records of modern enthusiast lore.

Besides, just think of the distances involved. The system at its peak covered well over 5000 km. In many countries it was half-jokingly said you could cross them without touching a main line. In Belgium the journey might have been a penance but it really was practicable. Just after the 1939-45 war, the SNCV even published timetables to prove it; they had staff holiday homes in the Ardennes and on the coast, and in those austere times the fare concessions for staff were really valuable. There was one route from Bruxelles, for instance, whereby you could get right out to the home at Wenduine on the North Sea. It involved five or six changes from electric to diesel and back again, and it took about eight hours as against two or three by the main line, but it was perfectly viable.

And the distances could lead to odd adventures. One former employee of the coastal operator SELVOP (see Appendix 2 for expansions of the initials used) recalls how, when they were short of power cars, the SNCV grudgingly found three bogie tramcars surplus to requirements at Charleroi - providing the coastal men went to fetch them. After various imbroglios (the local Groupe seemed loathe to lose the cars), they were run in convoy as far as Peronnes, boundary of the electric lines. From there a steam locomotive from Mons picked them up and towed them all along the rambling, industrialised route to Pecq - though not without further perturbations for the coastal crew, who were not accustomed to storming up and down such steep gradients and tended to apply the brakes at any opportunity. Setting out from Charleroi about 08.00 they staggered into Mons at 01.00 hrs the following morning in miserable drizzly rain. To the crew it was all foreign parts; as one of them rather unkindly said, "See Naples and die. That's all right, but I think I could have died without having to see Tertre" But, after a short stop, see Tertre they did, trailing along behind their steam locomotive through the grimy streets of Baudour, Tertre, Hautrage and Grandglise, and then out into the, thankfully more picturesque, countryside towards Tournai.

Alas the chateaux and woods didn't last. After reversing at Mainvault, they ground on through 'hills and quarries' to Tournai and on to the provincial boundary at Pecq - and that was the evening of the second day. Bright and early the next morning they were off again, behind a Vlaanderen Type 7 which dragged the cars all around the countryside by Bellegem, Moeskroen, Menen, Ieper and Dijksmuide to puff triumphantly into Oostende in the middle of the afternoon - only to be greeted by the Chef with ". ..they haven't got end-doors. They're no good to me; put them on that siding and we'll see what we can do next winter".

Ah well, you can't win them all and, alas, there is no space for most of the anecdotes which help to make a railway come alive. Still, when you do read of lines doing this or that, of heavy market traffic, or 'turned over to autorails' do try and envisage the reality: the long van trains setting out in the dark at 03.00 hrs to take smallholders into their nearest market town with produce, their huge acetylene headlamps throwing fitful gleams on the deserted roadside track; the hissing, steamy halts in darkened village squares as baskets of vegetables are dumped anywhere and new passengers join the fug round a pot-bellied coal stove under flickering oil lamps; the frantic turmoil at journey's end in the grey dawn as trains come in from all directions. Think a bit of the lone grumbling autorail as it pauses by the road in sunlight to pick up a farmer's wife or drop off a crate of chickens; or picture the bogie tram heading away out into the flat polders to an isolated turning loop by a couple of wind-blown trees and a red-brick farm illuminated by gleams of sun in a stormy sky. The reality of the SNCV was that it provided very personal local services and the same can be said of its successors even today, although almost everywhere it is a quivering bus that pauses where the tram once ran.

Chapter 1:   Before the Trams Came.

1.1   Introduction

The story of Belgian secondary transport is, in part, the story of 19th century Belgium itself - for its development was dependent largely on the nature of the land and its society. Belgium has always been a country with difficulties. Small as nations go, it is very heavily populated but with the population clustered in certain major conurbations, and with stretches of sparsely inhabited land even now. It has some coal, but most other minerals except clay and stone have to be imported. Geographically the country is a mix, from the reclaimed polders and sandy soils of the north and west, blending through alluvial uplands to the hilly, almost mountainous, woods and forests of the Belgian Ardennes in the south and southeast where the country abuts on France, Luxembourg and Germany. The coal, and hence the major heavy industry, lies mainly in a belt along the southern centre in Hainaut province.

A typical SNCV share certificate - albeit one apparently issued for raising additional capital, presumably for electrification
(SNCV)

Politically too, the country has always been divided. Trapped between Germany, the Netherlands and France, it is at once a natural gateway for east-west trade and, alas, a natural gateway also for any aggressor from almost any direction. Over the centuries this has had inevitable effects on its culture and population. The land has probably been fought over more often and more destructively than any other European state; indeed Belgium did not really emerge as a kingdom of its own until the 19th century. Because of its situation, it has also two almost distinct peoples - the Flemish-speaking northerners (Flemings or Flamands) who, in culture and language, relate closely to the Dutch; and the Walloons of the south and east, who are much more like the French and speak variants of that language. What happens in the middle is something of a mixup with the capital, Bruxelles/Brussel, as almost a neutral point. The country is divided into nine provinces of which four: Oost & West Vlaanderen, Antwerpen and Limburg are mainly Flemish; four: Hainaut, Liége, Namur and Luxembourg are largely Walloon; central Brabant is a real mixture.

This dual character has always been a problem when trying to ensure fair shares in the development of the country, and the geography does not help. The poor northern plains, used mainly for farming, were in the mid-19th century very backward and isolated because of transport problems and they were mainly Flemish. Industry was very much in the Walloon areas since the Belgian industrial revolution was based on coal; it was just as early and enthusiastic as the British one and just as messy in its legacy. Hence there was increasing contrast between the urban regions with their rapid development of railways, roads and canals, and the rural areas, where roads were often mere tracks or at best roughly paved with cobblestones (the dreaded pavé - or steenweg), and where local bulk transport away from the canal system was almost impossible. By the 1870s, therefore, there was strong political pressure for better transport, both socially - to even up the lot of the two races - and economically to move supplies from farming areas to the ever expanding cities.

1.2   The country and its provinces

To visualise the problem, it may help to start with an overall geographical/geopolitical survey of the nation, province by province (see map on page C-2). In the west, and occupying almost the entire coastline to the North Sea, were the two Flemish-speaking provinces of West and Oost Vlaanderen (West and East Flanders in English parlance) These were largely lowland and agricultural but with prosperous areas. West Vlaanderen was strongly oriented toward its coast and the development of a string of holiday resorts from De Panne in the south to Knokke in the northeast where it abutted onto a part of the Netherlands that occupied an enclave south of the Schelde/Escaut delta. The great river itself was basically international, at least as far the estuary of the River Schelde which provided Belgium with its biggest port, the extensive river harbour complex of Antwerp and its surrounding hinterland. Inland there were ancient towns such as Gent/Gand (in English terms Ghent) and Brugge, more familiar to the English as Bruges, while in the south, along the French border and the Yser valley, were the equally long-established wool towns of Ypres (or Ieper, in Flemish) and Furnes (Veurne) which would become all too familiar to the British during the 1914-18 war.

In the north, Antwerp city itself was capital of Antwerpen Province, an agricultural region flanked by the Netherlands to the north, the Flemish-speaking Limburg to the east and the pot-pourri of Brabant to its south - to both of which latter provinces it was joined by the River Dyle and a network of canals. The only real city other than Antwerp was Mechelen/Malines near the Brabant border but there were several substantial market towns such as Turnhout and Oostmalle. The other mainly Flamand province was Limburg, already mentioned, which abutted both the Netherlands and Germany and was, in general, a poor region with its administrative centre at Hasselt. It had a brief industrial period as late as the 20th Century with the opening up of the Campine coalfield east of Hasselt but this, alas, did not last. Its communications looked mainly to the Netherlands by Maastricht and the Maas river which flowed northward from the Ardennes.

To the south of Limburg was the great mass of the French speaking provinces, strung out along the same great river (which, naturally was here known as the Meuse) and its tributary the Sambre. Liége Province, dominated by its great fortress city of Liége, came first, stretching west to east and on to the German frontier which here was rather confused since three countries met at the neutral "Dreilandespunkt" enclave - and which changed hands several times during our period. Below Liége was the wooded and mountainous region of the Ardennes, sprawling across the Duchy of Luxembourg, the south eastern corner of Belgium and the French Ardennes Departement. Belgian Luxembourg was an area of large spaces, difficult terrain and occasional market towns where communication, before the railways came, was somewhat problematical and at its western edge it blended into the Province of Namur. Namur Province was centred on the old fortified city of Namur itself, at the confluence of the Sambre and Meuse rivers. Like others, it was basically agricultural but with a network of sizable towns that needed to be linked up and connected to the regions around it.

Perhaps the one of these provinces with the greatest potential for development was Hainaut, directly to the west of Namur and south of Brabant. Most of the country's mineral resources were here or hereabouts and it was the province that most quickly - and some would say grimly - became urbanised. The Belgian industrial revolution turned almost the whole province into a series of mining and factory towns and villages, from Charleroi in the east to the massive complex of the Mons-Borinage region toward the west - think Leeds-Bradford or the Lancashire mill towns. Only the area round Tournai, in the far west where it blended into Vlaanderen, remained relatively unspoiled.

In the middle of all these, like a spider in its web and abutting every province except West Vlaanderen, was Brabant, based round the National capital of Bruxelles/Brussel and the equally ancient city of Leuven/Louvain to its east. Again the eastern part was mostly agricultural - largely the ubiquitous sugar beet - but the west was, or soon became, suburban and sophisticated, its urban spread sprawling far outside the old city walls of Bruxelles and encompassing probably the most famous European battlefields of the 19th Century - Wavre, Mont St. Jean, Waterloo - where the ambitions of Napoleon Bonaparte were finally ended.

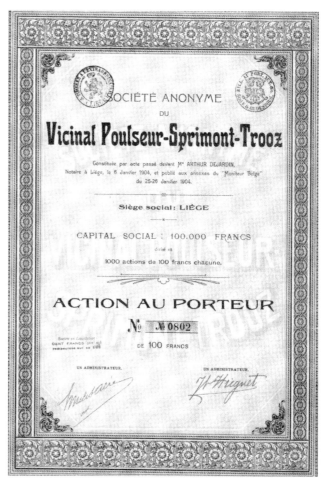

An example of the certificate issued by a concessionary company when raising its operating capital. (SNCV)

This, then, was the multicultural combination of widely disparate areas which, in the mid 19th Century, urgently needed efficient communication if they were to be unified and developed for the benefit of all their inhabitants. As in other countries, early attempts tended to try and persuade private interests to do the job, but these failed; in spite of a law in 1863 which offered some inducement to promoters of local railways, very few entrepreneurs could see a profit for themselves. The mainline railways were concerned mainly with major traffic flows, of which there were plenty, and so were not interested either. It was this situation, paradoxically, which led to national development of a unified secondary transport system that was unique in Europe.

1.3 Inception and constitution of the SNCV

While Belgium was pre-eminent in the development of her mainline railways, by the early 1870s these had almost reached the limit of what was economically viable. From about 1875, therefore, there were constant discussions as to how best to fill the gaps that were left. Further extension of the standard-gauge network was apparently rejected out of hand. It was pointed out that the big companies did not wish to get involved in minor traffic-flows, and that their bureaucratic structure would make speedy local developments difficult in any case. As to private interests, they clearly felt there was little profit to be made; up to 1875 only eight applications had been made for local lines, and even during the next nine years there were only sixty-two, of which most were "not serious" and the rest were urban tramways. Indeed only four genuine local railways were built privately and of these only one, from Taviers to Ambresin, was substantial enough to get contemporary citation.

Accordingly, in 1875, the first proposals were put forward for a *"Compagnie Nationale de Chemins de Fer Vicinaux"* which would coordinate the building of a secondary railway network; the idea was that, while keeping costs down, it would ensure that competition with the mainline railways was minimised. The proposals were, as usual, kicked around for a few years until a Commission was appointed in 1881 to consider three matters:

(a) the extent to which the state should intervene in the construction and working of local railways, and the possibility of joint action by the state, the provinces and the communes (local councils) likely to benefit directly from such lines;

(b) the latitude to be allowed to such railways in the matter of rolling stock and traffic regulations;

(c) the question of the possible competition which might arise between the local and mainline railways.

From this Commission came the concept of a national (but not nationalised) body to plan, build and administer the country's secondary transport system while at the same time not actually funding or operating it - a controllable monopoly, so to speak. The concept was based firmly on the notion that, while the state might need to subsidise a system, the main costs should fall on the areas through which a proposed line should run. Private interests were to be offered a chance to participate in two ways: by contributing up to a third of the initial cost (the Capital) of any given line, and by forming companies actually to operate such lines under a leasing system. The national body, in its turn, would carry out the planning, obtain the necessary legal authority from the state, build the line (usually by putting it out to tender), and supply the equipment to a standard pattern. It would also be expected to balance the "total" books, building up a reserve from its share of profits to support deficit-making lines in their early years.

During the first parliamentary term of 1884, the details were thoroughly discussed in the Belgian parliament, and on 28 May 1884 a law was passed authorising, on the above terms, the formation of a *"Societé Nationale des Chemins de Fer Vicinaux"* to be known in Flemish-speaking areas as the *"Nationale Maatschappij van Buurtspoorwegen"* (SNCV and NMVB). There was then a considerable pause while administrative matters proceeded, culminating in a slightly revised law of 24 June 1885 which required that the Societé be formed. It was officially created by Royal Decree a week later on 1 July 1885.

The structure of the new organisation was so unusual and worked so well that it is worth discussing it briefly here. It was at once a limited company set up for industrial purposes, and at the same time a non-profitmaking public cooperative given an effective monopoly which any private firm would have envied. It was to be independent of the state except in the two areas of obtaining initial authorisations and of controlling overall tariffs, where the state had power to raise or lower the top limits. In detail the organisation had four elements:

(a) a Council consisting of a President, appointed by the King, and four to seven members, of whom one had to be the Managing Director.

(b) a Comité de Surveillance (Watchdog committee) comprising six (later nine) members, one from each province.

We must not forget the personalities who made things happen. This is Constantin de Burlet, first director-general of the SNCV from 1884-1913   *(SNCV)*

(c) a General Assembly composed of members of the Council, the Comité de Surveillance, and public and private shareholders.

(d) an administrative organisation with a head office in Bruxelles and regional offices in each province, including regional engineering staffs to supervise work "on the ground"

The financial structure was fairly complicated since it had to operate at three levels: nationally, since the Societé had to support itself by claiming management expenses; regionally, since the provinces wanted to balance their books over all their lines, if possible; locally, since the several communes through which a line ran had to be satisfied they were taking only a fair share of costs. Theoretically there were also the private contributors to contend with, but in practice these were very few - even in early years they averaged only 4% of the Capital subscribed. It was based, therefore, on the principle of mutual assistance whereby profits from lines in surplus could be employed to cover losses on deficitary ones.

1.4 Practicalities of building the system

As we have seen, the SNCV's constitution required that, while it applied for routes, supervised building and provided the stock, it should normally neither operate its lines nor find the money required. The initial cost was to be found by raising capital from interested parties; to give private concerns a stake in the venture, operation was to be put out to tender, giving sensible-length concessions of about 30 years, with the operators paying a proportion of their gross receipts to the SNCV and to the Capital providers.

In practice this was not so easy. To start with, the procedures for initiating a new line, or even extending an existing one, were fairly lengthy and bureaucratic. First the SNCV had to "take under consideration" the proposed line(s), either on its own initiative or because it was asked to do so by

Bure, L'arrêt du vicinal

This is what the SNCV wanted to develop - a poor country village where modern communication has clearly only just arrived (author's collection/commercial card.)

Melreux-Hotton. — Panorama du village pris de la gare

And this is what it wanted to promote - a thriving town with standard and metre gauge connections (commercial card)

provincial councils. Some tentative planning was then done, mainly to ensure that the state was not likely to refuse the eventual concession on the grounds of competition with other forms of transport; quite a few proposals dropped out at this stage. If the go-ahead was given, the state's share of the Capital was then agreed. The next step was to obtain the agreement of province(s) and local communes to provide their share and to offer a token amount to private interests. The province usually agreed quite quickly - it could, after all, recoup from its internal taxes. The communes involved were often more cautious since they had to find their share directly from the parish rates. Thus one or more communes who could see others gaining more

benefit might prove very stubborn, and the proposals could be delayed for years or even eventually founder - although there were powers to compel agreement in certain cases. If and when agreement was reached, detailed plans were drawn up and formal application for a concession was made. This was submitted initially to the Department of Agriculture, Industry and Public Works and included:

(a)   a report on the prospects of the line;

(b)   a detailed estimate of cost;

(c)   a note on the proposed tariffs to be charged, with an estimate of the probable receipts;

(d) a specification of the project, together with maps and plans of various scales and degrees of detail;

(e) longitudinal and cross-sections of the line and detailed drawings of particular works and the type of permanent way adopted.

This submission was subjected to detailed study by appropriate Departments of State and could take up to three years to process in difficult cases. Some were refused even then or revoked after concession; an example was the proposed Yvoir - Ciney line authorised in 1892 but then re-conceded to the CF de l'Etat Belge. Furthermore, the whole procedure had to be repeated if the original line was authorised in several portions or if an extension was envisaged at a later date. In the latter case, it was usually given its own Capital, especially where new communes were involved, though this was often fused with the original Capital before the line opened. Other improvements and short branches were normally funded by augmenting the existing Capital in agreement with the various partners. Clearly this procedure was at times short-circuited - there are numerous instances of lines opening within three or four months of the concession being formally granted and several instances of the authorisation apparently being retrospective! Completion, however, could also be delayed by problems of negotiating building contracts; by legal disputes about the exact land needed where this was not public property; or by political and engineering problems caused by construction of river bridges, mainline railway crossings and similar features. Hence long lines often opened in sections over a period of years. In some cases they were never fully completed, and occasionally were not even started because the legal problems proved too great.

Since private interests rarely took up anything like their permitted one-third of the capital, a major problem was clearly the need for communes to raise substantial sums from their own revenue. They were, therefore, allowed to spread their contribution over a period of up to ninety years by promising a series of annual payments, the SNCV borrowing money against this security. This had the advantage that, if the promoters had judged right, the communes never actually had to pay anything, at least in theory; dividends from the line should cover the cost of annual payments. In practice, especially in the early years, this often proved to be the case, though later it was much less common (on the other hand inflation somewhat reduced the real cost of payment). The state and the provinces, subscribing on the same principle for a multitude of lines, were able to offset profits from some against losses from others; they thus had to find only the difference between the two and, since their main purpose was to develop the rural districts, this was perfectly acceptable.

So the SNCV eventually got its line funded, approved and, hopefully, built. Even then its problems were not over. In order to give private interests a look-in, its charter required that operation was put out to competitive tender. Specially formed companies usually calling themselves "Societé Anonyme pour l' exploitation du CFV de. ...", or its Flemish equivalent "Naamloze Maatschappij voor ...", put in their bids and the SNCV took the one likely to be most beneficial to the public purse. The bids were usually based on how profitable the line was likely to be and the terms were rarely over-generous, though they could be modified either after several years' experience or when the SNCV could not get anyone to accept the concession! In exceptional cases where no one was interested or where the line was long in completing, the SNCV operated the line itself, on a provisional basis.

It also wanted to develop access to the more difficult and remote parts, as typified by this scene at Bouillon near the French frontier
(commercial card / collection E de Backer)

In general the SNCV provided the line with equipment to a standard pattern, with all the advantages of bulk-buying; it also agreed to provide any extra stock and fittings such as sidings or extra stations that might be needed if and when traffic increased. The concessionaire held a repairing lease and was thus responsible for upkeep. Indeed part of the agreement was the deposit by the concessionaire of a guarantee of good behaviour. Initially this was charged at Fr 2000 per kilometre but proved too little. As a result it was later augmented by an agreed "renewal fund", raised by the operator and put at his disposal to carry out maintenance; the process was supervised by a small SNCV inspectorate.

The operating company could be a small local firm organised specifically for a single line, or a big concern operating a number of lines in a single province (eg the *Kempische Stoomtram Maatschappij* running a network in southern Antwerpen) or one operating scattered lines all over the country (eg the *Railways Economiques de Liége - Seraing,* whose original privately-sponsored tramway was quite the least important of its concessions). Where possible, the SNCV tended, as time went on, to grant linked "clusters"of lines to a single company for obvious reasons, though it was by no means unknown for separate companies to share stations and even have common stretches of track. For record purposes, these clusters were usually classed as operating Groups and named after their headquarters town (Groupe/Groep de .....). At the conclusion of the concession period, usually 30 years, the SNCV had the right either to offer a renewal or to take over operation itself; an original scheme whereby there was a break-point at 15 years was later less used as offering less incentive to operators. In practice, however, both SNCV and concessionaires sometimes ended contracts prematurely, either because the concessionaire was breaking the terms of his lease or because he found the burden becoming too

onerous. In such cases the line was again put out to tender. The SNCV also expected operators to provide welfare societies for employees and generally kept a watchful eye on its property through its regional engineers.

To go into great detail over financial arrangements is not appropriate here but it may be interesting to look at how a typical concession worked. To start with one must differentiate between the interests of the concessionaire and those of the actionnaire or capital provider. The concessionaire normally agreed to work the line for an agreed proportion of the gross receipts, typically a set percentage up to a given figure and then going down on a sliding scale for any excess. Thus for example the Liége - Seraing, for its Oostende - Veurne concession, got 70% of receipts up to Fr 4000/km/year, dropping in stages to 65% if receipts exceeded Fr 5500/km/year. Where a line was likely to run at a deficit, the SNCV would guarantee a minimum notional level of income, usually about Fr 2000/km/year, which was calculated more or less to cover expenses. There was no secrecy about these agreements, details being printed annually in the Societe's report. The actionnaires, providing the line was in surplus, received a first dividend which, if paid in full, covered the amount of the annual payment they would otherwise have to make. Anything left over was declared as a second dividend; divided in eighths, three went to a central reserve fund, two to a fund "de prevision"or advance-reserve allocated to that particular line as a first defence against unexpected losses or expenses in future years, and the remaining three were distributed in proportion to the actionnaires. For the communes this latter was profit and could be used to decrease their indebtedness; for the provinces and the state it could be used to offset their payments on unprofitable lines. The SNCV was thus in the position of being an impartial body, able to stimulate development without expecting or needing to make a profit itself.

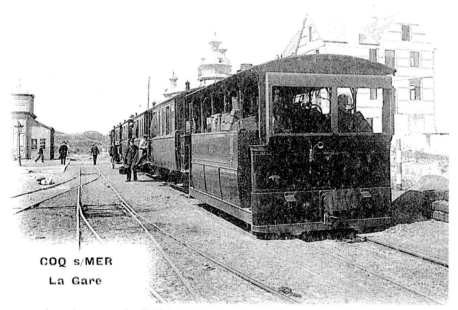

COQ s/MER
La Gare

... and on the coast, the SNCV went into the tourist business since the area was very popular with holiday makers

Chapter 2:   The First Thirty Years.

2.1   1884-1894: Work starts

The new Societé started its work very energetically. The legal procedures meant that the first batch of concessions, totalling 104 km, was not finally authorised until 27 March 1886, yet the SNCV in its first annual report covering 1885 recorded that two lines, Capital 2 from Oostende to Nieuwpoort in West Vlaanderen and Capital 1 from Antwerpen to Hoogstraten, in Province Antwerpen, had already been opened on 15 July and 15 August 1885 respectively. Indeed by May 1886 some 771km were under active consideration, and by the end of 1889, five years after the official start-up, 704.2km of these were operating, divided between 35 lines. Another 104.5km were under construction, and 45 lines totalling 790km were going through the process of planning. Yet the sifting process had worked so well that of all these only four: Deinze - Oudenaarde and Tielt - Aalter in Vlaanderen, Bourcy - Houffalize and Ethe - Arlon in Luxembourg, all in very poor districts, were in constant deficit. Even these were showing a slow improvement as they helped to develop their areas, and the overall operating ratio (costs expressed as a percentage of receipts) was a respectable 73.28%; note that on this basis, values over 100 are bad rather than good as in modern practice but it was the standard method at the time so has been used here. Five years later, at the end of 1894, no less than 62 lines totalling some 1249km were actually working, with an overall operating ratio of just over 70%, and about the same length was under consideration. Ten years after that, at the end of 1904, nearly 2680km were in full operation with a similar amount being considered. The rapid increase was undoubtedly much helped by the SNCV's monopoly position, and by the fact that it was .often possible to lay lines quickly along public roads. Even so it was a very rapid development.

These early lines set the pattern for all that was to follow. For the most part they ran alongside the public road, separated from it only by a kerb and even venturing into the carriageway itself when passing through villages or urban streets. A few had substantial sections on their own right-of-way, especially in hilly districts, but the majority deviated only to reach a terminus or to bypass a particularly steep gradient or narrow street. Hence they did serve their communities closely, and sidings were easily laid at intervals to serve farms or hamlets. The lines were never

sure if they were light railways or tramways. Buildings varied widely - in many cases they were almost non-existent outside termini, and in others they were more substantial than on the neighbouring main line. Suburban lines were mainly passenger-carrying, but in the country districts trains were often mixed and set off for the market towns at extremely early hours; a start at 03.00 hrs was nothing unusual. As briefly described below, the SNCV designed a family of double-ended 0-6-0 tram locomotives to suit varying conditions and provided standard patterns of four-wheeled coaches, vans and goods vehicles.

A typical operating company document: a freight waybill of the Kempische Stoomtram Mij. Note there is no mention of the SNCV since the concessionaire had full responsibility.
(SNCV)

In general the benefits to the rural economy were enormous. Previously the canal system had provided patchy if slow access to certain parts. Now, for the first time, holders of wide tracts of fertile but underdeveloped farmland were given easy access to the expanding markets of the industrial cities. This rapid and efficient provision attracted a good deal of attention outside Belgium among the advocates of rural light railways - especially those in the UK. The low average cost of construction and equipment, then about £2300 per mile in English terms; the ease with which routes along public roads could be agreed; the general administrative structure; all came in for much praise. The Belgians themselves were not quite so sure about some things; they regarded the concession procedures as very cumbersome, for example. On the other hand, they agreed that the arrangements did foster steady development of track and equipment on a scale that individual orders would never have done. The process also allowed economical distribution of equipment since spares could be provided quickly in case of need. The first ten years were, therefore, a time of very rapid growth but, unlike in other countries, the growth was properly coordinated and controlled.

2.2   Equipment standardisation and its benefits.

Manhay La Gare du Vicinal.

Operating companies normally had adequate provision: Even Mamhay terminus, in the rural Ardennes, shows a range of engine and carriage sheds with watering and office facilities (collection E de Backer)

The SNCV was unique, at least in Europe, in that it was a national organisation and was therefore in a position to determine what to provide and to ensure standardisation and interchangeability of stock between its various systems - the initial concessionaires got what they were given, not necessarily what they might, given a free hand, have stipulated. The advantages were manifold: buffing and coupling heights and types were standard, unlike in France for instance; interchangeability of stock meant that it could be swapped around to meet increasing or decreasing demand; bulk buying gave financial savings; in later years, at least, the electrical arrangements were standard nationwide. The disadvantages, fortunately few in quantity, were that if the SNCV made a misjudgement, everyone suffered. On the other hand centralisation meant that meaningful experiments with new concepts could be tried out in practice and their results taken on board - the single-phase ac electrification around the Borinage for instance proved, in the long run, to be not worth extending. On the other hand careful comparisons of early internal-combustion engined vehicles led to a very successful

And each company would have at least one central workshop for heavy maintenance. This is Turnhout in Antwerpen province. (SNCV)

standard design at a time when other countries were still groping. There were, therefore well defined trends in SNCV stock design and development and it may be worth highlighting them to illustrate how they affected - and were affected by - the overall system development.

2.2.1   Motive power development

The SNCV started with the premise that it was to provide local and sub-regional communication and that most of its lines would therefore run along or near existing roads since this was both cheaper than buying land and also, inevitably, served the villages and towns that the roads connected. Being initally committed to steam traction, it therefore wanted a tram-type locomotive that would give good visibility and be as safe as possible while being simple and robust (The Societé, quite rightly, never had a particularly favourable opinion of its concessionaires as maintainers and handlers of "someone else's" equipment -

An early train showing typical locomotive and stock   (SNCV)

that was one of the downsides of central provision when you were not using the equipment yourself). The eventual specification - which proved long-lasting - was therefore for a rugged six-coupled machine with two outside cylinders and motion and capable of being driven from either end so that the driver could always be at the front, while turntables or wyes would not be necessary. An overall canopy was intended to give shelter for the crew (and no doubt to make it look more like a carriage so as not to frighten horses) while side-skirts and fenders protected the motion from intrusion - and chickens, etc from the flailing rods; these skirts could be hinged up to provide access to the wheels and motion.

The SNCV therefore was clear about what it wanted and acquired a small number of light machines for its first railways. To be scrupulously fair, soon after it was formed in 1885 it then organised a competition at Antwerpen and, surprise, surprise, it was won by the big SA Metallurgique whose Tubize Works was already producing an 0-6-0 Tram design which met most of the requirements. Again being fair, examples were ordered from a number of manufacturers and, indeed, this became SNCV general policy. There were eventually some 23 different classes of which all but seven were of this general type; the others were mainly isolated groups or examples bought in for special purposes such as shunting. To summarise:

Types 1-4; 6-9; 13-14; were normal 0-6-0 tram locomotives of the type described above. The first two classes were basically an existing Tubize design and were built when bridge structures were comparatively delicate. They proved rather light for the work and once more robust infrastructure was decided on, they were superseded by the Type 3 which was the Tubize design that actually won the competition. Of these classes, Types 3, 4, and 7 were particularly successful, the two latter being heavier machines particularly suitable for goods and mixed train haulage.

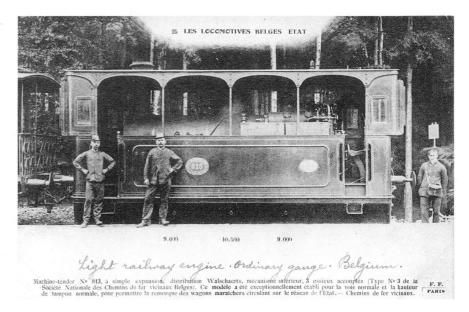

Type 12 was typical of the few standard gauge locomotives used on several isolated lines (SNCV)

Types 10-12; 15 were small classes of standard gauge locomotives, 10-12 being 0-6-0 tram machines - enlarged examples of the narrow gauge design - for line work on the few standard gauge branches and Type 15 a series of six bog-standard industrial 0-4-0Ts for shunting at the various Works.

Types 5 & 14 were conventional metre gauge 0-6-0Ts for special duties

Types 16 (enclosed) and 17 (conventional)
0-6-0Ts were single examples built to experiment with superheating which was eventually not thought to be worthwhile proceeding with.

Type 18 was the definitive, classic 0-6-0 Tram locomotive and was produced in considerable numbers by a variety of makers both large and small.

Type 19 was an anglicised Type 18, fifty being built in Britain for the War Department during the 1914-18 war and forty-eight being taken over by the SNCV after the war.

Types 20 & 22 were standard gauge equivalents of Types 5 & 14 - standard industrial shunters bought specifically for work in various interchange yards.

Type 21 was a series of twenty one 0-6-0 tram locomotives generally similar to Type 18 but built during the 1914-18 war by the American Locomotive Co (ALCO) in America.

Type 23 was the SNCV's one real experiment - two excellent Garratt locomotives built for the heavy coal trains in Limburg province but these did not come until 1928-29.

There were also the inevitable oddities taken over from failing concessionaires or other sources and fairly arbitrarily assigned to the nearest SNCV Type classification. It may be thought rather odd that the SNCV provided special classes for shunting. The fact was that there were quantities of sharply curved industrial sidings, especially in the major cities where the main workshops were also connected to the standard gauge system for obvious reasons and, in addition, there was a number of shortish sections - often on their own right of way - which were mixed gauge to serve industrial sites without the necessity for transhipment. Although taken out of chronological order here, the Garratts were a late development, specifically for hauling heavy coal trains on one of the few narrow gauge lines of any length that had heavy goods traffic.

It is clearly not appropriate here to go into great detail about the individual classes but the final "standard" pattern, the Type 18 and its doppelganger the Type 19 were such a classic design that they should be described and illustrated in any history. By the early 1900s the central engineering department

Type 5, on the other hand, was typical of the standard industrial types bought for shunting in yards and industrial sidings

had a clear idea of what was required and the Type 18 was the result. It was by no means the most numerous class but was generally considered the most efficient and the SNCV was proud of it. Indeed it said so in the official driver's handbook, calling it:

"this splendid locomotive, regarded with justification as a type remarkable for the elegance of its outline and the balance of its proportions"

127 in all were built, by a variety of makers large and small. The Type 18 was very much a refinement of earlier designs, incorporating all the features which had been found desirable for locomotives working longish distances over a variety of roadside and in-road routes. These tasks assumed the need for a two-man crew which removed many of the constraints of the one-man urban design. Hence the locomotive was a robust six-coupled machine with outside cylinders and Walschaerts valve gear and was fitted with both hand and vacuum brakes. It could be driven from both ends, the reverser, regulator and brake controls, plus the whistle cord, being duplicated and arranged so that the driver could always stand facing forward at the "front" end with an unobstructed view. Technically it was interesting, having a copper Belpaire firebox with a sloping grate designed to minimise maintenance problems; the wrapper was a single steel sheet mounting a pair of Ross or Wilson safety valves and a

An example of the "surbaissée" design.   (SNCV)

The Type 19 was almost, but not quite identical to the Type 18. This was because it was built in Britain during the 1914-18 war from anglicised Type 18 drawings, to a total of 50 examples for the British War Department and in order to use existing tooling imperial measurements were used. These locomotives, WD 201 - 250, were used mainly on the Yser front and 48 of them were taken into SNCV stock after the war. The SNCV numbered them in random order as they were acquired and put into service. The first 30 were built by Robert Stephenson, (3663-71; 3674-94) the remainder by Hawthorn Leslie (3215-34). ROD 201-09 are recorded as being built in 1916, the rest in 1917 - hence the break in works numbers.

2.2.2 trailer rolling stock

Passenger and goods rolling stock was equally standardised and the numbering system prefixed the actual number with a cipher: A for metre gauge; B for 1067mm gauge; C for standard gauge and D for...horse cars since they were always an anomaly. In the formative years stock consisted almost exclusively of four-wheeled vehicles in spite of their less than perfect riding qualities. Experiments were made with bogie coaches in the 1890s and again in 1911-12, but the Societé decided that their comfort was outweighed by lack of operational flexibility. If a two-axle coach "failed", there were usually others to carry the traffic; if a bogie coach had to be taken out of service, much more capacity was lost. Also, a two-axle coach could be added to or dropped from a train with less effect, and this was important when locomotives were not very powerful. The few bogie coaches that were built were regarded as curiosities and most ended up as trailers for electric services.

A posed view of a Type 18 with its proud crew
(the late JH Price)

neat steam turret supplied all the steamlines. Two restarting injectors were fitted, operated by the fireman. Again to rectify earlier problems, the boiler was all-steel, including the tubes, and particular attention was paid to provision of strong tubeplates, earlier designs having suffered from cracking. The dome was mounted on the front ring with a sandbox behind it. The overall canopy was open-sided but with bowed endscreens having sliding windows and the "cabs" had side doors giving the impression of a flush-sided vehicle. This impression was increased by the steel motion covers with four top-hinged sided doors for easy access. Four examples have been preserved, the remainder being scrapped over the years as the need for steam locomotives declined.

One advantage of a bogie coach, of course, was that different types of accommodation could be more readily combined within it. The SNCV, up to 1945, had two classes for passengers together with a need for luggage space and, in consequence, built 1st class, 1st/2nd composite, 2nd class, 2nd/luggage and all-luggage (fourgon) vehicles. Its general practice was to provide 2nd-class passengers with varnished-wood seats arranged transversely each side of a central gangway; 1st class had either upholstered benches arranged longitudinally along each side or had a longitudinal bench facing four-seat bays of upholstered seats. Vehicles might be divided into one, two or occasionally three saloons, but were not fitted with toilets; the official reason was that most journeys were short and that the standard was that of a tramway rather than a full-sized railway.

were many minor variations depending on manufacturer and date. Thirdly there were attempts to get greater capacity without requiring a bogie vehicle. These were long-wheelbase four-wheelers with patent De Rechter radial trucks and eight-window bodies but otherwise following the standard formula.

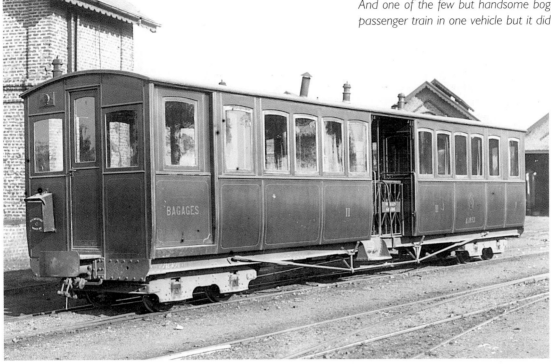

And one of the few but handsome bogie coaches - a whole passenger train in one vehicle but it did not find much favour (SNCV)

Throughout its development period, the SNCV was also unsure of what heating and lighting it should provide. Initially it used the stinking, flickering oil lamps common to most 19th-century minor railways, and in winter replaced one pair of seats in each coach with a portable solid-fuel stove. Gradually the latter was replaced by fixed hot-water thermic syphon heaters feeding radiator pipes and then, in the 1912 and 1920 types, by Charpentier hot-air systems fed from underfloor stoves. Lighting was difficult; the SNCV wavered for a long time between acetylene lamps, paraffin vapour lamps and battery powered electric lighting. In practice, while it decided in favour of the last, electricity was used mainly on long-distance trains,

It is not appropriate here to go into detail but for identification in photographs the SNCV steam-hauled two-axle coaches can be divided into four principal styles. First came the low-floor cars, or Surbaissées: These vehicles, built in 1885-86 for the first concessions, had a very low centre-of-gravity. Experience quickly showed that fears over the stability of narrow-gauge vehicles were exaggerated so the design was not perpetuated. Their main feature was that the frame, with wide steel solebars, was slung very low, the running gear being inside it with the wheel housings projecting into the passenger space. They had six-window saloon bodies with end balconies. They were followed by what might be called the standardised or "classic" pattern cars: This was the classic design built in considerable numbers between 1886 and 1911. There were two major variants, one with six equally spaced windows a side and the other ("à trumeaux") with three pairs of narrower windows separated by panels or trumeaux. Otherwise they were similar in general layout to their predecessors, with one or two saloons accessed by open end balconies although there

Forty-five were built between 1892 and 1899 for both narrow gauges and some were later modified for tourist uses with enclosed end-platforms and large square-cut windows. These conversions were equipped for relaying an audio commentary. Lastly there were the cars with glazed end-screens, or "à Paravents": Following construction of two prototypes in 1912 the SNCV decided that future coaches should be to a modernised design and eventually built four hundred and fifty three to this general pattern. Initial batches had substantial wooden saloon bodies with Charpentier hot-air heating and paraffin lamps but with open balconies protected by full end-screens. The final 215, built in 1920 were generally similar but had metal panelling over a wood framework. Many were later converted for use as trailers for electric cars. A small group of coaches was built for the SNCV standard gauge lines and followed a similar design. They were all end-platform two-axle cars with small round-topped windows, and looked like larger versions of contemporary narrow-gauge vehicles. They were built between 1888 and 1913, later ones having Charpentier warm-air heating. All vehicles remained in original condition until withdrawn as the lines closed. Two vehicles, C 1503 and C 2000 are preserved.

Inevitably, such a large organisation also had a collection of special passenger vehicles for unusual operations. These can basically be summarised in four categories: First there were the horse-drawn cars. D 1-12 (closed) and D 101-10 (open). Twenty of these vehicles (ten of each kind) were acquired with the Klapdorp - Merksem tramway at Antwerpen. From photographs, they appear to have been typical light horse-tramcars of the period, the closed cars having end-platforms with access to a single saloon, while the open cars had

A posed shot of a goods train in 1910, showing high and low sided wagons and a variety of the multi-purpose ventilated vans   *(SNCV)*

platforms for the drivers and either toastrack or back-to-back seating under an ornamental roof with long destination boards at each side. They were withdrawn in 1908. The other two were presumably those used to provide the odd shuttle service from Tielt station in Vlaanderen to the town centre (see chapter 6). Then there were Prison coaches B 1-7 (1067-mm gauge): The SNCV always had problems with vagabonds and other layabouts hanging around its property and occasionally getting run over by trains - the annual reports contained long lists of "perturbations" with notes of the appropriate penalties; "being idle on government property" seemed a favourite charge. For such as these and for more serious cases, the State maintained penal colonies, of which the most important was Merksplas in Antwerpen province, which was served by the SNCV. To transport felons, the SNCV operated seven cell-vans or coaches owned by the State Prison Authority. They were austere two-axle vehicles with vertically-planked sides and four small barred windows high up in each side. Access was from a gated platform at one end, with a small compartment for the escorting officers, and the whole affair had a home-made look; the builder was Verhaegen. At various times the SNCv also had two coaches fitted out as royal saloons - A 1625 on the coast and A165 on the Grottes de Han line in Namur province. Both were apparently rebuilds of normal coaches, A1625 being originally a 1st/2nd class composite and A 165 one of the tourist vehicles peculiar to the Grottes de Han. Lastly the SNCV in the 1930s converted nine or ten vehicles into camping coaches - and even advertised them at exhibitions. They were all rebuilt from 1912 or 1920-pattern coaches, mainly of the 2nd/luggage variety, the conversion consisting of stripping the interior and dividing it into two compartments. One contained four simple ambulance-type bunks; the other provided a small kitchen/eating room with a washbasin against one bulkhead; a large roof-mounted tank provided water. The vehicles were numbered from VC1 upwards, the prototype VC1 having been A 2121. Another photograph (not shown here) has an older vehicle marked VC 31, but it is not clear whether this was a prototype for a further series or whether more coaches were converted.

2.2.3 SNCV goods & service vehicles

The same principle of universal application applied to goods stock - as indeed it did throughout Europe. The "standard" four-wheeled metre gauge wagon or van could take the ten-tonne load of an average standard gauge wagon of the time so there was little point in going for bogies. Four-wheelers were more flexible to operate and easier to shunt. The SNCV therefore provided a standardised range of lowside, open and covered wagons of continental pattern - which in general meant that vans were dual purpose, with sliding ventilation flaps, and open wagons had the "Belgian" pattern of double, vertically-hinged doors in the centre of each side. In most cases continuous brakes were not fitted to rolling stock since it was expected that trains would be slow and undertake frequent shunting. Instead the locomotives had powerful steam brakes, all stock being fitted with parking brakes and a reasonable proportion with screw handbrakes operated either from the balcony (coaches) or from a brakesman's perch (goods stock). As with most large organisations there were standard varieties but, even so, the products of various makers differed in detail and local rebuildings over the years produced many other variants. In particular, underframes and bodywork were often adapted to serve specific functions such as weed-killing, permanent way equipment or mobile substations. The metre-gauge ("A" prefix) and 1067-mm gauge ("B" prefix) wagons were generally similar; the standard-gauge vehicles were similar to main line vehicles.

During its career, the SNCV owned a total of some 12607 goods vehicles, whose breakdown into principal types is shown below, For comparison, totals in the early years and almost at the SNCV peak are also shown. It should be noted that not all were in service at anyone time, and that some were built on the cannibalised remains of others,

		Quantities	
Type	maximum	in1894	in1912
2-axle open wagons	9327	978	6011
2-axle low-sided wagons	877	211	577
2-axle vans	2094	239	1067
6-wheel low-sided Wagons	10	—	
Bogie low-sided wagons	172	3	
Tank wagons	62	3	111
Match-wagons	30	2	
Misc service vehicles	45	—	

Inevitably there were also many special non-passenger vehicles: They included two-axle tank wagons of two types: with a cylindrical tank or a distinctive rectangular tank with cambered top and prominent fillers; six-wheel flat wagons of 15-tonne load; various patterns of heavy-duty bogie flatwagons, some fitted with stanchions (20-30 tonne load); and a number of special purpose two-axle vehicles such as hand cranes, snow-ploughs, match-wagons for coupling to standard-gauge vehicles, a single transporter, several tippers and a series of container wagons for the Liége-Limburg coal traffic. These last often featured in SNCV publicity, being distinctive vehicles with a long-wheelbase underframe carrying three removable "skips", specifically designed to be lifted and tipped into canal barges. Lastly, there were the various service vehicles, such as tower wagons, weed-killing tankers and a series of general purpose oddities under the designation of "trucks". They will be described in detail in a forthcoming volume.

As to standard gauge vehicles, there were very few SNCV goods vehicles on the standard gauge since mainline stock was used almost exclusively. For internal use, however, there was a total of 13 high-sided wagons, three low-sided wagons and five vans, all four-wheelers and, in appearance, bigger versions of their narrow gauge counterparts. There were also two handcranes and four match wagons. They were numbered in appropriate series prefixed by "C".

Lastly, for all stock, the "monopoly" aspect, of course, also meant that individual lines did not have to be over-supplied to start with; it was comparatively easy to provide extra stock from the ever-expanding central pool if a railway developed more rapidly than expected or indeed to reclaim items for use elsewhere if it stagnated.

2.3   Experiments with Electricity:

2.3.1   Early development of an electrified system

Returning to general history, the original concept of steam-hauled light railways had its limitations, particularly around the big towns and cities expanding rapidly with the rise of industry. By as early as 1894 several things had become plain, and one was that urban and suburban passenger traffic could not easily be handled by steam-worked tramways especially where, as in some Belgian cities, steep gradients had to be surmounted. The

SNCV, therefore, began experiments with alternative forms of traction. Light steam railcars of the Rowan type, battery-electric cars at Gent and Oostende, petrol-electrics at Bruxelles and Mons were all tried over the next twenty years without much success. What did, however, promise a useful potential was the overhead-wire electrification just coming into vogue for urban tramway systems. The SNCV was among the pioneers, electrifying and opening on 21 June 1894 a steeply-graded 11.2km line south from Bruxelles (Place de la Constitution, and later Place Rouppe) to the outer suburb of Petite Espinette. The line, and its later extension to Waterloo, were used as a testing ground for the electric tramway concept.

It proved so successful that the SNCV had little hesitation in building further lines around the large cities. From 1898-on, a largely-new network of lines criss-crossed the district around La Louvière in Hainaut (Centre I and II). The following year saw the start of converting the developing Charleroi urban system to electric traction. In 1904 Gent - Merelbeke (originally battery) and the Liége city system followed. The shape of the future was clear. At the end of 1904, the electric lines, though only 3.82% of the system in route length, were running some 22% of train-kilometres and earning nearly 20% of total receipts.

Table 2A: Development of electric lines 1904-13

Year	% of system	% of traffic	% receipts	km total
1904	3.82	22.00	20.00	97.03
1909	5.50	33.37	22.40	241.57
1913	10.00	42.37	29.64	409.80

Between 1905 and 1909, accordingly, electrification blossomed, route-km rising from 97 to 241.57, and by the end of 1913 (last complete year prior to the war) it had reached 409.8. Train-kilometres and receipts rose in proportion as the Table shows, for the lines chosen were either new urban ones or existing ones on which traffic was heavy, for example the coastal system. This was of particular interest since it had an enterprising (if sometimes irritating) concessionaire, lengthy routes with a heavy summer tourist traffic, and a generous

M19. one of the original series of twenty-four electric cars put into service from 1894
*   (SNCV)*

loading gauge - vehicles could for example be up to 2.40m wide as opposed to the normal 2.00m or 2.20m and the concessionaire wanted special stock to take advantage of this.

2.3.2. Early developments in electric rolling stock

Inevitably, these experiments also involved the SNCV in designing, trying out and modifying standard patterns of electrically powered rolling stock, almost all of which was four-wheeled. The history of the electric motor cars of the SNCV at this period is extremely complex and only a very superficial outline need be given here. It has to be said that, to the layman at least, the great majority of the earlier 4-wheeled tramcars were very similar, differing mainly in detail and in having some form of screen at each end - from about 1907 these were integral in the bodywork but earlier ones had improvised "bay-windows" often added retrospectively once they were in service. Most had trucks mounted beneath a sub-frame, some had conventional chassis and running gear; body styles differed in detail with the manufacturer as did the actual electrical equipment but they were all designed to do the same job - urban and inner suburban passenger workings requiring a shortish wheelbase and rapid acceleration. Six-wheelers incidentally were very uncommon, the only really successful ones being a small series introduced by the concessionaire

original number, and the A prefix was restored for some years. Subsequent cars were numbered in this 9xxx series and later in the 10xxx series. The first cars (M1-24) were designed partly for the single-phase lines in the Centre and Borinage and partly for the experimental route between Brussels and Petite Espinette/Waterloo and to some extent they set the early standard. This first identifiable pattern had six equal arched windows on each side and had completely open end-platforms with a waist-high dash; a neat panelled body very similar to that of contemporary trailer coaches was specified. From about 1906, full end-screens were fitted from new, and the earlier cars had local patterns of windscreen retrofitted above the dash. Ventilation was initially by drop-windows, which were supplemented by louvre ventilators in later series and were then sometimes squared off. In 1907, the SNCV drawing office clearly felt that the original design was becoming a little archaic and adopted another general body style which lasted until almost the end of our period. This had a panelled body with a short clerestory over the passenger saloon only and with six unequal, usually arched windows. End-platforms were partially enclosed with small side-panels, and there were three-window bow-end screens with the part below the windows often teak-panelled. The central end-window was usually narrower and was either an opening window or contained in a train-door. Both trucks and integral running-gear were again used.

Electrification was initially confined mainly to the urban areas but was vigorously pursued there. This is the old station square at Oostende with an Ostende-Blankenberghe four-wheeler and typical coastal system trailers.

(commercial card)

running the urban systems around Gent. From the 1920s-on, the majority of new cars were bogie vehicles and specifically intended to tow trailers, coming into use especially as inter city routes were electrified but that is a story best left to chapter 4.

The 4-wheeled cars eventually totalled some 874, most of those built during the period under review being second class only, for urban work. The first 24 or so were originally numbered in a series prefixed with A, but the prefix was soon altered to M. This was applied up to M168 and M200-4, but about 1904 they were renumbered by adding 9000 to the

Owing to delivery delays caused by World War I, series with this body style overlapped those with the body pattern more commonly seen in later photographs which was introduced just before the 1914-18 war. This next style, which was usually known as the "Manage" type, was hardly more modern since it had five unequal windows, usually arched, in the "iiwii" arrangement. Its main advantage was that it enabled the car interior to be divided into two unequal saloons: a small one for 1st class and a larger one for 2nd class. With various modifications, this style was used from just before 1914 until the mid-1920s. The other major variation was in the coastal routes for which special cars were designed, having large windows and being capable of towing a number of trailers in high season: the "OB" or Ostende-Blankenberghe type was the best known. Many of these cars, from the very earliest days, were intended to tow matching trailers, the coastal trains often consisting of a heavy four-wheeled passenger car or motor luggage van towing a whole gaggle of the things. There were also substantial numbers of open-sided toastrack or "baladeuse" cars for summer use including a set of handsome bogie vehicles bought after WW1 and originally destined for Oran.

2.3.3. Development of urban electric tramway systems

From the late 1890s on, as we have seen, the Societé also became embroiled in providing purely urban passenger services, although this was not its major function. It had applied as early as 1897 for a compact little group of routes in the heavily urbanised Borinage near Mons (the "Monophasé", described in chapter 9) and all through Hainaut as electrification flourished strings of short, purely passenger-carrying routes were established - though whether one should describe these properly as urban, suburban or commuter routes is a difficult one! Like Topsy, they just grew along with the industrialisation of the area. In addition, during the first decade of the 20th Century, a number of large cities all over Belgium already had or were acquiring town tramway systems largely run by private companies - Antwerpen, Bruxelles, Charleroi, Gent, Liége, Verviers were notable - but some were omitted. What they might well have was a network of SNCV steam tramways coming in from the surrounding countryside and ending up, perhaps, near the main market or railway station. It made sense both to the SNCV and to the municipal authorities to join these through the town streets by new links and to electrify the result plus, in some cases, the inner, suburban, sections of the steam lines. Thus, almost faute de mieux, the SNCV found itself with the task of organising full-blown urban trams. Oostende, Leuven/Louvain, Brugge and

In contrast, rural lines could be very basic. A simple wayside halt at Grune, marked by no more than a halt sign and, probably, a waiting room in a house across the road.
(E de Backer collection/commercial card)

Mechelen/Malines were among the towns to acquire purely SNCV networks at this time, much of them gained as noted above, by linking and electrifying the inner portions of existing steam lines. For these lines the SNCV initially provided related series of balcony-ended four-wheeled cars developed mainly from the originals of the Petite-Espinette experiment.

During this period the SNCV tended to build and, at least for a time, to work the new electric systems itself in order to assess the problems. It also experimented not only with current collection systems but also the type of electrical supply. Its 1897 plan for a network of lines in the Borinage, southwest of Mons southwest of Mons, eventually came to fruition in 1906-07 when some 20km were built on the then novel single-phase high-voltage system (Monophasé) in order to give it a proper trial. This however had no sequel for, by the time it was almost completed, the standard 600-volt dc equipment had proved both robust and reliable; its power could, moreover, easily be generated by the SNCV itself where required instead of having

And even junctions might have little more: Hotton, on the Manhay-Melreux line has a building which clearly doubles as staff accommodation and passenger servicing.   *(author's collection/commercial card)*

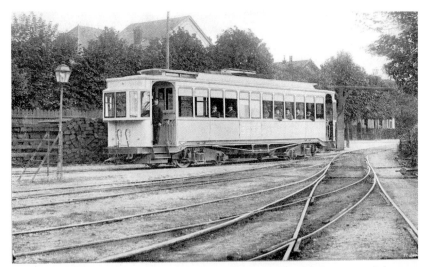

Voiture II. Pieper, type II, pour chemins de fer secondaires
(Modèle de la Société Nationale des Chemins de fer Vicinaux Belges)

to be bought from outside. The 1914-18 war intervened to prevent further experiments, and afterwards the Borinage lines were converted to the standard system.

2.4 Development of the non-electric system

Meanwhile back at the ranch (or down in the country) the much bigger steam-worked system was also expanding steadily. There were plenty of places where no more than two or three trains daily were needed, yet could support a basic railway. Even the four original loss-makers moved slowly towards equilibrium, and by 1914 very few of the 180-odd Capitaux were showing a consistent deficit - though rather more failed to pay any substantial dividends. From 1298km in 1894, the steam network rose to almost 2440km ten years later, and by the end of 1913 it had reached 3826.5km, a rise of no less than 2538km. The peak year for steam line construction appears to have been 1909, after which it slowly tapered off while the extent of electric lines rose. As with the electric lines, train-kilometres and receipts stayed more or less in balance as the length increased. The pattern of gauges had likewise been very firmly established. In effect, metre gauge was the norm almost everywhere; standard gauge (1435 mm) was used only for a few short lines with heavy interchange traffic to the main line, though there were instances of mixed-gauge track where local industry had to be serviced. The only other gauge used was the Dutch one of 1067 mm. This had originally been employed exclusively in Antwerpen province where cross-border connections were common, but by 1912 the SNCV was having second thoughts even there; the transhipment problem had just been transferred to junctions on its own system!

2.5 Early experiments with railmotors

The Societé was also having thoughts about urban and suburban traffic on those, mainly passenger-carrying, lines around the big cities which did not warrant electrification. Something more flexible than the conventional train was clearly needed and it started experimenting with railmotors. Two of the then fashionable steam cars on the Rowan system

were acquired and tried out but - like most of their contemporaries - proved rather delicate and not able to cope with fluctuations in traffic. The SNCV therefore turned to the ingenious M. Pieper who had designed a system which apparently combined the advantages of internal-combustion power without its undesirable mechanical complications. In the Pieper system an opposed cylinder petrol engine was coupled magnetically to a cardan shaft final drive but with an intermediate dynamo/generator. This in turn was linked to storage batteries and the idea was that, on level(ish) ground the petrol engine could propel the car over a range of speeds without requiring mechanical gears and the battery/generator combination would provide a boost on starting and when climbing gradients. Equally on a descent the petrol engine disengaged and the generator became a dynamo feeding current back into the battery via regenerative braking. The petrol motor's direction of thrust could be changed electrically thus removing the need for mechanical reverse gearing and allowing the use of a tram-type controller. The idea was tried out on a standard 4-w tramcar and a specially designed bogie vehicle and was sufficiently promising for SNCV to commission a small series of eight bogie cars which were used, notably, on the non-electrified sections of the lines south from Bruxelles through Petite-Espinette.

2.6 A review of the first thirty years and their achievements.

The SNCV at this time was unique in Europe. Other countries had laid down general guidelines for developing secondary transport systems to open up their rural areas. Some biggish, semi-autonomous provinces of a country, such as Saxony (Sachsen) in Germany, had gone further and developed systems built and run by the State. None, however, had gone to the extent of Belgium and set up a national organisation to select, build and coordinate a total network, retaining the powers to provide track and equipment while offering private companies the chance to operate them, hopefully at a profit to all concerned. The initiatives rightly attracted a good deal of international comment and praise; at this period, when road transport was not a real threat, it also produced considerable advantages. There was a central design bureau to standardise infrastructure and equipment; the Societé's share of profits from flourishing lines could (after establishing the necessary reserves) be spent on improving and supporting the less profitable - but essential - ones; size and centralisation permitted innovative experiments that would have been beyond the powers of small concerns. The result, by 1914, was an efficient network being developed with the most modern techniques of the period and still in a period of rapid expansion.

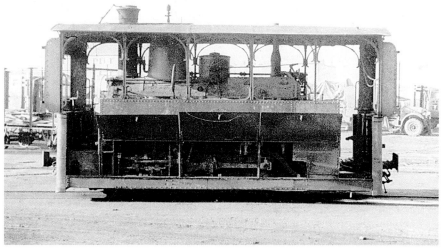

Type 4 0-6-0 tram locomotive 332 with its skirting raised to show the motion. Type 4 was the first heavy series for goods and mixed traffic. *(collection P Roovers)*

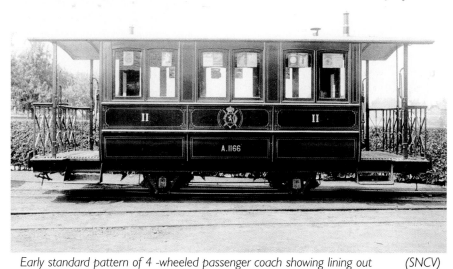

Early standard pattern of 4 -wheeled passenger coach showing lining out *(SNCV)*

An illustration of how SNCV equipment was moved: a standard goods van on a standard gauge wagon *(SNCV)*

Chapter 3:   1914, World War I and After.

3.1   The Position in 1914

It is fair to say that, by the end of the first decade of the twentieth century, the SNCV system had assumed its eventual shape. Indeed the great majority of steam-worked lines were complete before the outbreak of the 1914-18 war. At the end of 1911, the Societé published a list of its major connected systems. In so doing it divided them into the 30 so-called groupes. Note that this use of the term, which equated more or less to the French "réseau" or "system" simply indicated two or more connected lines, usually worked by a single concessionaire

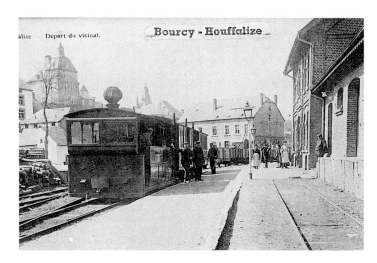

By 1914, even the rural concessions were looking fairly prosperous. This is a gleaming train on the little Bourcy-Houffalize line in Luxembourg.   (collection E de Backer)

from a common headquarters which gave the groupe its name; it should not be confused with the post-war, province-sized administrative Groupes of the SNCV itself. Table 3A shows the groupes listed by province. Of them, six (Antwerpen, Bruxelles, Littoral, Charleroi, Haine-St-Pierre and Liége) had substantial lengths of electric traction. Apart from the Groupes, the remaining isolated lines, such as Quiévrain - Roisin or Poulseur - Sprimont were regarded as separate entities and had their own headquarters. In accordance with SNCV practice, the Groupes are referred to by their French titles but Flemish equivalents have been added where appropriate.

Table 3A: SNCV major operating groupes in 1914

Province/length Groupe / Groep	No of lines or systems
Antwerpen (547.60km)	
* Turnhout	7
* Anvers/Antwerpen	3
* Itegem	4
Brabant (641.47km)	
* Bruxelles: south, west and north of city	6
* Louvain/Leuven	11
* Tremeloo/Tremelo	2
Westvlaanderen (663.72km	
* Courtrai/Kortrijk	6
* Littoral	8
* Poperinghe/Poperinge	6+
* Sweveseele/Zwevezele	6
+ including part of Roeselare - Diksmuide	
Oostvlaanderen (441.11km)	
* Aeltre/Aalter	4
* Audenarde/Oudenaarde	2
* Gand/Gent - Termonde/Dendermonde (east)	5
* Gand/Gent - Rabot (west)	2
* Oordegem	3
Hainaut (787.95km)	
* Boussu (around Mons)	8
* Charleroi	5
* Haine-St-Pierre	4
* Ath	2
Liége (475.67km)	
* Clavier	2
* Liége	3
* Waremme	6
Limburg (331.34km)	
* Hasselt	6
* Tongres/Tongeren	4
Luxembourg (417.98km)	
* Poix	4
* Wellin	3
* Arlon	3
Namur (364.11km)	
* Andenne	7
* Namur	4
* Petite Chapelle	3

It should be noted that there was also a substantial number of isolated lines run either by local concessionaires or by the SNCV itself where it had not proved possible to let any operating contract. More development was planned in 1914 and, indeed, earthworks were being constructed for several lines when the First World War broke out on August 4th and work virtually came to a standstill.

The electric lines were progressing even better. One of the new Titanic bogie cars with a summer train on the line to Waterloo.
(SNCV)

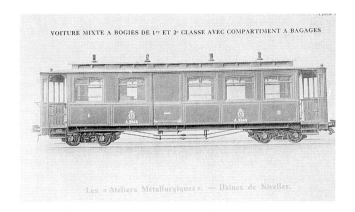

Again the SNCV experimented with bogie coaches - a whole train in one vehicle as seen here.
(SNCV/Ats Metallurgiques brochure)

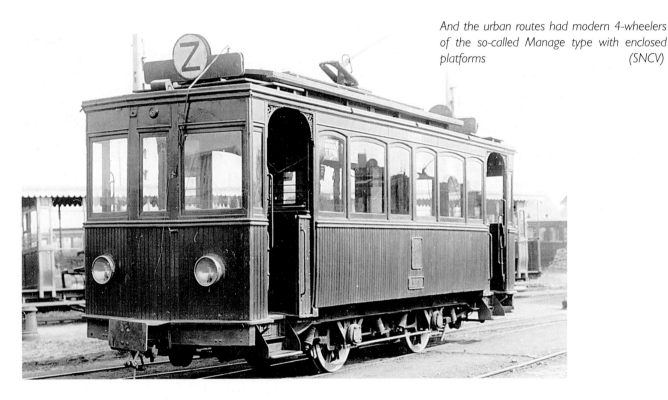

And the urban routes had modern 4-wheelers of the so-called Manage type with enclosed platforms
(SNCV)

3.1.1. General notes on a typical Groupe (Groupe de Louvain) prior to 1914.

As we have seen, in some ways this year was the high point of the SNCV as an organisation. Road transport was not yet a serious competitor, the organisation was still mainly a provider of rural transport and, uniquely for Europe, was operating at national level. The symbol of the SNCV, if there was such a thing, was the roadside light railway with its gleaming green steam tram locomotive and its gaggle of standard four-wheeled rolling stock. Fortunately some contemporary notes about the operation of Groupe de Louvain in 1914 have been preserved, and may be of interest in showing the position of a typical medium-sized concessionaire at this period. The Groupe then had some sixty steam locomotives of various types. First were fifteen or sixteen of Type 3, of which ten were the modified, or improved, variety and three, 147-9 with drive to the rear axle, were regarded as the "express" engines. Others known to be in use were 157-9, 201-5 and 210-11. There were twenty-four of Type 4, from No.226 on, and five of Type 6, No 400-4, plus the very similar 422/4 taken over from the Tramways

Bruxellois. The Groupe also had two of the notorious Type 13 survivors, 428-9, one equally unloved "mogul" of Type 9 (600) and "about ten" of the heavy Type 7, among which were 304, 323-5; 370, 484 and 563. To complement them there were about twenty four-wheel electric cars for the Leuven town services, six of which were moved to Schaerbeek for the Dieghem Lo route just before the war. Rolling stock comprised 150 four-wheel coaches and luggage vans, including some of the De Rechter radial-axle pattern, all at this period with the primitive oil lighting and heating by coal-fired stoves, plus about 1000 goods vehicles of assorted types.

There were major repair works at Leuven (Kessel-Lo), Aerschot (in the north east) and Chastre (down in the south) with subsidiary depots at Bruxelles (Rue Eenens), Haecht, Jodoigne, St-Joris-Weert and Tielt. Nevertheless the SNCV was constantly grumbling at its concessionaires for failing to keep the stock and lines in good order and the Leuven Groupe was no exception. Reading between the lines, it is easy to see why. Locomotive crews were largely untrained, putting considerable strain on the equipment; either to suit their own whims or to

The war changed all that. Typical of the results was the town of Ypres/Ieper, seen here with extensive damage.

(Courtesy the late Ir Debot.)

rectify what they saw as defects, the company's engineers had no qualms about making unauthorised modifications to "improve" steaming qualities. The standard of maintenance, too, was clearly not all that could be desired, though in fairness much of this could be blamed on design defects which made routine servicing difficult.

The infrastructure in this groupe was also typical of the SNCV at this time. Roadside track was normally wooden-sleepered with Vignoles pattern flat bottom rail of either 23kg/m or 32kg/m weight, town track, or other track embedded in the chaussée being of the type known as "à ornières" - basically 31kg/m or 45kg/m Vignoles rail screwed to sleepers embedded in the road surface and with a curved metal strip bolted at one side to form a groove for the wheel flanges. (an alternative sometimes used was replacement of the strip by creasoted wood blocks as spacers). The typical wayside station would have a loop and/or siding with a building combining railway offices, goods storage and accommodation for the stationmaster. Serving, as it did, a largely rural district the Groupe's stations often included ramped cattledocks or beet loading platforms, or else had mobile ramps available for

There are few views of the SNCV at war. Here ex-coastal stock forms a guardhouse "somewhere behind the lines" (SNCV)

use when required. At 1914 the Groupe was operating the following "country" lines:

* Wavre - Incourt - Jodoigne/Geldenaken
* Haacht - Aerschot - Tienen/Tirelemont
* Bruxelles - Haacht (regarded as running INTO Bruxelles)
* Bruxelles - Vossem (ditto: steam service)
* Leuven - Hamme Mille - Geldenaken
* Leuven - Diest
* Leuven - Tervuren
* Braine l'Alleud - Mont St Jean - Wavre
* Mont St Jean - Waterloo (link to Bruxelles - Waterloo)
* Tervuren - Hamme Mille -Tienen
* Courcelles - Chastre - Incourt - Gembloux

In addition it officially had responsibility for four urban routes within Leuven town, which used partly the inner ends of existing lines and partly new trackage. Three ran from the station to Grote Markt (the town square) before fanning out; the fourth was a cross-town route from Heverlee to Kessel Lo. Details will be found in chapter 8. It is worth noting that, with a single concessionaire, traffic patterns developed as the need indicated rather than according to the original Capitaux; thus, for example, there were through services: Bruxelles - Vossem - Hamme Mille, and Wavre - Incourt - Chastre.

3.2 War breaks out: The German attack and its consequences

The outbreak of war in August 1914 brought the golden era of the SNCV to an abrupt end. Belgium formed the natural invasion route to reach France, and the Germans acted accordingly. Despite fierce resistance, they swept through the country from east to west, being held by the allies only as they reached the country's southwestern corner. Hence, by the end of 1914, the SNCV and its constituent companies found themselves in a state of some disarray. The majority of the system was in German-occupied territory but in Westvlaanderen the trench zone cut a wide swathe through that system, and a small part was actually cut off from the rest in the allied-held sector around Veurne/Furnes and Ieper/Ypres.

This isolated part of the SNCV comprised parts of Capitaux 2, 29, 75, 107 and 115. Of these, the coastal line from De Panne (Capital 2) was truncated at Nieuwpoort, which was

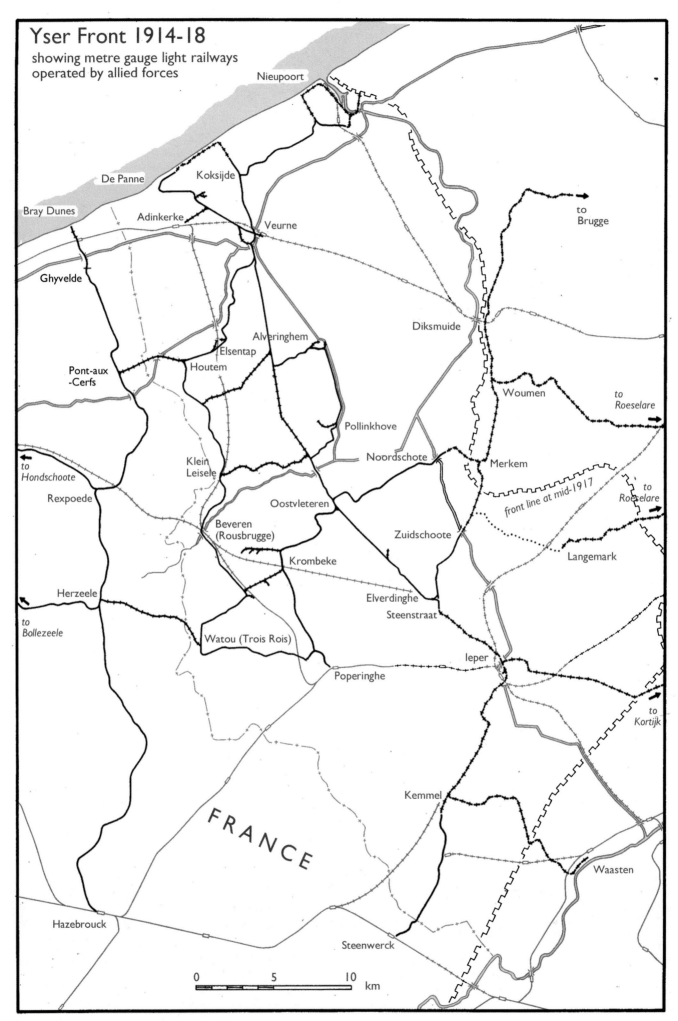

Yser Front 1914-18
showing metre gauge light railways
operated by allied forces

Nieuwpoort

De Panne

Bray Dunes

Koksijde

Adinkerke

Veurne

to Brugge

Ghyvelde

Alveringhem

Diksmuide

Elsentap

Houtem

Woumen

to Roeselare

Pont-aux
-Cerfs

Pollinkhove

Noordschote

Merkem

to Hondschoote

Klein
Leisele

Oostvleteren

front line at mid-1917

to Roeselare

Rexpoede

Beveren
(Rousbrugge)

Zuidschoote

Langemark

Krombeke

Herzeele

Elverdinghe

Steenstraat

to Bollezeele

Watou (Trois Rois)

Ieper

Poperinghe

to Kortijk

Kemmel

FRANCE

Waasten

Hazebrouck

Steenwerck

0   5   10
                          km

28

under constant bombardment, while the routes east from Oostvleteren junction toward Dijksmuide and south toward Ieper (Capitaux 29 and 107) were cut after only a few kilometres. All the lines from Ieper (Capitaux 41, 85, 121, 151) were either completely closed or in the hands of the German army, while the long line southwest from Ieper into France at Steenwerck was cut at Kemmel and could be worked only from its French connection. Capital 115 (Poperinghe - Veurne - De Panne) was largely within the allied sector and usable for military purposes, at least in part. The whole area then became a forward war zone, remaining as such for the rest of the war so that civilian services were abruptly terminated. Matters were complicated by the fact that the allied forces which held this sector were a mixture of Belgian and French toward the coast, with the British 1st Army overlapping them around Ypres; the back areas were even more thoroughly mixed. In practice, the remaining SNCV lines were split into northern and southern sectors, the latter being worked largely by a confused mixture of French and British military organisations, while the former was worked by the Belgians themselves.

3.3 The Section Vicinale de Chemins de Fer en Campagne (SVCFC)

The Belgian-operated lines became the responsibility of a unique organisation. Fortunately, as war became inevitable, Baron Edouard Empain, whose empire controlled many lines in Vlaanderen, had foresightedly made provisional plans to evacuate to the west much of his equipment and personnel. Soon after war started, he also set up, apparently as a semi-private army, the *Section Vicinale de Chemins de Fer en Campagne* or Vicinal field railways section. An initial grouping at Antwerpen was overtaken by the German advance in the autumn of 1914 but the SVCFC was reformed as the Front stabilised along the line of the river Yser. It was organised as an army Company, with a captain in charge and two platoons - one for operation and one for permanent way work - each commanded by a lieutenant. Repairs to material and installations were entrusted to the Belgian army's Railway Engineer Battalion, which ran the standard-gauge railways in this sector throughout the war and also developed some 60cm gauge lines.

Initially the SVCFC operated the whole remaining metre gauge system using existing depots at Veurne, Beveren and Poperinge, the last being converted to a repair shop. Nieuwpoort depot was unusable owing to its proximity to the front line, and indeed army engineers worked most of the Nieuwpoort line until early 1917, when the SVCFC took over. Conversely, at the end of 1914, all lines south of Beveren and Oostvleteren were effectively handed over to the French and British, the Poperinge shops being transferred to Beveren (Rousbrugge). The Section HQ was then at Houtem, on the Beveren - Veurne line, whence an east-west connection to French metre-gauge lines in the French part of Flanders (Flandres) was put in by French engineers between January and June 1915. Another, internal, link was put in soon after from Klein Leisele, north of Beveren, to Linde on the Veurne - Ieper route, and certain little-used sections, notably from Koksijde to De Panne, were lifted to provide materials. Transhipment points with the standard gauge were established at Klein Leisele and Veurne, a bypass route being built round Veurne town to allow trains to and from the coast to pass easily.

The SVCFC's main traffic centre was established at Veurne and the system was always controlled from there, although the operating HQ was moved to Klein Leisele in 1916. Veurne was very near the front line, and subsidiary depots were established further back at Elsentap and Klein Leisele - which was rapidly becoming very important. Rolling stock was almost entirely ex-

SNCV, Baron Empain having been able to evacuate some 80 locomotives, 330 coaches and 400 wagons from his own Groupe du Littoral and from the neighbouring Dijksmuide and Audenaarde Groupes. Some of this equipment was not in working order and a part, to clear congestion, was passed on into France, with consequent anguish when its owners tried to locate it after the war!

The traffic consisted of two distinct types. First there were scheduled services, run using normal SNCV procedures, to bring up supplies and provide leave transport for both French and Belgian troops. Secondly, as on all the military lines, there were regular mass movements of troops when one formation relieved another in the front line. On such occasions, Veurne and Klein Leisele depots were given five hours notice to produce twenty-two 14-coach trains running to and from De Panne. These would pick up the troops - up to a maximum of 6400 - and then run in one vast convoy "on sight" to the destination, a spare locomotive bringing up the end in order to take the last train back; to provide watering facilities, the first train took a motor pump which was connected to the nearest ditch at an appropriate point. The scheme proved efficient and was later adopted by other allied forces. The SVCFC continued to operate its lines up to the end of the war, although considerable difficulties were experienced and services were always likely to be disrupted by bombardment.

3.4 Allied use of SNCV lines around Ieper

The position on the southern sector was more complicated, involving not only the French and British military engineers but also several French secondary railway companies whose lines were either taken over entirely or "hired" from time to time. In the early part of the war, most work was done by the French 5th Engineer Battalion which was given the task of re-establishing communications between the forward zone and the rear areas in French Flandres. Apart from the Houtem line mentioned above, they also built a strategic link from the French system at Herzeele to Trois Rois on the SNCV Poperinge - Beveren line (3.35km) and a further cross-link from Proven, near Trois Rois, eastward to the old Poperinge - Dijksmuide line at Krombeke (7.02km). In addition, during the autumn of 1915, they rebuilt southwards from Woesten, on the Veurne - Ieper route, to Steenstraat on the outskirts of Ieper, while reopening the Elverdinge - Diksmuide branch as far as Zuidschoote.

At the year-end, operation of this area passed to the famous 10th Section of the French Field Railways Battalion, which appears to have more or less dispossessed the French light railway companies in French Flandres. At the same time, the British 1st Army was happily working its own trains over the same system and had even established a large depot at Ghyvelde near the coast. By mid-1917, after a short hiatus, the French were effectively running the east-west link lines while the British operated out of Poperinge to Beveren (Rousbrugge); to Oostvleteren and south from there toward Ieper. They also worked the detached stub of the SNCV's Ieper - Steenwerck route as far north as Kemmel from time to time but no details are available. The position probably reflects the relative numerical strengths of each national contingent. To do all this, the British War Department used available SNCV stock but also ordered 50 new 0-6-0 Tram locomotives based on the SNCV type 18, and 1200 wagons of SNCV pattern; 48 of the locomotives and 620 wagons later passed to the SNCV, the locomotives becoming SNCV Type 19.

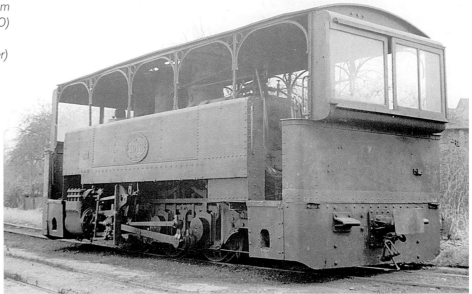

3.5   German military use of SNCV lines and equipment.

Although few details are available, it is clear that the German army also used many of the existing lines on their side of the battle zone - and also commandeered a fair amount of SNCV equipment for use on other parts of the front. For example, during the prolonged attack on Verdun in 1916, the Germans made considerable use of the former SE Réseau de la Woeuvre from Montmedy southward and also built a number of new spurs in the area. Since the SE (Societé Générale des CF Economiques) had evacuated its stock, all this had to be equipped "from new" and SNCV material formed part of that requisition. Certainly at the war's end no less than 14 locomotives, 53 coaches and over 700 goods vehicles were reclaimed from that area. Various items of stock were also recouped from systems on the Somme front and around the central front.

3.6   Other SNCV lines under German occupation

Meanwhile, what of the much larger portion of the network that remained within the general area of German occupation? Near the battle zones, the Germans also made some use of existing lines, as noted above but elsewhere the system rapidly regained a semblance of normal operation by the end of 1914. Indeed it had to, since the mainline railways were largely commandeered by the military, and the SNCV was the only practicable means of local communication. In the words of the SNCV's official history:

"Once assured of the approval of the Belgian Government in exile, the managers of the Société Nationale and those of the working companies strove with the willing help of all concerned, to restore the services disorganised by the invasion and to gather the scattered rolling stock. Formerly accustomed to organise only slow trains, they created faster long-distance passenger trains connecting big cities. To ensure the supplies of coal and food to towns, they ran night trains and used electric motor cars to haul goods trains. The maintenance work had to be done at night. All these innovations completely revolutionised the operation of the Vicinal railways."

Behind that laconic statement, however, lay a quite exceptional effort. Certainly only in Belgium with its countrywide network of standardised lines could it have been done at all. At the same time the "system" was, as we have seen, really a multitude of almost independent companies. All these companies, with their own problems, had to be persuaded to co-operate, the complicated costings had to be fairly apportioned, and the stock reallocated and maintained. If that was not enough, the Germans, quite justifiably from their point of view, realised that the "new" network was undoubtedly being used also for clandestine purposes. Therefore, they not only interfered constantly with its operation but, from om 1915 onward, began closing and lifting whole lines to re-use the material for their own purposes. Some 2230km, or over half the existing length, were eventually rendered useless by this means, and it is a great credit to the SNCV that the remainder in 1917-18 carried almost as much freight as the total system in 1913, while passenger receipts had nearly doubled.

3.7   The last days of the war and the aftermath

In the summer of 1918, following an abortive German offensive, the war became one of movement, and by the armistice on 11 November, the front line in Belgium had been pushed back well beyond the provinces of Vlaanderen; the SVCFC itself had advanced to an HQ near Brugge and, together with Belgian army engineers, was trying to restore some semblance of rail communication to the shattered region. The links forward via Nieuwpoort and Ieper were temporarily impassable owing to blown bridges and general devastation and the retreating enemy did not make things easy for the returning Belgians; infrastructure was damaged in a number of places and stock was wantonly vandalised. The SNCV, therefore, was faced with a herculean task in restoring its system to health and probably only a national organisation could have overcome the difficulties.

and don't forget the 60cm gauge feeder lines. ADELE (see ch 12) was used by the allies and picked up a useful war-surplus Simplex tractor for its seaside tramway.
(author's collection)

Chapter 4:   Between the Wars

4.1   Reconstruction and reclamation

In the aftermath of war, the SNCV found itself in probably the worst position of any European light railway organisation. Its territory had been constantly fought over and twice overrun by sweeping advances. The country's economy was in ruins and much of the secondary rail system had been damaged or dismantled; at the end of November 1918, only 1865km of track remained intact from a pre-war total of some 4095km. Furthermore, the rolling stock was heavily overworked and in need of serious maintenance even where it had not been actively sabotaged by the retreating Germans -

It took time for the system to recover and if things did not always go smoothly.... well, accidents happen everywhere. Here a train for Veurne has missed the swing bridge somehow.   (SNCV)

the experience of SVCFC, returning to Brugge only to find the entire Ostende - Blankenberghe fleet dumped in the open with controllers smashed by hammers, was not uncommon. Much of the equipment that had been evacuated to allied territory in 1914 and had been passed through to France for lack of storage had mysteriously "disappeared"; the SNCV was busy for several years reclaiming odd items from scattered lines along the western front. In addition, a large part of the fleet had been commandeered by the Occupier and much equipment removed to Germany. Most was quickly reclaimed but in mid-1922 some 60 locomotives, 145 passenger coaches, 484 wagons and 29 luggage vans were still recorded as missing although this may include material destroyed or otherwise written off owing to acts of war. The acquisition of some 48 locomotives and 620 or so wagons from the British War Department went only some way to balancing these losses.

Another indication of the scale of devastation is that, besides the efforts of SNCV workshops working at full capacity, some 385 locomotives, 1198 coaches and luggage vans and 2935 goods vehicles had to be repaired by outside contractors. These conditions had two immediate consequences:

Firstly, the postwar shortages and high prices made it very difficult for the Societé to obtain materials or to fund the production of replacement stock. The difficulty was compounded by a government ruling that the SNCV must obtain new equipment from outside manufacturers rather than from its own workshops. The measure was in essence a sensible one designed to protect heavy industry in its climb back to profitability, but it undoubtedly hampered development, though it was surprising what results could be obtained from rebuilding existing equipment, which was permitted.

Secondly, the financial collapse had disastrous effects on both the SNCV and its operating companies. Tariffs had been held down to an increase of only 100% to try and protect the ordinary passenger, while expenses generally climbed by up to 400% and continued climbing; by 1923 coal and other consumables were costing up to seven times as much as in 1913. As a result, many concessionary companies found themselves unable to continue. A law dated 11 October 1919 recognised this problem, allowing contracts agreed before the war to be given up under certain conditions.

Both big and small concessionaires hastened to take advantage of it. By the end of 1920, 3175km had been handed back to the SNCV, and two years later it had 3515km on its hands, although this included a few lines that had always been directly worked and some that were currently dismantled. Only 779km remained in private hands and, over the next ten years, even that dwindled until only four companies remained: The *Societé pour l'exploitation des Lignes Vicinales d'Ostende et des Plages Belges (SELVOP)*, with 144km, and the *SA pour l' Exploitation du CFV Rochefort - Grottes de Han - Wellin* (45.50km) both had profitable tourist traffic; the *Electrische Tramwegen van Gent* (17 km) had its own flourishing urban network to sustain it; the bits conceded to the *Tramways Bruxellois* (6km) and *Zeeuwsch Vlaamsche Tramweg Mij* (6km) were simply historical anomalies embedded in their owners' systems.

Perforce compelled to become a major operator, the SNCV decided to do the job properly, voluntarily taking over contracts that had expired instead of again putting them out to tender. Previously, cohesion had been almost impossible, with adjoining lines worked by different companies and with many big concerns having lines scattered all over the country. The SNCV decided to reorganise, basing control on a single administrative Groupe for each province or major part of a province; in Brabant, for example, two Groupes were established: Leuven/Louvain and Bruxelles/Brussel, while in Limburg one Groupe controlled the lot and eventually merged with the neighbouring province of Liége. Individual réseaux (the former operating groupes) still had considerable local autonomy but the major Groupe had overall control; thus it could deploy its equipment more efficiently, transferring material as required to meet peak demands. The most useful results were a reduction in the quantity of equipment needed as a reserve and the concentration of repair facilities at one or two big workshops per Groupe. As a bonus, the old system whereby each concessionaire had maintained its own workshops could be modified and, in effect, each major provincial SNCV Groupe was able to concentrate effort on one, or at most two, sites. Thus Hasselt became the focus of operations in Limburg and very soon proved to be very ingenious: its efforts in "rebuilding" existing stock into self-propelled railmotors became well-known, if not occasionally notorious. Equally Destelbergen for the inner parts of Vlaanderen, Cureghem in Brabant and Merksem Ijskelder in Antwerpen, for example, proved to be very adaptable and capable, when allowed to do so, of building new motive power from scratch, usually to the designs of the SNCV's own central drawing office.

One of the conventional Type 20 standard gauge 0-6-0Ts acquired for shunting.   *(author's collection)*

All this is was not done without great toil and trouble. The costs of reconstruction, and the inability of the public purse to increase its contributions, meant that the SNCV had to draw heavily on its devalued reserves and to spend all that it currently earned. Hence the yearly operating ratio, which up to 1913 had fluctuated comfortably between 65% and 75%, climbed steadily into the high 90s. In 1921, for the first time, it actually exceeded 100% (ie the Societé did not even meet its operating costs). Nonetheless it was the proud boast of the SNCV that it was able to carry through all this rebuilding without once contravening the terms of its original constitution. By the end of 1923 it had some 4383km, out of 5000 conceded, back in use, 3933km being steam-worked and 450km electrically worked, though steam trams worked through on some 84km of the latter. The operating ratio had stabilised at just over 97%.

4.2 Post-war Development and the effects of road and rail competition

The system was then very much on a "plateau". To develop and improve it, existing Capitaux would need to be increased (there was provision for this) and new ones formed. Agreement had been reached before the war on a revised share of costs in some cases, in the proportion of 50% to the state, 25% to the provinces and 25% to the communes concerned; now all lines were to follow this formula. It will be noted that private participation, always small, was now non-existent. The wild financial fluctuations of the early 1920s,

however, meant that even public money was in short supply and so little was done. At the same time, improvements were urgently needed, for the early 1920s also saw the emergence of serious road competition. With war-surplus vehicles plentiful, many local entrepreneurs had seized the opportunity to start short, local, road services which, inevitably, competed directly with roadside rural trams and, in towns, took traffic from districts the SNCV did not serve directly. A law of 11 August 1924 theoretically gave the SNCV preference in providing road services paralleling existing routes, in substituting buses on routes conceded but not yet built, and on new routes linking SNCV lines. These, however, were subject to all the rigours of the SNCV concession procedures, while private companies, although officially subject to licensing, could establish themselves more easily since their master was a different government department. As a result, by 1929, while the SNCV was running some 675 km of bus routes, either directly or leased to others, private - and often pirate - companies were running over 7000km. The situation did not stabilise until the early 1930s when new laws, especially that of 29 August 1931, gave the Societé powers to control the situation more closely. Even then its bus routes were considered very much as appendages to the rail network, and at the outbreak of war in 1939, the SNCV owned fewer than 80 buses in its own name.

So much for road competition. Fortunately, arrangements with the mainline railways were much smoother, especially after the *Societé Nationale des Chemins de Fer Belges (SNCB)* was formed in 1926. Previous planning had ensured that there was little serious competition, even though the SNCV was serving directly almost half the communes in the country (1200 out of 2670). Freight traffic, which might have been a bone of contention, was only 3 per cent of the national total, even though there were almost 800 industrial sidings on the narrow gauge. This was because SNCV lines were basically feeders to the standard gauge. Indeed, up to 1931, restrictive taxes discouraged the SNCV from running such freight as coal direct

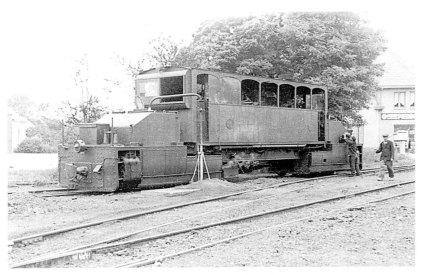

There were some attempts to develop the traditional steam power. Here is one of the two Garratt tram locomotives for hauling heavy goods in Limburg. (collection P Roovers)

4.3 Modernisation and extension.

4.3.1 Development of the i/c engined fleet

To take modernisation first, the SNCV had from 1925-on been experimenting with small petrol-engined vehicles that were essentially road buses on rails. Since outside manufacturers did not see a market for such vehicles, the Societé had to conduct its own experiments, initially using foreign equipment. The Societé was, as noted in chapter 2, interested in self-propelled passenger vehicles from quite early on. As we have seen, even before the First World War it experimented with two Rowan semi-articulated steam cars and with the Pieper i/c electrics. After WWI it realised quite quickly that it had to provide competition to the war-surplus buses that were proliferating on country roads and "dipped its toe in that water" so to speak by ordering a pair of railbuses and a pair of early double-ended cars with the intention of seeing which had most potential. Sadly, both designs were pretty crude and did not really provide enough evidence for a sensible decision so, as an interim measure, the SNCV bought two small series of developed railbuses from France (De Dion, Nos AR 5-10) and Germany (Bussing, AR11-12), the latter being heavy vehicles capable of towing a trailer. At the same time it commissioned its Hasselt Works, in conjunction with SNCV Cureghem, to build a series of double enders to its own design (AR13-35) - or rather, officially, rebuild them from trailer coaches as it was not permitted to build new. In practice Hasselt built chassis and some of the bodies, the others passing to Cureghem (Bruxelles) for completion; as an aside several sources mention that some at least of these motorised chassis processed solemnly from Hasselt to Cureghem under their own power, the drivers seated uncomfortably on a completely exposed box.

from producer to consumer, but then a new agreement allowed such traffic where it was clearly economic.

External pressures were, therefore, considerable throughout the inter-war period, and the SNCV needed to set its own house in order. The early 1920s, as we have seen, were largely a period of reconstruction, and the financial problems made it difficult to raise new capital; hence little fresh construction was undertaken. In 1927, however, the currency was stabilised and the SNCV started a new programme of modernisation and extension. The programme had two main directions: extension and electrification of routes likely to provide heavy passenger traffic, this for the first time including substantial new lines electrified from the start; and progressive modernisation of the existing rural system, replacing steam traction by petrol- and diesel-engined autorails.

but modernisation beckoned, especially with internal-combustion which offered many economies over steam: Here an early double-ended vehicle, AR3 or 4, is decorated to celebrate its debut at Mons.

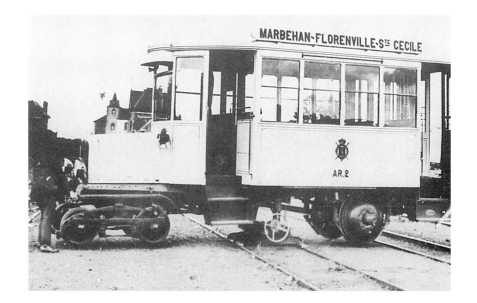

Early experiments, however, concentrated on railbuses: AR1 was a Saurer design, bodied locally (SNCV)

AR13-35 were the first really useful double-ended cars designed by SNCV Hasselt and built by them and SNCV Cureghem. This is AR27 with a Cureghem body (SNCV)

Before settling on a final design, the SNCV conducted controlled experiments as related in the text, This is AR38, one of a pair of i/c electric cars in which the transmission bulk required radiators to be moved to the roof (SNCV)

And this is AR 133 of the final metal-bodied design, caught drinking fuel at Martelange in the Ardennes. (late Ir. Debot)

The results of this second series of trials clearly showed that the double-ended vehicle had the edge but even so the Societé was not entirely satisfied. Should it use mechanical drive via gearing and cardan shafts? or final chain drive from a reversing gearbox? or even i/c electric which had by the mid 1920s developed into a reliable though cumbersome alternative. Three more pairs of slightly more sophisticated "homebuilt" double-ended cars (AR36-41) were therefore tried out against each other and the straightforward mechanical transmission won on points. As a result the Societé standardised on a neat four-wheeled double end car "externally resembling the electric cars" as it said in its reports. The SNCV itself built over a hundred of this type with a variety of wood or metal-clad bodies depending on the parent Works and, from AR 127 on, mostly powered by 100hp Brossel diesel engines. It then put the design out to commercial tender and, following a metal-bodied prototype by Baume et Marpent, another 154 examples were produced in the mid 1930s mostly by outside makers although SNCV Hasselt and Destelbergen got in on the act as well. At the same time the SNCV did experiment with bogie cars, a very neat Baume et Marpent prototype (AR 115) being followed by a small production series (AR 284-88, by Braine-le-Comte) used at first mainly in Brabant and Antwerpen and then later mostly transferred to the Ardennes. Apart from an odd abberation by Hasselt. who converted an old bogie coach to AR 283 in the 1930s, these were almost the final fling until a small collection after the 1939-45 war which will be mentioned in chapter 5.

These cars virtually replaced steam on rural lines for passenger work and transformed the operating results. In general service speeds were increased by about 50 per cent, train frequency was roughly doubled, and the operating cost per kilometre was almost halved. Passengers appreciated the new rolling stock, and loadings on some lines rose by up to 100 per cent, no doubt helped by the fact that fares were simultaneously lowered by about 25 per cent to encourage traffic! Those who

have ridden Vicinal autorails in their old age, experiencing the considerable noise and vibration, may well wonder what the users saw in them. It must be remembered, however, that the cars were very comfortable by comparison with the elderly steam trains they replaced, and also that travel on the often ill-laid pave or unsurfaced roads of the period was even more bone-shaking. Nonetheless the SNCV's autorail initiative was effectively a once-for-all effort. With the exception of the fine bogie cars built just before and after World War II, no further vehicles were provided, and the 1930s batch saw out both passenger and goods traffic on most rural lines.

4.3.2 Development of the electrified system & its equipment

The major effort of the late 1920s and 1930s was, however, put into extension and electrification, especially the latter. From 428km in 1923, the electrified system increased to no less than 1227km (almost a quarter of the total) during the next ten years; the peak period was during the early 1930s when new Capitaux added 123km (1930), 171km (1931) and 176km (1933) in successive years. By the end of 1934 no less than 1290km were in use, and by the outbreak of war in 1939 there were nearly 1500km of electrified routes. They spread from all the major cities and in some areas, such as Hainaut, formed a dense network which included long interurban services. Most were purely passenger-carrying, and to serve them there was a massive modernisation of rolling stock.

First came the penultimate standard pattern of two-axle car, usually known as the "Seneffe" or the "Braine-le-Comte" type after the manufacturers who first built it. The term "Seneffe" can most properly be applied to the 9695-714 series, which were a kind of intermediate stage. They had the general dimensions of later types and a distinctive arrangement of six almost square windows divided by a horizontal metal bar two-thirds of the way up. Their ends were of the "bow-end" type and the platforms were enclosed by double-leaf folding doors.

There was development on the electric side too. Several series were bought in from outside to fill urgent needs: Typical was the set of radial-axle four-wheelers originally intended for Odessa. *(SNCV)*

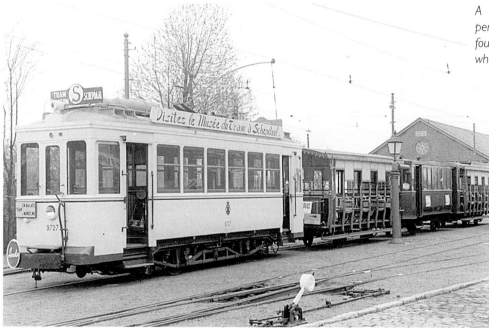
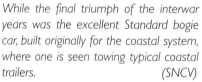

A preserved example of the penultimate, or 'Seneffe' series of four-wheeled cars, with typical four-wheeled stock. *(Author)*

While the final triumph of the interwar years was the excellent Standard bogie car, built originally for the coastal system, where one is seen towing typical coastal trailers. *(SNCV)*

later versions had sliding doors and squared ends which were similar to those of the "Standard" bogie cars then coming into service (see below). As with many earlier series, individual batches differed slightly in detail and some were modified in various ways during their careers. The final two-axle cars, and those of which the SNCV was most proud, were 10111-25, which were metal-bodied variants of the basic design. They had four large sidewindows and were similar in style to the later metal-bodied "Standard" bogie cars. Although widely publicised, they formed a very small proportion of the total cars built.

That having been said, the SNCV always had the habit of building retrospective series of "old-fashioned" designs to meet particular needs and there were of course various odds and ends - Oostende, Salzinnes and Hasselt for instance rebuilt new bodies on old equipment; the SNCV, post 1918, bought in series originally intended for such places as Odessa (4-wheelers with radial axles) and Taschkent; some German cars were taken over when the Aachen lines were assimilated post 1918; even before 1918 a few antiquated vehicles came from

design was formulated in 1913 but the outbreak of war delayed development until 1919 when it emerged as the type "Titanic", a series of twelve massive cars for use on mixed trains and high-density passenger routes. These cars, easily recognisable by their distinctive well-frames, had an eventful history for so small a class. The SNCV also acquired small groups of bogie cars from outside sources at this period: from Aachen, from Les Vicinaux Anversois, and from orders intended for Bogota and Odessa, while some Odessa cars had their radial axles replaced by bogies but no further indigenous cars were designed until 1930, when the first of the so-called "Standard" cars, eventually to number about 400, appeared.

It all started when SELVOP, then running the coast lines, asked the SNCV in 1927 to provide some radial-truck cars for fast services. Quick tests with the Odessa type, then running at Antwerpen, showed radial trucks to be unsatisfactory over about 45 km/h, and the SNCV Service Traction et Materiel drew up a tentative design for a large bogie car. This had a panelled wooden body with large windows and was mounted on a flat underframe; this was a departure from previous

The final prewar development: the metal-bodied standard car (SNCV)

the Etat Belge when the Mons-Boussu was taken over; some saloons and a small series of rather pretty open toastracks were acquired when the TEOL was taken over; there were even a few battery-electric cars round Gent and Oostende....but there were so many variations that they cannot be covered in detail here and must await a further volume.

In contrast to the four-wheelers, the story of the bogie cars is straightforward. The first SNCV bogie motor cars were "benzo-electrics" using the Pieper system. As we have seen they did not prove entirely successful and were converted to straight electrics in 1926. Even before that, however, as the electrified network spread, however, there was a need for large motor cars capable of pulling a substantial trailing load. A

practice and required the provision of small-wheeled plate frame bogies and new patterns of motor. Width was the generous 2.40 metres allowed by the coastal loading gauge. The cars were successful, and the news spread rapidly round other SNCV Groupes, which promptly decided one after the other that they too urgently needed bogie cars. Their orders raised a sizable problem, for many of the cars could be only 2.20 metres wide, and the proposed plate-frame bogies did not have enough play in the narrowed chassis. It was therefore decided to equip the whole series with a heavy Pennsylvania-type bogie manufactured by Haine-St-Pierre. In passing, one may note that the SNCV never had occasion to regret this decision, the bogies proving almost indestructible and forming the later basis for many type "S" cars in the 1950s.

The SNCV also indulged in what one might call peripheral activities: one venture was an early series of camping coaches, seen here at the 1935 Bruxelles exposition. (SNCV)

The standard series, built between 1930 and 1933, eventually reached a total of 152 and proved so successful that Baume et Marpent were asked to produce a metal-bodied version. This series, recognisable by its riveted panels, was built between 1934 and 1938, reaching a total of 185; all except forty were equipped with roller-blind destination indicators and, although initially fitted with the Pieper oleo-pneumatic brake common to previous SNCV vehicles, were retrospectively fitted with Westinghouse air brakes. They were followed between 1942 and 1948 by a final 63 cars with welded steel bodies.

As before, many of these cars were expected to tow trailers when required to increase their capacity. Even the final batches of four-wheelers had the facility and from 1917 a separate number series, the 19XXX series, was allocated for trailer use. It included many improvisations including bought-in designs, further conversions of steam stock and, eventually of early railcars but was made up mainly of standard bogie trailers to match the appropriate motor cars. The later volume will cover all these in detail.

4.4   Results of modernisation

The widespread introduction of railcars saved many rural services that would otherwise have been completely economical, even though they meant that day-to-day freight traffic dwindled rapidly; only the seasonal agricultural traffic - in particular beet and timber - and the limited mineral traffic remained faithful to rail for obvious reasons. At least it did allow a large part of the ageing steam locomotive fleet to be retired or put into reserve for high days and holidays while keeping open lines that

otherwise would have closed. The electric services that developed at the same time, however, were a positive advance. They were far superior to contemporary bus provision, and contributed greatly to keeping the overall operating ratio below 100% (ie in surplus) for most of the period. By the mid 1930s the electrified system, though totalling only about a quarter of the whole, provided over two-thirds of the receipts. This development therefore continued steadily, if rather more slowly, through the depression years and up to the outbreak of World War II. The combined system peaked in 1940, with 3333 km of non-electric and 1479 km of electrified routes. Notable

Interior of an SNCV camping coach looking through the kitchen/washroom to the dining/bedroom. No space was.wasted. (SNCV)

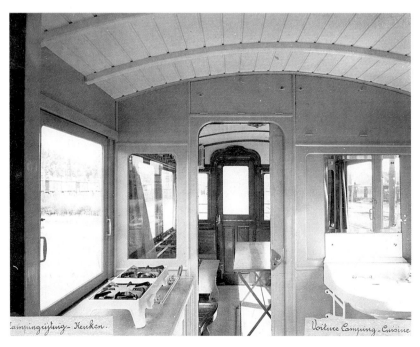

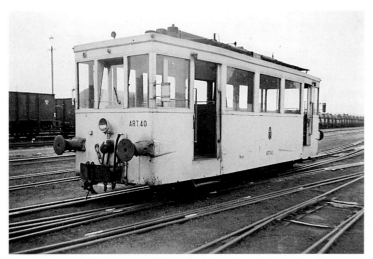

A typical autorail-tracteur fitted with dual gauge buffing/coupling gear for shunting standard gauge sections.
(P de Backer)

was the development of true interurban fast services linking a number of major towns and cities. For instance in Antwerpen, the Turnhout - Antwerpen and Antwerpen - Mechelen routes benefited; in Brabant, Bruxelles - Leuven and in Hainaut Mons - Charleroi services were greatly improved by such means to which the new standard bogie cars contributed greatly.

An interesting by-product of all this electrification was a fresh development of purely urban tram services. Not only did existing towns like Leuven or Oostende benefit - which they did, since electrification of existing country lines allowed new routes, including short suburban workings for commuters. Several other towns found themselves, almost by default, with an infrastructure that encouraged such developments. Thus Tournai and Kortijk had electrified lines coming in from the country and criss-crossing the town centres; urban services were a natural development. In other cases such as Antwerpen and Liége the SNCV wanted to join the inner termini of its existing railways for operational purposes which, in turn, led to provision of new services; in addition big cities such as Bruxelles simply expanded to engulf their neighbouring settlements so that the lines toward Londerzeel and Grimbergen for instance became, faute de mieux, urban tramways with intensive services. The inevitable result was the shift toward the SNCV which was familiar to most modern enthusiasts - a, largely passenger-carrying, collection of urban, suburban and interurban electric tramways with a diminishing hinterland of traditional rural light railways, rather than the network of rural development lines which had been its original raison d'etre.

Although this particular view is post WW2, a typical sight on the coastal route throughout the period (and familiar with British tourists) was a 4-wheeled motor luggage van towing a gaggle of 4-wheeled trailers: this was almost unique to the coastal system but there it was common.
(WJKD)

Chapter 5:   World War II and After.

5.1   The war and its immediate effects

In some ways, World War II for the SNCV was simply an action replay of the earlier conflict. Well before any fighting actually reached Belgium, its inevitability had been recognised and various measures had been considered. These included the possibility of systematically destroying all major SNCV installations in the event of an invasion, and of evacuating to the western provinces as much rolling stock as possible, as in 1914. Fortunately it was recognised that the network would be unlikely to be of much use to an occupying power but would be vital to the country's economy, while the German Blitzkreig over Poland raised doubts as to whether 1914-18 style trench warfare was a likely outcome of any attack! Hence, when the German army did invade on 10 May 1940, the SNCV system

The German invasion of 1940 brought disruption with damage and blown bridges - here a railcar is (rather shakily) moved across a canal to allow services to be resumed on a cut-off stretch of line.
(author's collection)

was still largely intact, with its material and personnel in place. The rapid pace of the invasion and immediate requisitioning of all road vehicles and their fuel threw the whole system into chaos, most services being temporarily suspended. Nonetheless, the network did play a large part in evacuating vital government departments and their records to Oostende for eventual transfer to England.

Only hours after the German motorised troops had passed through Bruxelles, some local services were restored and during the following weeks personnel worked all hours to

patch up the extensive war damage and get long-distance trains running again. Work was hampered by destruction of no less than 167 bridges, most of which had to be replaced or bypassed before services could be restored. Yet, as in the earlier war, these were vital. With the mainline railways either damaged or commandeered, and with road transport almost non-existent through lack of fuel, the SNCV was the only means of averting crises all over the country. Long coal trains ran through from Liége to Bruxelles and into Antwerpen province; vegetables and other foodstuffs passed from Brabant to the almost starving industrial centres of the south. Above all, in the autumn, the essential sugar-beet harvest had to depend almost entirely on the SNCV. Accordingly, during 1940 especially, freight traffic more than doubled, from 6 to over 13 million tonne-km per month; although it settled down as some mainline capacity became available, long-distance traffic especially remained very high for the rest of the war. Passenger traffic also increased greatly, though this was local rather than inter-provincial. Even so, long-distance expresses were organised between Bruxelles and all the major provincial cities, and passenger totals rose sharply from 190 million in 1939 through 340 million in 1942 to some 403 million in 1943. Doubtless the rise would have continued had not the eventual disorganisation and liberation in 1944-5 rather upset the statistics.

All this effort, as in World War 1, was achieved under very difficult conditions. By no means all the vital bridges were repaired - in the Kempen and along the major arteries such as the Albert Canal, only fragmentary services were possible. The Germans, while not taking over the system, nevertheless added to its problems in many ways. The Hague Convention allowed their personnel free use of the trains, which did not help receipts, and they imposed the same regime as the Belgians had imposed on Germany during their occupation of the Rheinland after 1918. As in the first war, they also requisitioned numerous rural lines with the intention of lifting them and sending the rails off to the Ukraine. Delaying actions by the SNCV prevented

The war also brought disruption of another kind: Place d'Armes at Namur in 1943 after a bombardment. *(P Guyot, courtesy SNCV).*

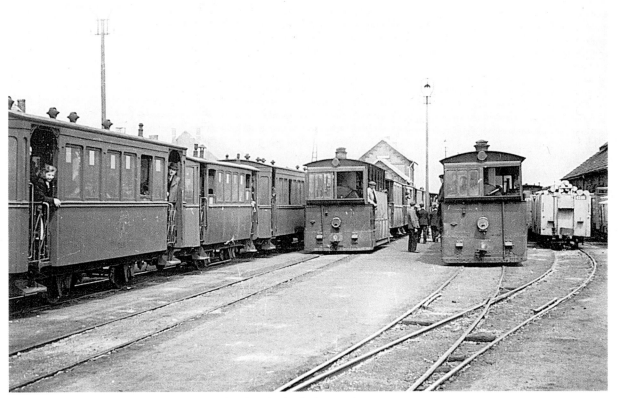

But services continued and even increased - they had to! A typical wartime scene at OLV Tielt with trains crossing. (collection P Roovers)

and many steam locomotives came back into use to handle the urgently needed goods traffic. (collection P Roovers)

KH10295

On the electric lines even cars formerly relegated to goods work reappeared to handle the passenger demand. A Titanic, rebuilt for goods work after the 1937 Haacht depot fire, runs a commuter train in Antwerpen.   (collection P Roovers)

the first "batch" of 429km being lifted before Spring 1943, and this material was still on Belgian soil when the Germans requisitioned a further batch of lines at the beginning of 1944. By then Russian advances had made the need for Ukranian light railways rather academic, and only St-Niklaas - Doel, in Vlaanderen, was actually dismantled. The personnel were, in the main, discreetly found employment elsewhere by the SNCV to avoid transportation to Germany as forced labour, though some 785 SNCV employees were thus treated at various times out of a total of 1308 "notified".

The Germans, inevitably, also reclaimed the border lines round Eupen, complete with much of their rolling stock. After the SNCV refused to sell them equipment, they simply requisitioned twenty tram sets to replace material damaged in the Ruhr. All in all, however, the SNCV came off comparatively lightly, especially as the occupying forces, quite justifiably from their point of view, constantly suspected it of subversive activities and of collaboration with the Resistance!

In other ways, the SNCV had a hard war. It was badly affected by lack of petrol and diesel oil, hundreds of steam locomotives having to be brought out of retirement to replace autorails, but the electric services proved their value. The Societé even managed to complete one major electrification, from Antwerpen to Turnhout, in 1941 and to build a new series of all-welded "Standard" bogie motor cars plus over a hundred matching steel-bodied trailers. As in the first war, its major headaches were that, even with increases in traffic, costs far outstripped receipts since it was prevented from raising fares and charges by more than 25 per cent, and the equipment and track were very heavily used while few materials were available for maintenance. Yet, even during the allied advances in 1944, some 77 per cent of the total system was kept in use; the only real disaster befell the Luxembourg lines, most of which were effectively closed by the German Ardennes offensive in December and not fully reopened until the war's end. It is worth remembering that, up to this time, the SNCV had not received any subsidy from the state, depending entirely on its overall receipts and interest on Capitaux to balance the deficit-making lines against those in profit. On a minor note most Groupes abandoned 1st class from 15 January 1945 (Antwerpen had dropped it in 1937 but SELVOP only followed suit at the end of 1947).

A rare view of a railcar in wartime, fitted with producer-gas system
(SNCV / E de Backer collection)

After the war there was some attempt to modernise the country routes: This handsome bogie car of the AR29X series was designed and built by the SNCV at Hasselt (where else!)

(SNCV)

There was a also brief renaissance on the electric lines: Here a "pre-N" prototype car for Bruxelles runs on the Observatoire route   (E de Backer)

But eventually only the systems in the big conurbations survived. This is Gare du Sud at Charleroi with a virtual fleet of S -types   (WJKD)

5.2 Postwar revival: 1945-1952

1946, therefore, found the SNCV in much the same position as in 1919, with tariffs artificially held down and with operating costs rising fast against a background of a rapidly devaluing Franc. Unlike 1919, however, those lines which had been dismantled were not reinstated, most being replaced by buses under the provisions of the 1931 legislation. Indeed this removal was probably something of a relief since most had been in deficit even before the war. On the other hand, in the first flush of post-war euphoria, a grandiose electrification and expansion scheme known as the "1946 Plan" was drawn up. It envisaged considerable extensions to the system around major cities and included some provision for modernising the autorail fleet. The horrendous financial results of the 1946 financial year, however, quickly showed that such ideas were unrealistic. The ingenious Hasselt Works did at least propose a modernised bogie railcar for unelectrified commuter lines and, after constructing a mock-up "AR 301", was allowed to build six semi-streamlined lightweight cars as AR 291-96 (numbers 289-90 were never allocated). Finally four modernised four-wheelers were constructed new as railcar-tractors (AR 297-300) to help fulfil a need for goods haulage and for shunting mixed gauge sections in replacement for the various non-standard steam locomotives which had done those duties so far. They were not entirely successful and future needs were met by ballasting existing cars and upgrading them with 180hp motors. In the years after 1945 the following were converted to tractor railcars: ART 36-37; 40-71; 80; 83-90; 92-93; 96-97; 99; 100-112; 118-126; 135; 155-58; 225; 230; 281. Some were fitted with dual gauge buffing-coupling gear for shunting mixed gauge sections.

1947 and 1948 were also very bad years financially and for traffic, and they reinforced the proposition that large-scale retention and expansion of the rail system was a dubious financial possibility. Even as early as 1949, some of the more rural and remote branches were reluctantly turned over to buses or their services simply discontinued entirely. Yet at the same time all was not gloom. Where there appeared to be traffic potential, the SNCV continued to develop its electrified network, including a certain amount of new construction, especially in the densely-populated Hainaut. The electrified system did not actually "peak" until 1952, when at 1511km it constituted just over half the contemporary operating length; even after that, a major stock replacement programme was undertaken. In particular the pre-war series of metal-bodied standard cars was followed between 1942 and 1948 by a final 63 cars with welded steel bodies. Concurrently with the production of this final series of standard cars, the SNCV experimented with various prototypes of a high-capacity semi-streamlined car for town services. This, later finalised as type "N", was a two-motor car with cardan-shaft drive designed for solo operation. Six "pre-N" cars were built to test out various ideas and were followed by 85 cars of type "N". These were of two distinct series: one seating 23 and standing 67 with a 2.20-m wide body, and the other the definitive 2.32-m wide version. All were built by the SNCV itself.

At about the same period, the SNCV ordered two batches of non-standard types. A series of 21 single-ended semi-streamlined bogie cars with automatic doors came from Braine-le-Comte in 1949 for Charleroi town services but were not entirely successful since the cars were very lightly constructed and their frames tended to distort. Following evaluation of an

P Niederbaum 1959

For a few years the real country routes persisted, as illustrated by this charming shot of a standard railcar nosing across the village street at Libin. (M. Niederbaum)

American-built prototype, especially on the coastal system, a series of 24 PCC-cars with American body design was built by Nicaise et Delcuve in 1950, partly for Bruxelles - Leuven and partly for Charleroi. The next, and perhaps the best-known SNCV bogie cars, however, were of SNCV design and construction. These were type "S" and their origin was as follows. By the early 1950s, the wooden-bodied "Standard" cars in particular were showing signs of body wear, and it was decided to replace them by four-motor streamlined cars, generally similar to type "N". The first batch were built new but all succeeding ones were built around the bogies and equipments of the old "Standard" cars or other spare sets of equipment. A number of the cars was specially built as type "SO" for the wider loading-gauge of the coastal lines, while those built for the 1958 Bruxelles Exhibition were denoted "SE". The type "SO" cars were single-ended, with arm-rests fitted to the seats, and some were modernised with air-sprung bogies; they were provided with matching trailers converted from surplus type "N" cars. Further development of type "S" was still, up to the end of the SNCV, in progress at Charleroi where a number of cars had been modernised for use on the semi-metro. Some were slightly modified as type "SM" with changed step arrangements, while drastic rebuilds at Jumet produced a small series as type "SJ", liveried to match the newest articulated cars.

The final SNCV passenger cars were type "BN" articulated cars in two series: 50 single-ended six-axle cars for the coast and 55 double-ended six-axle cars for Charleroi. Five double-ended cars were used for short-workings on the coast, supported by 6102 modified to an eight-axle car as a demonstration car for overseas visitors; the centre-section was still owned by the manufacturers. These new cars incorporated the most modern LRT technology but lacked adequate ventilation for hot summer weather. Since 1991 even more developments and improvements have taken place but they are without the scope of this volume.

It may be worth reminding ourselves that, besides the "indigenous" designs of the SNCV, there were also several smallish classes bought in before WW2 from outside or assimilated when concessions were taken over - the Cie North (TEOL), Taschkent, Bogota and Odessa all featured at one time

or another. Most of these cars, excepting the Ns and the later BN types, were also expected to pull trailers and over the years a large collection of these was accumulated. They were all numbered into the 19XXX series and ranged from converted "Standard" motor cars and "N" class cars surplus to requirements to purpose-built designs for the Braine-le-Comte lightweight cars and extempore modifications - for example a batch of Odessa-type trailers were converted to bogie vehicles.

5.3   The long decline

So much for the post-war developments. In the mid 1950s, however, the last of the SNCV's chickens came home to roost when it took over the remaining Gent lines (1954), the Groupe de Wellin (1955) and the complete coastal network (1956). There then existed in private hands only some 8km of Bruxelles urban tramway (reduced to 1.9km in 1961) and the short tourist line to Grottes de Han in Namur province.

In general the 1952 "flowering" was illusory as Table 5A shows. The rise of private road transport in the 1950s was so rapid that even the most modern electrifications soon proved to be of dubious viability, while goods traffic - the staple of most surviving country routes - plummetted. From over 4 million tonnes in 1938, contributing some 16% of total receipts, it had dropped to just over 1 million tonnes in 1957, a mere 2.6% of receipts, and was mainly seasonal agricultural traffic. Even that did not last and, with closure of the last goods-only lines serving the sugar-beet and timber industries (1961-2), the amount carried became negligible; it was restricted mainly to transfer traffic on the few standard and mixed-gauge sections. In the same ten years (1952-61) the length of non-electric lines in use dropped from 1486 to 112.5km, and even the electrified lines went down from 1511 to only 708.5km. Some of the major electrifications lasted less than five years and the decade saw complete disappearance of passenger-carrying light railways from five of the nine provinces: Namur (1957); Limburg (1958); Liége (1961); Luxembourg (1961) and Oostvlaanderen (1959). What remained was concentrated on the coast and in the conurbations of Hainaut, Bruxelles and Antwerpen.

But soon the country lines decayed too: A very grubby autorail pauses at Oetingen on the cross-country route from Leerbeek to Ninove; note the shabby concrete shelter and overgrown tracks .*(author's collection)*

And eventually they too descended to pottering around with local goods where bulk traffic kept this viable. Even there the fight was hard; here a timber train at Bouillon has to share its tunnel with the ever encroaching road traffic. (E de Backer)

It must be said that, just because light rail transport became less viable, the SNCV as a whole did not abdicate its responsibilities of providing local public transport. The road network, with its increasingly familiar red and deep cream vehicles, spread as rapidly as the rail system declined. From only a few hundred kilometres just before the war, the bus network had reached 4716km by the end of 1951 and ten years later it was running over 10500km of regular services with about 30000 km of "specials" - for workmen, schoolchildren, etc. Map (inside front cover) shows how coverage of the country was sustained and even improved. Moreover, in so doing, the SNCV had reduced its personnel to under 8000 (as against 9000 or so for a rail network half the size) and managed to keep its operating ratios in the high 90s; thus it may not have built up reserves, but at least it did not make an operating deficit, and for public transport this was something of an achievement.

The road services of the SNCV warrant a book to themselves and cannot be dealt with here. So far as the rail network was concerned, alas, the steady decline continued. 1968 saw the final withdrawal of services from Antwerpen province, an event not entirely of the SNCV's making, but caused partly by dock and road improvements. With the exception of standard-gauge spurs round Cureghem works, which also went in 1968, the Bruxelles suburban network, though severely cut back, lasted until 1978; it was doomed when the city decided to build a standard-gauge light metro linked to the town trams, and the metre gauge became an inconvenience. That removed the last SNCV rails from Brabant, leaving only West Vlaanderen with its coastal lines, and the much-pruned electric tramways of Hainaut. These, oddly enough, appeared to have a brighter future. In the late 1970s there began a slow renaissance of urban rail transport throughout Europe, and in 1977 the SNCV decided to develop its remaining properties to upgrade them and to re-equip with modern articulated cars.

Under this regime, the coastal line flourished. Reduced to its basic minimum of an express line from De Panne via Oostende to Knokke, it was steadily realigned, fitted with new heavy-duty catenary and equipped with modern two-section six-axle articulated cars of the 6xxx series. In Hainaut, events were rather more mixed. The original project, seen partly as an unemployment relief programme, was to build a light metro in the Charleroi area, putting the metre gauge on its own exclusive rights-of-way and providing a "star" pattern network with easy links into the remaining tram routes out to Trazegnies, Binche and La Louvière - which were, themselves, to be modernised. Unfortunately, recession in the basic industries and population falls made nonsense of the original traffic predictions. By 1984 its future was very uncertain.

5.4 The last six years of the SNCV - 1985-1990

The first edition of this book took the story up to the end of 1984 but of course the SNCV did not stop there. The year 1985 was dominated by the Centenary celebrations of the Vicinal, and coincidentally, the 150th anniversary of the mainline railways in Belgium. The national government proclaimed 1985 to be the year of Public Transport and numerous festivities commemorated the centenary. These included the production of a special postage stamp showing a type 18 steam locomotive, several local exhibitions, special theme exhibitions in all transport museums, etc. Special funds were made available for the restoration of rolling stock. The most impressive achievements included the restoration of two steam locomotives to running order and the reconstruction of an authentic 1920's tram of the coastal route. Highlights of the celebrations were the official Centenary procession in Oostende on 15 July and the Tram Festival on the Anderlues-Thuin line on 15 August.

On the coast a cavalcade of historic trams ran between Oostende Station and the Mediacenter at Mariakerke. Steam locomotive 979 headed the procession, pulling a train of five authentic coaches. This included royal saloon A.1625, which had not been used as such since the days of King Albert I, with Queen Fabiola as its distinguished passenger. It was followed by a tram of Belle Epoque electric stock, a tram of the 'Standard' era, a 1950's tram and two modern BN articulated cars. During

47

A train of traditional early electric stock at Schepdaal Museum before the collection was split up
(AMUTRA

A steam train of the Tramway Touristique de l'Aisne in its early years   (author)

A train of the ASVI (Lobbes - Thuin)   (courtesy ASVI)

15-18 August a large collection of preserved trams was in use between Anderlues and Thuin. A frequent service was operated using the steam tram, autorails ART.89 and ART.300, and several electric trams from A.9073 of 1901 to 'Standard' trailer 19405 of 1944.

Two notable intended events, however, were cancelled, a foretaste of things to come. On the much trumpeted light metro at Charlerol, the inauguration of two new routes to Gilly and Chatelet, and the opening of Fontaine l'Eveque and Petria stations on route 90, did not take place. As time would prove, the new extensions, although finished, would not open until after the demise of the Vicinal.

When life on the Vicinal returned to normal in 1986, the state of the three surviving tramway systems set the pattern for the coming years: gradual improvements on the coastal tramway, continuing decline in Hainaut, leading to a 'network' of just one route at the end of the decade, and the onset of improvements at Han sur Lesse, once it had been decided to retain the tramline. The problem was partly one of declining patronage but even more a political matter. For most of this century, Belgian internal politics have been dominated by the effects of what is sometimes called the 'language battle', a complex of social, cultural and economic tensions between the French speaking and the Dutch speaking communities, Wallonie and Vlaanderen. The recent developments date from the early years of this century, and matters came to a head with the forced abdication of King Leopold III soon after World War II. This event marked the start of the gradual change from the old unitary state constituted in 1830 towards a federation of Vlaanderen, Wallonie and the bi-lingual Brussel/Bruxelles agglomeration within the Kingdom of Belgium.

This conflict of views came to a head during the 1980s when important constitutional changes were introduced, culminating in setting up of regional parliaments and governments for Wallonie, Vlaanderen and Brussels. Although the national government kept control of several State functions such as Foreign Affairs, Defence, Finance, and, among others, the mainline railway system, many other institutions were split up, among them being regional and local public transport.

5.5   The end of the SNCV.

Following legislation of 8 August 1988, three new bodies were created. Although in practice the situation in Bruxelles remained unchanged, the SNCV and the other municipal operators, known usually as the "MIVs and STIs", were to cease to exist. The arrangement was that the Vicinal groups in the Flemish provinces of West-Vlaanderen, Oost-Vlaanderen, Antwerpen, Limburg and much of Brabant were combined with the local operators in Antwerpen (Maatschappij voor het Intercommunaal Vervoer te Antwerpen or MIVA) and Gent (Maatschappij voor het Intercommunaal Vervoer te Gent or MIVG) to become the new VLAAMSE VERVOER MAATSCHAPPIJ (VVM) with headquarters in Mechelen, while the SNCV in Hainaut, Liége, Namur, Luxembourg and the Walloon part of Brabant merged with the Societé des Transports Intercommunaux de Liége (STIL), the Societé des Transports Communaux de l' Agglomeration Vervietoise (STIV) and the Societé des Transports Communaux de Charleroi (STIC) to became the SOCIETÉ REGIONALE WALONNE DU TRANSPORT (SRWT) based at Namur. The new companies chose separate trade names: the VVM, founded on 1 October 1990, is universally known as DE LIJN (literally: the Route), while the SRWT, founded on 1 January 1990, adopted the acronym TEC, for TRANSPORT EN COMMUN (Public Transport).

These new bodies took over as operators on 1 January 1991 at which point the SNCV effectively ceased trading, though as more time was needed to finalise the legal and financial details of the split-up the Societé was not disbanded until 1 January 1992. Curiously, among the most difficult problems to be solved were the ownership of three 61XX series BN cars based in Oostende and the future of the Schepdaal museum collection which has regrettably been split up.

In the reorganisation, the old SNCV operational Groups were replaced by 'Entities', which in general incorporated the functions of the old Group plus those of the municipal operators in its geographical area. A notable exception is the former Groupe de Hainaut which was joined with the STIC. For operational purposes two entities were created: TEC Charleroi for the Charleroi conurbation, and TEC Hainaut, based in Mons, including Mons, La Louvière, Tournai and the rural areas. Although outside the scope of this publication, it should be noted that this, together with the fact that Charleroi route 90 crossed into TEC Hainaut in Binche would lead to the closure of Anderlues-La Louvière on 29 August 1993.

Belgian trams : the current position

Both the LRTA and myself are aware that, in ending this volume with the demise of the SNCV, we left open the question of what has happened since - and what is the current position.

Fortunately, a Belgian group has just republished a very comprehensive summary of the situation as at 2006 which can be heartily recommended. It includes basic details of all working urban tram, trolleybus and metro systems, with maps, depot layouts, stocklists and notes on timetables. etc., plus contact points. There are also notes on existing museum and preservation activities and lists of ex-SNCV vehicles preserved, both in Belgium and abroad, with their current locations.

Since most of the information is tabulated, ignorance of the language is not a great handicap

Publication details:
FLASH 2006: Atlas of Beglian Tramways, Metros and Trolleybusues as at March 2006
Published by Tram 2000 and available from LRTA Publications at 9 Hinderwell Road, Scarborough YO12 4BD

Table 5B: Changes in SNCV fleet 1952-61 and 1966

	1952	1953	1954	1955	1956	1957	1958	1959	1960	1961	1966
Electric stock											
Motorcars	932	892	885	812	798	739	701	641	604	572	401
Trailers (enclosed)	705	702	684	628	625	559	558	470	440	425	300
Trailers (open)	107	98	87	72	68	38	19	18	15	13	10
2nd/luggagecars	3	3	3	3	3	3	3	1	1	1	1
Motorluggagevans	31	30	30	29	25	25	25	21	21	21	21
Luggagevans	1	1	1	1	1	1	1	1	1	1	1
Locomotives	1	1	1	1							
Special vehicles	1	5	6	6	6	6	6	6	6	6	
Steam/dieselstock											
Autorails/tractors	250	222	220	208	170	119	110	73	68	52	22
Locomotives	139	103	54	40	30	29	19	17	14	13	11
Coaches	547	423	374	211	155	92	61	27	26	15	5
2nd/luggagecoaches	55	50	45	34	25	22	15	9	9	9	24
Luggagevans	154	135	114	79	66	55	47	44	32	29	4
Goodsvans	1725	1658	1502	1299	1113	875	759	541	435	295	164
Open wagons	5030	4923	4558	4231	3796	3340	2391	2449	1779	1036	328
Flatwagons	669	649	636	576	513	448	407	337	222	153	64
Special vehicles	150	150	148	136	131	125	122	101	89	64	33
Road fleet											
Buses	352	411	523	718	821	941	1070	1192	1355	1490	1896
"Road Trains"	—	—	1	1	1	1	1	1	1	1	1
Other vehicles	*	*	*	*	3+	3+	4	4	183	178	178

NOTES: * not recorded; + gyrobuses. See also Appendix 3
The "road train" was an articulated vehicle for conveying trams between systems.

A BN articulated car on the Hainaut system in orange/cream livery. (SNCV)

50

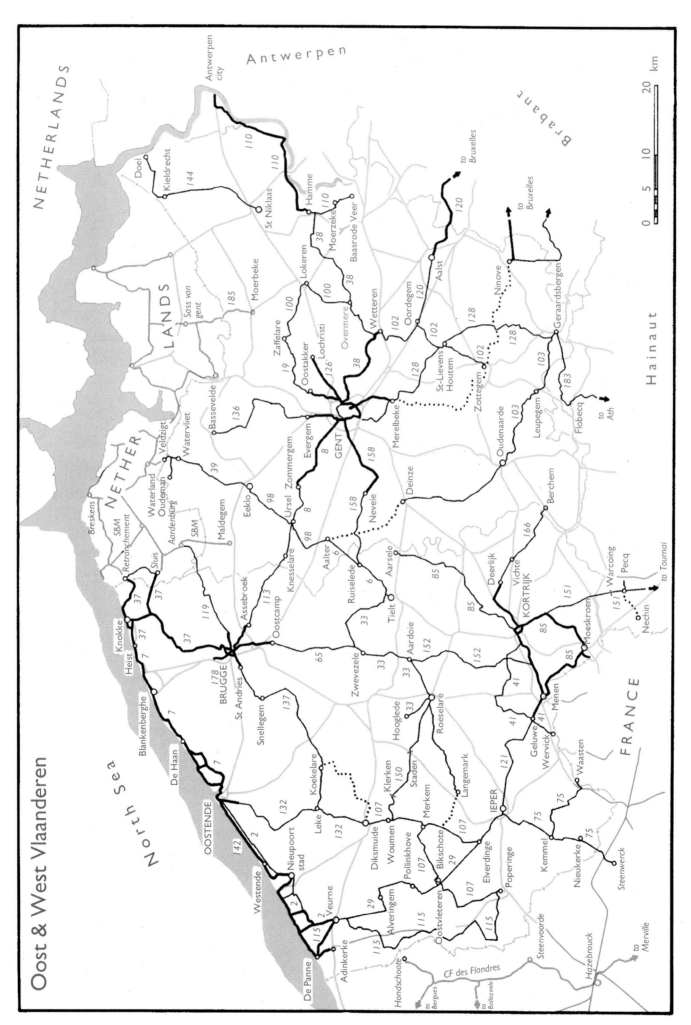

Oost & West Vlaanderen

NETHERLANDS

Antwerpen

Antwerpen city

Brabant

to Bruxelles

Hainaut

North Sea

FRANCE

Chapter 6:   The SNCV in Oost & West Vlaanderen

6.1   Vlaanderen: Introduction

The two provinces of Oost and West Vlaanderen form a pattern of development different from other SNCV operations and can best be taken together. The provinces occupy the whole west part of the country and monopolise its only seaboard. Except for the coastal strip with its many resorts and its two major ports of Oostende (Ostende to the Walloons, Ostend to the British) and Zeebrugge, the provinces were in 1884 still largely agricultural. They had between them a small number of biggish, and ancient, towns - Veurne/Furnes, Ieper/Ypres, Brugge/Bruges and Kortrijk/Courtrai in West Vlaanderen; Gent/Gand in Oost Vlaanderen were the most important. In between these lay large tracts of sparsely-populated countryside and the SNCV system developed very much piecemeal to suit these conditions.

The provinces were very early in promoting tramways, and the first three lines set the pattern for what was to follow. **Capital 2 (OOSTENDE - VEURNE** and actually the first line opened) connected many of the fashionable resorts along the North Sea coast; **Capital 6 (TIELT - AALTER)** was an isolated inland rural line running from nowhere to somewhere very similar but with a main line junction; **Capital 8 (GENT - ZOMERGEM)** was a suburban tramway bringing people and products into a large city. After this promising start Vlaanderen was slow to develop, only thirteen Capitaux in all opening during the decade to 1894, but those that did open followed the pattern. The coast line was completed (Capital 7) and sent off long antennae from each end to the nearest big towns inland (Capital 29 to Ieper and 37 to Brugge). **Capitaux 28 (DEINZE - OUDENAARDE), 33 (HOOGLEDE - TIELT), 39 (EEKLO - Dutch frontier) and 59 (ST-NIKLAAS - DOEL)** perpetuated the honourable tradition of loss-making rural branches that would nonetheless enormously develop their neighbourhoods. From Gent, Capitaux 19 to Zaffelare and 38 to Wetteren and Hamme, and from Kortrijk Capital 41 to Menen began slowly to extend the suburban lines which eventually became a feature of the network. Even the next decade, to 1904, saw only a cautious extension round Gent, Kortrijk and Ieper, with long rural lines (Capitaux 65, 98, 100, 103) beginning to extend and connect the previously isolated ones.

Inevitably the provinces gained one truly private company for a while, the slightly eccentric *Tramways Electriques d'Ostende - Littoral (TEOL)*, also known as the Cie North after its English promoter. As a early overhead-electric tramway, it ran south from Oostende along the sea wall (or Dijk/Digue) until 1905, when the government ordered the SNCV to take the line over and assimilate it into their system. The decade, too, saw the rise of a few large operating companies which gradually acquired most concessions originally allocated to small local concerns. The most important were the *SA des Transports Urbains et Vicinaux (TUV)* and the *SA des CF Provinciaux (CFP)* in Oostvlaanderen; the *Mij tot Uitbating den Buurtspoorwegen van het Noorden van West Vlaanderen in Westvlaanderen (NWV)*; the *SA Intercommunale Courtrai (IC)* and the *Buurtspoorwegen van den Om trek Diksmuide - Ieper (ODI)*, whose spheres of action are obvious; and, almost inevitably, the *SA des Railways Economiques de Liége - Seraing (LS)*, which spread throughout Belgium, busily forming a string of subsidiaries to look after its interests.

It was, however, the next decade which saw the real expansion. The coastal routes themselves developed steadily to connect the few remaining untapped resorts, and several lines were electrified to cope with increasing traffic. Indeed they became very much a separate entity in that they were profitable, with a big tourist traffic, and the concessionaire saw no reason to hand them back to the SNCV. They therefore have a virtually separate history right up to 1956 when the SNCV finally reclaimed them, and it makes sense to deal with then as a unity up to that point.

In the hinterland, the picture was different. What on maps appears to be a loose network, spread right across the province, theoretically linked the Ieper region with Brugge via Diksmuide and connected from all directions into the centrally placed Hooglede - Tielt - Aalter group of rural lines. From Brugge, Kortrijk and, even more, from Gent, new suburban lines snaked out in all directions, including several routes that would eventually become interprovincial links. Two, Capitaux 151 and 183, would link with Tournai and Hainaut; the third would eventually give a direct route into Brabant, completing a chain stretching from Bruxelles to the sea. Since in practice these networks fall into no easily organisable pattern it has seemed sensible to use the SNCV's own division into operating groupes or reseaux as a basis for their early history.

The total length, in both provinces, rose sharply, to 1061km by 1914. Apart from the coastal lines, one or two suburban lines at Gent and some town lines in Brugge, however, there was still little electrification, the total of 81km being a reflection on how poor the provinces were in real terms at this time. The end of the 1914-18 war, when most of the concessionaires relinquished their contracts, is also a convenient time to pause when looking in detail at the

The SNCV came early to the old city of Veurne/Furnes. Here a steam tram on the Oostende line crosses the Niewpoort bridge. (SNCV/commercial card)

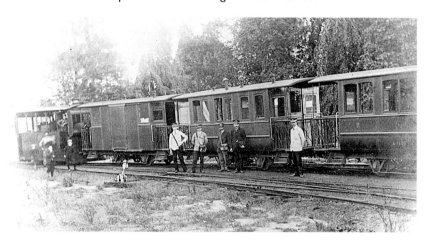

The original face of the coastal system: An early steam passenger train poses for its photograph. (SNCV)

development of individual lines other than the coast, in both Flanders. Their early history will therefore be considered under the separate operating groupes and later history under the overall SNCV grouping.

6.2 Vlaanderen Coast. 1885 to 1956

6.2.1 Groupe du Littoral, 1885 - 1920 (Map ref C-3)

Capital	Name	Auth km
2	Oostende - Nieuwpoort - Veurne	36.95
7	Oostende - Blankenberge - Heist en Uitbreidingen	*45.03
37	Brugge - Sluis - Heist	29.08
142	Oostende - Westende (retrospective)	14.70
193	Koksijde - De Panne	n/k

* includes both lines to Blankenberge

For what would initially appear to be four simple lines, the history and geography of this group is very tangled. The lines were subject to various "paper" changes of operator; they sprouted various spurs which cannot definitively be assigned to a particular Capital; they were all subject to modifications of their alignments; they also, at various times, included steam, battery and conventional electric traction, and took over or replaced several horse trams.

* initial developments south from Oostende

In the beginning, if one is not being irreverent, was **Capital 2 (OOSTENDE - NIEUWPOORT - VEURNE)**. It ran southwest from Oostende through scattered villages crouching below the long line of dunes to Nieuwpoort town and thence southward to Koksijde and the lovely old inland town of Veurne/Furnes. First tentative plans for this were laid as early as 1875 by a private company calling itself the *Tramways de la Flandre Orientale* (most early companies in this very Flemish region had French titles). In practice nothing was done until the SNCV came along, virtually taking over most of the planning as its Capital 2. It was authorised retrospectively in two stages, from Oostende to Nieuwpoort (Stad) on 27 March 1886 and from Nieuwpoort (Stad) to Veurne on 16 July 1886. The first part, from Oostende through Mariakerke Dorp, Middelkerke Dorp and Lombardsijde to Nieuwpoort Stad was actually the first SNCV line to be officially opened, to Middelkerke on 5 July 1885, although shortage of stock delayed public services until 13 July. It was formally opened on to Nieuwpoort (Stad) on 15 July 1885. The extension to Veurne followed on 22 July 1886, and operation of the whole line was ceded to the *Liége-Seraing* and its partner the *Cie Générale des Railways à Voie Etroite (CGVE)*; both these companies were part of the complex owned by Baron Empain which later became "Electrorail". The line was steam-worked, some 32.50km long, and had depots at Veurne, Nieuwpoort and Oostende. For most of its length it faithfully followed the main road and was a genuine all-purpose tramway.

Oostende was always the focus of the coastal lines. The old station Square in the early days, with steam trams waiting to depart.   *(author's collection / commercial card)*

Tourism, however, was obviously profitable business and short spurs soon followed (an authorisation of 25 October 1887 probably refers to these). At Nieuwpoort the SNCV was initially pre-empted by the mainline railway, which ran down to Nieuwpoort Bad (bathing place or, perhaps, lido) station, but the SNCV apparently soon followed suit on mixed-gauge track, running the service by agreement with the *CF de l'Etat Belge*. This appears to have happened in summer only from 1889-on (it was after all for holidaymakers) but was never satisfactory and, on 12 December 1902 the SNCV got authorisation for a new loop from Nieupoort Stad to Bad and on to Groenendijk back on the "main line" a little south of Nieuwpoort Stad; the EB/SNCV agreement was terminated on 31 December 1902 and the new line was opened on 31 May 1903. Soon afterwards, two enterprising local resort companies joined in, the *SA de Coxyde-Plage* opening a narrow-gauge horse line from Koksijde SNCV down to the beach on 24 July 1904, while in 1910 the similar *SA de St-Idesbald* put in a detached horse-tramway from its name town along the coast to the growing resort of De Panne, which in turn had quite a famous 60cm gauge tramway inland to Adinkerke station (see chapter 12). The SNCV clearly could not let all this private enterprise go unchecked, so in 1906 it started laying plans which resulted in **Capital 193 (KOKSIJDE - DE PANNE)**. The Coxyde Plage tram was replaced by SNCV steam trams on 4 July 1909 and eventually, on 1 July 1914, the SNCV replaced the horse tram line to De Panne with its own spur from Koksijde Dorp through St-Idesbald and along the dunes to De Panne (authorised 28 July 1914). It was intended to go through to Dunkerque but the war stopped that - though the existing line was heavily used by the military during the war. Not, if one may comment, that the takeover did the SNCV much good. A month later the war came, and that line was promptly closed and lifted again. Needless to say, the LS took all this manoeuvring in its stride, though it officially passed the concession to its wholly-owned subsidiary, the *CF Electrique d'Ostende - Blankenberghe et Extensions (OB)* from 17 November 1905. Before investigating the OB and its developments, however, we really need to describe what had been going on around the town of Oostende itself.

* tramways in and around Oostende: the "Cie North"

Now the story of internal tramways in Oostende and its immediate surroundings is so complex that it really warrants a book to itself - the locals have a habit of constantly renaming streets for instance and local politics at the period were fierce,

to say the least (and complicated again because of Royal politics as well, King Leopold having a palace in the area). It will, therefore, only be summarised here.

Contemporary developments in and around Oostende were twofold. Firstly, in 1896 a private company, based on Antwerpen but promoted by an Englishman, Colonel T. North residing in Eltham, Kent, had been formed to run electric tramways in Oostende and along the coast. This was the *Cie des Tramways Electriques d'Ostende - Littoral (TEOL)*, otherwise known as the Cie North, d'Ostende after its promoter - a potentially confusing title for historians since its lines were planned to go southwards from the town!

The background to this enterprise was that Colonel North was apparently a close friend of King Leopold and, despite resistance from the SNCV and to a lesser extent the local council (which was ambivalent since it did not want to annoy the king) his company was granted a concession on 11 March 1897 to build and operate an electric line from Oostende (Waterhuis) south along the sea wall to Middelkerke (Bad). The first edition of this book recorded it as initially run by battery cars but that was not so. It used the standard 600v DC with overhead collection via trolley poles and had a fleet of some fourteen closed and three open-sided power cars plus twelve trailers. Ironically Colonel North died in May 1896 but his company continued, running a service from Oostende Handelsplein to Mariakerke Dijk from 19 July 1897 and on to Middelkerke from 31 July. The official opening was on 2 August and the service, which initially was summers only, ran until 31 October 1897. The line was damaged by storms that November but was restored in time for the next summer season, reopening on 15 May 1898. From then on it ran usually from about mid-May to mid-October with occasional variations. It was extended to Westende with effect from 29 June 1903 and a limited winter service is noted as operating during the 1902/3 and 1903/4 winters.

Clearly this was not satisfactory and, after the summer service ceased on 1 November 1904, negotiations started to sell the whole concern to the SNCV. After some delay, the deal was finalised on 20 April 1905, the official takeover, as **Capital 142 (OOSTENDE - WESTENDE)** taking effect from 29 May. The concession was handed to the LS (and then to the OB), services starting again from 10 June. The SNCV then upgraded, and partly realigned, the route during the winter of 1906/7 and it was during this period that battery cars were used to run a limited service. The battery cars themselves had an interesting history, having been bought in 1897 for use by the LS on Oostende local services under Capital 2, mainly in the summer. There were eventually five of them and they worked until 1907, when the town lines were electrified using bow collectors. Originally Nos 1-5, they became SNCV 9480-84.

* urban tramways in Oostende town

The Oostende town lines appear to have started with a route from Sweepplaats (leter Feysplein) by the old railway station, to Slijkens in July 1897. There were various changes over the years, complicated by the fact that urban routes only ran in summer anyway and that much of the trackage was used by the LS mainly for transporting sand and other commodities

Place Léopold 1er, Ostende

The earliest use of electricity appears to have been when the Liége-Seraing asked for some battery cars to run town services in Oostende. There were five, which later became straight electrics as SNCV 9480-84

(collection P de Backer)

And even before SNCV went electric, there was the odd case of the "Cie North". In SNCV days this is an open motor car from TEOL, with open trailers.

(The late G Desbarax)

Westende   L'arrivée du tramway électrique.

and here a Cie North enclosed train, hauled by a motor car of TEOL series 1-14 after acquisition by the SNCV pauses at Westende

(collection P de Backer)

rather than passengers (who, reading between the lines, were a bit of an annoyance). Certainly the LS/OB acquired two town routes at Oostende, the Slijkens one already mentioned, which had been extended to Marie-José Plein in 1905, and a route from Marie-José Plein to Vuurtoren (lighthouse) opened on 20 or 21 September 1903 with steam traction and apparently forming part of Capital 7; when electrified, from 15 May 1909, a special class of car, known as " Phare" was built for it.

* developments northward from Oostende

Outside Oostende town, the Ostende - Blankenberghe company itself came quite late on the scene

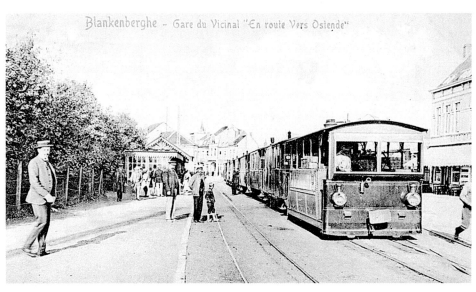

North from Oostende, too, the lines were originally steam. A typical train pauses at Blankenberghe on its way south. *(Commercial card)*

and, as recorded above, was a result of some earlier manoeuvring among the concessionaires. The first SNCV concession northeast from Oostende was actually an inland line through Slijkens and Bredene villages to the coast at De Haan and thence along the dunes to the thriving resort of Blankenberge and was very definitely steam-worked. As **Capital 7 (OOSTENDE - BLANKENBERGE - HEIST)** it was originally authorised retrospectively on 9 November 1886, being opened in advance on 8 August of that year; operation was ceded to the *Liège-Seraing*. It was always regarded as being a tourist line, but its amble through the villages was no advantage for the tourist traffic. Consequently in 1900 the SNCV started planning a more direct route which was authorised on 22 February 1905 under the same Capital. Opened on 9 July 1905, it ran from the old railway station at Oostende along the dunes to connect with the existing line at De Haan. The SNCV also insisted that a special company must be formed to operate its new treasure and the LS obligingly came up with the *SA du CF Electrique d'Ostende - Blankenberghe et extns (OB)*. A special design of handsome four-wheeled tramcar was produced, and the concession was subject to elaborate conditions. With an eye to the future, it was built as double track and electrified from the start; these features were

also incorporated in the old line from De Haan onwards, the modernisation being completed in the summer of 1908 - though delays in building the new power station meant that electric services did not start until 29 May 1909 at which time the Oostende terminus was moved to Marie Joseplaats. Initially, electric operation was confined to passengers and the summer months, steam being then used only on the inland loop and for goods on to Blankenberge; steam locomotives ran the whole service during the winter.

Meanwhile...the Westende route, though initially assigned to Capital 142, was soon merged into Capital 2. Back on the main line northward, completion of the electric route to Blankenberge also gave fresh impetus to a long standing SNCV plan to build a tramway on to Heist. It had been angling hopefully for a scheme involving mixed-gauge track on an existing railway but this was turned down "for safety reasons". It eventually got a line of its own authorised on 10 May 1909 and lost no time in constructing the extra few kilometres, and laying a third rail on the standard gauge track between Blankenberghe and Zeebrugge (Mole). This is noted as not completed until 7 October 1908 although SNCV also recorded opening the line throughout with steam traction on 1 October

Once the SNCV took over the TEOL electricity spread. Here a typical early coastal tram proceeds along the digue at Raversyde, south of Oostende. *(commercial card)*

1908! The overhead was extended on 1 July 1911, from which date the line was electrically worked, a distinctive feature of the coast lines being that electric motor luggage vans were used for most goods haulage. From 15 July 1909 trams ran through from Oostende via Heist and Capital 37 (see below) to the Dutch border at Sluis, where the Dutch *Stoomtram Breskens-Maldegem (SBM)* took them on to Breskens with a steamer connection to Vlissingen. Apparently this service was mainly for the thursday market at Middelburg in the Netherlands.

At Heist, the route from Oostende met an already existing line with its own history and an international flavour. This was **Capital 37 (BRUGGE - SLUIS - HEIST)** which was authorised as early as 24 May 1889 and which opened its major routes the following year. The "main line" started at the old 't Zand railway station in Brugge and ran first northwest to the tiny village of Westkapelle, then north to the equally small but ambitious coastal village of Knokke and then west to Heist where it terminated. There was a goods-only branch to the river quays at Brugge - passengers went via the town centre - and the line opened throughout on 18 March 1890; a direct route was later opened from Brugge Oostendepoort to Brugge standard gauge station on 11 June 1912.

Meanwhile again, an international branch east from Westkapelle (between Brugge and Knokke) to the Dutch frontier at St-Anna-ter-Muiden and then to Sluis followed on 1 May 1890. It again gave direct connection with the Dutch *Stoomtram Breskems - Maldegem (SBM)* company, opened in 1887, which was specially built to metre gauge so that traffic could be interchanged. The SBM also ran another spur south from Sluis into Belgium for about 5km to terminate at Maldegem standard-gauge station, but the 5km on Belgian soil was never owned by the SNCV; the Sluis line was, so as to speak, part of a quid pro quo. The SNCV Capital 37 then totalled 30.20km, and on 11 July 1890 it was ceded to the *Antwerpsche Maatschappij voor den Dienst van Buurtspoorwegen (AMDB)*, presumably because that concern had experience of cross-border lines in its own province. Its lease lasted only until 1 January 1905 when it was reclaimed by the SNCV and reallocated to the LS/CGVE duo; it was transferred to the *OB* with effect from 17 November 1905 which is why it gets treated with the coastal lines.

Although steam-worked, the Brugge - Heist route and its Dutch connection were fairly important, and the SNCV looked for ways of extending them. Once again its eye fell on a successful horse tram which the *SA du Tramway de Knocke-s-Mer* had opened on 2 April 1904 from Knokke village to the beach at Bunnenlaan. This 1.70km line was too tempting to leave, and on 20 May 1912, the SNCV was authorised to replace it, extending it to the new resort of Het Zoute/le Zoute and opening it as a branch from Knokke SNCV station a month later on 29 June. It was electrified from the start, electrification between Knokke and Het Zoute coming into use the same day and the line being included in the OB domain. It was the last extension before World War I.

* ***World war I and after on the coast***
The 1914-18 war hit the Littoral group very hard; as related in detail in Chapter 3, all its lines south of Middelkerke were either destroyed or taken over by Allied military forces. A section between Zeebrugge and Heist was wrecked by war damage and the rest was much interfered with by the Germans. At the war's end the whole system was in a parlous state, though restoration work had high priority. Records indicate the following major changes:

Section	reopened
Capital 2 (whole route closed 19 Oct 1914)	
Oostende - Veurne	
* Oostende (statie) - Mariakerke	24 Feb 1919
* Mariakerke - Middelkerke (dorp)	8 Mar 1919
* Middelkerke (Dorp - Krokodiel)	10 May 1919
* Krokodiel - Westende (dorp)	28 May 1919
* Westende - Lombardsijde dorp	21 Jun 1919
* L'sijde - Nieupoort Palingbrug	26 Jul 1919
* Palingbrug - Veurne	23 Aug 1919
Oostende local routes (limited service)	Dec 1920
(full service)	15 May 1921
Nieupoort (Stad) - Gronendijk	
* Nieupoort (Stad - Bad) only	10 Sep 1922
Capital 7	
Zeebrugge - Heist (closed 26 Oct 1914)	
* Zeebrugge - Heist (sluizen)	15 Jun 1919
* Heist (sluizen - Statie)	29 Jun 1919
Oostende - De Haan (both routes closed 1 Sep 1918)	
* Oostende - Blankenberghe	19 Jan 1919
* Blankenberge - Zeebrugge	15 Jun 1919
Oostende - Vuurtoren (closed 1 Sep 1918)	1 Jun 1919
Capital 37	
Brugge - Heist (closed 26 Oct 1914)	
* Brugge - Dudzele	20 Feb 1919
* Dudzele - Heist	10 Mar 1919
Westkapelle - Sluis (closed 26 Oct 1914)	1 Jan 1921
Het Zoute - Heist (closed 30 Oct 1914)	29 Jun 1919
Capital 142	
Oostende - Westende (closed 18 Oct 1914)	
* Oostende - Middelkerke	24 Mar 1921
* Middelkerke - Westende	8 Sep 1921
Capital 193 (closed throughout 19 Oct 1914)	
Koksijde (Dorp) - De Panne	1 Oct 1920

Most routes had some damage and the Koksijde - De Panne line had to be completely reconstructed. Nonetheless, the whole group of lines remained firmly in the grasp of its concessionaires, who had every intention of retaining their concessions.

6.2.2 Groupe du Littoral 1920-1939

The Vlaanderen system which saw most development in the 1920s and 1930s was, inevitably, the coastal one, where tourist traffic increased rapidly. At the end of 1918 it was still largely run by the OB and its associates, but the position was regularised and the system limits finally defined in 1927 by the promotion of a new operating company. This was the *Societé pour l' Exploitation des Lignes Vicinales d'Ostende et des Plages Belges (SELVOP)* formed in Bruxelles on 8 February 1927 to take over existing contracts. It had an even longer and more difficult Flemish title but was usually known by the initials of the French title. It was still "all in the family", so to speak, being wholly owned by Baron Empain's "Electrorail" group which, among its other international activities, ran the Liége-Seraing and the Charleroi and Gent town trams (LS, TEPC and ETG respectively).

As from 9 March 1927 SELVOP took over all existing coast lines (Capitaux 2, 7, 37, 142 and 193) plus that part of Capital 115 between Veurne and De Panne. It also took over operation of any new branches as they were built, while the SNCV, for its part, consolidated the various Capitaux over the following few years. Briefly, Capitaux 2, 142 and their extensions combined from 1 January 1930 as Capital 2 "Oostende -De Panne (Grens) -Veurne", while to the north Capitaux 7 and 37 were combined in 1930. Through trams De Panne - Oostende - Knmokke - Het Zoute were introduced from 16 September 1931. Adinkerke - De Panne (see below) became Capital 201 when it was regauged and electrified in 1932 and was then assimilated into Capital 2 as "Oostende - De Panne (Grens) - Veurne - Adinkerke" in 1935.

Electricity soon took over northward on the coast as well. A typical train of an OB 4-wheeled car and coastal trailers in the dunes *(author's collection)*

* postwar developments south from Oostende

This is anticipating matters, however. To take the southern lines first, a project to extend electrification to De Panne and Veurne had been put forward in 1913 but cut short by outbreak of war. In 1919 it was taken out once more and in due course submitted for authorisation, received on 23 September 1927. It proposed a mixture of new and old lines within the existing Capitaux, leaving Oostende over the existing electric sea-wall route to Westende. From there it would swing inland to Lombardsijde, joining the existing steam route for about 800m and then diverge to join the old trackbed to Nieuwpoort Bad. From there it was to run directly along the coast to De Panne Grens (frontier), first on new trackage, then over a doubled stretch of the Koksijde Bad - St Idesbald Bad - De Panne Bad line with a further new spur at the southern end to bring it to the frontier. Inland, a short section of the old route 2 between Nieuwpoort and Oostduinkerke would be virtually abandoned and replaced by a new spur from Oostduinkerke Bad through the village and over existing track to Koksijde Dorp, whence Capital 2 would be electrified to Veurne. The former Nieuwpoort Bad - Groenendijk route, never reopened after the war, would be formally abandoned, which it was in 1930. To join all these lines together, the former Koksijde (Dorp - Bad) line and the section of Capital 115 from Veurne to De Panne would also be electrified, and this was done. The dates of opening are below:

Section	Electrification
Westende - Lombardsijde - Nieuwpoort Bad+	1 Jul 1928
Nieuwpoort Bad - De Panne (Grens) via the coast++:	
* Nieuwpoort - Koksijde Bad (steam from 11 Jul 1926)	7 Jul 1929
* Koksijde Bad - St-Idesbald Bad	23 Jul 1929
* St-Idesbald Bad - De Panne Grens	1 Aug 1929
* Oostduinkerke Bad - Dorp - Koksijde Bad	8 Jun 1930
* Koksijde Dorp - Veurne	16 Jul 1929
* Koksijde (Dorp - Bad)	16 Jul 1929
* Veurne - De Panne	1 Aug 1930
+ double track, 12.4 km	
++ double track	

In addition, after considerable negotiations, the SNCV took over the rights to a 600mm gauge tramway between Adinkerke and De Panne as noted above, providing a metre-gauge electric replacement with a connection to the Veurne line from 25 June 1932. The new lines were largely passenger-carrying although several series of motor luggage vans were built for parcels and small-goods haulage. The steam line through the villages was retained for general use as far as Nieuwpoort, but its passenger service was effectively withdrawn; in the 1930s it had one train in one direction three times weekly for market-goers, returning as an unadvertised freight service.

* further developments north of Oostende

The lines north from Oostende were also extended and improved, though mostly at a rather later date. The major alterations were at the northern end, where through trams from Oostende to Breskens had been reintroduced as early as 28 July 1921. The Knokke routes were extensively reworked to provide a network of local services. The first one was a simple extension from Knokke (Van Bunnenplein) on the seafront to Albertplein, a little way to the north, opened on 1 January 1927. This route was again extended, on 1 July 1928, to the Restaurant Siska at Oosthoek, and from there to the Dutch border on 4 July 1929. Finally the line, electrified from new, was extended over the frontier to Retranchement on 19 July 1929; from that date through services were started between Knokke SNCV station and Breskens, replacing the Oostende through service. The track north from Oosthoek was used mainly during the tourist season from 1 July to mid-September, and the through stock was provided by the Dutch SBM, whose steam locomotive handed it over to an SNCV motor luggage van at Retranchement. There was a further modification to the line on 21 July 1929, when what amounted to a huge loop was brought into use in Knokke, running from Albertplein back to Lippenlaan via Zoutelaan and Elisabethlaan; as seemed to happen quite regularly at this period, the project did not actually receive Royal approval until two months after it was opened.

The northern end was further improved in 1930 when the line from Brugge to Knokke station was electrified in two stages, from Knokke to Dudzele on 1 July 1930 and Dudzele - Brugge on 19 July 1930; its branch from Westkapelle to Sluis followed on 1 August 1934, although its international importance had been diminished by the more direct route via Retranchement. Finally, a new link was put in during summer 1935 between Knokke (Albertplein) and Heist (Duinbergen), using existing track as far as Lippenlaan and new track from there along Bayauxlaan and H Consciencelaan. It was opened on 23 August 1938 and it was then possible to organise a complete local network in the area with routes as listed in the adjoining table.

Nieuport-Bains Café Léopold.

In later years, the standard bogie cars largely took over the fast workings. Here is one at Niewpoort, Cafe Leopold.
(SNCV/commercial card)

No	route
1	Oostende - Knokke Stn - Knokke (Albertplein)
10	Brugge - Westkapelle - Knokke Stn - Knokke (Albertplein)
11	Brugge - Westkapelle - Knokke Stn - Heist Stn
12	Heist (Duinbergen) - Oosthoek (Siska)
13	Knokke Stn - Oosthoek (Siska) - Retranchement
14	Sluis - Westkapelle - Knokke Stn

Meanwhile, back along the coastal main line, two small additions had been made. At Bredene, an electrified branch had been opened on 24 July 1923 linking the village alongside the new Renbaan (racecourse) to the main line of Capital 7, and at Zeebrugge a spur was laid along the famous Mole. Opened on 5 June 1930, it was apparently built at the request of the British

London & North Eastern Railway (LNER), many of whose Harwich - Zeebrugge passengers were destined for towns along the coast.

* development of Oostende town services

Lastly, the local electric tram system around Oostende was reorganised, partly on existing lines and partly with new track. It will be recalled that routes 4 to Slijkens and 3 to Vuurtoren already existed before the war, while routes 1 and 2 were always the main north and south routes. On 24 July 1923, route 5 was created by electrifying the "villages" line of Capital 2 as far as Mariakerke (Ruslandstraat), running in from there along Nieuwpoortse Steenweg and Adolf Pieterslaan to the SNCV station by the fish quay; thence it passed round the existing major loop to cross over itself at Klein Parijs and out along the Dijksmuide line of Capital 132 as far as Elisabethlaan; the latter route was electrified from Klein Parijs. Route 6 was effectively an extension of route 5 to Mariakerke (Dorpstraat) at the western end (9 November 1932) and to Stene at the other,

And Knokke, the last real town before the frontier, had its own urban network based on Albertplein. (author's collection)

Knocke-Zoute   Place Albert, Hôtel Memlinc.

though the latter section was apparently not brought into use until 1949. There was a depot at Stene, but the ground was subject to flooding and it was little used. Route 7, not introduced until near the end of World War II, was simply a short-working from the SNCV station along A Pieterslaan and on to Elisabethlaan via a new curve at Klein Parijs, while route 8 ran from the SNCV station along route 3 tracks until just after the latter crossed the inner harbour on a mixed-gauge bridge. It then swung sharply northwards along Vismijnlaan to terminate at Vismijn (Minque); this spur was opened on 21 December 1936 but possibly only for goods and in any case ceased operating from 16 May 1940 owing to bomb damage. Its original route number is not known to the writer. There remains only to mention a short goods branch inland to the coke works and chemical plants at Zandvoorde, laid by the Germans during the 1914-18 war and officially taken over by the SNCV in 1927. It was steam-worked and saw occasional Sunday passenger workings in season in connection with the boat races on the Brugsche Vaart; trains of open sided trailers followed the race along the shore and seats were reservable in advance. The workings apparently ran between 1927 and 1939 and again from 1945 to 1951.

*   *general expansions along the coast & route allocations*
    The coastal lines remained in SELVOP control throughout this period, and were steadily developed so far as that company's resources allowed. For a period during the 1930s there was even a through service from Oostende via Sluis to Breskens on Thursdays (Middleburg market day in Walcheren) and "boat trams" to and from De Panne connected with LNER sailings at Zeebrugge. The company's Oostende shops, at Nieuwpoortse Steenweg, were comprehensively equipped and, besides rebuilding their own cars, carried out work for other elements of the "Electrorail" organisation. The company was also instrumental in persuading the SNCV to design and build the excellent bogie motor cars which developed into the "Standard" series. Nonetheless the characteristic SELVOP train of the period was probably an OB four-wheel passenger car or motor luggage van towing a string of distinctive deep-windowed Oostende-pattern trailers.

The allocation of route numbers on the coastal system was potentially confusing since changes were made from time to time to "rationalise" the system. Thus bus routes were initially designated by letters (A, B etc) while route numbers 7-9 were used around De Panne. When Oostende routes were extended, during and after the war, these numbers were acquired, giving the southern routes allocations in the 20s, and this in turn involved renumbering the Sluis services. Route numbers 15-19 appear always to have been used by buses. Note also that, as tram routes closed, variations were again made. In particular, route 9 was used for a new service out towards the lighthouse, route 11 became a new bus service to Maldegem, while route 14, apparently transferred to a Knokke local service after closure of the Sluis branch, was discontinued. Bus route 15 to Klemskerke replaced the "Over de

Dorpen" inland route to De Haan. The table below shows typical alterations but services varied with the years!

Table 6A: Coastal routes numbering before and after World War II

1935	1950	Route details
1	1	Oostende - Knokke
1	+1	Oostende - De Haan (inland)
2	2	Oostende - De Panne
2	2	Oostende - Westende Bains
3	3	Oostende - Vuurtoren
4	4	Oostende - Slijkens
5	5	Mariakerke - Oostende - Elisabethlaan
6	6	Mariakerke (Dorpstr) - Oostende - (Elisabethlaan) - Stene
	7	Oostende - Elisabethlaan
	8	Oostende - Vismijn
*7	22	Koksijde Bad - Koksijde Dorp - Veurne
8	20	De Panne - Veurne
*9	23	Oostduinkerke Bad - Dorp - Koksijde Dorp Veurne
10	10	Brugge - Westkapelle - Knokke
11		Brugge - Westkapelle - Knokke - Heist
12	11	Heist - Knokke Bad - Oosthoek (Siska)
13	13	Knokke Dorp - Bad - Oosthoek (Siska)
14	21	De Panne - Adinkerke
21	14	Westkapelle - Sluis

6.2.3: Coastal system to 1956 & the end of SELVOP

The war did not have as much effect on the coastal system as it did inland. Some lines, however, closed for other reasons. The Nieuwpoort Stad - Oostduinkerke link, reduced from 1932 to a thrice-weekly mixed train in one direction only, was closed entirely on 16 November 1940 and then dismantled. The less essential frontier lines, too, were obvious candidates when the Germans demanded a supply of rails, and many saw their second abrupt closure in thirty years. The following lines were thus treated:

Capital	Section	km	Date
2	Koksijde towards Veurne (airfield works)	1.70	12May 1941+
2	Mariakerke -Middelkerke -Lombardsijde		18 Nov 1944
	Koksijde (Dorp - Bad)		Sep 1944
	Koksijde (Dorp) - Oostduinkerke (Dorp & Bad)		Sep 1944
	Track in Oostende	1.00	1940-44?
7/37	Oostende -Vuurtoren cut back & lifted		16 May 1940
	Oostende - Vismijn		16 May 1940
	Zeebrugge Mole abandoned	1.30	1943
(5/40)	Knokke (Bad) -Oosthoek (Siska)	1.20	1943++
	Oosthoek -Retranchement (lifted)*		1943
	Bredene Renbaan link abandoned May 1940, lifted		1944

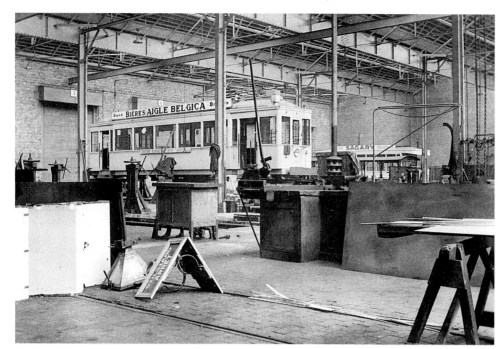

SELVOP always had its own Works at Oostende which carried out repairs for both the coastal system and other Empain concessions.

(the late Ir. Debot)

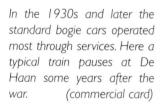

In the 1930s and later the standard bogie cars operated most through services. Here a typical train pauses at De Haan some years after the war. (commercial card)

And here a similar train loads at Oostende itself. (SNCV)

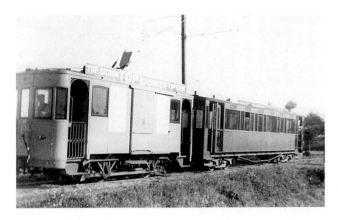

A shot on the frontier: An SNCV motor luggage van and SBM bogie trailer prepare to depart from Retranchement in 1932. Photo WJ Baron d'Aulnis. (Collection Paul de Backer)

The wartime closures proved permanent, and in addition there were some postwar cutbacks as shown below:

Section	closed
Heist (Duinbergen) - Oosthoek (Siska)*	30 Jun 1951
Westkapelle - Sluis	6 Oct 1951
De Panne - Adinkerke**	5 Sep 1954
De Panne - Veurne	5 Sep 1954
Oostende - Bredene - De Haan (inland route)	17 Jun 1955

NOTES:

* all trains now running via Knokke village.

** It appears these closures were somewhat protracted. On 22 May 1955 buses took over but some trams ran during the summer season, rail service was discontinued from 19 September but four journeys were reinstated on 2 October and final closure was from 2 June 1956. In addition various internal modifications and extensions were made to the Oostende urban routes at sundry times between 1945 and 1949

* ***the end of SELVOP and its effects***

All goods traffic on the SELVOP lines ceased from 1 February 1952 and at the end of 1955 SELVOP finally gave up its coastal concessions, the SNCV reorganising the provinces into Groep West-Vlaanderen, based on Brugge and Groep Oost-Vlaanderen based at Destelbergen. In spite of a very conscientious approach to its work, the SELVOP company was not rich and, as a senior member of the staff remarked, the SNCV takeover on 1 January 1956 was "like the opening of a new door". The SNCV did have resources and fully intended to make the coastal routes the pride of its system. It immediately reorganised Vlaanderen services to take account of this, splitting them into two groups. Eventually, Groupe 20 became Groep Vlaanderen and kept most of its former responsibilities, with its headquarters at Gent, where most of the remaining electric lines were situated. A new *Groupe du Littoral (Groupe 21)* was formed to operate the coastal region and the bus routes immediately inland, with headquarters at Brugge. It took over a system that was essentially sound, though in need of modernisation, and one that had already lost most of its less profitable branches - for the Littoral, too, had suffered since 1945. The coastal livery gradually changed from the Electrorail light-cream with blue lining to SNCV deep cream (almost beige). Even so, the SNCV felt the system could be further pruned if it was to survive, and made extra closures both at the northern end and at Oostende. At the northern end, Knokke - Brugge went on 29 September 1956, and the spur to Albertplein followed on 30 June 1957, thus finishing all local rail services in the area. In Oostende the town routes were shut as follows:

Route No	Section	Closed
3	Marie-Jose Plein -Vuurtoren	2 Jun 1956
4	Marie-Jose Plein -SJijkens	2 Jun 1956
5	Station -Mariakerke	13 Mar 1955*
6	Station -Stene	13 Mar 1955*
7		31 Mar 1955
8	Marie-Jose Plein -Vismijn	30 Jun 1958

* Route 7 probably also closed in March 1955; buses started replacing trams after 13 March. Vuurtoren tracks remained in occasional use until summer 1963

This reduced Oostende to being virtually a stop on the mainline routes 1 and 2, and enabled the stub ends of the old Lombardsijde, Diksmuide and Bredene lines to be lifted, though a connection from the Westende line was left in for depot access at Nieuwpoortse Steenweg. As compensation, the SNCV re-equipped the system with the magnificent type "SO" tramcars, which took full advantage of the wide coastal loading-gauge. They also took advantage of the fact that the line was now a continuous run with turning circles at strategic points, and built these as single-ended cars. The modern history of this line will be found at the end of this chapter.

Oostende town in the postwar years. On the left the prototype US-built PCC car; on the right a battery car rebuilt and modernised in Oostende Works (SNCV)

Outside the tourist coast, illustrations are less frequent. This is the Aalter horse tram with its bilingual notices.

(SNCV/author's collection)

62

6.3 Vlaanderen: major rural groupes to the 1920s

6.3.1 Introduction.

The coastal group of lines was a distinct entity for both political and geographical reasons. The same, alas, cannot be said for the tangled web which occupied the inland areas of both Vlaandern provinces; so how to cover their history in any kind of a coherent manner? They all started as isolated lines to serve areas identified as needing transport; most developed organically from that beginning and, inevitably, eventually made contact with developments in neighbouring areas but apparently not on any master plan. Two grew up around the major cities of Brugge and Gent and so can be treated separately as unities; the rest simply filled in the gaps and eventually emerged as four operating groups in the centre and south and a couple of detached lines in the north.

7 December 1886; it was one of only a few lines to link Oost and West Vlaanderen. Operation was ceded to the *SA des Railways Economiques de Liége -Seraing et Extensions (LS)* but they got little joy from this extension. It was, from the start, one of the SNCV's most consistent loss-makers; if there is a Belgian equivalent to the traditional story of the peasant preferring his donkey to the tram "because it was so much quicker", then this must be its origin. The local communities refused to desert the canal system because they found it "so much more convenient", and both passenger and goods traffic were, the SNCV sadly reported, "minimal". Even a short extension past Aalter station to a canal wharf on 1 October 1887 only gradually persuaded the locals that there might be something in these new-fangled ideas, and it was not until 17 July 1899 that the tramway really came into its own. At that date a 1.16km extension was opened from Tielt Markt to the standard-gauge station, and suddenly there was a thriving

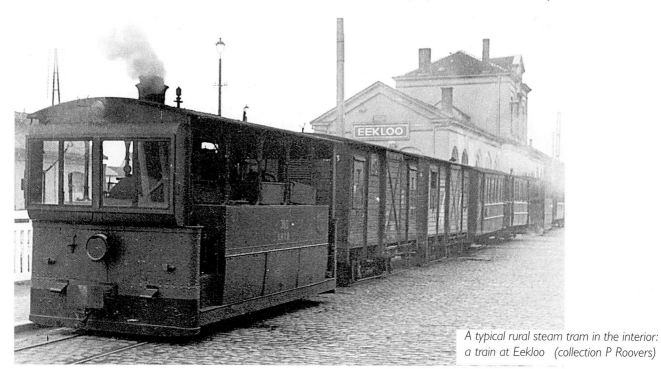

A typical rural steam tram in the interior: a train at Eekloo   (collection P Roovers)

6.3.2 Groupe d'Aeltre/Aalter. 1886-1917

Capital	Name	Auth km
6	*Tielt - Aalter*	*18.06*
39	*Eekloo - Watervliet - Grens*	*15.80*
98	*Aalter - Eekloo*	*12.64*

This first group sprang from one of the SNCV's earliest attempts at rural development and consisted effectively of a direct line of rails from Tielt, in the centre of Flanders, northeast to the Dutch frontier; just why the SNCV did not also include the later branch from Ruiselede to Gent is something of a puzzle. It was worked by the same people and initially had very little connection with the Gent system as a whole.

The trunk line of the system was **Capital 6 (TIELT - AALTER)**, a short, largely roadside route from the small market town of Tielt, almost in the centre of Vlaanderen, to the equally small market town of Aalter/Aeltre some 18 km to the northeast. It was authorised on 30 April 1886 as one of the first "batch" of concessions, and opened from Tielt town square through Ruiselede to Aalter standard-gauge station on

commuter traffic, or so it would appear. It is just possible that there was an existing route between Markt and station and that the SNCV "improved" it. Certainly the SNCV took the extraordinary step of starting a regular service between station and town and, to operate it, it appears that the concessionaire provided two horse trams. Furthermore, presumably in deference to everyone's linguistic sensitivities, the tram was bilingual. "Thielt -Aeltre" proclaimed the car sides, in French (a lie because the tram never ventured outside Tielt, but presumably you could transfer to the steam tram at Markt); "Van de Statie naar de Markt en vice versa" on big fascia boards was presumably for the local Flemish-speaking population. On 15 October 1902 the line was taken over by the *SA de CF Provinciaux (CFP)*, created in Bruxelles in December 1900 for a 30-year term, and was assimilated in that company's network. The SNCV provided new trams (actually ex-steam tram trailers) in 1905 and the horse tram lasted until 1914, being discontinued on 30 September of that year when the motive power was requisitioned for military use. As with other parts of the group, the whole line suffered considerable turmoil during World War 1, as shown below:

Section	fate	date
Tielt (Markt - Statie)	suspended	30 Sep 1914
Tielt -Aalter	suspended	13 Oct 1914
	restored	24 Nov 1914
	closed	16 Mar 1916
	reopened	1 Jun 1919

The second line in the chain, **Capital 39 (EEKLOO - WATERVLIET - GRENS)**, was actually the northernmost and was originally isolated. It ran from a station of the Brugge - Maldegem - Gent railway up to and across the Dutch frontier. It was authorised from Eeklo through Watervliet to the Dutch frontier on 9 April 1890, running initially from Eeklo town to the village of Watervliet (15 km, opened on 6 April 1891), and on to the Dutch frontier at Veldzicht about 1km further; At Veldzicht it connected with a branch of the Dutch *Stoomtram Breskens - Maldegem (SBM)*. As with Capital 6, traffic was slow to develop, needing a short extension south to Eeklo Canal on 10 June 1892 (authorised 31 October 1891) before matters improved - although the Capital name deteriorated, becoming the cumbersome "Eecloo à la Frontière vers Schoondyke et extension au canal d'Eecloo". The concessionaire was a local company, the *Societé en Nom Collectif du CFV d'Eecloo - Watervliet et Extensions (EW)* which was then running some 15.97km. The SNCV records give a further authorisation, on 3 October 1892, but it is not clear what this involved. It may refer to a short spur to the main line station at Eeklo opened on 10 December 1900, but if so, no real traffic resulted. The company did not prosper and surrendered its lease on 12 June 1901. The CFP took over from 15 October 1902, the SNCV presumably running the line itself in the interim. The new spur, however, quickly became a godsend. The line very soon became recognised as part of a useful route to Vlissingen (in the Netherlands) via Breskens, so that both passenger and freight traffic, particularly coal, increased rapidly. Unfortunately it was fought over during the German invasion of 1914 and was so badly damaged that it remained out of use throughout the war; with the Dutch connection discontinued as a result of the war, its main raison d'etre was gone anyway. Some 11.57km had to be rebuilt when war ended, and it was reopened from Eeklo town northward in three stages during 1919 as follows:

* Eeklo - Bentille   19 Mar 1919
* Bentille - Watervliet   1 Apr 1919
* Watervliet - Grens   1 Jun 1919

The canal and station links followed in June. The SNCV, which had taken control from the concessionaire in 1917 in what can only be described as high dudgeon, even extended the line slightly over a previously privately owned 2.21km goods branch from Watervliet to Waterland-Oudeman on 1 October 1923; this was authorised retrospectively on 17 December 1925 to regularise the affair!

Third and last line of this groupe was **Capital 98 (AALTER - EEKLOO)**, the connecting link from Aalter through Ursel to Eeklo or, to be more exact, Aalter Canal to Eeklo Canal, though services naturally ran through; hence the authorised length of 12.64km against an operational one of 16.68km. Authorised on 16 January 1899, and technically in Oost Vlaanderen, it was opened on 12 March 1900 and was operated by the SNCV until handed over to the *CF Provinciaux* from 9 January 1903. It was just a useful link and appears to have been built mainly because it was felt the rising township of Ursel ought to be on a line to somewhere; in fact Ursel very soon became a stop on a through route between Gent and the

coast, so its north-south links became comparatively insignificant. Like its neighbours, the line was extensively damaged during World War I and was restored during January 1919 (exact dates unknown to the writer). It should be noted that the CFP clearly did not see eye-to-eye with the SNCV about the way these lines should be run and the SNCV took advantage of the 15-year breakpoint in 1917 to request a revision of the contract. At about the same time, the lines were partially damaged and the concessionaire, quite reasonably, declined! The SNCV, therefore, had to take over the group and operate what remained under direct control.

6.3.3. Groupe de Dixmuide/Diksmuide, 1888-1920

Capital	Name	Auth km
29	*Veurne - Ieper*	36.89
75	*Ieper - Waasten - Steenwerck*	30.19
107	*Diksmuide - Ieper - Poperinge*	41.80
115	*Poperinge - Veurne - De Panne*	46.18
132	*Oostende - Diksmuide*	26.13
150	*Roeselare - Diksmuide - Bixschoote*	39.9

Following on from the Tielt-Aalter line - though not connected to it - came a collection of rural tramways immediately inland from the coast and grouped around old wool towns along the French frontier. Although not radiating from one particular town, these six lines were classed as a Groupe by the SNCV since they eventually came under the same concessionaire. They occupied between them the whole southwest of Vlaanderen, and their history was even more turbulent than that of the coast, though in early days they were closely related to it through the original concessionaire, the *SA des Railways Economiques de Liége - Seraing (LS)*. The LS operated both Capital 29 with that part of Capital 115 joining it to De Panne, and also the two-branched system running south from Ieper towards the French frontier as Capital 75. Later on the group was physically connected to the coastal system and ran trams into both Oostende and De Panne.

The first two lines in the district were both based on the old town of Ieper (Ypres to the French & British). The first line to be built was **Capital 29 (VEURNE - IEPER)**. Authorised on 22 March 1888, this ran first northwest from Ieper along the main road through hamlets like Brielen, Elverdinge and Oostvleteren to Linde where it suddenly diverged northeast in a big loop. This took it through Pollinkhove, Lo and Alveringem before rejoining the main road for a straight run north into Veurne standard-gauge station on the east side of that ancient town; somebody in the communes en route clearly had a lot of political clout. Capital 29 was opened throughout on 15 July 1889, with a total length of 36.44km and depots at each end. It was soon linked to the coast, though not to the coastal routes, by an early spur of Capital 115, 7.17km from Veurne to De Panne, authorised on 23 December 1901 and opened on 25 July 1901; operation of this was again given to the LS, which in due course handed the whole lot over to its coastal subsidiary, the *Ostende - Blankenberghe (OB)*.

The LS also got the district's second line, **Capital 75 (IEPER - WAASTEN - STEENWERCK)**. Plans for this dated from as early as 1888, it being projected to join Ieper to a French narrow-gauge line some 25km or so southwestward across the frontier. Initial authorisation, on 24 Dec 1895, provided for that part entirely within Belgium, consisting of a main line from Ieper through Kemmel and across the gently rolling plain to Nieuwkerke/Neuve Eglise with a branch from Kemmel through Messen/Messines to Waasten/Warneton; as might be expected this is largely a French-speaking enclave, and both names were in common use. It was opened throughout on 22 December 1897, an unexceptional rural line largely following minor roads and with its main depot at Ieper station. It may be mentioned here that the long-awaited French connection was not authorised until 19 March 1904 for the Belgian part and 11 September 1906 for the section in France. Even then it was not opened until 1 May 1909, when a 3km extension from Nieuwkerke Seule/Le Seau was intended to link the system to the *CF Economiques du Nord (CEN)* at Steenwerck for passengers only. It appears this connection never materialised.

That was later. After the main part of Capital 75, there was then a pause before a whole new batch of lines came into being around 1906-07. This time the LS did not get the concessions; they went to a local concern styling itself the *NM voor de Uitbating der Buurtspoorwegen van de Om trek Dixmude - Yper - Poperinghe* (Capital 107) to which it rapidly added "Veurne - Poperinghe - De Panne" (Capital 115) and "Dixmude - Oostende en uitbreidingen" (Capital 132). By that time the firm's title was getting somewhat out of control - no-one really wanted to correspond with a company address of that length - and there was a general sort-out. The concessionaire emerged in February 1910 with a new name, the *NM voor de Uitbating der Buurtspoorwegen van dem Om trek Dixmude - Yper (ODI)* (which can be roughly translated as the whole collection of lines round Diksmuide and Ieper). It also acquired title not only to its own lines but to the Veurne - Ieper and Ieper - Steenwerck lines, which it took over from the OB on 22 October 1910. There remained to the OB only Veurne - De Panne, and this in turn came under ODI control on 1 July 1914.

All this history has taken us to 1914 too quickly. A rapid survey shows that the first part of Capital 115 **(POPERINGE - VEURNE - DE PANNE)** , authorised retrospectively on 23 December 1901, was the first ODI line to open, on 25 July of that year. The major part followed in two sections: Poperinge to Roesbrugge (Haringe) on 24 October 1905, and Roesbrugge to Veurne on 1 July 1906, an operating total of 40.91km. It had depots at Poperinge and Veurne, and was a long, rambling line which ran for the most part in sight of the French frontier. From Poperinge standard-gauge station it ran first west to the hamlet of Watou and then rambled generally northwards, detouring first east, then west, then east again to link dozens of minor hamlets. Proven, Roesbrugge, Leisele, Houtem, Lez Moeroes and Bulskamp were only the major clusters on its wandering way, and it must have been something of a nightmare to work in any rational fashion. It was soon joined, however, by one branch of **Capital 107 (DIKSMUIDE - POPERINGE - IEPER)**, which ran south from the pleasant old Vlaanderen town of Diksmuide along the main Ieper road through Woumen village before splitting into two branches at a cluster of farms known as Merkem. The northernmost branch ran southwest along minor roads to cross Capital 29 at Oostvleteren and thence to Krombeke before turning south for its last lap to Poperinge. The other branch went almost due south from Merkem to Elverdinge, where it met the Veurne -Ieper route once more, with running powers into Ieper. The whole system was authorised on 25 March 1901, opened on 25 September 1906, and was worked in sections.

The ODI then looked to extend its empire northwards to the "bright lights". **Capital 132 (OOSTENDE - DIKSMUIDE)** had been mooted since 1889 by various communes but without success. Then the SNCV applied for and got authorisation on 19 March 1904, opening the 26.13km line three years later on 29 June 1907 (one of the few where the final length agreed with that authorised!). It ran northeast from Diksmuide through Beerst and then to Leke, which was later a junction for a long cross-country line to Brugge (Capital 137). From Leke, Capital 132 generally followed the main road through little villages like St Pieterskapel and Leffinge across typical bleak Vlaanderen countryside to the outskirts of Oostende at Stene. From there it ran into Oostende over OB tracks to terminate at Sweepplaats (later Feysplein) by the old railway station. It was a typical rural line providing a vital if not lucrative service to its villages, and completely uneconomic even with autorails once road transport became reliable, Main depots were at Diksmuide and Stene.

Last but by no means least, the ODI acquired the first part of a line planned to develop country to the southeast of Diksmuide. This was **Capital 150 (ROESELARE - DIKSMUIDE - BIKSCHOOTE)**, with two branches based on Roeselare, a station on the existing route from Hooglede to Tielt (Capital 33). The most important line ran through Roeselare town and then northwest alongside the road to Staden (15.48km) whence it struck across country via Klerker to join Capital 107 at Woumen (11.97km) for a common run-in to Diksmuide. It was authorised on 2 May 1908, being opened in stages from Roeselare to Staden on 15 February 1911, and on to Woumen on 1 October 1911; depots were at Roeselare and Diksmuide. The other branch was never completed; opened on 1 March 1913, it ran roughly west by various lanes to the mainline railway at Langemark. It was intended to carry on to Bikschoote on Capital 107, a total of 19.15km, and most of the work was actually done, but the standard-gauge crossing at Langemark delayed matters; war stopped further progress in 1914 and it was never revived, although there are indications that the roadbed was used for military light railways. Alas for the ODI, it was still building its empire when World War I broke out, and three months later all its lines were in the battle zone and out of its control. All routes were officially closed from 16 October 1914.

* **the 1914-18 war and its effects**
The overall story of the SNCV in the war is told in Chapter 3. In brief so far as this groupe was concerned, Capital 29 was used by the allied military from Veurne to a point near Elverdinge from where it was destroyed. Capital 75 was mostly smashed very early on, only the southern bit from Steenwerck up towards Kemmel seeing occasional military trains. Capital 107 ran right across no-mans-land. Its northern section was largely destroyed by the fighting and artillery duels; the southern portion from Poperinge to Oostvleteren with a couple of dead-end spurs northward from Capital 29 was used by the allies along with most of Capital 115. Big store dumps, new cross-links, even a bypass round Veurne, and a line to cut out the Alveringem detour were built, and the lines were busier than they had ever been. In German-held territory the picture is not so clear. It is known that Capital 132, the Oostende - Diksmuide line, was used by the army field railways as far south as Beerst with new spurs round Vladslo, just northeast of Diksmuide and out along the Brugge route from Leke. As for Capital 150, It is likely that parts of the Roeselare

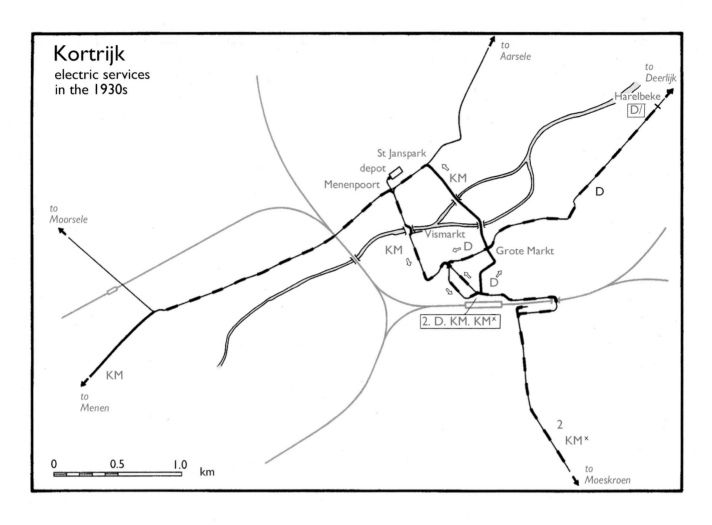

Kortrijk
electric services
in the 1930s

to
Aarsele

to
Deerlijk

Harelbeke
D/

St Janspark
depot
KM

Menenpoort

to
Moorsele

D

Vismarkt

KM

D

Grote Markt

KM

D

2. D. KM. KM×

to
Menen

KM

2
KM×

to
Moeskroen

0   0.5   1.0   km

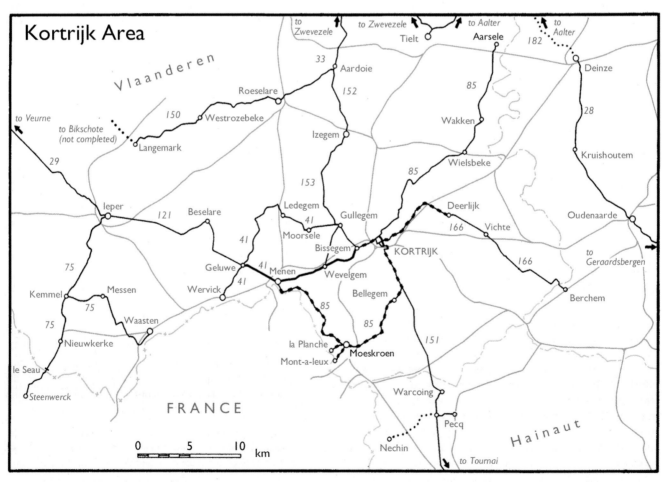

Kortrijk Area

to
Zwevezele

to Zwevezele

to Aalter

to
Aalter

Tielt

Aarsele

182

Vlaanderen

33

Aardoie

Deinze

Roeselare

152

85

150

Westrozebeke

Wakken

28

to Veurne

to Bikschote
(not completed)

Izegem

Kruishoutem

Langemark

29

153

85

Wielsbeke

 Ieper

121

Beselare

Ledegem

Deerlijk

Oudenaarde

41

Gullegem

166

Vichte

41

Moorsele

Bissegem

KORTRIJK

to
Geraardsbergen

75

Geluwe

41

Menen

Wevelgem

166

Kemmel

Messen

41

Wervick

Bellegem

Berchem

75

85

Waasten

75

85

151

Nieuwkerke

la Planche

le Seau

Mont-a-leux

Moeskroen

Steenwerck

FRANCE

Warcoing

Pecq

Hainaut

Nechin

to Tournai

0   5   10   km

line saw occasional military use, though later on they were out of use through damage between Diksmuide and Klerken and between Roeselare and Langemark. Certainly, after the war, all were reconstructed as soon as conditions allowed, but by that time the ODI was finished. Although it did accept a short-term lease in 1920, it really could see little point in trying to rebuild its former possessions, and took advantage of the 1919 law to change its mind and surrender its leases. The SNCV took control from 1 January 1921, services being restored as shown below:

Capital	Section	Date reopened
29	Veurne - Alveringem (Fortem)	19 Dec 1918
	Alveringem - Lo - Oostvleteren	22 Mar 1919
	Oostvleteren - Elverdinge - Ieper	24 Apr 1919
75	Ieper - Voormezele	17 Sep 1919
	Voormezele - Kemmel	15 Sep 1920
	Kemmel - Menen	1 Oct 1920
	Menen - Waasten (village)	1 Feb 1922
	Kemmel - Nieuwkerke (village)	25 Dec 1920?
	Nieuwkerke (village) - Seule	7 Dec 1922
	Seule - Steenwerck	14 Jan 1923
107	Poperinge - Oostvleteren	22 Mar 1919
	Oostvleteren - Merkem - Diksmuide	26 Jun 1919
	Elverdinge - Ieper	24 Apr 1919
	Elverdinge - Merkem*	3 or 8 Mar 1922
115	Poperinge - Veurne - De Panne	4 Dec 1918
132	Oostende - Leke - Diksmuide	1 Aug 1919
150	Roeselare - Staden - Woumen	7 Sep 1919
	Roeselare - Westrozebeke	15 May 1920
	Westrozebeke - Langemark	15 Aug 1920

* All military branches were removed and it is difficult to see why Merkem - Elverdinge was ever reconstructed. Certainly it had virtually no traffic, and by the 1930s was down to one train a day in each direction, with extras on market days.

6.3.4 Groupe de Courtrai/Kortrijk, 1891-1927

Capital	Name	Auth km
41	Kortrijk - Wervick - Menen	29.07
85	Aarsele - Kortrijk - Moeskroen - Menen	50.90
121	Ieper - Geluwe	17.70
151	Kortrijk - Pecq	18.80
153	Izegem - Wevelgem	13.95
166	Kortrijk - Berchem	24.31

NOTE: This area was partly French and partly Flemish speaking.

The only town-centred group of Vlaanderen lines with serious electrification, other than the major ones at Gent and Brugge (qv) was that based on Kortrijk in the southeast of Vlaanderen. It filled the gap along the French frontier between the Diksmuide group and the odd little Groupe d'Audenarde to be described later.

The Kortrijk lines were fairly straightforward. They had their origin in the local *SA pour l' Exploitation du CFV de Courtrai - Menin - Wervicq (CMW)* formed in December 1892 to operate the line of its title. This, authorised on 7 June 1890 after a four-year hassle, was **Capital 41 (KORTRIJK - WERVICK - MENEN)**. It ran from Kortrijk standard-gauge station via Menenpoort and then in a generally southwesterly direction to Bissegem, Gullegem, Moorsele and Ledegem, where it met and crossed the standard-gauge Menen - Roeselare railway. It was never far from a road, but from Gullegem onwards it followed a stream which required several deviations. At Ledegem it swung southeast by the main road to run alongside country

lanes through Dadizele and Geluwe where it joined the main road; it terminated at Menen standard-gauge station. Wervik was reached by a short branch from Geluwe which, though only a village, had a subsidiary depot. The line was opened in two stages, the central part from Ledegem to Geluwe and Menen on 8 December 1892, and the two ends on 13 February 1893. Again the SNCV recorded a further authorisation on 6 March 1893, possibly for amendments at Kortrijk. As a means of getting to Menen it was not particularly brilliant, running over some 26.81km as against 13km by the direct road. Nonetheless the CMW prospered and, in anticipation of further concessions, changed its name in 1899 to the more imposing *SA Intercommunale Courtrai (IC)*.

Its confidence was justified, since all succeeding lines around Kortrijk were allocated to the company. The first of these was the long **Capital 85 (AARSELE - KORTRIJK - MOESKROEN - MENEN)** which ran from Aarsele, some 29 km northeast of Kortrijk, through Kortrijk town and on south to reach Menen/Menin from the east in another great loop via Moeskroen. As shown below, the line was authorised and built in rather leisurely fashion in sections. The northern line, with depot at Kortrijk, ran northeast on its own right-of-way, following the canalised River Leie to Oyghem whence it broke away to follow minor roads via Wielsbeke (standard-gauge crossing) and Wakken to terminate at the standard-gauge station of Aarsele on the Tielt - Gent railway. The southern line was physically separate, starting on the south side of Kortrijk mainline station and leaving town along a paved road to what was officially Bellegem but could more correctly be called Bellegem Road. There it swung southwest across country on its own right-of-way to Moeskroen town, crossing but not connecting with the standard gauge. The short spur to Mont-a-Leux, right up against the French frontier, left the main line at Moeskroen while the main track continued northwestward, first on private track and then along roads to Menen town square.

Section	authorised	opened
North line		
* Kortrijk - Wakken	8 Sep 1897	1 May 1900
* Wakken - Aarsele	20 Jul 1903	14 May 1906
South line		
* Menen - Moeskroen	8 Sep 1897	8 Aug 1900
* Moeskroen - Kortrijk	8 Sep 1897	15 Jun 1902
* Moeskroen - Mont-a-Leux	17 Sep 1904	4 May 1906

Almost simultaneously with this line, the SNCV applied for and got a route to link the Ieper lines with the burgeoning Kortrijk system at Geluwe. **Capital 121 (IEPER - GELUWE)**, authorised on 24 June 1902, started at Geluwe SNCV station and ran almost due north to Ieper town with only one short deviation just before the wayside station of Beluveld to serve the hamlet of Beselare, an oddity since the more important Zillebeke had to make do with a station some way from its village. The line was opened throughout on 14 July 1905, although the SNCV also quotes a date of 1 June 1907, which may refer to linking at one or other of its ends (probably Ieper). The main depot was at Geluwe, which was rapidly becoming an important junction, and the length, including some running powers over other lines, was 18.30km.

The three remaining lines were all from or near Kortrijk. First was **Capital 151 (KORTRIJK - PECQ)** which formed part of an SNCV "plot" to link Kortrijk with Tournai in Hainaut. Authorised on 29 May 1905, it was eventually 18.78km long, opened on 27 September 1909, and ran almost due south along the main road for most of its route. As far as Bellegem its tracks were common with the Moeskroen line and then it served Kooigem, Espièrres (standard-gauge link), Warcoing and Estaimbourg before terminating at Pecq town centre. Here, eventually, it met a tentacle of Capital 95 reaching north from Tournai and threw off a short branch to Pecq standard-gauge station, opened on 25 October 1909. At Warcoing was a sugar refinery with its own branch and, to serve it, four-rail mixed-gauge track was laid over 4km to Espièrres.

Capital 153 (IZEGEM - WEVELGEM) was a minor oddity. It was the southern portion of an 1899 project for a line from Aardooie to Izegem and Wevelgem. Authorised on 5 July 1906 and opened on 11 April 1911, it ran north from Wevelgem on the Kortrijk - Menen railway, through Gullegem where it crossed the SNCV Menen route (Capital 41) and thence northwest along minor roads to Izegem town, where it terminated some way short of the "northern section" from Ardooie, which was baulked by the Roeselare - Lys canal. It was not until 1930 that the two were united. The line as opened was some 13.31km long, and the services appear to have been based on Kortrijk.

Last but not least was **Capital 166 (KORTRIJK - BERCHEM)**. Authorised on 31 May 1908, it was 24.20km long and was opened in two stages. The first stretch to Deerlijk and Vichte (13.40km) was opened on 20 February 1912, and it was reported that the usual problems with "bridge works" crossing the Etat Belge railway would delay the extension to Berchem (10.90km) for "a few months". The war intervened before the dispute was settled, and the remainder did not open until ten years later on 1 February 1922, though it appears that most track was at least laid, since it is recorded as lifted by the Germans during the war. The war also affected the other Kortrijk lines badly. Kortrijk was in the rear battle zone on the

German side of the lines. All tramways, except possibly parts of those to Izegem and Aarsele, were out of use, various sections being damaged and others lifted by the Germans. They were restored as (in the table below) :

NOTE: Of these lines, Capital 41 had been badly damaged south of Moorsele and Capital 121 was badly damaged throughout while Capital 151 was also damaged between Bellegem and Pecq.

Unlike most other companies, the IC decided to hang on to its lines and resumed working them, though the SNCV made it hand back the Kortrijk -Pecq line from 1 January 1923. The rest were not handed back until 1 July 1927, although working arrangements until then were made on a year-to-year basis.

6.3.5 Groupe d'Audenarde/ Oudenaarde, 1888-1920

Capital	Name	Auth km
28	Deinze - Oudenaarde	19.00
103	Geraardsbergen - Oudenaarde	25.52
182	Deinze - Aalter (not built)	16.00

This small operating group was originally isolated and even at its maximum consisted only of two routes - one running north west and one southeast from the small town of Oudenaarde in the southeast corner of Oostvlaanderen; as such it was typical of the SNCV's more rural and unprofitable lines in Vlaanderen. The trunk line was **Capital 28 (DEINZE - OUDENAARDE)**, a roadside tramway from Deinze, where it made a standard-gauge connection, through agricultural country to the market town of Oudenaarde some 19km to the south. It was authorised in two parts, on 18 November 1887 from Deinze to Oudenaarde (Markt) and on 15 June 1888 to the river bank at Deinze (Brug); it was opened throughout to Deinze Brug (18.94 km) on 14 October 1888 and an extension over the river to Deinze (Grote Markt) was authorised on 30 October 1888. Construction of a bridge over the Leie river delayed the final portion, but at the end of 1891 it was pushed through to Grote Markt, an operating total of 19.6km. Initially the SNCV negotiated with a local body, the *Sté en Nom Collectif Balat et Leclercq (BL)*, but from 24 July 1889 the *Sté pour l'Exploitation des CF Regionaux en Belgique (CFRB)* took over the lease on terms that did not prove very advantageous. The line, alas, was one of the SNCV's more embarrassing ventures from the start, being consistently in deficit for many years. Even though matters slowly improved, it was never able to do more than cover its first dividend, and the CFRB surrendered its lease at the earliest opportunity, with effect from 27 September 1903. There was then a short gap before the big *SA des Transports Urbains et Vicinaux (TUV)* took over on 30 December 1903 as part of its policy of collecting lines in Vlaanderen to form a unified system.

The TUV's immediate interest was caused by a recent (1899) authorisation of a further line connecting with Geraardsbergen about 25 km south east of Oudenaarde. This branch, **Capital 103 (GERAARDSBERGEN - OUDENAARDE)**, eventually totalling 26.74km, was authorised on 19 October 1899 and opened in stages, from Geraardsbergen town to Leupegem on 1 April 1905, and on to Oudenaarde standard-gauge station on 20 November 1905; it connected en route with

Cap	Section	closed	reopened
41*	Kortrijk - Ledegem	9 Nov 1914	19 Mar 1919
	Ledegem - Dadizele	9 Nov 1914	21 Mar 1919
	Dadizele - Geluwe	9 Nov 1914	1 Apr 1919
	Geluwe - Menen	9 Nov 1914	25 May 1919
	Geluwe - Wervik	9 Nov 1914	1 Jul 1919
85**	Menen - Kortijk	1 Jul 1917	1 Jul 1919
	Kortrijk - Ooigem	1 Jul 1917	Mar 1919
	Ooigem - Wakken	1 Jul 1917	1 Jul 1919
	Wakken - Aarsele	1 Jul 1917	29 Dec 1919
	Moeskroen - Montaleux	1 Jul 1917	9 Mar 1919
121	Ieper		
	(Statie/Menenpoort)	9 Oct 1914	5 Oct 1919
	Ieper - Zillebeke	9 Oct 1919	1 Sep 1919
	Zillebeke - Geluveld	9 Oct 1914	14 Aug 1919
	Geluveld - Geluwe	9 Oct 1914	25 May 1919
151	Kortrijk - Bellegem+	31 May 1917	24 Feb 1919
	Bellegem - Pecq+	31 May 1917	19 Mar 1919
	Izegem - Gullegem	9 Nov 1914++	24 Feb 1919
	Gullegem - Wevelgem	9 Nov 1914++	14 Apr 1922
166	Kortrijk - Vichte	1 Jul 1917+++	12 Dec 1919
	Vichte - Berchem (new opening)		1 Feb 1922

*   all lifted Jun 1915
**   services suspended 27 Oct - 23 Nov 1914, then irregular.
+   suspended 9 - 27 Oct 1914
++   lifted Gullegem - Wevelgem?
+++ suspended 27 Oct - 5 Dec 1914

the Deinze line at or near its terminus in the market place, and the two lines were worked as an entity with main depot at Oudenaarde and a shed at Geraardsbergen. The branch, alas, had the same problems as its predecessor, having been offered around by the SNCV in both 1902 and 1904 without success before the TUV took it on. It was never very profitable, and even up to 1914 was able only to cover part of its first dividend, though by then linked to Capital 128 at Geraardsbergen. Nonetheless the SNCV persevered with ideas for expansion, and in 1911 even obtained a concession for a Deinze - Aalter link (Capital 182). Perhaps fortunately, the 1914-18 war intervened before it could be built. The system was therefore an obvious choice when the Germans were looking for lines to dismantle. Geraardsbergen - Oudenaarde was closed and lifted in December 1917, the Deinze branch following soon after, and the operating company lost no time in surrendering its lease as soon as the post-war law of November 1919 allowed it to do so. The SNCV clearly did not consider the system a priority for reconstruction, Deinze - Oudenaarde reopening to Deinze (Brug) only on 14 February 1921 and being extended to Grote Markt on 26 March 1921. Geraardsbergen - Leupegem (29 February 1922) and Leupegem - Oudenaarde (21 December 1922) followed, and the system once more settled down to a sleepy existence.

6.4 Lines around Brugge

6.4.1 Brugge: introduction

The network of lines centred on the ancient city of Brugge/Bruges is probably the next logical cluster to examine. They were, in effect, the northern equivalent of the Groupe de Dijksmuide, being just behind the coastal area in the north of Flanders with strong links into the Littoral system - indeed one important line some might think of as in this cluster, **Capital 37 (BRUGGE - HEIST)**, was allocated to the coastal concessionaires. Brugge was one of the Belgian cities which started with suburban and rural lines and then developed their inner portions into a electrified urban network. The history follows this pattern.

6.4.2 Groupe de Swevezele/Zwevezele 1889-1920

Capital	Name	Auth km
33	Hooglede - Tielt	32.84
65	Brugge - Zwevezele	19.96
113	Brugge - Knesselare - Ursel	20.47
119	Brugge - Middelburg - Aardenburg	21.90
137	Brugge - Leke - Diksmuide	32.90
152	Ardooie - Izegem	6.53
178	Lignes Electriques de Bruges	5.75

Although the SNCV officially classed this as a single group, it appears in early years to have been something of a mixture. It had originally three different concessionary companies operating various lines from various headquarters, though in later years all operated from Assebroek and were probably connected. To the south were two intertwined routes with headquarters at Roeselare. The other lines all centred on Brugge and the two companies concerned seem to have had close links.

To take the southern lines first, these were **Capital 33 (HOOGLEDE - TIELT)** and Capital 152 (ARDOOIE - IZEGEM). They were both run from the start by the *SA pour l' Exploitation du CFV Thielt - Hooghlede (TH)* which opened its trunk line on 24 December 1889. This was a rambling rural

Brugge town: 4-wheeled car 9432 on route 1 in the Wollestraat; the silhouette in the arch is the tram stop sign! (photographer unknown. collection Paul de Backer)

route authorised on 12 December 1888 and 20 March 1889, springing from the Tielt -Aalter line (Capital 6) and running north, west and then south in a huge semicircle along minor roads. At Hille (in the commune of Zwevezele) it later met a link to Brugge (Capital 65); between Koolscamp and Ardooie it crossed the standard gauge, and at Roeselare standard-gauge station it met the Menen - Brugge main line railway before swinging briefly northwest to the commune of Hooglede - in all, 33.31km with a depot at Ardooie. Its own history was uneventful, though Roeselare became quite an important junction with routes to Diksmuide and Langemark.

The Thielt-Hooglede Company did, however, almost by accident, acquire a second line, from Ardooie to Izegem. This, **Capital 152 (ARDOOIE - IZEGEM)** was originally part of a much larger project which was turned down by the Belgian state. Instead, on 5 January 1906, (SNCV: another source says 6 July 1906) the 6.01km stretch south to Izegem was granted "as a branch of Tielt - Hooglede". This was not nearly so attractive a proposition, and four years elapsed before it was finally opened on 1 October 1910. Even then it stopped short on the north bank of a canal, and its final section to Izegem standard-gauge station - and a link to Kortrijk - was not put in until 1930. Meanwhile, as with so many other lines, it was closed and lifted during World War I, not being reopened until 1 February 1922. The same fate befell the parent line, Tielt - Hille being lifted completely and the rest left derelict or in military use. It was reopened earlier, from Roeselare to Zwevezele (Hille) on 8 February 1919, on to Wingene on 24 May 1919, and to Tielt Markt on 1 July 1919. The short branch to Hooglede was not reopened until 19 December 1919, by which time the SNCV had taken over control.

The main part of the group, however, consisted of a cluster of lines centred on the old town of Brugge/Bruges. The first of these northern lines, **Capital 65 (BRUGGE - ZWEVEZELE)** was the result of continuing machinations from 1884-on. It was originally proposed as a part of various schemes in the area but took its final shape only after Capital 33 (Hooglede - Tielt) had been formed. Authorised on 3 July 1894, it was actually opened on 22 January 1896 with a total length of 19.91km. It ran from a connection with the Hooglede - Tielt line at Zwevezele (Hille) northwards along the main Brugge road via Oostkamp and Assebroek (Steenbrugge) where it made contact with the standard gauge. It entered the old town of Brugge at Gentpoort and by a roundabout route eventually reached the mainline station. The depot was at Hille and operation was ceded to the local *NM tot Uitbating van den Buurtspoorweg Brugge - Swevezeele (BS)* formed at Brugge four days before the opening! There is some doubt as to whether the company operated the line for its whole independent life or whether it later passed fleetingly to the NWV concern (see below). The companies may, in any case, have been have been associated. Like its neighbours, it was closed and lifted during the 1914-18 war except for rails within Brugge. It was restored on 29 January 1919 and came into SNCV control either later that year or in the following year; the BS was certainly the concessionaire until 1 October of that year.

The other three lines, Capitaux 113, 119 and 137, were also based on Brugge and were worked from new by the *Maatschappij tot Uitbating der Buurtspoorwegen van het Noorden van West Vlaanderen (NWV)*, a company formed in 1903 with headquarters at Assebroek and with most of its capital subscribed by local councils. **Capital 113 (BRUGGE - KNESSELARE - URSEL)** was authorised on 5 July 1901 as a line from Brugge through the northern part of Assebroek commune to the provincial boundary at Knesselare, the line actually being opened on 18 January 1904. Its extension to Ursel, where it eventually met Capitaux 8 from Gent and 98 from Aalter, followed on 15 March 1908 (some local sources suggest that public services did not actually start until 21 March), giving a working total of 21.45km. The increase over authorised length was probably due to sections in common with other lines within Brugge town where the authorisation had been altered in June 1903 to run from Garenmarkt to Gentpoort; this modified trace was opened on 1 July 1905. Completion also gave an SNCV link between the coast and Gent parallel to the standard gauge, though not frequently used, one imagines. The line was straightforward, was closed for a period during the 1914-18 war with the Knesselare - Ursel section badly damaged, and was restored in two sections: Brugge - Knesselare on 22 December 1918, and Knesselare - Ursel on 11 January 1919. It reverted to SNCV control at the end of that year along with the other NWV operations. It may be mentioned that in 1931 it was effectively extended, the SNCV taking over the unelectrified stretch of Capital 8, from Ursel to Zomergem, previously worked by the ETG. Its own depot was at Assebroek, which also became the main one for Brugge town services after the inner part from Assebroek was electrified under Capital 178 (qv).

Capital 119 (BRUGGE - AARDENBURG) was slightly more complex. The original portion from Brugge via St-Kruispoort and St-Kruis village to Middelburg by the Dutch frontier was authorised on 22 May 1902, and opened on 4 September 1904. On that date, also, it was extended from the frontier for 5km to a junction with the Dutch Stoomtram Breskens - Maldegem (SBM) at Aardenburg. This link, as we have seen, was in the nature of a quid pro quo, the SNCV having allowed the Dutch company to put in a 5km line on Belgian soil to Maldegem in 1887. Through links were provided with the SBM, and on 30 May 1913 the inner part to St-Kruis-Kerke was electrified as part of Capital 178 (see below); electrification was extended to St-Kruis-Doornhut on 22 February 1914. This became route 6 of Brugge, but the whole line was out of use during World War I because it was taken over by the German army. It was restored to public use in two sections: Brugge - Moerkerke on 11 November 1918 (which was fairly rapid) and Moerkerke - Aardenburg on 1 June 1920. In fact Moerkeke - Aardenburg had been briefly reopened in 1918 but was closed again on 26 November of that year when the trackbed was found to have been mined. For a brief period the line is said to have been part of an improvised postal link between Paris and Amsterdam.

The third line, **Capital 137 (BRUGGE - LEKE - DIJKSMUIDE)** was originally intended to be longer than it turned out. It was planned to run from Brugge station westward via St-Andries to Snellegem along the main road. Thence it was to swing south and west across country on its own right-of-way to Koekelare where it would split. One branch was to go due west to Leke on Capital 132, the other curving south by Bovekerke and Vladslo to reach Diksmuide itself. In practice, authorisation for the Leke line was given on 5 October 1904, and it was opened on 22 March 1910, a total of 32.09km; trains worked through to Diksmuide over Capital 132. The Koekelare - Diksmuide branch was not proceeded with, though the Germans came near to building it in 1914-18. As with other lines, the Brugge end, from St-Andries, was electrified in 1913 as part of Capital 178. The line was effectively put out of use during World War I, though the German army worked at least the Leke -Koekelare section with additional spurs. It was restored on 6 December 1918, and all three lines out of Brugge reverted to SNCV control in 1920.

6.4.3 Brugge urban & suburban network: inception & development (Map ref C-4)

This leaves us with **Capital 178 (LIGNES ELECTRIQUES DE BRUGES)**. In the first decade of the 20th century, internal public transport in Brugge, despite various ephemeral "tramway" companies, was virtually non-existent. Only an odd horse bus plodded from station to canal via Grote Markt, supplemented by occasional trains on the inner ends of existing SNCV steam-worked lines. So far as contemporary maps show, these were as follows.

* **Capital 37** from Heist came in at the northeast corner via Fort Lapin to enter the city at Dampoort. Thence it ran part way round the northern boulevards and then split. A goods branch ran on via Ezelspoort or Oostendepoort to Scheepsdaalbrug; the passenger line turned south via Schouwburgplatz (Theatre square) to skirt Grote Markt and run west to the old railway station at 't Zand. A second long goods branch diverged at Dampoort and skirted the eastern and southern boundaries alongside a canal to reach Katelijnepoort and possibly Gentpoort.

* **Capital 65** from Zwevezele came in at Katelijnepoort in the southwest corner and, according to maps, ran first north and then east through the lower town via the "New Gent Road" to join Capital 113 on its way to Grote Markt.

* **Capital 113** from Ursel came in from the southeast via Gentpoort, and ran north via Grote Markt to join Capital 37 near Schouwburgplatz.
* **Capital 119** from Middelburg and St-Kruis came in part way along the Capital 37 goods branch at St-Kruispoort, where it originally terminated, and appears to have used the ring line to reach the old station either via Dampoort to the north or via Gentpoort to the south.
* **Capital 137** from Leke came in through Smedenpoort on the west side, and went along Smedenstraat, turning into Consciencestraat where it terminated near the old station at 't Zand.

It is not surprising, therefore, to see the town council deep in conclave with the SNCV from 1906 onward, with the idea of producing an urban electric tram system. A plan was concocted which electrified the inner portions of existing lines and joined them by a new network of tracks through the narrow twisting streets of the old town centre, this being authorised on 5 August 1910 as **Capital 178 (LIGNES ELECTRIQUES DE BRUGES)**. Initially the SNCV awarded its contract to the OB, presumably on the grounds that they had experience with electricity and their parent companies ran one of the lines coming into Brugge (Capital 37). The following year, however, both the SNCV and the town council had second thoughts. The lines were reallocated to the local *NWV*, which was certainly the major operator and over whose existing routes most of the town trams were to run. The concession, unusually, was for a short period to terminate on 3 October 1919, when the NWV's other concessions were also due to run out. The routes involved seven new sections of track and were opened during 1913 as follows, the railway station then being at 't Zand:

Rte	Section	Opened
1	Station - Stevinplein - Grote Markt - Gentpoort - Assebroek with parallel link	
	Grote Markt - Schouwburgplaats - Station	2 Feb 1913
2	Station - Stevinplein - OL Vrouwkerk - Katelijnepoort - Steenbrugge with a link between OL Vrouwkerk and the St-Salvatorkerk	10 Feb 1913
3	Station -Eiermarkt -Ezelspoort - Scheepsdaal	19 Feb 1913
4	Station - Schouwburgplaats - Dampoort	2 Mar 1913
5	Station - Smedenpoort - St-Andries	24 Apr 1913
6	Station -Stevinplein - Grote Markt - St-Kruispoort	30 May 1913

The parallel sections allowed one-way working at crucial points. The section of Capital 65 along the New Gent Road appears to have been abandoned for passenger traffic but electrified on 2 February 1913 nonetheless, being used mainly for stock transfers. The following year, route 6 was extended to St-Kruis (Doornhut) over Capital 119 on 22 February 1914 and route 4 was extended to Warandebrug on 2 May 1914.

The whole system appears to have been out of use for at least part of the 1914-18 war since it is recorded as having been restored piecemeal thereafter. Some local services were working by 22 December 1918; the St-Kruis route was restored on 11 May 1919, and the link from Markt to Gentpoort on 12 February 1920. The electric service from 't Zand to Warandebrug apparently had to wait until 18 December 1923. To complete the picture, it should be mentioned that the Knokke line was electrified throughout in 1930, and route 3 was extended north into the St-Pieters district on 14 July 1935. In 1938-9, as part of a general reconstruction, a new road was built round the northwest of the city, and the railway station moved several hundred metres to the south. Cars from Knokke then ran in over the northern ring but out via the town centre, while all routes were extended to the new station from 1 April 1939 over a new link from the old 't Zand terminus. The subsequent history will be found under section 6.8.2

6.5 Development of Lines around Gent to 1920:

6.5.1 Gent: Introduction

The second biggest collection of lines, after the coastal system, was around the ancient walled city of Gent/Gand in Oostvlaanderen. With the short-lived exception of the Cie North, Gent was the only place in Vlaanderen where the SNCV had to contend with an existing local tramway company. This was the *Electrische Tram van Gent (ETG) or Tramways Electriques de Gand (TEG)*, which used both versions of its name. It was an LS subsidiary which took over an existing municipal horse tramway on 4 January 1898. The municipal undertaking already worked an urban system of seven routes plus an SNCV steam line to Zomergem, and the ETG not only acquired these but added a new SNCV concession, Capital 79 to Merelbeke, to its empire. It was early in the field of electrification, trying out accumulator cars on its town system and on Gent - Merelbeke as soon as it took over. When they proved unsuccessful, it provided overhead electrification on the Merelbeke line as an experiment in 1901. It was a success, and the remaining lines soon followed. So far as the SNCV was concerned, the ETG was a friend rather than a rival, for all SNCV lines terminated near or outside the former city walls and were not interconnected. Up to 1920 or so, they were indeed classed as separate systems, the three eastern lines being Groupe de Gand (Chaussée de Termonde), and the western ones Groupe de Gand (Rabot), from the locations of their headquarters, though from 1911 they were all run by the same firm. Gent - Zomergem and the steam-worked Gent - Merelbeke - Herzele - Geraardsbergen line (Capital 128) were treated separately.

6.5.2 Gent lines ceded to the ETG

Capita	Name	Auth km
8	*Gent - Zomergem - Ursel*	20.83
79	*Gent - Merelbeke*	7.43

Capital 8 (GENT - ZOMERGEM) was one of the earliest SNCV concessions, being authorised on 22 November 1886 and opened westward from Gent (Rabot) to Zomergem Kanaal the following day! There was then a distinct pause owing to bridging problems before it reached Zomergem Dorp on 15 June 1887. The 14.30km route was a straightforward roadside line starting from the Rabot district in the northwest of Gent, and was ceded for operation to the *Liége-Seraing*. In the late 1890s it was extended west again to Ursel (authorised 18 August 1897 at the same time as an extension from Gent (Rabot) to Gent (Bruggsche Poort), an operating total of 21.07 km. At Ursel it eventually met a line from Brugge (Capital 113) and crossed Capital 98 from Aalter to Eeklo. Its depot was at Mariakerke in the Palinghuizen district of Gent, with subsheds at Zomergem and Ursel. The extension opened on 2 October 1898, by which time the concession had been transferred to the ETG (from 21 April 1898), which worked it as a single route. Its early history was uneventful, traffic more than covering expenses and being sufficient to ensure that it remained open throughout World

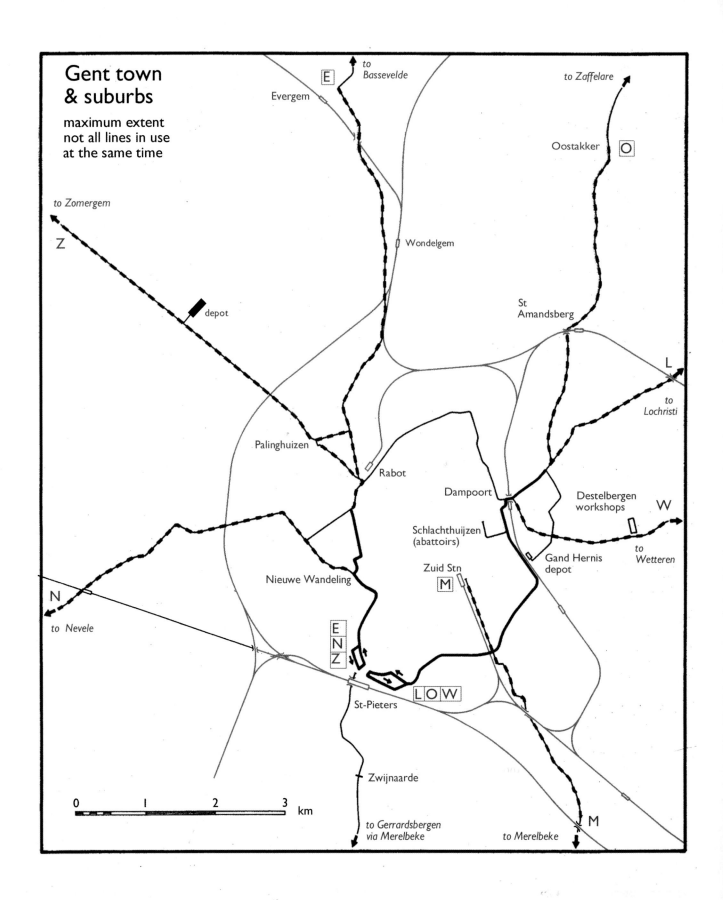

Gent town & suburbs

maximum extent
not all lines in use
at the same time

to Zomergem

Z

depot

E

Evergem

to Bassevelde

to Zaffelare

Oostakker

O

Wondelgem

St Amandsberg

L

to Lochristi

Palinghuizen

Rabot

Dampoort

Destelbergen workshops

W

Schlachthuijzen (abattoirs)

Gand Hernis depot

to Wetteren

Nieuwe Wandeling

Zuid Stn

M

N

to Nevele

E
N
Z

LOW

St-Pieters

Zwijnaarde

0   1   2   3   km

to Gerrardsbergen via Merelbeke

to Merelbeke

M

War I. It is a curiosity in that an industrial customer, the SA des Usines d'Evergem, proposed in 1911 that it should use transporter trucks. It is recorded that three were actually delivered but loading gauge problems prevented their use and they were transferred to Limburg in 1914; the idea was finally abandoned two years later.

Capital 79 (GENT - MERELBEKE) was a little more confusing. To start with, there were two SNCV routes to Merelbeke, this more easterly one and the inner end of Capital 128 (qv) which took a more circuitous route. Capital 79 was built in from its depot at Merelbeke, being authorised on 3 January 1897, opened with steam traction to Ledeberg on 16 January 1898 and on to Gent Zuid station on 1 July 1899. It was originally conceded to the LS but this terminated its claim on 1 February 1899 and the SNCV took over until it was completed when it was provisionally ceded to the *ETG*, which promptly introduced battery cars for the passenger traffic. They were not very successful, steam trams being reintroduced as a temporary measure on the outer sections from 2 November, and in 1901 the ETG, whose tenure officially dated from 19 August 1899, electrified it at 600 volts dc, using trolley poles for current collection and running it as such from 1 December 1901. Meanwhile, five battery cars had been provided by the SNCV in December 1899 (M 200-4) to replace ETG ones and they were converted for overhead supply and became 9200-4 in due course. The line had some goods traffic to begin with but, after Capital 128 opened, became simply a suburban passenger tramway. Like the Zomergem route, it paid its way and was useful enough not to be affected by World War I. Both lines remained under the control of the ETG during this period.

6.5.3 Gent eastern lines (Steenweg op Dendermonde/Chaussée de Termonde)

Capital	Name	Auth km
19	Gent - Zaffelare	16.50
38	Gent - Wetteren - Hamme	39.06
100	Overmere - Lokeren - Zaffelare	20.70
126	Gent - Lochristi	9.90
	plus (in the eastern part of the province	
110	Hamme - Zwijndrecht - Hamme - Moerzeke	36.31

The countryside to the east of Gent was the first area in Vlaanderen to have a connected series of lines, operating from a single depot at Heirnis, just to the east of Gent (Dampoort) mainline station. The first, **Capital 19 (GENT - ZAFFELARE)**, ran northeast through the suburb of St-Amandsberg to Oostakker and then swung northeast to the little town of Zaffelare, a total of 16.30km. It was authorised on 13 July 1887, opened throughout on 6 May 1888, and was initially conceded to a businessman named Octaaf Groverman, the concession being transferred to the *SA des Vicinaux en Flandres (VF)* in 1892. A typical rural feeder line, with just sufficient stock to cover its needs, it struggled along to the 15-year breakpoint in 1911, when operation was transferred to the big TUV. The line was closed and lifted by the Germans during 1917 and 1918, and its lease was surrendered late the following year. The SNCV did give its restoration some priority since Gent -Oostakker (Slotendries) was reopened on 27 April 1919, a short stretch in Oostakker being added on 16 May 1919, and the rest on 15 January 1920.

The next route was **Capital 38 (GENT - WETTEREN - HAMME)**. This long line was built to connect Gent with two major

market centres to its east. It started at Dampoort station, passing Heirnis depot before swinging southeast via Destelbergen (later a major SNCV works) and through the villages of Heusden and Laame to reach Wetteren town centre (20km). Thence it turned northeast to Overmere and Hamme (37.50km). It was authorised on 24 June 1889 and opened throughout on 17 April 1891, operation being ceded initially to *Ingenieur J Heintz (HJ)* of Termonde and then, from 1893, to the *VF.* After some debate, a short extension from Wetteren town (Kapellendries) south to the standard-gauge station was authorised on 28 December 1896 and opened on 1 May 1902, thus providing a reversing spur and linking the line to Capital 102 to Oordegem; Capital 110 then tended to be worked in two portions with a depot at Kalken for the eastern branch. As with Capital 19, operation was transferred to the TUV in 1911, and most of the line was closed and lifted during the 1914-18 war. Hamme - Kalken went during 1917, and most of Kalken - Dampoort in 1918, a total of some 34 km. The TUV gave up its concession in 1919, and the line was painfully rebuilt as shown below.

Section	km	Date
Gent (Dampoort) - Heusden	6.90	18 May 1919+
Heusden - Laarne	4.50	4 Jul 1919
Laarne - Wetteren	2.94	15 Aug 1919
Wetteren - Kalken	1.49	21 Sep 1919
Kalken - Overmere	3.50	22 Oct 1919
Overmere - Zele		*1 Dec 1919
Zele -Hamme		*1 Aug 1919

+ to Destelbergen two days earlier
* these dates are uncertain

Next line of the group was **Capital 100 (OVERMERE - LOKEREN - ZAFFELARE)**. Without being unkind to the SNCV, one wonders just why this line, or at least its final section, was ever built. It had a long inception, several communes being very reluctant to contribute, and was originally intended simply to go to Lokeren with a possible extension to the hamlet of Eksaarde. Authorised on 6 July 1899, the 4.10km to Lokeren were opened on 14 November 1901, with operation ceded to the VF, and the line was in deficit from the start. It was treated as a branch of the Wetteren - Hamme line, trains apparently working through to Wetteren. Almost incredibly, although the Eksaarde branch did not materialise, on 29 May 1905 a further extension was authorised to connect with Capital 19 at Zaffelare, another 11.08km. This was opened on 29 April 1911, and at the same time operation was transferred to the *TUV.* With an empire like this, it was little wonder that the *Vicinaux en Flandres* went bankrupt, and even the SNCV was moved to comment that "it is hoped the new concessionaire will be able to improve matters". If so, it did not have much time, since war came, the line being closed and lifted between June 1917 and April 1918. Re-acquiring the lease in 1919, the SNCV showed some reluctance to relay but eventually did so, reopening Zaffelare to Doorselar on 1 July 1920; Doorselar -Lokeren on 7 August 1921, and Lokeren -Overmere on 13 January 1922.

Capital 126 (GENT - LOCHRISTI) was actually the next line in chronological order. A short suburban route, the 9.90km line was authorised on 22 May 1903 and opened on 20 August 1903, running northeast from Heirnis through St-Amandsberg to Lochristi village. Operation was initially by the VF, replaced by the TUV from 22 November 1904. The route from St-Amandsberg was closed and lifted in 1917, a total of 9.31km, but was reopened on 23 March 1919.

The odd man out was **Capital 110 (HAMME - ZWIJNDRECHT - HAMME - MOERZEKE -**

BAASRODE VEER). This system was always classed by the SNCV as an extension of the Gent lines since it was controlled from Chaussée de Termonde. It was in practice an Antwerpen suburban line on its inner part, but one which had somehow got separated from its associated lines by the River Schelde; its traffic patterns were biased accordingly. It was first mooted in 1897 but not authorised until 13 May 1901. It was started from the Hamme end in 1904, and even then took a long time to complete. The first section, from Hamme to Temse was opened on 17 November 1904, followed by Temse - Bazel on 1 March 1906 and Bazel - Zwijndrecht - Antwerpen on 15 May 1908, a total of 29.27km. Zwijndrecht is the first station out of Antwerpen on the railway to Gent. The Hamme - Moerzeke spur, with its extension to Baasrode Veer was authorised on 4 May 1908 but was not opened until 1 February 1910, and was never very successful. The main depot was at Hamme and operation was entrusted to the ill-fated VF until 1911 when the TUV took over. Oddly enough only a short part was actually lifted in World War I, the Hamme - Tielrode section being removed between May and October 1917. This was reopened in two stages, from Elversele to Tielrode on 1 September 1920, and Elversele - Hamme on 1 October. By that time the SNCV was in control of the whole group, having taken over the TUV's concessions the previous year. Hamme - Moerzeke which had apparently been closed but not lifted, followed on 1 March 1922. The actual years of take-over varied because, although a concessionaire might formally surrender a concession on a given date, there was always some form of take-over period to allow for staff adjustments, etc.

6.5.4   Gent western lines (Rabot)

Capital	Name	Auth km
36	Gent - Bassevelde	25.84
158	Gent - Drongen - Ruiselede	26.60

NOTE: Capital 128 which eventually nearly connected to these lines came into Gent from the south and was considered part of the Groupe d'Oordegem.

These two lines were built for different reasons but both started at Rabot. **Capital 136 (GENT - BASSEVELDE)** was a straightforward rural feeder reaching out northward via Evergem into the polder country near the Dutch border - or, rather, reaching in, since, although authorised as a whole on 5 May 1904, it was constructed from the Bassevelde end in stages. The 15km or so from Bassevelde village to Evergem was opened on 6 July 1910, followed on 1 October 1910 by the 10km from Evergem via Wondelgem suburb into the industrial area of Gent

Gent St Pieters (terminus for lines toward Rabot) in 1956. Wood bodied standard car 10030 on a Nevele train; N-type 41000 bound for Evergem; S-type & trailers. In the background is an ETG car.   (Paul de Backer).

(Industrie) just north of Rabot. The final short spur to Rabot (Begijnhofbrug) was opened on 8 December 1910, giving a total length of 25.6km in use. Operation was initially entrusted to a local company, the *SA Intercommunale du Vicinal Gent - Bassevelde (GB)* but it either defaulted or withdrew since the concession was almost immediately transferred to our old friend the TUV. As with most Gent lines, this one suffered during the 1914-18 war. Even though it was apparently not lifted, the installations were badly damaged during the German invasion, and the line remained out of use until taken over by the SNCV. It was restored in three stages: Gent to Evergem on 1 April 1920; Evergem - Oosteeklo on 17 June 1920, and on to Bassevelde on 18 July 1920.

Capital 158 (GENT - DRONGEN - RUISELEDE), on the other hand, was intended as a link to the Aalter group of lines, though it was three years in building and opened in numerous stages as shown below. It was always a difficult line to work, there being a good commuter traffic into Gent but very little beyond Nevele, which contained the depot and became, in effect, an intermediate terminus. The line was authorised on 16 January 1907, was ceded to the TUV from its opening and, as shown below, suffered the same fate as its neighbours in the 1914-18 war.

Note: all lines listed were closed during 1917-18

Section	Opened	Reopened
Gent (Rabot) - Drongen	6 Jun 1909	1 Apr 1920
Drongen - Drongen (Baarle)	15 Oct 1910	18 Jul 1920
Baarle - St-Martens-Leerne	20 Nov 1910	6 Aug 1920
St-Martens-Leerne - Vosselare	26 Dec 1910	21 Aug 1920
Vosselare - Nevele (Kanaal	28 Jan 1911	21 Aug 1920
Nevele (Kanaal-Stelplaats)	28 Jan 1911	during 1927
Nevele (Stp) - Ruiselede	29 Feb 1912	10 Oct 1921

6.5.5   lines in the Gent hinterland: Groupe d'Oordegem, 1903-1920

Capital	Name	Auth km
102	Wetteren - Zottegem	20.50
120	Assche - Aalst - Oordegem	25.70
128	(Gent) -Merelbeke -Herzele - Geraardsbergen	36.80

In the southeast corner of Oostvlaanderen was a cluster of three lines, all run for most of their independent careers by the *SA des CF Provinciaux (CFP)*, a Bruxelles firm formed for this particular purpose in 1900. First was **Capital 102 (WETTEREN - ZOTTEGEM)** which ran south from Wetteren on the Gent - Hamme line (Capital 38). Starting from a connection with the latter at Wetteren Etat station, it went first southeast to neighbouring Oordegem and then swung south across country by way of St-Lievens-Houtem to end at the town centre of Zottegem, a complex standard-gauge junction whose station the SNCV did not quite reach. It was authorised on 23 September 1899, opened throughout on 1 April 1903, and worked from the start by the *CF Provinciaux*. Otherwise there was little memorable about it. It was just a small, sleepy rural line with minimum stock: 3 locomotives, 7 coaches and 19 wagons. It made a steady annual loss but kept its villages in touch with the outside world. Inevitably it was closed and lifted during the war, in 1917, and its trackbed duly came back into SNCV possession in 1920 when the CFP gave up. The SNCV not only faithfully restored it to life, on 15 April 1922, but added a small stretch from Zottegem centre to the standard-gauge station on 18 May 1924 in the hope, alas unfulfilled, that it might generate traffic. The main depot was at Oordegem with a sub-shed at Zottegem.

Capital 120 (ASSCHE - AALST - OORDEGEM) was something rather different, an inter-provincial line which ended up as part of a through route from Bruxelles to the coast, but it started out modestly enough. The first section, from a junction at Oordegem southeast to Aalst/Alost on the provincial boundary, was authorised on 27 May 1902, and opened on 1 May 1904. It was soon extended across the border to Asse/Assche in Brabant on 1 February 1905, a total of 25.5km. (SNCV gives an additional opening date as 01 March 1910 but it is not clear to what this refers). It was run from the start by the *CF Provinciaux* and was planned to extend further. Unfortunately war intervened, the whole line being closed and lifted during 1916-17. Its restoration clearly had low priority, the Asse/Assche -Aalst section not being reopened until 30 December 1921, while the line on to Oordegem stayed closed until 15 April 1922. Its future history belongs mainly to Brabant, but it should be noted that both this and Capital 102 came into SNCV hands in 1918 when their concessions were terminated at the 15-year breakpoint.

Last in the group was **Capital 128 (GENT - MERELBEKE - GERAARDSBERGEN)**, as it eventually became. This long route south from Gent was very much a strategic link in its later years but had a curious and confusing early history. It started life as a detached line from Merelbeke through St-Lievens-Houtem, where it met Capital 102, and on southeast to Herzele, a total of 18.8km. In that form it was authorised on 22 October 1903, and opened throughout on 23 June 1907, being ceded to the *CF Provinciaux*. This was rather a second-best arrangement, original proposals to go through to Ninove on the outskirts of Bruxelles having been turned down on the ground that it would compete with the mainline railway. Instead, after a decent interval, a 14km extension was built south to Geraardsbergen where it simultaneously provided a potential link into Hainault over Capital 183 and brought the Deinze group of lines into contact. Authorised on 19 January 1909, it opened on 1 May 1912. Presumably the SNCV was hoping to reach Gent via its existing line from Merelbeke. Equally the ETG was presumably unhappy about all those messy steam trains on "its" line, for a further 8.10km link was built into Gent to the west of it, terminating at the Sterre district just

south of the main railway line. Authorised on 15 May 1912, it opened on 11 October 1913 and, surprisingly, escaped almost immediate closure in the war. The remainder was not so lucky, closing in 1917 and only reopening from Merelbeke to Herzele on 9 April 1921 and onto Geraardsbergen on 1 October 1921. By that time it was in SNCV hands.

6.6 Detached lines in the north of Vlaanderen

Capital	Name	Auth km
59	*St-Niklaas - Kieldrecht - Doel*	23.18
185	*Moerbeke - Grens*	5.70

In the north of Vlaanderen there were two detached lines which do not fit neatly into any group. **Capital 59 (ST NIKLAAS - KIELDRECHT - DOEL)** was a simple, if long, dead-end branch, starting from the standard-gauge station at Sint-Niklaas, northeast of Gent, and running northward into the polder area around the Schelde estuary. The first portion, 15.69km to the small market town of Kieldrecht, was authorised on 26 September 1892 and opened on 1 October 1893 (SNCV records cannot decide between that date and 24 September 1893 but the latter was probably simply an "official" opening). As with other Vlaanderen lines, the concession was not very attractive, and the SNCV even had fruitless discussions with the standard-gauge *Compagnie du Chemin de Fer de Malines à Terneuzen* (Malines - Terneuzen railway company) before grudgingly conceding operation "on revised terms" to a M *Lamquet* on 9 August 1893. Reading between the lines, they were hoping for the concession going to the Terneuzen line so that that company could lay it to standard gauge and use its own stock, since the "revised agreement" made great play of the fact that the SNCV must now supply the material. Even so, M Lamquet evidently quickly thought better of being a one-man band since a local company was formed, variously termed *SA du Tramway Vicinal de St-Nicolas - Kieldrecht et Extension* or *SA pour l'Exploitation du CFV de St-Nicolas - Kieldrecht et Extensions (SNKD)*. The "extensions", in the form of a further 7.44km to Doel on the banks of the river Schelde, were authorised on 22 February 1903 and opened on 15 February 1905, giving a working total of 23.15km. The company gave up at the 15-year breakpoint in its lease, the big *TUV* taking over on 29 November 1908 with a guarantee of the total receipts up to Fr 1700/km/year. The line was obviously proving better than expected since it proved "very useful for local traffic" in World War 1 and thereby escaped closure. The TUV surrendered its lease at the end of 1919 along with its other lines, and the SNCV took control. As a detached line, its later history can be quickly summarised here. It was converted to autorail operation early, receiving most of the batch of De Dion railbuses in the AR 5-10 series and retaining them to the end. That came on 13 July 1944 when the line was the only one of a second batch requisitioned by the Germans actually to be closed and lifted. The material was left on site but the line was never reopened, buses being substituted after the war. The main depot was at St-Niklaas with a sub-shed at Doel.

Capital 185 (MOERBEKE -GRENS) was an oddity, being really the Belgian end of a Dutch tramway. In 1915, the *Zeeuwsch Vlaamsche Tramweg Mij (ZVTM)* opened its branch south from Drieschouwen to the Belgian frontier at Roodesluis. Roodesluis was nowhere in particular, and the ZVTM had previously negotiated with the SNCV for an extension south to the Etat Belge junction of Moerbeke, a total of 10.30km from Drieschouwen. The SNCV obtained

75

authorisation for this on 4 January 1912, but war delayed construction and it was not opened until 9 November 1915, and then only for goods. It was worked as a ZVTM branch, the only SNCV presence until 1926 being 15 wagons for local goods traffic. Passenger service started on 18 January 1926 and continued until July 1940 when it was withdrawn; one of its last functions was to carry 20,000 Belgian prisoners-of-war on the first stage of their journey to captivity in Germany. The remainder of its history is rather vague, but it had a resurgence of beet traffic during the war and remained open for freight traffic until 1949 when the ZVTM finally closed. Like other cross border connections in Vlaanderen, it was always metre gauge. Unlike most of them, the concessionaire appears to have operated it until the end which came on 30 December 1949, final day of the sugar beet season.

6.7 Vlaanderen between the wars

6.7.1 General situation away from the coast

After the 1914-18 war, when it assumed control of most of its system, the SNCV in Vlaanderen was in a very messy position. Over half the lines had been put out of use, either through war damage or because they had been closed and lifted by the Germans. The rolling stock had suffered much more than in other provinces and three large concessionaires, the ETG, OB and IC, had every intention of retaining "their" lines - which were the profitable ones - and of getting them modernised. Moreover Vlaanderen, both Oost and West, had been fought over twice from end to end, so the task of civil reconstruction was likely to absorb all available money without even considering the trams. In the circumstances, both the SNCV and its concessionaires did a very praiseworthy job in getting the tramways substantially restored by the end of 1922. Although most of the outstanding pre-war projects such as Langemark - Bikschoote and Deinze - Aalter were never completed, the remaining system was conscientiously brought back to life. The main problem was administrative; the coastal system was such a large proportion of the whole in terms of traffic and revenue that, without it, the SNCV could not form a viable group of its own for Westvlaanderen alone. It therefore left the coast to its concessionaires and organised the rest into a single *SNCV: Groep de Beide Vlaanderen/Groupe des Deux Flandres*, with headquarters at Gent and main workshops at Gent (Destelbergen) and later at Kortrijk. The coastal lines continued in private hands throughout this period as already recorded.

6.7.2 SNCV Groupe des Deux Flandres/Groep der Beide Vlaanderen (Groupe 20)

Unfortunately, Vlaanderen without the lucrative coastal lines was a very poor region indeed for the SNCV, and very little improvement or extension was undertaken outside the big towns. What development there was came in two areas - urban and suburban electrifications and the "motorisation" of rural routes. Because of its poverty, Vlaanderen was similar to the Limburg group in its ingenuity. It was early in the field with autorail development. As a result of the De Dions' success at St-Niklaas and the promising results being achieved elsewhere with the "rebuilds" of the AR 13-35 series, standard four-wheel autorails were introduced quickly throughout the province.

The Group's major workshops at Destelbergen became a major producer of the wooden-bodied version, and even the prototype bogie car AR 115 worked out of Hamme for a time. As regards electrification, this was much less intense than in other Groupes. It was confined to Gent and Kortrijk, apart from two lines where there was sufficient traffic to justify it, and both were atypical.

Capital 120 (ASSE - AALST - OORDEGEM) was during this period linked to Bruxelles by new work, and electrified out from that end as far as Aalst; operation of the electrified section was transferred to Brabant (qv). **Capital 110 (HAMME - ZWIJNDRECHT)** was really an Antwerpen suburban line which just happened to be cut off by the River Schelde. It had a heavy commuter traffic into Antwerpen and it is not really surprising that the line was electrified in stages from the Antwerpen end. Zwijndrecht - Temse was electrically worked from 1 September 1931, and in 1935 a short extension from Zwijndrecht took the inner end to Antwerpen (Linkeroever); total length is then quoted as 37.80km. Finally, on 15 October 1937 electrification was extended to Hamme. Traffic justified the expense, especially at peak hours when standard bogie cars hauled three or four trailers to carry the load. The same, alas, cannot be said of the Moerzeke branch which was closed in 1936.

6.7.3 Gent SNCV urban and suburban network gevelopments

Meanwhile, probably the most important extension and electrification had slowly been taking place in Gent (Page XX). The SNCV was not satisfied with its outer suburban termini and, soon after the war, started building inwards. The northeastern lines were given a new link from St-Amandsberg across a new bridge to the west side of Dampoort station in 1921, replacing the St-Amandsberg -Heirnis stretch; this was initially left in for depot access but dismantled about 1937. Equally, the Geraardsbergen route (Capital 128) was extended from Sterre under the railway to terminate beside St-Pieters station from 1 April 1925. The major modernisations, however, were in the early 1930s, involving construction of a network of new routes round the old town to link everything to St-Pieters, and to provide a crosstown link for freight along the canalside from Rabot to Dampoort. The main works are shown below.

Capital	Section	Electrified
8	New link: St-Pieters - Palinghuysen	3 May 1931
	Rabot - Palinghuysen	3 May 1931
	Palinghuysen - Lovendegem	1 Nov 1930
	Lovendegem - Zomergem (Canal - Dorp)	29 Mar 1931
19	Dampoort - Oostakker as route O	16 Dec 1930
38	Dampoort - Heusden	16 Jan 1931
	Heusden - Laarne	10 Jan 1932
	Laarne - Wetteren (Etat) as route H	*13 Feb 1932
126	Dampoort - Lochristi as route L	*7 Dec 1930
	Gent (Begijnhofbrug) -Evergem as route E	10 May 1931
158	New link: St-Pieters - Nieuw Wandeling (part in common with Capital 8)	(5?) 3 Apr 1931
	Rabot - Drongen	5 Apr 1931
	Drongen - Drongen Baarle	6 Dec 1931
	Baarle - St-Martens-Leerne	14 Feb 1932
	St-Martens-Leerne - Nevele	20 Mar 1932
* some sources say 31 January 1932 and 1 November 1930 respectively		

Note that Nevele -Ruiselede was never electrified and was but poorly served by autorails. On the other hand, in Gent, new sections of track were laid and completed as below:

St Amandsberg - Gent (Dampoort)	16 May 1931
Gent (Dampoort - Rabot)	21 May 1931
Gent (Dampoort - Slachthuizen)	6 Oct 1933
Gent (Dampoort - St Pieter)	24 Nov 1933
Gent (St Pieter - Nieuwe Wandeling)	29 May 1929

Zomergem -Ursel was not electrified and was surrendered to SNCV control in 1931. The stock on Gent - Zomergem was ex-ETG cars modified by the SNCV plus two three-axle passenger/luggage cars (10055-6). It became Gent route S (for Somergem). The eastern routes shared track from Dampoort to St-Amandsberg; the northern and western ones had a common final section into St-Pieters. The various routes did not physically connect at St-Pieters, except via the town tram tracks, each having its own terminus in the station square. The depot was at Destelbergen, routes being worked mainly by cars of the 9880-9 series with some Standard cars to Wetteren. There is some confusion over the Evergem route, the concession to ETG not being accorded until 29 October 1936, while SNCV steam trains from Bassevelde ran over it right into town. Those Gent area lines not electrified were slowly converted to autorail operation for passengers; in most cases interchange was made at the outer end of the electrified portion.

6.7.4 Expansion in the Kortrijk area: Kortrijk urban services

The other major area of post-war expansion in inland Vlaanderen was the development of a suburban network around the town of Kortrijk. The local politicians were very keen on developing communications, and in 1923 they suggested electrifying from Kortrijk station to Wevelgem (7.20km); to Moorsele via Gullegem and new track (9.20km); to Kuurne (4.3km) and to Deerlijk (9.00km). The SNCV investigated and came up with slightly different proposals which were eventually accepted and are described below. First, within Kortrijk itself, a section was added in 1926 from Kortrijk station to Veemarkt and another to Montaleux; later, a new electrified line was built from the station through the town centre via Kornmarkt and Grote Markt to St-Janspark on the west side; here it connected with the line from Aarsele. Authorised in 1932, it provided an urban service for the town and was opened on 16 April 1933 as part of a new direct electric route to Menen. This, authorised on 6 July 1933, followed the new line to St-Janspark, thence swinging south over the Aarsele line as far as Menenpoort, whence it carried on for a short distance over Capital 41. At Bissegem, however, it struck off on its own, a new 7.6km. stretch heading directly south through Wevelgem to a connection with the Moeskroen - Menen branch at Menen (Grote Markt). It was not the first electrification to be completed, the Berchem line (Capital 166) being electrified on 27 March 1932 as far as Deerlijk (Kerk) over the original route, and extended to Deerlijk (SNCV) 0n 19 August 1933. Kortrijk, while not having a proper urban network, did then at least have a cross of lines with a good service; this was supplemented on 25 May 1939 by the provision of electric trams over Capital 85 to Moeskroen, a connection apparently being put in across the SNCB at Kortrijk to the other lines.

This, in effect, completed an electrified circle since, back in 1932, isolated development had taken place between Moeskroen, Menen and Geluwe. It involved a short link at

Moeskroen to give a big triangular junction between the MontaLeux branch and the Menen route, together with a minute dead-end spur of the MontaLeux line to a locality called La Planche rather than De Plank. (Names get very mixed up in this area.) All new parts and the relevant old lines were electrified as shown below:

Section	Date
Moeskroen (Risquons Tout) - Menen (Barakken)	19 Jun 1932
Moeskroen (Risquons Tout - Station)	3 Jul 1932
Moeskroen - Mont-a-Leux	3 Jul 1932
Menen (Barakken - Grote Markt)	10 Jul 1932
Menen (Grote Markt) - Geluwe (via SG station)	2 Oct 1932
Moeskroen (La Marliere - La Planche)	24 Dec 1932

The apparently isolated development was actually part of the scheme for a direct route to Menen, coming into service early only because that route took longer than expected to build. Kortrijk routes were then:

letter	colours	Section
KM	Br/Br	Kortrijk - Menen
KMx	Red/red	Kortrijk - Moeskroen - Mont-a-Leux
D	Gr/gr	Kortrijk - Deerlijk
D barré	Gr/red	Kortrijk - Harelbeke
MM	Blu/Blu	Moeskroen - Menen - Geluwe
MP	?	Moeskroen - La Planche
MMx	Pk/pk	Mosekroen - Mont-a-Leux
MB	?	Menen (station) - Menen (Barakken)

Apart from the two short extensions at Brugge, mentioned above, Kortrijk was the last real expansion within the Vlaanderen Group. Even there, a foretaste of what was to come occurred on 9 November 1937 when the short branch from Gullegem to Wevelgem was closed and abandoned. Services to Ardooie, extended via Izegem since 1930 by a 1.20km spur across the canal and village, were based firmly on Kortrijk. Elsewhere in the region, the rot set in even earlier. On Capital 75 the French connection from Steenwerck to Seule/Le Seau was abandoned from 20 May 1932, the Waasten branch following six years later on 5 December 1938 (passenger service may have ended rather sooner, on 18 May 1936 if SNCV records are correct). Hooglede - Roseelare closed to passengers from 12 April 1936 and to goods on 27 November 1936, not entirely surprisingly since it closely paralleled the Woumen line. In 1936, too, the Moerzeke branch from Hamme closed.

A standard railcar running Kortrijk country services; note the pantograph needed for working points and signals on the electric town lines.
(P. v Campenhoudt.)

77

6.8 Vlaanderen: later history

6.8.1 The 1939-45 war and its effects

The 1939-45 war simply hastened the process of closures. On 30 August 1939, with threats of war looming, the international link from Oosthoek to Retranchement on the coast closed early that season and - as it proved - for good. All services into the Netherlands were suspended from 10 May 1940 and traffic on other lines was suspended for several days but actual war damage does not appear to have affected the Vlaanderen lines much except for the inevitable blown bridges and for a section of the coast line near Middelkerke where the Germans forced dismantling of the overhead in 1942-43 to give coastal guns a clear field of fire. At first steam trams replaced electric services but these were soon discontinued and all trams had to go via the inland route, being hauled by steam between Oostende and Lombardsijde. The electric services were restored only in mid-December 1944 after liberation.

On the other hand there were various minor adjustments. The Westkapelle - Sluis service was reduced to two trips, weekdays only, from 1 October 1939 and was not fully restored until 26 June 1940 while, following closure during the invasion, the Aardenburg line did not reopen until 25 August 1941. From 25 July 1940, however, a direct autorail service was started between Brugge and Kortrijk, presumably to take strain off the main line railways, and at Brugge the eastern rung line was electrified in two stages: Gentpoort - Dampoort in 1943 and Gentpoort - Kruispoort in 1944, although used only for goods traffic. Otherwise the more hopeless inland lines were obvious candidates when the Germans demanded a supply of rails and many were abruptly closed as shown (in table below)

6.8.2 1945 to the end of SELVOP

The war's end in Vlaanderen saw none of the optimism current in other SNCV groups. This time the lines that had been closed and lifted were not relaid. A few, the Oudenaarde group, St-Niklaas - Doel, Deerlijk - Berchem and Overmere - Zaffelare (- Lochristi) were replaced by SNCV buses, while concessionary bus networks sprang up round Diksmuide -

Ieper and from Brugge towards the coast. Even the "1946 Plan" left Vlaanderen virtually untouched. Only four new electrifications were proposed: a partly new line using the Aarsele route as far as Dentegem with new track on to Tielt. : Kortrijk - Pecq - Doornik; Wetteren - Hamme; Gent - Zwijnaarde - Merelbeke; Kortrijk - Dentergem with a new line on to Tielt replacing Dentergem - Aarsele; and the last two of these were little more than ideas.

None came to fruition. Instead the more rural lines in the Vlaanderen group were steadily closed, at least for passenger traffic. As early as 1949, Ieper lost all but its route north to Veurne; the Veurne - Poperinge line was cut back to Roesbrugge, and the long route from Tielt to the Dutch border was broken between Aalter and Eeklo. The next four years saw disappearance of virtually all the hinterland lines, leaving only the big towns with their interconnecting links, and even one of these, Brugge, had closed all but one route by 1953. It is true that Brugge was something of a special case. The cars were old, the routes were inconvenient to operate in the narrow streets, and the system had been in deficit for years. In 1950, therefore, the SNCV started experiments with one-man buses (replacing two-man trams) and these were so successful that closure came quickly. The final route allocations with their closure dates are given below:

No	Route	Closed
0	SNCB station - Grote Markt	14 Jul 1951
1	Grote Markt - Assebroek	
	(depot retained)	23 May 1950
2	Assebroek (Steenbrugge) - Oostkamp	14 Mar 1950*
2 barré	't Zand - Assebroek (Steenbrugge)	15 Apr 1950
3	Eiermarkt - St-Pieters	14 Jul 1950
4	SNCB station - Gistatabriek	31 Jul 1950**
5	't Zand - St-Andries	5 Apr 1950
6	Grote Markt - St-Kruis	23 May 1950

Most common sight in the 1960s and 70s were the handsome SO series cars with their matching trailers (often converted from demotorised N-series cars). (WJKD)

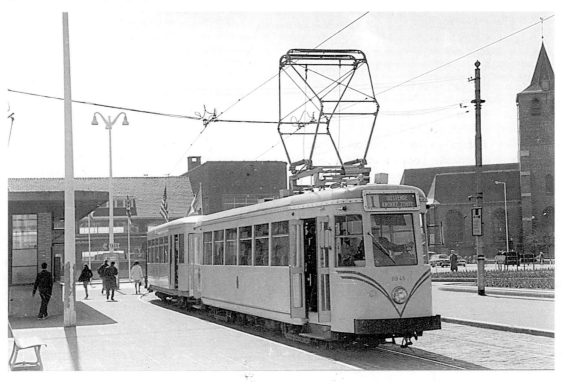

* another source says 6 April 1950 with some trams retained to connect with Oostcamp - Zwevezele autorails until 24 May.
** Gistafabriek - Dampoort from 8 April 1951

On the other hand the circular town service at Kortrijk, discontinued since May 1940, reopened on 1 February 1951 and from 26 October 1954 Capitaux 41, 85, 151 and 166 were merged under the new title "Lijnien van het Kortrijkse". Of the associated steam-worked lines, those to Diksmuide and to Kortrijk via Hille closed down almost simultaneously; elsewhere, the Ursel link had to operate from Gentpoort from 1951 but lasted another two years. The total Vlaanderen closures up to the end of 1955 when the provinces were reorganised were as shown in the table below:

Westvlaanderen		km	date
6	Ruiselede -Aalter	9.00	5 Jan 1943
41	Geluwe -Wervik	4.00	16Dec 1942
75	Kemmel -Waasten lifted**	12.00	9 Nov 1942
107	Merkem -Elverdinge***		20 Jan 1941
119	St-Kruis -Aardenburg (lifted)	15.00	18Mar 1943
150	Roeselare -Langemark	15.00	22Feb 1943
151	Pecq (Village - Gare)	abandoned & lifted 1944	
166	Deerlijk -Berchem	16.00	3 Dec 1942
Oostvlaanderen			
28	Deinze -Oudenaarde	19.90	1 Mar 1943
59	St-Niklaas -Doel	24.20	13 Jul 1944
100	Overmere -Zaffelare	15.80	30Nov 1942
102	St-Lievens-Houtem -Zottegem	?	22Feb 1943
103	Geraardsbergen -Oudenaard	25.52	15Apr 1943
110	Moerzeke branch lifted**		1942?

NOTES:
+ lifted 1944;
++ one track lifted;
* overhead remained in situ to 1951
** closed, but still in place at the time
*** lifted May 1944

6.8.3 The end of (most) trams in Vlaanderen

Meanwhile, the few remaining lines in the Vlaanderen group proper were slowly but surely closed. On 1 July 1954, the ETG concession came to its end, and the lines were repossessed by the SNCV; Route S became route Z though the ETG continued to operate route M, to Merelbeke, (Capital 79) until the end of April 1955 when it was replaced by SNCV buses. There was an interesting sequel to this, the SNCV using the latter route for trials of the "Gyrobus", an electrically-powered vehicle deriving its power from energy storage in a massive internal gyroscopic flywheel which was periodically boosted to full speed at charging stations en route; the experiment lasted from 10 September 1956 to 23 November 1959, after which conventional buses took over. By 1956 the SNCV system at Gent thus consisted of seven routes, all except that to Bassevelde being electrified and even partly equipped with type "N" and "S" cars, but over the next three years they all went, leaving the ETG and its successor the *Mij voor Intercommunaal Vervoer te Gent (MIVG)* in full possession. Passenger closures were as in the following table (all from St-Pieters).

Cap/Route		Section	closed
136		Evergem - Bassevelde (autorails)	2 Jun 1956
126	L	Gent - Lochristi **	29 Nov 1957
19	O	Gent - Oostakker	** 29 Nov 1957
38	W	Gent - Wetteren station	** 28 Sep 1958
8	Z	Gent - Zomergem	1 Jun 1959
158	N	Gent - Nevele*	1 Jun 1959
136	E	Gent - Evergem	1 Jun 1959

NOTE:
* cut back to Nevele Brug from 3 October 1954.
** another source says 29 Sept for all

All the surviving Gent area lines with goods traffic also closed down during this period, between October and December 1958. Apart from those above, they included the goods lines around Rabot and across the city to Dampoort, which closed on 29 December 1958. They had already been preceded by two lines in the Kortrijk area: to Deerlijk (to passengers 10 September 1957 and to goods on 14 March 1958), and the direct line to Menen on 14 October or 15 November 1957. Local Moeskroen - Mont-a-Leux services had ceased from 1 October 1954, through workings from Kortrijk continuing until 29 May 1960.

Meanwhile on 19 September 1959 the electrified line between Hamme and Antwerpen (Linkeroever) (Capital 110) was replaced by a bus which reached central Antwerpen via a road tunnel under the Schelde. The last line to go was the final vestige of Capital 85, from Kortrijk to Moeskroen station on 25 March 1963 which had been kept on because the roads were unsuitable for buses. (Goods had gone already, on 17 March 1958, while Moeskroen to Mont-a-Leux had closed even for through passenger traffic on 29 May 1961).

Apart from the Littoral, Vlaanderen was then entirely without trams. On the coast, the northern end was cut back to Knokke station in the 1960s; It appears that Knokke council wanted to reduce tram traffic during the summer season and in 1962 restricted it to single cars between Station and Het Zoute. In 1963-65 the service finished from 1 July and was only resumed from 1 September each year. Alas, in 1966 this was not allowed to happen, local services effectively finishing for good from 30 June. Indeed for some years the whole system was under threat. Then in 1977 the SNCV decided to upgrade it and started a policy of systematic improvement. Extensive modifications to the permanent way and power supply were carried out; all track between Knokke and De Panne was relaid with heavy rail, the yard at Oostende Kaai was entirely refurbished to act as a running depot and Zeebrugge got a direct link across the canal with a double track round the basin to act as a diversionary route when required. Six new substations were installed, existing ones upgraded, and heavy duty catenary and associated equipment provided. New two-section articulated trams were ordered from BN and these have recently been mainly upgraded and converted to three-section vehicles. By 1991, when the SNCV finally ceased to exist, this ensured that the future of the coast line was safe and so it has proved. It is still one of the more spectacular inter-urban services in Europe and well worth a visit; the closed Adindkerke - De Panne line has even been relaid and reopened.

Table 6C

Capital	Section	passenger	goods
		1949	
115	Roesbrugge - Poperinge	10 Apr	12 Jul 1954
	Poperinghe - Watou	8 Sep	12 Jul 1954
75	Ieper - Kemmel - Seule	25 Apr	29 Dec 1951
121	Ieper - Geluwe	7 Sep	x
107	Poperinge - Oostvleteren	7 Sep	17 Jul 1953
41	Geluwe - Moorsele	16 Sep	x
98	Aalter - Eeklo	2 Oct	x
		1950	
39	Eeklo - Watervliet	Oct	x
185	Moerbeke - Grens (goods only)		1 Jan 1950
		1951	
132	Oostende (Stene) - Diksmuide	18 Mar	29 Dec 1951
137	Brugge - Leke	18 Mar	29 Dec 1951
33	Roeselare - Ardooie	15 Jul+	x
150	Roeselare - Diksmuide	15 Jul	29 Dec 1951
		1952	
65	Brugge - Zwevezele (Hille)*	6 Apr	x
33	Tielt - Roeselare	6 Apr	x
33	Tielte - Zwevezele - Ardooie*	6 Apr	x
152	Ardooie - Izegem*	6 Apr	x
153	Izegem - Gullegem*	6 Apr	x
115	Veurne - Roesbrugge	10 Aug	15 Oct 1953
29	Veurne -Ieper	4 Oct	30 Jan 1953
		1953	
38	Wetteren - Overmere - Zele - Hamme	18 Apr	4 May 1955
151	Bellegem - Pecq**	16 May	29 Sep 1955
113	Brugge (Gentpoort) - Ursel - Zomergem	16 May	x
	Brugge - Oedelgem		17 Jul 1957
	Oedelgem - Ursel - Zomergem		28 Feb 1956
107	Diksmuide - Oostvleteren	27 Jun	20 Jul 1953
119	Moerkerke - Middelburg	6 Jul	
	Brugge ring (Gentpoort - Dampoort)	17 Jul	
6	Ruiselede - Tielt	8 Aug	28 Dec 1953
158	Nevele - Ruiselede	8 Aug	28 Dec 1953
19	Zaffelare - Oostakker	4 Oct	30 Aug 1954
		1954	
128	Gent - Merelbeke	6 May	4 Feb 1955
41	Geluwe - Menen	22 May	
85	Moeskroen - la Planche	30 Sep	17 Mar 1958
128	Merelbeke - St-Lievens - Houtem	2 Oct	14 Feb 1955
85	Moeskroen - Menen	26 Oct	22 Nov 1954
		1955	
85	Kortrijk - Aarsele&	31 Jan	21 Oct 1954
79	Gent - Merelbeke	30 Apr	X
41	Kortrijk -Moorsele	21 May	29 Aug 1955
102	Wetteren - St-Lievens - Houtem - Zottegem	1 Oct	18 Dec 1954
128	St-Lievens-Houtem -Geraardsbergen	15 Oct	14 Feb 1955

(local sources give 15 Dec 1955 and 13 Jan as the "real" dates for this last line)

NOTES:
*   as part of Brugge - Kortrijk link;
+   as part of Gent -Tielt link;
** track retained for inter-provincial transfers until late 1955;
x   as for passengers

Improvisation. A special working in the wake (literally!) of the disastrous 1953 floods with a power car at each end.
(the late G Desbarax)

BN articulated car 6102 was specially modified with a centre portion to test out the feasibility of increasing capacity. *(M R Taplin)*

Chapter 7: The SNCV in Province Antwerpen

7.1 Antwerpen: Introduction

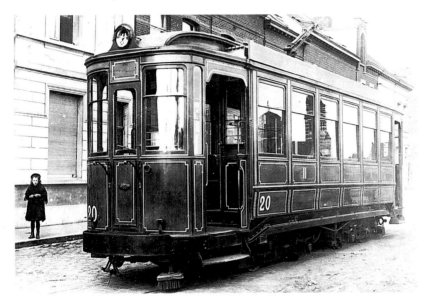

LVA20, one of the famous "red cars" which were used by both the Vicinaux Anversois and then the SNCV. (SNCV)

ANTWERPEN is a lopsided province with its two major population centres on the west side and its major industries between them. From this area, a plain spreads eastward from the River Schelde along the top of Brabant and across the Dutch frontier which forms the province's northern and eastern borders. There is some industry, massive international docks on the river at Antwerpen itself and a few sizable towns, but the ruling occupation in the late 19th century was agriculture; that meant a widely spread population, for the soil is often poor . Hence the SNCV network developed in long straggling lines which crossed each other frequently and tended to link at focal points. The two major towns were Antwerpen/Anvers itself and Mechelen/Malines, both on the western side, but Turnhout in the east, and Westerlo and Oostmalle to south and north of the province centreline, all developed to have five or six lines meeting, but without ever having sufficient traffic to justify much electrification.

Antwerpen province has always been a Flemish-speaking region and tended to look towards the Netherlands; hence its unique feature in SNCV history that many lines were initially built to the Dutch 1067mm gauge to facilitate cross-border interchange. Apart from two systems north from Antwerp town, which connected with Dutch metre gauge tramways in a

bight of the Netherlands cut off from the remainder by the Schelde/Escaut river, only a few internal lines connecting into Brabant were metre gauge from the start, and the SNCV initially classed those operationally as belonging to Brabant anyway. These characteristics of the SNCV network (locally referred to as the NMVB net) make it very difficult to provide a comprehensible chronology. Fortunately, like Gaul, Antwerpen province can be divided roughly into three parts, corresponding to the territories of the major concessionary companies which eventually emerged and which formed the operational groups of Turnhout, Antwerpen and Itegem - the latter, to confuse matters, was simply a headquarters part-way along a line and did not have routes radiating from it. These three companies were:

* *Antwerpsche Maatschappij voor den Dienst van Buurtspoorwegen (AMDB)*, which concentrated on the north and east of the province with headquarters at Antwerpen (Zurenborg) and an operating base at Turnhout;

* *Societé Les Vicinaux Anversois (VA)*, also based in Antwerpen which eventually ran the local networks in and to the north of Antwerpen city;

* *Kempische Stoomtram Maatschappij (KSTM)*, with headquarters at Itegem, which operated out of nearby Heist-op-den-Berg, mainly in the south and west of the province in the area known as "Kempen" ("backwoods" is probably a reasonable translation).

There were two other smaller concerns but they were special cases. All concessionaires gave up soon after World War I when the 1067mm gauge lines were, in any case, regauged to metre and unified. This chapter is therefore by operating Groupes up to 1920 and by the *SNCV Groep Antwerpen* thereafter. The first Groupe was undoubtedly that of the AMDB, which boasted Capital 1 as its foundation

7.2 Antwerpen: The early concessions to 1920s

7.2.1 Groupe de Turnhout (AMDB), 1885-1921 1067mm gauge

Capital	Name	Auth km
1	Antwerpen - Hoogstraten - Turnhout	53.25
31	Antwerpen - Zandhoven - Broechem - Lier	37.99
57	Turnhout - Arendonk	15.39
64	Turnhout - Mol - Westerlo - Zichem	56.77
70	Brasschaat - Brecht - Westerlo	52.00
84	Turnhout - Merxplas - Hoogstraten - Grens	42.31
133	Turnhout - Poppel	21.64

* **development of the AMDB network**

The very first SNCV line to be authorised, though the second actually to be opened, was **Capital 1 (ANTWERPEN - HOOGSTRATEN - TURNHOUT)**. Part of it was actually built and opened without official blessing,

Key to colour map symbols

▬▬▬▬▬▬	SNCV electric
▬▬▬▬▬▬	SNCV non-electric
· · · · · · · · · ·	SNCV authorised but not built
────────	main line railways
— + — + — + —	national borders
— — — — —	provincial borders
～～～～	waterways

Colour map key and SNCV logo

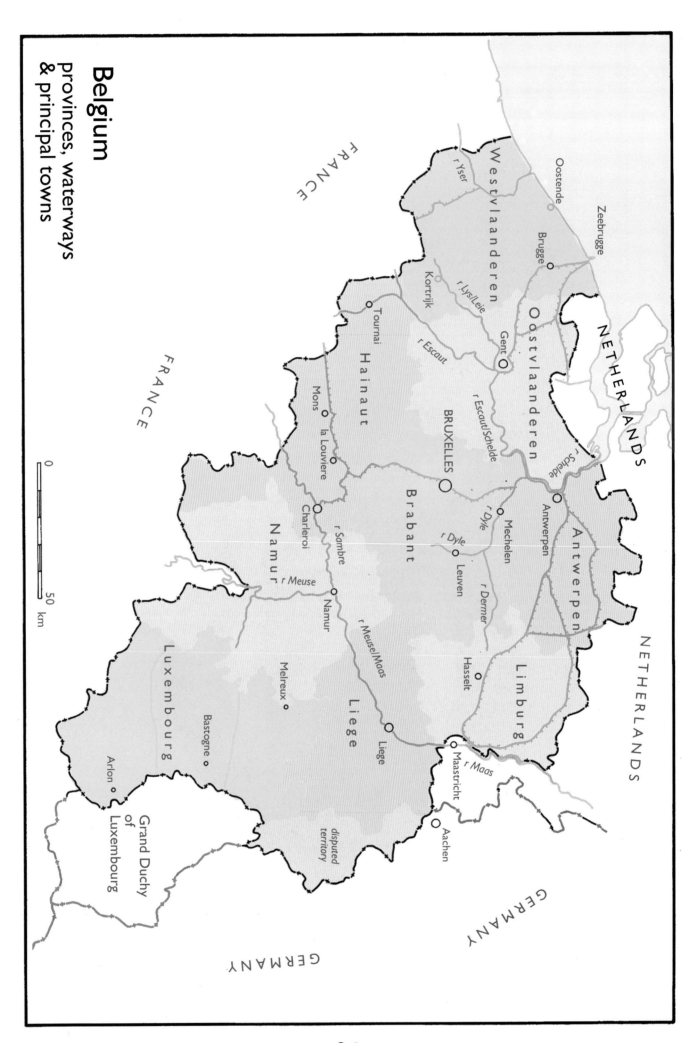

Belgium
provinces, waterways & principal towns

Westvlaanderen
r Yser
Oostende
Zeebrugge
NETHERLANDS
Brugge
FRANCE
Kortrijk
r Lys/Leie
Oostvlaanderen
Tournai
Gent
r Escaut
Hainaut
r Escaut/Schelde
r Schelde
Mons
BRUXELLES
la Louviere
Brabant
Antwerpen
r Dyle
Mechelen
Antwerpen
Charleroi
r Sambre
r Dyle
Leuven
Limburg
Namur
r Meuse
r Dermer
FRANCE
Namur
Hasselt
r Meuse/Maas
Melreux
Liege
Luxembourg
Bastogne
Liege
r Maas
Maastricht
Arlon
Grand Duchy
of
Luxembourg
Aachen
disputed
territory
GERMANY
NETHERLANDS
GERMANY

0
50
km

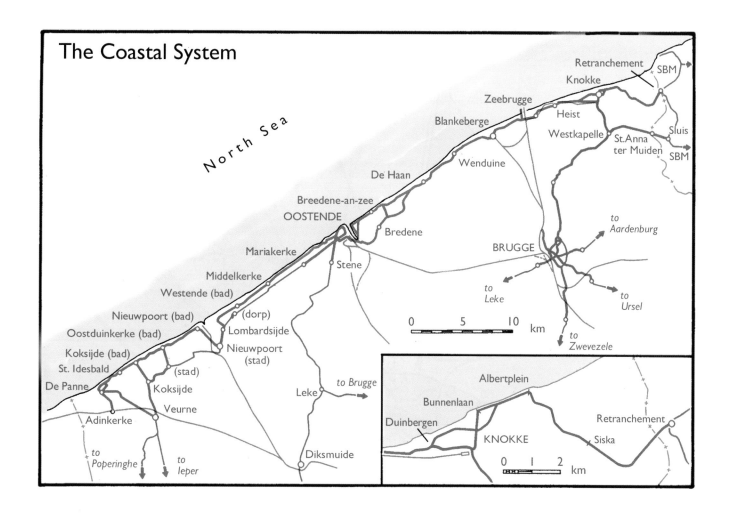

The Coastal System

North Sea

Retranchement
Knokke
SBM
Zeebrugge
Blankeberge
Heist
Westkapelle
Sluis
St.Anna
ter Muiden
SBM
Wenduine
De Haan
Breedene-an-zee
OOSTENDE
Bredene
BRUGGE
to
Aardenburg
Mariakerke
Stene
Middelkerke
Westende (bad)
to
Leke
to
Ursel
Nieuwpoort (bad)
(dorp)
Oostduinkerke (bad)
Lombardsijde
Koksijde (bad)
Nieuwpoort
(stad)
St. Idesbald
to Zwevezele
De Panne
(stad)
Koksijde
Leke
to Brugge
Adinkerke
Veurne
0   5   10 km
to
Poperinghe
to
Ieper
Diksmuide

Albertplein
Bunnenlaan
Duinbergen
Retranchement
KNOKKE
Siska
0   1   2 km

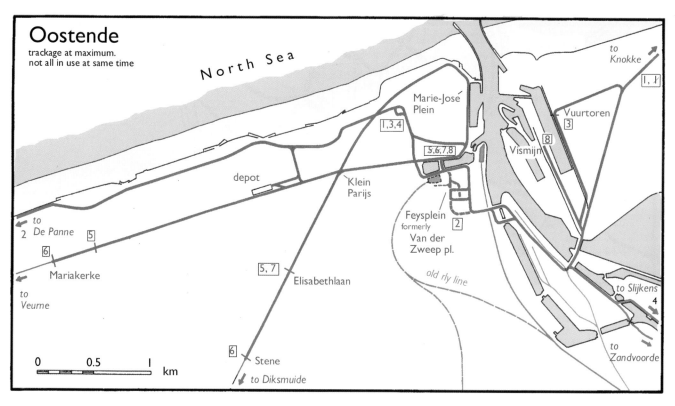

Oostende
trackage at maximum.
not all in use at same time

North Sea

to
Knokke

Marie-José
Plein
1, 1
1,3,4
Vuurtoren
3
5,6,7,8
8
Vismijn
depot
Klein
Parijs
Feysplein
formerly
Van der
Zweep pl.
2
old rly line
to
2 De Panne
5
to Slijkens
4
6
5, 7
Elisabethlaan
Mariakerke
to
Veurne
6
Stene
to Zandvoorde
0   0.5   1 km
to Diksmuide

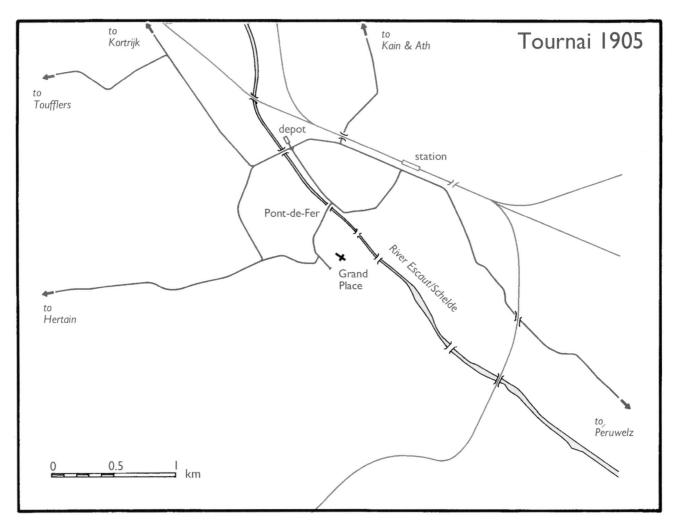

Tournai 1905

to Kortrijk

to Kain & Ath

to Toufflers

depot

station

Pont-de-Fer

Grand
Place

River Escaut/Schelde

to Hertain

to Peruwelz

0   0.5   1 km

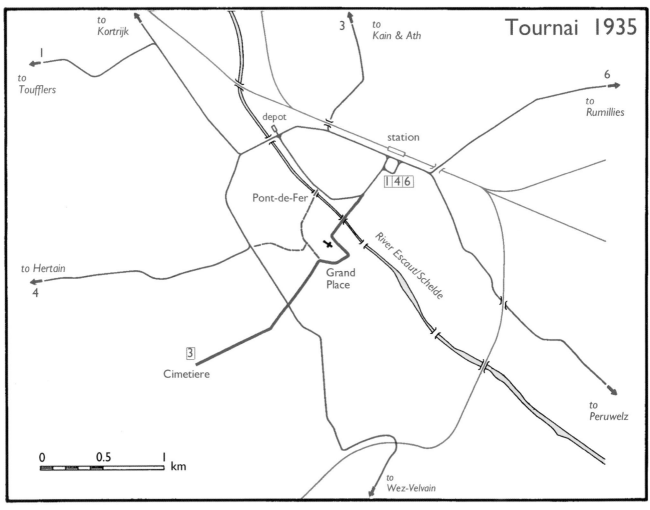

Tournai 1935

to Kortrijk

3   to Kain & Ath

1

to Toufflers

6

to Rumillies

depot

station

1 4 6

Pont-de-Fer

Grand
Place

River Escaut/Schelde

to Hertain

4

3

Cimetiere

0   0.5   1 km

to Peruwelz

to Wez-Velvain

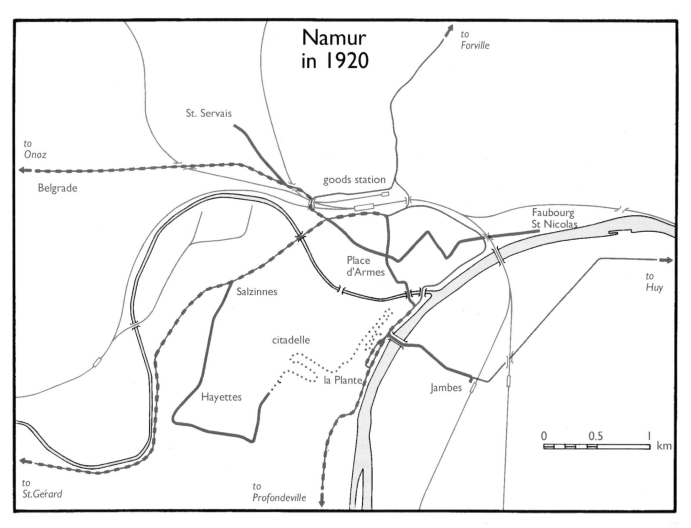

Namur
in 1920

to Forville

St. Servais

to Onoz

Belgrade

goods station

Faubourg
St Nicolas

Place d'Armes

to Huy

Salzinnes

citadelle

la Plante

Jambes

Hayettes

0   0.5   1 km

to St.Gérard

to Profondeville

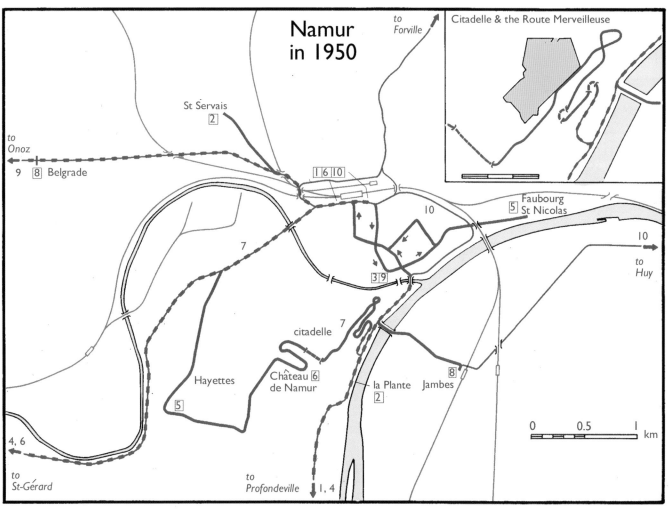

Namur
in 1950

to Forville

Citadelle & the Route Merveilleuse

St Servais
2

to Onoz

9 8 Belgrade

1 6 10

10

Faubourg
5 St Nicolas

7

10

to Huy

3 9

citadelle 7

Hayettes

Château 6
de Namur

la Plante
2

Jambes 8

5

0   0.5   1 km

4, 6

to St-Gérard

to Profondeville 1, 4

C-7

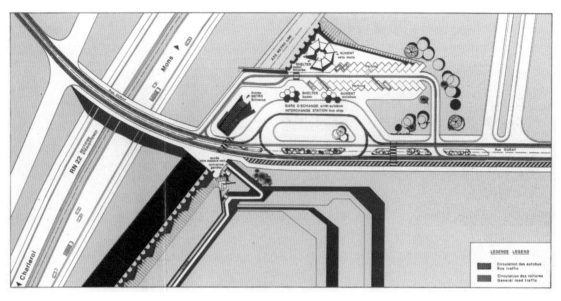

SNCV proposal diagrams
Lower - original metro design; Upper - typical station

Le métro léger de Charleroi • The Charleroi light metro

POUR MIEUX VOUS TRANSPORTER

FOR BETTER TRANSPORT

S.T.I.C.
SOCIÉTÉ DES TRANSPORTS INTERCOMMUNAUX DE CHARLEROI

S.N.C.V.
SOCIÉTÉ NATIONALE DES CHEMINS DE FER VICINAUX

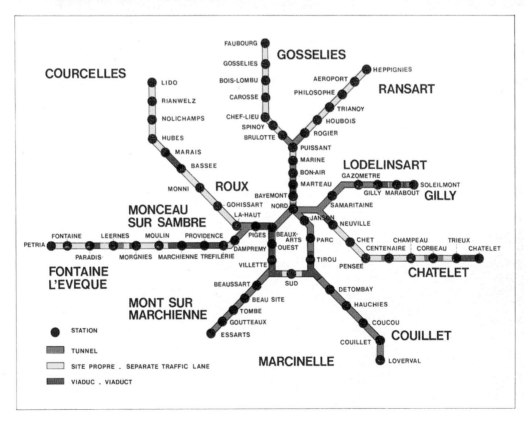

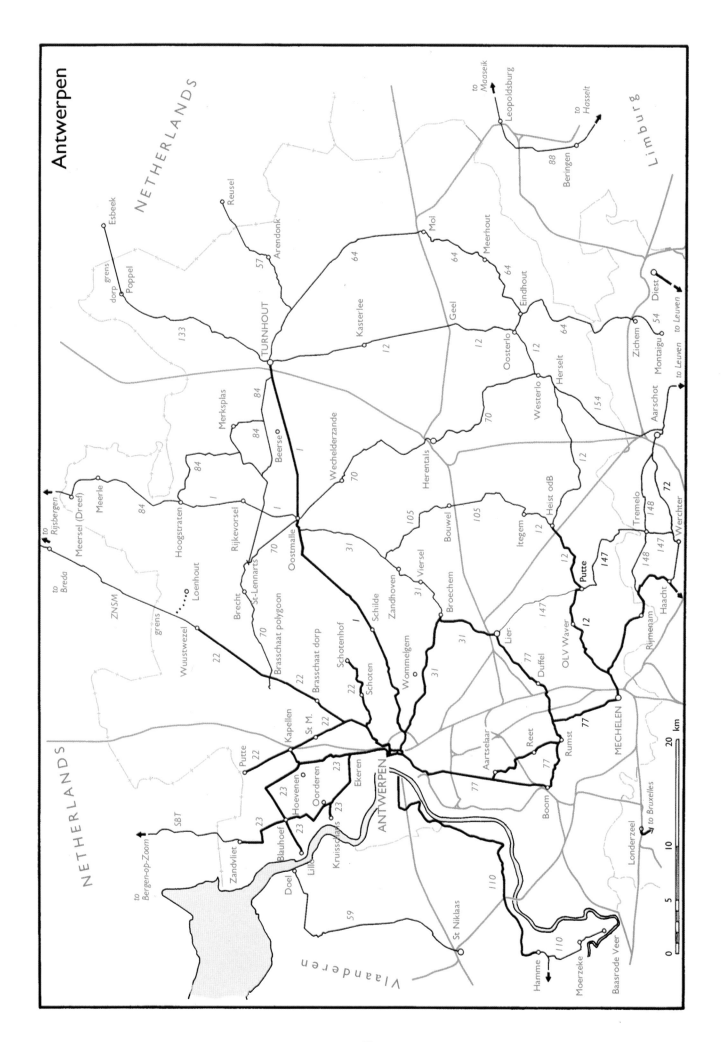

Antwerpen

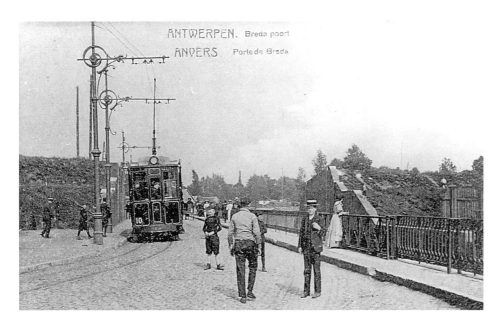

River bridge at Antwerpen city,
with a VA-type red car
(commercial card)

the first short section, from Antwerpen's Turnhoutse Poort (Turnhout Gate) to Wijnegem Canal being opened for restricted traffic on 15 August 1885; the route east to Oostmalle and then north on to Hoogstraten by the Dutch frontier followed on 20 September 1885 "amid much local rejoicing" - although the SNCV never officially admitted that it had not been opened in August!. The original authorisation, obtained retrospectively on 27 March 1886, was for the line from Antwerpen (Turnhoutse Poort) to Hoogstraten, but a branch from Oostmalle east to the market town of Turnhout was authorised on 19 April 1886 and added to the Capital before being completed. This branch was opened on 18 August 1886 and appears quickly to have become the main line. There was a fairly heavy goods traffic and the route provided a cheap and practicable link between east and west of the province. The line did not really penetrate the centre of Antwerpen at all, stopping for all practical purposes at the standard-gauge Zurenborg interchange station. This was reached via a short spur south from the Turnhoutse Poort.

There followed some complications. In 1887 the State agreed with the SNCV to transport inmates of a penal colony at Hoogstraten, when required. There was a similar colony at

Merksem standard gauge shunting with conventional 0-6-0T
(probably 821) by the Albert Canal in 1965.   (P de Backer)

Merksplas, a few kilometres south east from Hoogstraten, and a 9km, privately-arranged, spur was therefore laid from Rijkevorsel (Vaart) on Capital 1 north of Oostmalle to the prison colony of Merksplas via a cement factory; it appears to have been sanctioned by an authorisation of 30 April 1888. In due course the commune of Merkspas decided it wanted rail access of its own and applied for an extension of the prison branch, the whole thing to be operated as a public light railway. The line was officially authorised on 5 May 1893 and opened on 2 April 1894, being initially attached to Capital 1. It was transferred to Capital 84 (qv) in 1900. It was for these lines that seven prison-cars (B 1-7) were built.

Capital 31 (ANTWERPEN - ZANDHOVEN - BROECHEM - LIER) was the second line in the AMDB repertoire. It was basically an alternative route to Oostmalle, running in a huge curve south of Capital 1 and opened in stages from 1889. The initial authorisation, on 25 August 1888, was for Antwerpen - Broechem - Zandhoven with a branch southward from Broechem to Lier, a total of 26.1km. The line ran south and east from Zurenborg to Broechem, where the Lier branch diverged, and then swung northeast to reach Zandhoven, the whole being opened on 31 October 1889. The Oostmalle extension, first mooted in 1892, was authorised on 27 July 1895 and opened on 12 April 1896; it brought the total length to 39.06km including elements at each end in common with other lines and the Capital title then became **Antwerpen - Zandhoven - Oostmalle - Lier.**

Both the above used Antwerpen as their base. **Capital 57 (TURNHOUT - ARENDONK)** was the first development in the east, a simple dead-end branch authorised on 29 August 1892. It ran from Turnhout standard-gauge station first southeast and then east across flat agricultural land to Arendonk Canal (15.39km, opened 1 May 1893). An 0.47km extension on 1 July 1894 brought it to the Dutch frontier at Arendonk Grens and then, on 15 August 1894, across to Reusel (Grens) on the Dutch side where it terminated. In 1897 it was physically linked to a Dutch 1067mm gauge line from Eindhoven, the *Tramweg Maatschappij De Meijerij* (app 5) although, for legal reasons, there was apparently no through-working.

The next development was also from Turnhout and was **Capital 64 (TURNHOUT - MOL - WESTERLO - ZICHEM)**. Authorised in stages, this long rambling line struck south from Turnhout. Its first few kilometres were common with the existing Arendonk route, and the line on through the standard gauge junction of Mol to the small village of Meerhout was authorised on 19 April 1894 and opened on 4 May 1895; a 4km spur between Mol standard-gauge station and Mol (Donk), authorised on 31 December 1894, was laid as four-rail mixed gauge to serve local industries. From Meerhout the "main" line was extended southwest via Eindhout to Oosterlo, whence trains could run over an existing SNCV line (Capital 12) to reach Westerlo. It was authorised on 11 June 1895 and services started on 15 February 1896. Lastly, on 5 April 1900, a 14.5km branch, authorised on 5 November 1898, was opened from Eindhout south to the town of Zichem just over the border in Brabant. The operating length, including the common elements, was then given as 54.94km.

The next AMDB concession was a branch from an existing Antwerpen line latterly run by someone else. **Capital 70 (BRASSCHAAT - BRECHT - WESTERLO)** was typical of the wandering rural lines of the province. It started from the end of one route, connected with three others and then straggled off on a long ramble across country to join up with two more lines at its far terminus. It was initially proposed on 18 October 1894 as Brasschaat - Brecht with a length of 10.39km, was officially authorised on 15 August 1895 and was opened as such on 10 June 1896. From a junction with the *Vicinaux Anversois (VA: Capital 22)* at Brasschaat Polygoon, to the northeast of Antwerpen, it ran eastward to the village of Brecht and, so far as the AMDB was concerned, was an isolated branch. The much longer extension south to Westerlo via Oostmalle, authorised on 17 May 1904, however, brought it properly into the AMDB fold. It ran first easterly to St-Lennarts for a junction with Capital 84 and then southeast through Oostmalle and

Herentals. It was opened as far as Wechelderzande on 3 September 1907, and thence to Herentals on 14 March 1908. There it met the southern end from Westerlo, opened previously on 23 April 1907 and till then worked as a detached extension of Capital 64. The route length was 52.87km.

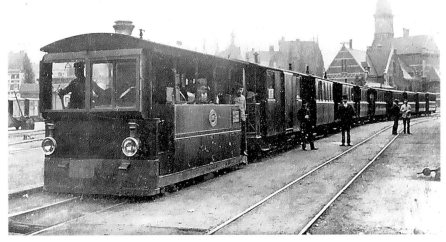

Antwerpen Zurenborg with an express interurban steam train for Turnhout   *(SNCV)*

The next line, **Capital 84 (TURNHOUT - HOOGSTRATEN - GRENS)**, had a very complex gestation, being built in sections between 1899 and 1912 with links to both the Dutch frontier and various AMDB lines. The project was initiated as early as 1890, but discussions dragged on until 16 June 1897 when a line was authorised from the existing SNCV terminus of Capital 1 at Hoogstraten to run north via the village of Meerle to the Dutch border at Meersel (Dreef), with a link thence to the Dutch town of Rijsbergen. This latter town was on a Dutch tramway from Wuustwezel to Breda already in being and operated by the *Zuid-Nederlandsche Stoomtram Mij* (app 5). The Dutch section was actually conceded to a specially formed SNCV subsidiary the *"Exploitatie van Buurtspoorwegen in Nederland"* and was then handed over for the AMDB to operate. The line as far as Meerle (12.3km) was opened on 20 March 1899, the Rijsbergen stretch following on 1 September 1899. The next section, from Turnhout west along the Kempische Canal to Beerse (Brug 4) and thence northward via Merksplas to Hoogstraten, was authorised on 31 January 1900 and opened in two sections: Hoogstraten - Merksplas on 1 October 1901, and Merksplas - Turnhout on 28 August 1904. On the way it

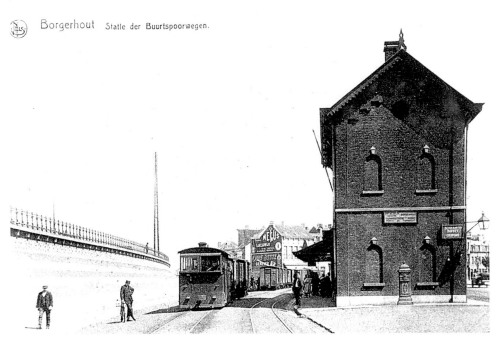

Borgerhout   Statie der Buurtspoorwegen.

Borgerhout station on the Antwerpen - Oostmalle - Turnhout line (author's collection)

Northern frontiers 1: Zandvliet in steam days with Dutch train on the left. (SNCV)

Northern frontiers 2: Zandvliet in early post-war years with a rebuilt Odessa car
in front of the customs post.
(E de Backer)

Northern frontiers 3: S-type car almost drowned by road traffic
at Wuustwezel.
(WJKD)

1891 and certainly by 1893, operation was then joint between our old friends the AMDB and the ZNSM, this extending to 3 September 1907 when the ZNSM withdrew. The VA (see below) then took over the Belgian routes.

In the meantime, a short extension from Schoten to Schoten Vaart had been authorised on 22 June 1905 and opened on 16 July 1905, and in the following year discussions were started to see if the city tramways would take over the whole set-up, together with Capital 23. On 17 November 1906 an agreement was reached whereby the CGTA formed a wholly-owned subsidiary, the *SA Les Vicinaux Anversois (VA)*, which agreed to "operate, electrify and maintain" the existing SNCV lines of Capitaux 21, 22 and 23 and to provide its own rolling stock as part of the bargain. This organisation officially took over on 3 September 1907.

There was then a discreet pause while the CGTA workshops assembled a fleet of 20 bogie cars, 5 four-wheelers, 26 passenger trailers and 3 luggage vans, painting them in a distinctive livery of carmine red; they were henceforth known to Antwerpen locals as the "red trams". On 6 June 1908, the Klapdorp route was worked for the first time under VA control as an electric service, and on 21 June that year, electrification came to the Schoten branch, extended from that date to a terminus at Schotenhof (authorised 7 November 1907). The same year, a branch from Wuustwezel to Loenhout was authorised but never built. Electrification, however, was extended to Brasschaat (Dorp) on 18 May 1909 and a new branch from Merksem (Kleine Bareel) to Sint-Mariaburg-Hoogboom Kruis, electrified from the start, was authorised on 10 February 1910 and opened on 5 August 1911. This branch appears to have partly replaced, or taken over from, a 600mm gauge steam tramway laid down by the estate company which was developing the district. This latter actually ran from Ekeren Station via St Mariaburg to Brasschat (Kaart) and lasted until the outbreak of war in 1914; the remains were lifted by the Germans in 1914/15 for military purposes. Finally, electrification was extended to Brasschaat (Polygoon) on 15 July 1912 to simplify connections with the Brasschaat - Brecht line. This completed the line while under VA control although there were further extensions after World War I, which took Capital 22 on from St Mariaburg through Kapellen to Putte on the frontier.

The VA also took over the existing **Capital 23 (ANTWERPEN - ZANDVLIET - LILLO)**. The SNCV had apparently considered this line one of its first priorities, requesting authorisation almost as soon as it was formed. The authorities clearly saw no hurry since they took almost two years to agree. Since authorisation on 9 August 1887, at the same time as Capital 21, was "followed" by opening of the first section on 4 September the same year, there was presumably some collusion (one notes several instances of lines

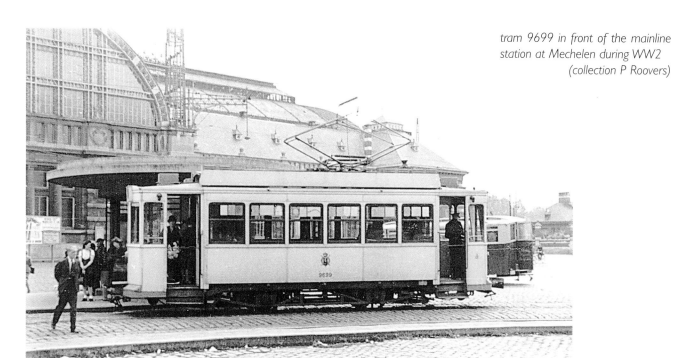

*tram 9699 in front of the mainline
station at Mechelen during WW2
(collection P Roovers)*

opening only weeks after authorisation was formally granted or even of authorisation being granted retrospectively). The first section was from Merksem (IJskelder) via Ekeren, Hoevenen & Blauwhoef to Zandvliet frontier where it met an existing Dutch tramway from Bergen-op-Zoom which had arrived on 1 May 1887. The latter's operator, the *Stoomtramweg Mij Bergen-op-Zoom - Tholen* (app 5) was quick to arrange through workings with the *Tramways du Nord d'Anvers* who took up the SNCV concession. Unusually, they were allowed to provide their own stock of Dutch pattern. The Belgian line was opened throughout by 4 September 1887 and through services started on 7 September of that year.

The companies worked very closely, the Dutch one adding Antwerpen to its title, and the locomotives being numbered in one common series. The system was soon developed, a loop line from Ekeren through Wilmarsdonk to Lillo Vaart being authorised on 16 April 1888, opened on 1 October 1888, and extended west to Lillo harbour on 22 July 1892 (authorised 29 February 1892); it connected with the Zandvliet line at Blauwhoef where there was a four-way crossing; in later years through trailers between Lillo and Zandvliet were apparently exchanged at this point.

The SNCV formally ended the mutual arrangement in 1894, taking over its share of the joint stock but the through services continued up to the first world war; the route was much used by refugees fleeing from Antwerp when it came under siege and it is said (but not officially confirmed) that some SNCV locomotives and stock were caught on the Dutch side of the border when Belgium was occupied and were interned for the duration. The complex came under VA control in 1907 but was not electrified by them. All VA lines remained intact during the 1914-18 war and through services were resumed for a short period after the war. They were terminated finally on 23 August 1921 because the Belgian trackage was regauged to metre. Meanwhile, the VA had surrendered its concessions in 1920 and its stock had been partitioned between the CGTA nand the SNCV - which in particular acquired ten of the "red trams".

While describing this area, It must also be mentioned that the SNCV built its Merksem Ijskelder station and workshops

on the site of an earlier standard gauge siding off the Antwerpen - Roosendaal railway line. About 1896 it appears that standard gauge interchange arrangements were put in there for SNCV use, the SNCV buying the freehold in September 1903 and providing some of its few industrial locomotives (Types 20 and 22) to work them.

7.2.3 Kempen. Groupe d'Itegem (KSTM), 1887-1920 1067mm gauge

Capital	Name	Auth km
12	Mechelen - Itegem - Westerlo - Geel - Turnhout	72.26
77	Antwerpen - Boom - Mechelen - Duffel - Lier	40.48
105	Itegem - Zandhoven	18.33
154	Aerschot - Westerlo	14.90
184	Stadsdiensten van Mechelen	3.30

The third early concessionaire, the *Kempische Stoomtram Mij (KSTM)*, was a company formed in 1890 with operating base at Heist-op-den-Berg specifically to operate SNCV "and other" lines in the south and west of Antwerpen province. From its inception it clearly had political clout since it was immediately able to take over an existing line and to obtain favourable treatment in acquiring the concessions for others. It eventually held four lines forming a connected system.

Capital 12 (MECHELEN - ITEGEM - WESTERLO - GEEL - TURNHOUT) was the first. It was, perhaps, inevitable that this, the second line to be ceded in Antwerpen province, was from its second largest city to Turnhout, providing another east-west link through agricultural country. The old city of Mechelen (fr. Malines) was the market town for a wide area, and it is not surprising that a line was promoted in 1887 to tap the area to its east. The Mechelen - Heist-op-den-Berg - Itegem branch was authorised on 11 January 1887 and opened from Itegem to Mechelen (Nekkerspoel) on the eastern side of the city on 27 June 1887. Operation was ceded initially to the big *SA pour l'Exploitation des CF Vicinaux (CFV)*, already active elsewhere. The line proved successful, with a heavy market-garden traffic and an extension from Heist eastward was soon promoted to Westerlo, a total of 35.54km.

Authorised on 24 April 1889, this was opened on 7 April 1890 under the control of the KSTM, which had taken over the rest of the line at the beginning of that year. A short extension to Mechelen station was authorised on 23 March 1892, but not built, but then five years passed before the next section was authorised on 13 June 1897. This ran east from Westerlo and then northeast to Geel (Vaart), on the standard gauge Herentals - Mol railway, being opened on 1 July 1898; it served the numerous farming "colonies" for mentally disturbed patients in that area. It was not until 5 October 1904 that the final section was authorised, being opened from Geel northward to Turnhout SNCV station on 15 September 1906, the last bit being over common track with the AMDB's Capital 1. Meanwhile, a project had been in existence since 1890 to connect the Mechelen end to the town station, being authorised on 23 March 1892 as noted above but it was not until 17 January 1911 that a new bridge at Nekkerspoel allowed it to connect via the existing ring line of Capital 77 (see below) and thus gain access. There is a record of a further authorisation on 10 August 1908 which may refer to a modification of this route.

Capital 77 (ANTWERPEN - BOOM - MECHELEN - DUFFEL - LIER), the next acquisition, was also a complex system, parts of which were not built until the inter-war years. In essence it was shaped like a cross, with a main line from Antwerpen to Mechelen and branches going en route from the little town of Rumst west to Boom and northeast to Lier. The first sections were authorised on 23 June 1896, a political squabble about who was to operate them being resolved in favour of the KSTM. At its southern end, the stretches from Rumst south to Mechelen (Katelijne Poort) on the northwest edge of the town, and west to Boom (St-Anna-Kapel), were opened on 6 May 1900 and 1 October 1900 with a short extension through Boom town to Boom (Tuyaertstraat) on 14 October the same year. The eastern branch from Rumst to Lier followed officially on 1 January 1902 (some sources give 13 January as the real date) where it met the AMDB line from Broechem, a link being installed for goods traffic only. A ring line round Mechelen to the standard-gauge station was opened on 22 June 1902. Finally, under the original Capital, the line was authorised on 18 March 1899 to go north from Rumst to Reet (opened 1 October 1900) and on, via Aartselaar, to a terminus at Antwerpen Brederodestraat near Antwerpen Zuid station which it reached on 15 September 1901. After some haggling this was extended to the port at Antwerpen (Zwemdok) over track common with the Sté des Tramways Anversois from 15 September 1903. Besides serving a fertile agricultural region, this line was profitable from the start because it served the rapidly expanding brick industry near Rumst. The first private siding was put in during 1908 and was followed by many others. Even up to the end of World War 2, the brick traffic, mainly to the standard gauge at Reet and Mechelen, was very large, and the "Titanic" bogie motor cars of series 9499-510 are said to have been built at least partly to haul this traffic.

Capital 105 (ITEGEM - ZANDHOVEN), the next concession, was back in the provincial centre and was a simple south-north link from Itegem through the Kempen to link up with the AMDB's southern Antwerpen - Oostmalle line (Capital 31) at Zandhoven. Authorised on 22 December 1900, it was opened throughout officially on 15 January 1904 (some local sources cite 14 May 1902 which might have been for local goods traffic?); its operating length of 19.87km included the common section of track between Zandhoven (Herkant) and Zandhoven (Dorp). It had a placid existence at least up to 1914. The same comment applies to the KSTM's last branch, **Capital 154 (AERSCHOT - WESTERLO)**, authorised on

28 July 1906 and opened throughout rather tardily on 8 July 1911. It too had a common section, this time with the KSTM line from Mechelen between Herselt (Kwadestraat) and Westerlo, but was otherwise unmemorable except for crossing into Brabant at its southern end.

* KSTM in and after World War 1.

As with other companies, the KSTM lines suffered during World War 1 and some closed and then reopened actually during the war - presumably the parallel main line railways were otherwise occupied. In brief:

Capital 12 was badly affected by bridge damage at Geel and Itegem. Mechelen - Heist-op-den-Berg was summarily closed on 1 May 1915 and, after a considerable struggle, the remainder stopped operation on 1 October 1917.

Capital 77. The sections of line from Rumst to Antwerpen and to Mechelen and also the branch to Lier were also affected by war damage during the early campaigns and temporarily closed, but were brought back into use on 1 January 1915 (Rumst - Antwerpen) and 1 October 1915 (Rumst - Mechelen); presumably the brick industry required transport. The Lier branch was reopened also, but the Germans charged tolls over a bridge at Lier. The SNCV terminus was therefore cut back to the Rumst side of the bridge; the branch was in any case closed and lifted in March 1918 to provide materials for military lines.

Both the other KTSM lines, Capitaux 105 (Itegem - Zandhoven) and 154 (Aarschot - Westerlo), were closed during 1915, although the Zandhoven branch reopened for a short time before closing finally in October 1917.

After the war the damaged lines were slowly rebuilt, but to metre gauge. Itegem - Zandhoven reopened in two stages: from Itegem to Bouwel on 1 May 1921, and thence to Zandhoven on 27 September 1921; Aerschot - Westerlo came back on 1 May 1921, and Rumst - Lier on 30 September 1921 but Capital 12 had bridge problems. Its reopening was as shown below (depot and works were at Heist). Like the other Antwerpen companies, the KSTM felt unable to continue after the war and surrendered its concessions in 1920.

Section	Date
Heist-op-den-Berg - Putte	4 Aug 1919
Putte - OLV Waver	17 Aug 1919
OLV Waver - Mechelen	31 Aug 1919
Heist-op-den-Berg - Westerlo	15 Apr 1920
Westerlo - Geel Canal	30 Jul 1920
Geel Canal - Geel station	1 Oct 1920
Geel (Vaart) - Kasterlee	21 Jan 1921
Kasterlee - Turnhout	9 Apr 1921
Heist-op-den-Berg - Itegem	21 Jan 1921

7.3 Mechelen urban network (1911 - 1953) (Map ref C-5)

Also associated with the KSTM was **Capital 184 (STADSDIENSTEN VAN MECHELEN)**. There is some confusion over this concession. Discussions certainly started in 1909 between the state, the SNCV and Mechelen city council regarding provision of an urban tramway system. An initial limited programme was agreed during 1911, partly utilising existing tracks and partly new trackage, the whole to be electrified at 600 volts dc with bow collectors. The system was authorised on 13 December 1911 but the concession was not finalised until June 1913 when The Societé d'Electricité du Nord de la Belgique (EN) was commissioned to provide current and,

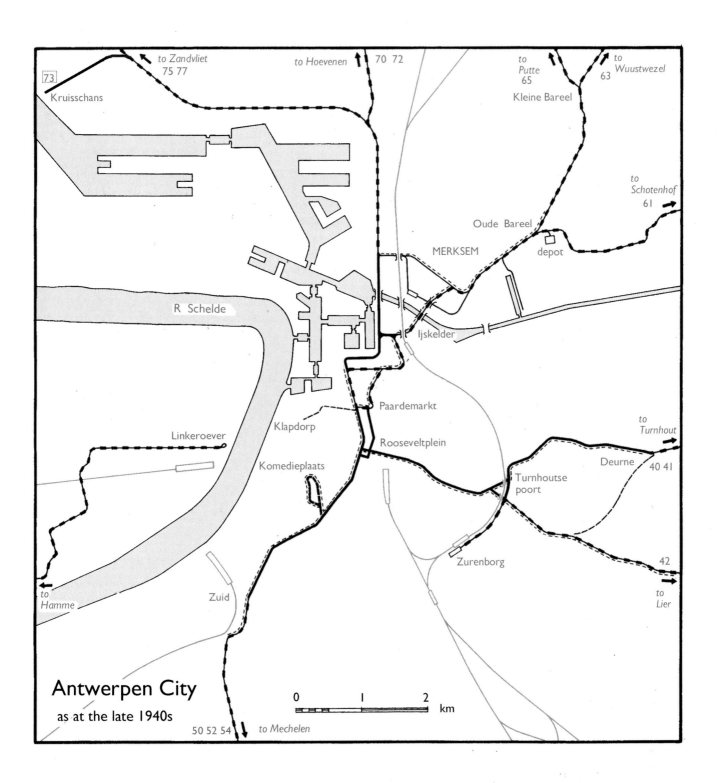

to Zandvliet
75 77

to Hoevenen

70 72

to Putte
65

to Wuustwezel

63

73

Kruisschans

Kleine Bareel

to Schotenhof
61

Oude Bareel

MERKSEM

depot

R Schelde

Ijskelder

Paardemarkt

Linkeroever

Klapdorp

Rooseveltplein

to Turnhout

Komedieplaats

Deurne

40 41

Turnhoutse
poort

Zurenborg

42

to Hamme

Zuid

to Lier

Antwerpen City
as at the late 1940s

0   1   2
km

50 52 54   to Mechelen

Mechelen Route 2 with car 9489 in the town (collection P Roovers)

officially, to operate the lines. An SNCV note of March 1912, however, indicates that the concession was to be transferred to the KSTM, which is logical since their tracks were being used, but apparently this was never done. There were two routes. Route 1 ran from the standard-gauge station over new track north via Grote Markt and then northwest to contact the Rumst line at Schietbaan where the urban lines depot was located. Route 2 took the same route to Grote Markt and then swung east to Nekkerspoel, intending to reach Pasbrug over the tracks of Capital 12. Work started on 26 March 1912, the routes being opened on 25 June 1913 and 18 November 1913 respectively. The Pasbrug extension followed in 1915 (1.425km), and the system was further extended in postwar years (see below).

The Mechelen town lines, like many others, suffered during World War I, all services ceasing on 1 November 1917 because of electricity supply problems and complications on the associated rural lines. It does not appear that any track was lifted, and all routes were restored to operation on 5 October 1919. By that time, the EN was certainly the official concessionaire, and indeed it hung on to the services until May 1932 on short-term leases before it passed control back to the SNCV. Operation was then initially passed to the SNCV Groep de Leuven (Louvain) until 1 March 1933 when Antwerpen took over.

For continuity, the inter-war development of Mechelen town trams is given here, although out of chronological sequence. The main improvements started in 1932 when the SNCV took over. First, Route 3 from Grote Markt north to the existing ring route at Oude Liersebaan (Kerkhoflei) was opened on 1 November 1932, with an extension north to Elzenstraat on 21 April 1933, short workings to the original terminus being 3 barré. To the west of routes 1 & 2 and broadly paralleling them, a new link from the station to Grote Markt followed on 21 April 1935, giving the southern section of route 3 its own trackage. This enabled improvements to be

made to routes 1 and 2 during 1936, Route 1 being extended to become Racing - Station - Brusselse Poort and routes 2 and 3 being effectively combined. Route 2 became Elzenstraat - Station - Pasbrug and Route 3 was the reverse. As before a Route 3 barré provided short workings to Oude Liersebaan while all these modifications also allowed the Rumst country lines to penetrate directly into Mechelen centre from 1932 onward. Mechelen town routes retained their route numbers of 1, 2 and 3, throughout the period, though track was doubled from station to Grote Markt, and country routes H, T and 52 used it. Route 52 then continued over route 3 tracks to the ring route and turned along the boulevard. The postwar decline, however, was swift. Routes 1 and 3 of Mechelen closed on 21 December 1952, leaving only route 2 to Pasbrug; that was probably because it could be treated as a short-working of the eastern country routes. It lasted only until 28 February 1953, being replaced by methane gas-powered buses. The town tracks were lifted soon after.

7.4: 1920-39 SNCV Groep Antwerpen (Group 10)

The end of World War I saw the Antwerpen provincial lines in some disarray with many requiring reconstruction and with costs rising rapidly. Two major changes resulted in the next few years: Firstly, the SNCV seized the chance offered by major reconstruction to abandon the 1067mm gauge. It was clear that development would be internal, rather than via links with the Netherlands that had not produced much traffic anyway. Between 1919 and 1921 the existing lines were therefore relaid to metre gauge, stock being altered to suit, while all reconstructed lines were laid to that gauge from the start. The immediate extra cost was not great, since war neglect and

Intermediate stage: Oorderen station in the 1930s with a steam train from Zandvliet and an Odessa-type radial axle car by the station building at the limit of electric working from Antwerpen. *(SNCV / commercial card)*

damage meant that much work was needed in any case, while gains through standardisation were considerable

Secondly, one by one, the concessionary companies surrendered their leases, taking advantage of the law of November 1919. Initially the VA surrendered the concession for its electric lines, from 23 January 1920, thereby precipitating a crisis because the lines were then still 1067mm gauge; the VA's fleet had, from 1931-on actually been owned by the CGTA and hired from them, and the SNCV and CGTA apparently could not agree terms for its use! It took an intervention by the Minister for Agriculture to allow SNCV to buy part of the fleet, including ten bogie motorcars which became SNCV 9636-45, and to

Antwerpen - Turnhout line, too long to electrify, received an allocation of ex-British Type-19 steam locomotives, and from 1 September 1924 had an upgraded service consisting of expresses and semi-fast trains together with short suburban workings; the expresses took 95 minutes for the 40km, which was quite fast in the circumstances. New vestibuled four-wheeled coaches of the 1919-20 batches were used, equipped with electric light and Westinghouse brakes, and the whole affair was very successful indeed; receipts per kilometre were four times the average for steam lines, and from then on Turnhout always had favoured treatment. In the 1930s a special series of bogie autorails, AR 284-88, was even built so that standards could be maintained against bus competition.

During the war many steam locomotives were pressed back into service to handle the increased goods traffic. Here one shunts wagons at Mechelen Nekkerspoel. (collection P Roovers)

restore services from 7 June 1920; even then, the SNCV was dependent on the CGTA for maintenance, depot space and power supply until its own depot and workshops at Merksem (Oude Bareel) were completed on 1 January 1923. Meanwhile it appears to have taken back the ex-VA steam lines with effect from 1 January 1921.

Of the other concessionaires, The KSTM gave up on 1 April 1920. A month later, the AMDB relinquished its concessions, and in 1923 the *SA des Vicinaux et Tramways (VT)*, operating two cross-border lines from Brabant, (see chapter 8) did likewise. One of those lines, **Capital 147 (LIER - WERCHTER)**, came under Antwerpen control.

As a result, in 1924, the SNCV formed its *Groep Antwerpen* to take over all provincial lines. Initially there were three operating divisions, based at Merksem (ex VA), Turnhout (ex AMDB) and Heist-op-den-Berg (ex KSTM and VT) but after the Mechelen urban routes were assimilated from Groep Leuven in 1933 operation was centralised, with headquarters at Antwerpen (Zurenborg) and major works at Merksem. The Groep conscientiously rebuilt even the remote country branches, though doing little to improve them except by introducing autorails, or railmotors, from 1933 onwards. These took over passenger services between Broechem, Zandhoven and Oostmalle on 16 July 1933 and, later the same year, appeared on the unelectrified lines from Turnhout. The last steam passenger trains on this system were replaced in 1938.

In the more industrial and populated areas, however, the SNCV started to expand and electrify. To start with, the

In Antwerpen itself a new link between Borgerhout (Driehoekstraat) and Deurne (Drie Koningenstraat) was authorised on 20 October 1924 and joined the Antwerpen - Lier and Antwepen - Turnhout lines from 1 May 1925. The other main routes out of Antwerpen and, to a lesser extent, Mechelen, bit by bit became high-capacity electric tramways. At this period, letter route codes were employed, normally using the initial of the outer terminus (eg E for Ekeren; B for Brasschaat; P for Polygoon). It may be of interest that the Antwerpen group made considerable use of mobile substations to provide power as electrification was extended.

The first lines to benefit were those from Zurenborg, the Broechem branch being electrified to Wommelgem on 15 March 1926, followed by the Turnhout line as far as Schilde on 7 June 1926 for suburban services; the event marked a change from trolley poles to bow collectors although these, in turn, were changed to pantographs in the early 1930s. Broechem itself was reached on 13 February 1928, and the branch to Lier on 28 June 1930, while a short Station - Village spur was added at Wommelgem on 5 June 1931. Meanwhile, on the already partly electrified northern lines, the track to Ekeren (Dijk) on the Zandvliet line was electrically worked from 19 June 1927 and when electrification reached Zandvliet the line was actually extended across the Dutch frontier to Ossendrecht (Kabeljouw). On the parallel route to St-Mariaburg, a completely new electrified extension to Kapellen was opened on 31 July 1927. On 1 December 1928, the Kapellen line was extended again, to Putte Grens on the Dutch border. (It is important not to confuse this with Putte in the south of Antwerpen province).

The remainder of the Zandvliet system followed in stages: first the loop to Oorderen and to Lillo (Haven) on 18 November 1929 and 4 January 1931 respectively, then the "main line' to Blauwhoef and Zandvliet on 31 May 1931, and a new short spur to Kruisschans near Oorderen on 18 July 1932. Finally the main line was linked to Kapellen by a new spur from Hoevenen on 1 March 1934, giving Putte trams a quicker route into Antwerpen. The lines received most of the war-surplus "Odessa" type motor cars thriftily bought by the SNCV in 1926.

Simultaneously, the network south from Antwerpen had also been attended to. Apart from a short length from Mechelen (Pasbrug) to Rijmenam on 2 August 1931, the first section electrified was in the middle of Capital 77, from Rumst to Boom on 11 December 1931. It was very quickly followed by the line north from Rumst into Antwerpen on 6 March 1932, a new alternative route from Boom direct to Antwerpen via Aartselaar being opened the same day. The Rumst - Lier line had to wait until 16 April 1933. Clearly the heavy brick traffic was making itself felt.

The remaining lines to be electrified were all around Mechelen. A short length of Capital 148, from Mechelen to Rijmenam, had been electrified on 2 August 1931. Then Capital 12 was electrified for suburban traffic as far as Heist-op-den-Berg on 31 July 1932. Mechelen - Rumst (Capital 77) followed in two stages, to Walem (Brug) on 9 April 1932 and on to Rumst on 2 October 1932, completing a link through to Antwerpen, while the Mechelen town system was gradually upgraded with new routes as described in section 7.3. As part of this, the Rumst lines gained entry to Mechelen town centre from 1932 on.

Lastly on the prewar programme, the line from Rijmenam to Keerbergen, on the provincial boundary, was electrified on 5 June 1938 as part of a projected link to Bruxelles . The eastern routes from Mechelen were then given letter route codes: H for Heist, and T for Keerbergen (they hoped to extend electrification to Tremelo).

The SNCV also took advantage of its expansion plans to tidy up the situation in Antwerpen city. It will be recalled that the lines there had three widely separated termini: Zuid/Zwemdok, Zurenborg and Klapdorp. By an agreement with the *Tramwegen van Antwerpen en Omgeving (TAO)*, dated 6 October 1933, the SNCV was permitted to bring its northern lines down from Merksem via Italielei to Victorieplaats (later Rooseveltplein) in the centre of town and, similarly, to bring the eastern lines in from Tumhoutse Poort; the City Council confirmed the agreement on 6 August 1934, work beginning in February 1935. The eastern routes operated over the new link from 3 June 1935, Route S (Schilde) becoming route 40 (see table 7A for route numbering), Broechem becoming route 42, while the former spur to Zurenborg became first route 41 and then an unnumbered shuttle. The northern routes to Kapellen followed on 1 July 1935 and the rest on 19 April 1936. Klapdorp was largely superseded, but remained in use at peak hours until at least 1938; a few workings on routes 75 and 77 remained until after the war.

Equally, on the south side, the southern routes were extended up Britischelei and northwest over Leopoldstraat to a huge return loop at Komedieplaats from 4 November 1935; a service link was put in to Victorieplaats along the Frankrijklei, and the trams were brought on along this from 15 July 1940 to pass Victorieplaats ; Some sources note that from 1 February 1942 they were extended even further north, terminating at the

Osystraat loop but others suggest Osystraat was used only as a layover point, services actually departing from Victorieplaats.

The TAO was not entirely happy about this invasion, and another agreement of 16 March 1937 included arrangements whereby they could run some suburban services over SNCV lines; in one case the SNCV even abandoned its own track from Borgerhout to Deume, and used TAO track with consequent overhead-wire complications. At the same time, the SNCV brought into use a series of route numbers as shown in Table 7A; these started at 40 to avoid confusion with the urban lines. Other significant changes were the elimination of 1st class from 1 January 1937 and the closure of three rural sections as their Dutch connections closed. These were:

Cap	section	pass	goods
22	Brasschaat - Wuustwezel	11 Feb. 1939	-
84	Meersel (Dreef) - Rijsbergen	7 Oct.1934	Jan 1937
133	Poppel (Dorp) - Esbeek	15 Sept.1935	1936

Elsewhere, the link between routes 65 and 72 at Kapellen was abandoned on 31 August 1936 as being hardly ever used. Merksem, however, saw a considerable increase in traffic and by the late 1920s the SNC owned some 2.7km of track and served 33 separate sites involving over 20 industrial concerns. Narrow gauge operations, however, were largely transferred to Oude Bareel and Blauhoef from the mid-1920s on.

Table 7A: Antwerpen routes in 1937

No.	Route details
40	Victorieplaats - Schilde
41	Borgerhout - Zurenborg (transferred to Turnhout route
42	Victorieplaats - Broechem - Lier (change at Broechem)*
50	Comedieplaats - Boom
52	Comedieplaats - Boom - Rumst - Mechelen**
53	Rumst - Lier
54	Rumst - Artselaar (- Antwerpen in rush hours)
60	Klapdorp - Merksem (from 1935 to 1939 only)
61	Victorieplaats - Schotenhof
63	Victorieplaats - Brasschaat
64	Allocated to Wuustwezel; used from 23 Dec 1951
65	Victorieplaats - St-Mariaburg - Kapellen
70	Victorieplaats - Kapellen via Hoevenen
70 barré	Victorieplaats - Ekeren
72	Victorieplaats - Hoevenen - Kapellen - Putte
73	Victorieplaats - Kruisschans
75	Victorieplaats - Ekeren - Lillo
77	Victorieplaats - Oorderen - Zandvliet

NOTES:
* used ex-VA cars because of clearance problems
** fast workings, passenger only, electric signalling.

At much the same time, vast extensions to Antwerpen docks completely altered the northern approaches. A direct double-track route was laid down the new Noorderlaan, and a high-level road between Merksem and Yserlaan got rid of most remaining awkward crossings. All this brought the electrified route length to 207 km, which remained the position until World War II.

7.5   Groep Antwerpen (Group 10): The final years, 1939-1968

Antwerpen province, as always in the European wars, was badly affected by the fighting. The German Blitzkrieg of May 1940 left smashed bridges all along the Albert and Kempische waterways so that the SNCV was for some months restricted to running local services - and even to shipping equipment

a WW2 electric service for Zandvliet waits at Antwerpen (Paardemarkt). Standard car with a mixture of stock to increase capacity *(Collection P Roovers)*

across canals to provide for isolated sections. The full story is too complex to detail here and serious students are referred to the bibliography. In brief, all services had to be suspended for a period in May 1940 because of damage caused by the German invasion. No less than seven branches or sections were closed completely during the war and never reopened, a total length of some 78 km. They included, among the northern country lines,

*   St-Lennarts - Oostmalle (22 February 1943);
*   the spurs from Rijkevorsel to Merksplas (Colonie) and Beerse (22 February 1943), thus cutting the east-west link between Brecht and Turnhout;
*   Hoogstraten north to the frontier.

One other northern line, Brasschaat - Brecht - St-Lennarts - Rijkevorsel, lost its passenger service, at least for a time, but stayed open for freight, at least in part. In the south, those closed included:

*   Lier - Putte (22 February 1943),
*   Heist-op-den-Berg - Westerlo (15 March 1943),
*   Keerbergen - Aerschot (in Brabant; 22 February 1943)

In Antwerpen itself, the Kruisschans branch, route 73, lost its passenger service on 31 August 1939, its overhead equipment being reused to electrify an extension of route 61 (to 's Grevenwezel, opened 8 May 1941 as a steam line). It closed completely on 30 June 1940 and did not reopen. On the other hand all was not gloom, for on 28 April 1941 electric trams reached Oostmalle from Schilde, (opened in two stages: the first being Schilde -

Some quite complicated working took place on the northern lines. Here two trains exchange trailers at Bloeuhof where the Lillo and Zandvliet routes met. (E de Backer)

St Antonious Brecht from 24 February 1941) and on 2 August 1941 they were even extended to Turnhout; the route then had long-distance express services and a heavy freight service, the latter worked by rebuilt "Titanic" cars converted to motor goods vans. In fact, as in the first war, the Turnhout route became very busy indeed and this continued for some years after the war: it is recorded that, on weekdays, no less than 70 workings left Rooseveltplaats on routes 40 and 41 alone and other traffic included a nightly newspaper tram bringing news to the rural areas. Meanwhile, on 18 August 1943, electrification on the northern lines from Schotenhof to 's Gravenwezel extended route 61, and the SNCV in general certainly saw very heavy use. Most diesel services were replaced by steam, though the Turnhout ones continued up to electrification, cars being towed over electrified stretches to save fuel.

The end of World War II thus found the system in a worse state than in most other provinces. There were various plans for electrification, including among others Oostmalle - Hoogstraten but only two short electrification projects were actually completed. First was a link to the Bruxelles system via Keerbergen and Haecht on 1 June 1949 which allowed a direct

In the final years fast trains between Turnhout and Antwerpen were run by S-type cars with one or more trailers (E de Backer)

Typical of the mixed gauge interchanges. On an industrial branch at Mol Donk are two patterns of tractor:ART40 has double buffing/coupling gear for handling both gauges; ART69 has metre gauge equipment but is working with a match wagon.
(Paul de Backer.)

Antwerp town in the final years. S-type cars at Roosevelt Platz.
(E de Backer.)

Bruxelles - Mechelen service (Groep Leuven route M). The other, on 23 December 1951, was a direct service to the Dutch frontier, achieved by electrifying the section between Brasschaat and Wuustwezel Grens which had revived its passenger service from 27 May 1945 and modernised it with diesel railcars from 9 May 1948. The electrification used materials from Rumst - Lier and Broechem - Lier which closed as noted below. In Antwerpen, the Victorieplaats terminus was renamed Franklin Rooseveltplein in 1945, the SNCV offices being moved there in 1952.

Elsewhere the rot set in very early. Apart from the Wuustwezel branch, none of the closed lines were reopened, most being replaced by buses when fuel became available. In the south, Rumst - Lier (always the weak part of Capital 77) went on 4 September 1945, and the stub of the Lier - Werchter line, from Putte to Werchter, followed on 15 December 1947. The Turnhout area was next. Passenger services were withdrawn from the lines to Poppel (16 June 1948) and Arendonk (15 May 1949). Turnhout - Mol - Westerlo was cut back by closure to passengers of Mol - Westerlo and its branch from Eindhout to Zichem, both on 4 June 1949, though the mixed-gauge at Mol remained in use.

East of Antwerp, Oostmalle lost much of its old importance from 31 August 1949, when the lines north to Hoogstraten and south to Herentals closed to passengers, though they stayed open for freight for a short time. On the same day, Turnhout suffered again, Turnhout - Geel - Westerlo and Turnhout - Merksplas - Hoogstraten losing their passenger services, and the latter closing completely. This left the eastern half of Antwerpen province bereft of SNCV rail services save for the Turnhout electrics and a spur thence to Mol. The following year, Westerlo lost its last passenger service with closure of the truncated line to Herentals on 30 June 1950, and the next day Broechem - Oostmalle and Broechem - Lier (electric) closed too. Zandhoven - Itegem and probably Heist - Itegem closed completely on 28 September 1951, and lifting was authorised almost immediately, being completed in 1952

There was then a respite of some eighteen months until, as recorded in section 7.3, routes 1 and 3 of Mechelen closed on 21 December 1952, leaving only route 2 to Pasbrug which lasted only until 28 February 1953, being replaced by methane gas-powered buses. The town tracks were lifted, so that SNCV trams once more plodded round the outer boulevards. Aerschot - Westerlo followed on 11 April 1953, its goods services ending on 15 October the same year, and all southern lines were clearly in danger. Rumst - Reet - Artselaar closed on 31 December 1953, breaking the most direct route to Antwerpen, and Keerbergen - Tremelo closed to passengers on 3 October 1954. As an autorail-operated stump of a longer line, it is surprising it lasted so long. One should at this point perhaps mention the disastrous floods in February 1953 which affected most of the low countries. Routes 70 and 72 were badly damaged, some sections having to be worked for a time by buses and others reduced to peak-hour services.

The stumps of truncated lines tended not to last. Mol - Westerlo closed even to goods on 12 July 1954; Turnhout -

Mol, excluding the now isolated mixed-gauge spur, closed on 12 November 1955, followed by Rumst - Mechelen on 10 November 1956. The electric lines east from Mechelen followed: to Heist-op-den-Berg on 30 April 1957, and to Keerbergen on 1 June 1957. Only the electric lines radiating from Antwerpen and the Brabant link line to Haacht/Haecht from Keerbergen remained, but the latter was no longer viable. It closed on 31 May 1958 and, when it went, the south too had lost its tramways.

Antwerpen city had only a short respite. In spite of an allocation of the new type "S" cars for the interurban routes, closures continued. Antwerpen - Broechem closed on 27 September 1958, last vestige of Capital 31. The "flagship" line was cut back from Turnhout to Oostmalle on 31 August 1960 and, two months later on 5 November, the first of the northern routes between Ekeren, Oorderen and Zandvliet followed, part of a closure programme the SNCV did not want. The trouble was that Antwerpen docks were expanding once more, and most of the land on which the older lines ran was needed. The remainder was not really viable, especially as the operation involved drastic alterations at Merksem. Its extremities suffered again on 27 May 1961 when the Blauwhoef - Lillo branch went, and Kapellen - Putte closed on the same date. Hoevenen - Blauwhoef followed on 1 October 1961, leaving only the Merksem - Hoevenen - Kapellen stretch. On 26 May 1962 Oostmalle lost its last SNCV link with Antwerpen and the eastern lines were gone.

There was then a three year gap, after which the SNCV virtually admitted defeat; by then it was running a mixed tram and bus service on most lines. The 's Gravenwezel extension closed on 29 May 1965, while closure of route 52 to Boom and Rumst on 21 May 1966 removed the last of the southern lines. In the north, Antwerpen - Hoevenen - Kapellen went on 2 April 1966, and was followed on 1 October 1966 by Brasschaat - Wuustwezel after an electrified life of only 14 years. Closure of Merksem - St-Mariaburg - Kapellen concluded the history of the north-western lines on 27 May 1967, and there were left only the Brasschaat route and the truncated spur to Schoten. They followed on 4 May and 25 May 1968 respectively, and SNCV rail passenger services were then extinct in Antwerpen province.

It should be said that the TAO and its successor, the *Mij voor Intercommunaal Vervoer te AntWerpen (MIVA)* were interested in taking over all these northern lines, and offered to do so provided that the SNCV terminated its buses at the outer termini to act as feeders. The SNCV apparently did its sums and decided it would be uneconomic not to run buses right into the city centre. Nonetheless, tracks were maintained in situ for some years in the hope of a mutually acceptable agreement. Meanwhile, since the standard-gauge shunts at Merksem had finished on 16 June 1967 when the SNCV got notice to quit its workshops and depot in favour of the SNCB, there remained just the short goods line at Mol worked by ageing autorail-tracteurs. At its peak this had handled some 230 000 tonnes a year, and it survived in SNCV hands until 26 June 1970. It was then taken over by a local firm but it was little more than a ghost.

Chapter 8:   The SNCV in Brabant Province

8.1   Brabant: Introduction

All the Belgian provinces had their own patterns but Brabant was always special. Situated in the centre of Belgium, it is a transition area between the Flemish and Walloon cultures, containing the capital Bruxelles/Brussel and one other large city, Leuven/Louvain. In the late 19th century the province was largely agricultural, being devoted particularly to the growing of sugar beet. Of all provinces it is, therefore, the most confusing linguistically since Flemish and French names abound, apparently indiscriminately. Since some of the French ones, especially in Bruxelles, may be more familiar to British ears, they tend to be given preference in this chapter. In areas which are so Flemish that most traces of the French name have vanished in the present day, particularly around Leuven, the Flemish names have preference. Absolute consistency is impossible.

The SNCV did not enter Brabant until 1887 and, initially, was focussed round the capital city of Bruxelles. Brabant, however, despite what the Bruxellois tend to think, is not just Bruxelles and appendages. Indeed the major, then rural, part of the province is well out to the east of the city and, if it had a focus, it was the equally ancient city of Leuven, from which three main routes went: west to Vossem and Bruxelles; east to Tielt and Diest; south to Hamme Mille and Jodoigne/Geldenaken. En route they each met and crossed a whole series of lateral light railways that were much more concerned with joining their villages to the nearest market or main line railway than with either of the big cities; further in the east Brabant had a whole spider's web of rural light railways and many of them connected into other provinces

From the historical point of view, Brabant was divided initially into two major Groupes, based on Bruxelles and Leuven and with a few independent "hangers on". These groupes were formed through allocation of lines to two large concessionaires, the *SA pour l' Exploitation des Voies Ferreés en Belgique (VFB)* in the west and the *SA des CF Vicinaux (CFV)* in the country districts to the east of Bruxelles and around Leuven; the same pattern was retained when the SNCV took control and they fused into the Groupe de Brabant only in 1954. The position, however, was slightly complicated by several detached lines conceded to other operators and by inter-provincial links which were sometimes classed as "Brabant" and sometimes as belonging to another province.

The chapter is therefore written following the histories of the two main groups up to their fusion, with notes on other lines where appropriate. The main exception is due south of Bruxelles where lines of both groupes formed, in effect, a linked whole and where two Groupe de Leuven lines came across to the Bruxelles Groupe once the SNCV took over direct operation. The SNCV did not bring everything together into its Groupe de Brabant until 1954, when services were already in decline.

8.2.   Bruxelles Area - general introduction

Bruxelles and its immediate surroundings is not an easy area to cover coherently. Because of the city's size, and because local politics decreed that the urban trams were conceded to a variety of operators, the SNCV in general penetrated little further than the line of the old city walls. Its five inner termini, reading clockwise from north, were essentially:

* the main line Gare du Nord whence lines went off to north and northwest (via a later link to Molenbeek).

* the ancient Porte de Schaerbeek, and Place St.Josse, in the north-east, into which area lines came from the Leuven direction.

* Place Rouppe down in the south, the only terminus well inside the old walls, from which a detached but important line went due south toward the battlefields of Waterloo and Wavre.

* Boulevard Jamar, by the main-line Midi station, which hosted lines to the south-west via Leerbeek, to Hal and to Enghien on the borders of Hainaut.

* Porte de Ninove in the west, from which the first line in Bruxelles struck out due west to Schepdaal and Ninove.

Of course it was not quite so simple as all that. The Porte de Schaerbeek lines originally terminated a bit further out at Eglise Sté. Marie, were later linked to those at Place St.Josse and were in any case regarded as a Groupe de Louvain operation (ie: they came into Bruxelles, rather than starting from it); the SNCV terminus at Gare du Nord was later moved to Place Rogier when the main line station was resited in the 1920s. In the south, Boulevard Jamar was joined to Place Rouppe as a common terminus; and various cross-links connected the Enghien line to the Ninove one and on to the north-western batch while serving such vital destinations as the city abattoirs

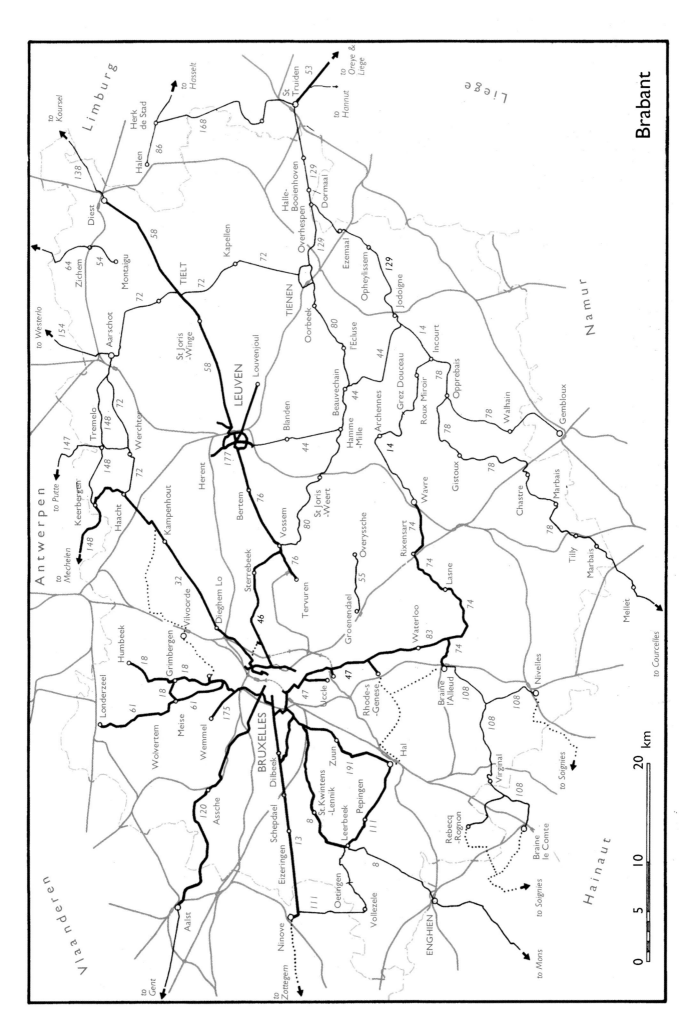

Brabant

99

But in 1894 came the first electric line, to Petite Espinette and on to Waterloo: early motor car & trailer at Espinette Central   (E de Backer collection/SNCV)

Rhode=Saint=Genèse.   Espinette centrale

So far all was comparatively simple, but there was a heavy passenger traffic throughout, especially at the inner end where the line tangled with routes of the standard gauge *CF Economiques (CFE)*, which worked part of the Bruxelles city trams (see appendix 6) and eventually had some mixed gauge stretches. The line from Porte de Ninove to Scheut was electrified in tandem with the CFE in 1905, a section of mixed-gauge being involved at Porte de Ninove, and 4-wheeled cars 9123-31 being allocated to carry the SNCV share of the traffic. Five years later, on 22 March 1910, electrification was extended to Dilbeek (6.71km) and, very soon afterwards, a new electrified link (2.19km, authorised 21 May 1909) was built up north from Vandenheuvel almost parallel to the old walls through the industrial district of Molenbeek to the Gare du Nord where it met Capital 18. It opened on 20 September 1910. There was a fair goods traffic at this time and a spur was also put in to the Etat station of Bruxelles Ouest at Molenbeek St-Jean. Soon after, on 4 January 1912, a further 1.75km spur was authorised south from Dilbeek (Chaussée de Ninove) via Avenue de Scheut and Avenue de l'Acetylene to the Pont du Canal at Anderlecht (Cureghem canal). It is noted by SNCV as opened in 1915 and among other things it finally served the municipal abattoirs at Anderlecht. Meanwhile the final section of the Capital was opened on 19 February 1913, this being in common with Capital 111 (see p.) and joining Burchtdam to the centre of Ninove at Quai de la Dendre. Operating total was then approximately 32.2km.

The other early southwestern line was **Capital 16 (BRUXELLES - ENGHIEN)**, which was seen from the start as an inter-provincial link into Hainaut. Authorised on 21 May 1887 and opened on 1 February 1888, it started from a simple terminus in the Rue de l'Instruction, turning then south west

into the Chaussée de Mons to cross the canal by Cureghem station and carry on through Anderlecht district, the original depot being just west of the canal on a site later occupied by the municipal fire services. This depot was later replaced by the final Cureghem depot and Works in Rue Eloy (this is current spelling although at various times it has been spelled Eloi). Capital 16 then left the city south-westward via the inner

And electric lines soon proliferated; "Manage" type 4w car of series 9287-9335 and trailers at the suburban depot of La Roue/Het Rad.   (SNCV)

suburb of La Roue/Het Rad where there was an intermediate terminus and depot. From there it struck out to Lennick St.Quentin/St-Kwintens-Lennik, reached on 1 February 1888, thence to the then-small town of Leerbeek and on to the provincial border at Enghien on 22 September 1888. There it met Capital 66 and, via Horrues and Casteau, eventually provided a through link to Mons. This, however, was later; the main early links were at the Bruxelles end.

First, in 1888, the SNCV came to an agreement with the urban *Tramways Bruxellois (TB)* whereby the latter's north-south line from Laeken to Anderlecht would be converted to metre gauge, the SNCV having running powers which enabled it to link the radial lines to Enghien, Ninove (in the west) and Humbeek (to the northwest from Gare du Nord; see below). Then, on 28 June 1891, following an authorisation of 19 December 1890, the Bruxelles end of Capital 16 (the Enghien line) was extended from Rue de l'Instruction north to Place du Conseil, then along the rue Rossini to its junction with Rue Bara, north along Rue Bara to Place Bara, then via Boulevard Jamar and Avenue du Midi (later Avenue de Stalingrad) to Place Rouppe/Rouppeplein giving a more convenient town terminus and a total length of 30.28km. Place Rouppe was also inner terminus for Capital 47 to Petite Espinette, opened in October that year; at the Rue Rossini/Rue Bara junction, Capital 16 was joined by a link from the new depot at Rue Eloy which was now being developed to serve Capital 47(qv) and eventually became the main SNCV base in the area; indeed from 1894 the link to Place Rouppe was electrified and, about the same time, a further non-electrified depot link joined Rue Eloy to Rue de l'Instruction via Boulevard de la Revision. A metre gauge goods connection from the Enghien line at Chaussée de Mons into Anderlecht Abattoirs (slaughterhouses) was established at this period also, together with other industrial spurs.

As with the Ninove line there was a considerable inner-suburban traffic, and on 25 November 1909 the section from Place Rouppe through Anderlecht to a subsidiary depot at La Roue/Het Rad was realigned and electrified. The realignment ran down Rue Bara with a subsidiary terminal spur at Midi railway station, past Rue Eloy depot (using the old depot link) and then along Rue E Carpentier, joining Chaussée de Mons near Cureghem railway station; through passengers normally changed trains at la Roue and, though out of sequence, this is probably the best place to note that after WW2 a new underpass below the main railway linked Chaussée de Mons with Rue Carpentier and the SNCV took advantage of this to cut the corner! (at about the same time the electrified line past Midi station was modified to incorporate a long loop via Rue de France to give better interchange). Meanwhile, back to the 1890s. After the realignment the old line via Rue de l'Instruction was discontinued apart from the Abattoirs goods siding which continued for some years - most authorities say until about 1925 but the former Abattoirs administrator noted it as in use up to World War 2. The Enghien line itself escaped closure during World War 1 owing to its strategic value and was handed over to the SNCV along with the other VFB lines in 1920; it was linked to the Ninove line in 1924 by a further spur to Dilbeek from Bon Air.

This is probably the best place, geographically speaking, to mention that the SNCV further complicated this tangle of lines with standard and mixed gauge industrial sidings. One started at an exchange point with the mainline railway just behind Gare du Midi. It ran north and then west to Rue Eloy depot with a spur northward from Rue Eloy to an industrial site (later the Côte d'Or chocolate factory) in Rue Bara. This siding connection faced to Rue Eloy depot, was electrified and used odd home-made tractors "concocted" at Rue Eloy depot. It served various customers but one peculiarity was that the chocolate works had no overhead wire; in consequence, the shunting tractor carried a long reel of feeder cable, one end of which was clipped to an outlet at the works gates, and which provided power rather in the manner of a domestic lawnmower. The other siding was a four-rail mixed gauge affair which ran from the resited Ouest station goods yard in rue Vandermeeren eastward via a bridge over the canal to Anderlecht Abattoirs where it mingled with the sidings coming up from Chaussée de Mons.

The final lines of this cluster were those reaching in from Hal/Halle, down in the south south-west across to Leerbeek and Ninove and northeast into Bruxelles at Anderlecht. They are really out of sequence but are taken here for clarity. The first line was **Capital 111 (HAL - NINOVE)**. It ran from Hal/Halle some 19 km south of Bruxelles, northwest to Leerbeek on the Bruxelles - Enghien route and then, via a dog-leg, west to Vollezeel and north to Ninove (Burchtdam). It had been talked about fairly vaguely since 1886 but was not authorised until 26 June 1901, and even then took a further five years to open its first section. The Leerbeek - Ninove branch started first, from Leerbeek to the hamlet of Oetingen ("Oetingen Road" really) on 14 April 1906 and on to Vollezele on 8 September 1906. On that date, too, the Leerbeek - Hal branch opened and the Vollezele - Ninove section followed on 22 May 1907. It was extended to Ninove (Quai de la Dendre/Denderkaai, by the canal side) on 19 February 1913, trains from Bruxelles (Porte de Ninove) also using this section.

The next line, **CAPITAL 191 BRUXELLES - HAL**, the direct link between Hal and Bruxelles (Anderlecht La Roue) had a slightly more complicated genesis. The SNCV first applied for it in March 1909 but was turned down on grounds that it competed with the mainline railway. A modified trace was submitted the same October but was again refused unless the SNCV agreed to indemnify the main line railways company against loss of revenue. The SNCV promptly agreed but even so, authorisation was not given until 19 February 1913, when the concession was awarded to the VFB. The war then caused further problems. An electric service from Place Rouppe was started as far as Zuun from 23 December 1914 but the link on to Hal (18.4km) was not completed until 1 May 1916 - and with steam traction only; full electrification came only in 1931.

b) Lines north and northwest from Gare du Nord (pl.Rogier)

The first SNCV development north from Bruxelles was **Capital 18 (BRUXELLES - HUMBEEK)**. This line had been discussed since 1886 in the form of a line northwest to Londerzeel with a branch from Humbeek to the town of Grimbergen. The final proposal allowed only for the Bruxelles - Grimbergen - Humbeek line and this was built in two parts. The first section, authorised on 2 July 1887, actually started in the suburb of Laeken at Rue de Vriefe/De Vrierestraat near the railway station. Thence it ran north and east to Gros Tilleul/Dikke Linde and north again through what was then countryside to Grimbergen before turning north east to the little town of Humbeek. It was opened throughout on 14 September 1889.

Clearly, however, a line commencing in an outer suburb was not satisfactory, and over the next few years it was extended inwards to Bruxelles Nord mainline station. Official authorisation was not given until 24 March 1891 but by that time the line had already been extended eastward via Rue Marie-Christine to Pont de Laeken/Laken-brug on 15 May 1890, thence to the Antwerpen road and down the Allée Verte/Groendreef to reach Gare du Nord on 1 May 1891. In the early 1900s, harbour work at Bruxelles docks along the Canal de Charleroi, however, made this section difficult to work and an authorisation of 7 June 1906 allowed a deviation from Nord along what is now Ave Leopold II, splitting off at Place d'Yser and running west via the Place Sanctelette to swing north and rejoin the original route at Laeken (Pl Emil Bockstael). It also permitted electrification and track doubling via this route with some realignment as far as Gros Tilleul. The new deviation was brought into use with steam traction on 1 April 1908 and converted to electric working on 21 April 1909, when the original route was discontinued. Later the same year, on 17 September 1909, electrification was extended to Grimbergen, the depot being transferred there from Laeken, and the electrified section then became purely a passenger line; the Humbeek branch retained a goods service. At this period, operating lengths were given as 11.1km electric and 6.27km steam-operated.

The SNCV had not forgotten its Londerzeel project, and in 1891 applied once more for it as a branch of Bruxelles - Humbeek. This was authorised on 20 March 1893 as **Capital 61 (GRIMBERGEN - LONDERZEEL)**, to run west from Grimbergen to Meise (or Meysse as it was then known) and thence north to Londerzeel via Wolvertem and Impde with an exchange siding at Londerzeel Ouest mainline station (12.75km). It was opened in three stages; Grimbergen - Meise on 24 September 1893; to Wolvertem on 26 June 1894 and on to Londerzeel itself on 1 December 1894. The alignment of this final section was lightly modified before opening under an amendment to the authorisation on 14 May 1894.

These lines effectively completed the Brabant empire of the VFB which settled down to run its various concessions. The only further development up to 1914 was a short branch, originally authorised on 29 October 1910 as **Capital 175 (LAEKEN - WEMMEL)** but soon subsumed in Capital 18. It left the Bruxelles - Humbeek line just north of Laeken depot and ran northwest for 3.6km to Wemmel where there was a subsidiary depot. It was opened on 9 July 1911, being electrified from the start. Meanwhile electrification had spread from Nord to Laeken (Gros Tilleul) on 21 April 1909 and on to Grimbergen via Meise on 17 August of that year.

* *The 1914-18 war and its aftermath*

The Groupe suffered from the 1914-18 war as heavily in proportion to its size as any other concessionaire. First section to be closed and lifted was that from Leerbeek to Hal in April 1916, presumably thought disposable as the direct line Bruxelles - Hal was opened at the end of that month. Capital 61, and Capital 18 north of Grimbergen, went in June 1916 and were followed in September 1917 by Leerbeek - Ninove and Dilbeek - Ninove which were not yet electrified; the Enghien route was spared since it formed a major inter-provincial link with Mons. The *VFB* was one of the first concessionaires to surrender its leases, the SNCV taking physical control early in 1920. It was therefore left to the latter to rebuild and operate both the existing lines and sundry others which came into its new Groupe de Bruxelles. It also applied for a link between Gros Tilleul and Meise, receiving provisional approval on 22 February 1920. Exact opening dates are not available for all lines.

Capital	Section	reopened
13	Dilbeek - Eizeringen	Jun 1919
	Eizeringen - Pamel	Apr 1920
	Pamel - Meerbeke	Aug 1920
	Meerbeke - Ninove	Oct 1920
18	Humbeek - Grimbergen	23 May 1920
61	Grimbergen - Londerzeel	23 May 1920
111	Hal - Leerbeek	Apr 1921

8.2.2 Detached lines of Bruxelles area up to 1920

Not conceded to the VFB, but essentially part of the Bruxelles area lines, were three separated Capitaux worked by small companies or the SNCV itself. One, Capital 47, was physically linked at Place Rouppe, the others (Capitaux 55 and 106) were detached systems. Their early history is interpolated here as they were assimilated into the SNCV Groupe de Bruxelles from its inception as a direct operation in 1919. They were:

Capital	Name	Auth km
47	*Bruxelles - Petite Espinette - Waterloo et Extensions*	18.72
55	*Groenendael - Overyssche (1435mm gauge)*	6.40
106	*Nivelles - Braine-l'Alleud - Virginal et Embranchements*	39.08

Capital 47 (BRUXELLES - PETITE ESPINETTE - WATERLOO et EXTENSIONS) was a very interesting line in many ways. It was a pioneer of SNCV electrification, being its first electric line in service, and also served for experiments with early "benzo-electric" railcars. It eventually had more short branches than any other SNCV line and it was one of the few in Brabant not conceded to a big company. A possible branch to Ixelles (Pl. St Croix) was apparently projected but never built.

Originally the SNCV submitted a project for a single route from Bruxelles to Petite Espinette and then east through Groenendael to Overyssche in the royal forest of Soignies but

 Leerbeek Station.

While, as a link between past and future this is Leerbeek station after electrification in the 1930s - a typical outer Bruxelles junction, with ex-Benzo-electric cars converted to straight electrics. (SNCV)

locomotives of the period, especially at peak hours, and "Le Vert Chasseur" was a very popular rendezvous with the Bruxellois from the southern part of the city. Consequently the SNCV decided to use the line for a trial of the new-fangled electricity and to extend it to Petite Espinette, another favoured weekend spot. It came to an agreement with the *Union Electrizitats Gesellschaft (UEG)* of Berlin to build and electrify the whole line. A new operating company, the *SA pour l'Exploitation du CF Vicinal de Bruxelles à Petite Espinette et Extensions (BPE)*, was formed on 25 January 1892 and resumed steam operation of the existing line as an interim measure on 6 February that year. Electrification was on the Thomson-Houston system, with current at 500 volts dc supplied from a substation at Anderlecht depot via overhead wires and collected by trolley poles; the first cars resembled motored six-window SNCV standard coaches. They were built by Verhaegen and Franco Belge.

politics intervened, the Petite Espinette - Groenendael section being refused. This indeed was a running sore to the SNCV for many years; it was always trying to link Groenendael direct to Bruxelles and, as we shall see, never succeeded. Making the best of a bad job, the Societé put in a bid for the line to Petite Espinette and shelved the rest. As built the line ran from Place Rouppe, the only SNCV terminus actually inside the old walls, southeast through suburbs, parkland and then open country to reach, eventually, the old battlefield of Waterloo and was entirely roadside or in the street. The first part, 11.2km from Bruxelles (Place Rouppe) to Petite Espinette/Klein Hut, was formally authorised on 21 April 1891. Its first section, 6km to a cafe called "Le Vert Chasseur"/"Groene Jager", was tentatively opened on 1 October 1891, together with an access spur to Cureghem depot over Capital 16. It was provisionally operated by the *VFB* with existing equipment, but because of disagreements with the local authorities, they gave up, services ceasing again on 2 November 1891.

There was then a pause while the SNCV considered the matter. The major problem was a steep and long gradient from "Le Vert Chasseur" which put far too much strain on steam

With such a novel technique, progress was slow and hesitant. Official trials were carried out on 19 May 1894 and the line was opened officially on 5 June 1894 as far as Le Vert Chasseur. Public services began on 21 June but were marred by a series of electrical defects and broken axles. They had to be suspended on 14 July to sort things out, steam trains taking over until the full electric line to Petite Espinette was reopened on 1 October. The line then settled down, becoming sufficiently popular to need trailers on most trains; because of the gradients such trains had air brakes supplied by an axle-driven compressor on the trailer. The traffic was such that the line from Place Rouppe to Vivier d'Oie, about 8km, was doubled in 1895, and in 1901 a short spur was built at the inner end from St Gilles (Turkijestraat) to Place Loix just outside the old walls. Special workings to Petite Espinette left there on high days and

holidays, thus escaping the congestion encountered between Place Rouppe and the Porte de Hal. The spur was authorised on 8 May 1900 and opened on 1 May 1901.

Once electrification had proved successful and profitable, the SNCV naturally planned to extend the line further. The original intention had, in any case, been for a long line through Petite Espinette and Waterloo down to Braine l'Alleud and thence east to Wavre - all the old battlefield territory of 1815 in fact! The concentration on experimental electrification had thrown this into the background but nevertheless discussions on at least the Braine l'Alleud - Wavre bit had been going on simultaneously and it was actually built in 1897-98, a short line from Waterloo (Gare) to a junction at Mont St Jean following on 15 June 1901, though allocated to the *CF Vicinaux* and so not strictly within this section of the story. The SNCV's intention, however, was to connect with these existing lines so their early history is interpolated here.

l'Alleud - Wavre route, to the village of Waterloo, ending at Waterloo (Gare). It was a very modest affair with an operating length of only 5.47km. Authorised on 13 June 1897 and opened on 15 June 1901, it ran due north into Waterloo village, pausing at the church (Waterloo Eglise) before turning west to the standard-gauge station. It became important only when Capital 47 was extended south from Espinette Centrale to Waterloo (Eglise) on 13 August 1910 to give a through link between Bruxelles and the southern lines.

Back, however, to Petite Espinette. A first bid for extension in 1900 brought long arguments with the Railways Ministry which claimed that the line would offer unfair competition, so authorisation to extend to Waterloo (Eglise) and the connection to Capital 83 (Waterloo - Mont St.Jean) was not obtained until 4 August 1910. The extension was opened to Waterloo Eglise with running powers to Waterloo Gare on 13 August 1910, suspiciously soon afterwards, though still electrified only as far as Espinette Centrale/Midden Hut which

Detached lines 2: The Nivelles - Virginal - Brain-le-Comte system was quickly converted to autorails as they became available. A typical train with ex-steam trailer at Virginal Canal (collection E de Backer)

In fact, the first part of the chain to open was a complete system which had been authorised and built down in the south of the province west of Wavre. This was **Capital 74 (BRAINE-l'ALLEUD - WAVRE)/(EIGENBRAKEL - WAVER)** which had been argued about since 1886-7 with various proposals. It was finally authorised on 27 November 1895 but not opened until three years later, in stages: Braine-l'Alleud (Etat station) east through Mont-St-Jean to Renipont (Chapelle-St.Lambert) on 22 March 1898; on to a standard-gauge junction at Rixensart on 16 July 1898, and finally, on 11 March 1899, to Wavre (Etat station) where it linked to Capital 14. The depot was at Lasne between Mont-St-Jean and Renipont, the operating length was 21.56km, and there was a private branch to Wavre sugar refinery. At Braine-l'Alleud it terminated on the east side of the standard gauge, and between Rixensart and Maransart (west of Lasne) mixed gauge was laid to serve local industry; the mixed gauge was removed in 1936.

Last link in the eventual chain was a short one, authorised as **Capital 83 (WATERLOO - MONT-ST-JEAN)**. It ran north from Mont-St-Jean (Monument Gordon), on the Braine-

was a convenient transfer point. The remainder was to be steam-worked to minimise the competitive element and was provisionally operated by the SNCV itself. Application had, however, also been made for a branch west from Espinette Centrale through Rhode-St-Genese/St-Genesius-Rode to Alsembourg which had also been approved on 4 August 1910. The first 2km of this line into Rhode-St-Genese village was opened on 7 November 1911, and the SNCV then entrusted operation to the *Cie Internationale d'Electricité* of Liége on 1 February 1912 "at least until 30 April 1916" when the Bruxelles - Espinette concession would come up for review. The reason was that the concessionaire was promoting thermal-electric railcars (Benzo-electriques) on the Pieper system and was providing eight for the SNCV. The concession was granted in order to give the company as good a chance as possible of trying out and proving its products, and it was expected that arrangements would also be made with the CFV for the "Benzos" to work south from Waterloo over Capital 83. In practice it appears they took over the Espinette Centrale - Waterloo section of Capital 47 from 1911.

Meanwhile other short extensions and improvements were in prospect. The original line had been doubled as far as Petite Espinette in 1909 and the projected Rhode-St-Genese - Alsembourg branch was opened to Rhode standard-gauge station on 20 September 1913, being electrified from the start, but went no further. Just prior to the outbreak of war, however, a totally new branch was authorised on 3 February 1913 to run from St Gilles (Ma Campagne) near the inner end of Capital 47 southwest to the state observatory (Observatoire/Sterrewacht) at Uccle/Ukkel. It was electric from the start, the first section to Avenue Longchamps opening on 18 October 1913 but the remainder was not opened until 1 November 1915 when other lines were about to be torn up. It brought the operating length to 26.94km. These lines appear to have been handed over to the BPE, which clearly did not give satisfaction. In 1916 the SNCV terminated the concession under pressure from the public shareholders, but the war prevented a new tender. The SNCV had, perforce, to renew the concession on the same terms "until six months after peace is declared". Presumably the line was worked with steam traction since fuel shortages prevented use of the benzo-electric railmotors. The BPE complex survived the war intact and even slightly extended except for the Rhode St.Genese branch which was closed in September 1917. The lines run by the CFV, however, fared much worse, the Braine l'Alleud - Wavre section being closed and lifted in 1916-17.

a solo railcar in a typical village setting.   (B Y Williams)

The BPE gave up its concession as early as possible, in November 1919, and the SNCV took over the whole complex, attaching it to the Groupe de Bruxelles. The "Benzos" were used again, briefly, Espinette Centrale - Rhode-St Genese was restored to service from 24 May 1922 and on 30 December 1923 the remaining stretch was electrified right through to Mont St. Jean (Monument Gordon), the spur at Waterloo (Eglise - Gare), disused since the war, being abandoned under an authorisation of 10 February 1922. Capital 83 was assimilated into Capital 47 and came under the Groupe de Bruxelles. The proposed extension from Rhode-St-Genese to Alsembourg was quietly dropped, as was a proposed line from Alsembourg to Braine-l'Alleud/Eigenbrakel. The system was completed on 17 October 1927 with a short branch off Capital 47 from Vivier d'Oie (between Vert Chasseur and Espinette) to Place St-Job (authorised 16 June 1926), but otherwise became

just a link in the southern chain of lines. The rest of its history will be found under section 8.5.

Of the other two detached lines, **Capital 55 (GROENENDAEL - OVERYSSCHE)** was one of only four standard-gauge railways operated by the SNCV, though it was originally planned to be metre gauge and about twice its eventual length. In 1887 the SNCV proposed a line from Bruxelles to Overyssche/Overijse via Petite Espinette and Groenendael/Groenendaal. The section between Espinette and Groendael through the royal Foret de Soignies was refused firmly and finally: no rail "pollution" through the forest. Since the remaining length to Overyssche was only some 6.5km and there was likely to be a heavy goods traffic, the SNCV decided to make the line standard gauge with a connection to the Etat Belge's Namur - Bruxelles railway at Groenendael. It was authorised on 15 February 1892 and, after a fairly leisurely building period, the line opened on 15 July 1894 with a total length of 6.71km. Operation was initially conceded to the specially formed *SA La Ruche pour l' Exploitation de Chemins de Fer Vicinaux en Belgique (LR)*, which quickly found the task not to its liking and surrendered its lease two years later. The SNCV perforce had to take over direct control from 1896 to 29 May 1901 when it persuaded the *SA de CF Provinciaux (CFP)*, then busily acquiring concessions in Vlaanderen, to take it on. The CFP presumably did not regret it. The line had a steadily increasing traffic in coke and manure to service an expanding industry of growing grapes under greenhouse conditions. It also took the products away in bulk and had no less than seven industrial sidings of one kind and another; at its peak, some 28,000 wagon loads a year moved over its rails and there was also commuter traffic to Bruxelles via the main line railway.

Its route was simple, through the pleasant Yse/Ijse valley with only one serious gradient, on the approach to Groenendael station. Only two stations, Hoeylaert (later Hoeilaart) and Overyssche itself, where the depot was, had any substantial buildings but the line was solidly built and adequately equipped with 8xx-series locomotives and appropriate stock. Just prior to the 1914-18 war the SNCV even applied for a 4.9km extension to Huldenburg but nothing was ever done. Instead, war came and most of the stock was requisitioned for military use (a disadvantage of being standard gauge!) while in October 1917 the occupying power closed the line entirely and lifted the track. After the war, SNCV took over direct control, reopening the line on 2 October 1919 with most of the original equipment painfully reclaimed, though the Etat Belge had to help out for a while and even sold the SNCV a wagon (C 5100). Its "loan engine", however, was soon replaced by 823, one of the few SNCV conventional locomotives. The line was nominally attached to the Groupe de Bruxelles but in practice continued its independent existence.

Its decline started in 1925 when the SNCV began a direct Bruxelles - Overyssche bus service, though an attempt ten years later to turn this into a trolleybus was refused; "no electric wires through the forest", even though the vehicles had been bought. Despite a reported trial in 1926 of a petrol railmotor, passenger traffic dropped sharply, even more so after a parallel bus service was introduced in 1937, and even goods traffic declined slowly from about 1930 onward. World War II actually had little effect save for a short break in 1940, though locomotives were "borrowed" from time to time to shunt military installations in the forest. After 1945, however, the decline continued, passenger trains being finally withdrawn from 13 February 1949. Even the economy of a new diesel locomotive, rather speciously numbered ART 500, could not save it, the line losing nine-tenths of its goods traffic at a stroke in May 1955 when new tariffs came into force. From then on the only big customer was Hoeilaart sawmills, and in December 1962 the last regular trains ran; the goods service was officially withdrawn on 1 July 1963. A few special workings enlivened the following year, but in April 1964 the axe fell. The Groenendael - Hoeilaart section (2.06km) plus ART 500 was sold to the sawmill on 19 March 1964, and the remainder lay derelict until scrapped in mid-1966. The sawmill never used its acquisition, and the section was lifted in May 1968, ART 500 being sold.

The other detached system south of Bruxelles, **Capital 106 (NIVELLES - BRAINE-L'ALLEUD - VIRGINAL et Embrts)**, was one of the odder rural systems in Brabant, and was a sprawling system which would have been even more straggling if all its projected extensions had materialised. For most of its life it was at least theoretically separated from its nearest neighbour by just the width of a standard-gauge railway. It was planned for electrification from the start but always remained steam and diesel; the electrification proposals found no takers. The area lies south of Bruxelles, a little south and west of the Waterloo battlefield. The original line, authorised on 23 November 1900, after the usual to-ing and fro-ing, started from the industrial town of Nivelles, famous for its rolling stock factory, and ran north to a country junction at Bois-Seigneur-Isaac. This section was opened on 6 September 1903 and work started on branches east to Braine-l'Alleud/Eigenbrakel and west to the village of Virginal. The Braine-l'Alleud branch was opened fairly quickly thereafter, on 9 October 1904, and was quite straightforward. It terminated on the west side of the Bruxelles - La Louvière main line railway and thus did not quite connect with Capital 74 to Wavre which started on the other side of the tracks. The Virginal branch got as far as Ittre by 1 May 1904, but then had to wait for three further years of arguing before it was allowed through to Virginal standard-gauge station on 10 August 1907 (23.04km).

The SNCV could not find anyone willing to operate it, so assumed direct control. In spite of this, the Société appears to have been determined to extend the system, and as early as 1901-02 had obtained permission for a branch southwest from Virginal through the industrial area round Braine-le-Comte (equally famous as a railway town). Originally this was to carry on to Enghien out to the northwest. Then it was modified to reach for Soignies, not very far to the southwest, but both projects were turned down; they paralleled state railway branches and would undoubtedly have offered unnecessary competition. Moreover they twined back and forth across the provincial boundary, leading to possible financial complications.

What did transpire was 14.9km of line from Virginal through Planoit and south to Braine-le-Comte/'s Gravenbrakel by a roundabout route, with a spur en route northwest from Planoit junction to Rebecq-Rognon/Roosbeek. It was authorised on 21 September 1907 and built slowly, with long arguments, in bits. In 1910 a service link with the Wavre line

was put in at Braine l'Alleud; a short link at Virginal (station - village) opened on 14 February 1911; a detached section from Rebecq to Planoit junction on 20 March 1912, and the line on to Braine-le-Comte on 1 June 1912. Finally the branch opened throughout from Virginal on 20 March 1913. Once more the SNCV offered its property around, and once more there were no takers. Yet simultaneously the SNCV had received authorisation for two further lines, allocated to Hainaut but connecting to Capital 106 at various points. One, Capital 169, was a wandering, east-west link of 29.16km between Soignies and Nivelles. The other, Capital 174, revived the Soignies - Braine-le-Comte project but took it wide of the standard gauge in a roundabout ramble via Steenkerke and Pt Roeulx, with an equally rambling branch from Steenkerke to Rebecq-Rognon, a total 23km. Not surprisingly, the communes concerned were unwilling to contribute, and the projects died stillborn on the outbreak of war in 1914.

The existing lines were closed and lifted during 1916-17 and the SNCV clearly did not regard their restoration as a priority. Braine-l'Alleud - Nivelles was reopened on 9 April 1921, Bois-Seigneur-Isaac to Virginal on 1 November 1921, and the branches not until 16 April 1922, the system coming under operational control of the new *SNCV Groupe de Bruxelles*. There was no more talk of extension but the lines were "motorised" during the 1930s, and in 1939 the idea of electrification surfaced again, possibly to help provide a Nivelles - Bruxelles link. The 1939-45 war put paid to that idea and also to the western branches. The lines from Planoit junction to Rebecq and to Braine-le-Comte were closed on 2 February 1943 and lifted; they were never restored. The remainder kept running with standard four-wheel autorails, though bus replacement began as early as 1949. On 10 September 1953, the line was even formally joined to the main system by an electrified spur over the railway at Braine-l'Alleud, just in time to be assimilated into the new Groupe de Brabant. It lasted another six years, the whole surviving system closing with effect from 5 July 1959, although goods services had been withdrawn between Nivelles, Braine l'Alleud, Virginal and Planoit the previous autumn from 13 October 1958.

8.2.3 SNCV Groupe de Bruxelles 1919-1954 (Groupe 70)

* *post-war assimilation of various lines*

As it took over the lines in Brabant province, the SNCV made some adjustments to their "ownership". In particular, the Bruxelles group in due course took over Capitaux 47, 83 (combined with 47 in 1923) and 74 (BRAINE-L'ALLEUD - WAVRE). It also assumed responsibility for the two detached lines, Capital 55 (GROENENDAEL - OVERYSSCHE) and Capital 106 (NIVELLES - VIRGINAL et EMBRANCHEMENTS). By 1923, therefore, all SNCV lines in the Bruxelles area were under direct SNCV control, and it was decided in principle to electrify them as soon as money became available. As a start, several series of post-war electric motor cars were drafted in to bolster numbers, among them a group of bogie cars originally destined for Bogota in South America (the "Bogotas" 9623-8) used mainly to Uccle (Observatoire) and lasting till 1928 when they went to Oostende; a series of motor luggage vans (9967-71) was produced to handle the considerable market-garden traffic which still existed.

As noted above, first electrification was the branch to Rhode-St-Genese on 24 May 1922 and this was followed by Espinette Centrale - Waterloo (Eglise) - Mont-St-Jean

The link to the Leuven group after modernisation. Wavre station with: railcar AR 213 for Jodoigne; electric car for Bruxelles; a connecting franchised bus. (JW Smith)

(Monument Gordon) on 30 December 1923; at the same date, the short spur to Waterloo station, virtually unused since 1910, was officially closed. The line became route W, with short workings to Espinette (route E) and Rhode-St-Genese (route Rh and then R). It was very popular with summer visitors to the Waterloo battlefield, and nine bogie toastrack trailers ("Oran" class) were bought to serve it, hauled by bogie motor cars of the Titanic class. It was about this time, too, that cream livery was adopted for electric stock in place of the former dark green. To provide the extra power that was obviously going to be needed, the SNCV built its own generating station at Rue Fransmann; all Bruxelles lines except Haecht used trolley poles at this time to collect the current and the southern line was double-track as far as Waterloo.

The group also tried another ploy to link the Groenendael - Overyssche line to Bruxelles. In 1924, as previously related, the SNCV was permitted to submit bus routes for authorisation where it felt that a tramway was too expensive. The first of these was actually Etterbeek - Overyssche, for which the SNCV already held a rail concession, and the bus route was inaugurated the same year with the Societé's very first bus AB 301. It solved the problem of "wires or steam" through the forest, but was not much help to the existing tramway since it simply funnelled off passenger traffic.

* ***development between the wars***
The inter-war years history of the Bruxelles lines is mainly concerned with electrification since it was carried out even in the unstable early 1920s. In the west, the first "country" part of Capital 13, Bruxelles - Ninove, was electrified from Dilbeek to Schepdael on 15 September 1925, followed on 15 March 1926 by the section to Eizeringen and on 16 April 1927 to Ninove (Burchtdam), giving routes D and N (later Ni). The final part, over Capital 111 to Ninove (Quai de la Dendre), was not electrified until 31 December 1933, but the line was notable for a number of innovations in the mid-1920s. The SNCV's first automatic substation was established at Eizeringen to provide current for the outer sections, and a new pattern of automatic signalling was introduced; in 1929 the line was used for early multiple-unit trials. These involved four-wheelers of the 9695-714 (Seneffe) class working in formations of two motor cars with three trailers sandwiched between them. It was not very successful, and the rakes were soon split up and sent elsewhere, replaced first by 9715-28 series (Braine-le-Comte)

four-wheelers towing trailers and later by Standard bogie sets. The reason for all this was an intensive suburban traffic which was worked through to the Gare du Nord over the link through Molenbeek. Meanwhile, to provide extra power, the eight "Benzo-electric" cars had been converted to straight electrics with maximum-traction bogies in 1925, and allocated mainly to the eastern routes. In the north, Grimbergen - Humbeek was electrified as route H on 6 August 1925, and the branch through Meise to Wolvertem followed on 1 May 1926 as route L barré. The remainder to Londerzeel followed on 26 October 1930, but Wolvertem was always the logical terminus for most suburban traffic.

1927 saw quite a spate of work. On Capital 47, a new road between Espinette and Waterloo allowed double track to be placed in the centre of the carriageway, and, as recorded elsewhere, the short 0.6km branch was opened from Vivier-d'Oie to Place St-Job on 17 October 1927, being worked from Place Rouppe as route V; the Dilbeek - Ninove section was electrified on Capital 13 and a new link line, mainly for goods, was put in from Itterbeek to Anderlecht on Capital 16 (15 May 1929). There was then a pause until the early 1930s when a steady programme of improvement began. First, perhaps, was the development of the "Standard" bogie cars in concert with SELVOP. Bruxelles urgently needed such equipment for the suburban passenger traffic and got an initial batch of ten (9732-41) which it used mainly on the Espinette line, releasing the Titanics for workings to Haecht. In the north, a new link, from Gros Tilleul to Meise, was authorised on 10 September 1928 and opened in stages by 25 April 1932 as described below. Several sections of busy track in the suburbs were doubled.

Over the next few years, electrification affected most of the lines as can be seen from Table 8A. Basically the Braine - l'Alleud - Wavre line was linked directly to Bruxelles as route W between 1930 and 1933, trains running out to either Braine-l'Alleud or Wavre as timetables dictated. The inner section of Capital 16 was electrified to Leerbeek in 1931-32 for suburban traffic, and in the northwest an entirely new line was built from Capital 18 near Place d'Yser westward through Zellik to join Capital 120 (Vlaanderen) at Asse/Assche on 9 May 1936; for nearly a year the last section from Zellik (Molen) to Assche/Asse was run by autorails until electrification to Aalst was completed on 25 July 1937. A turning circle was laid in at Place d'Yser to take the heavy rush hour trains.

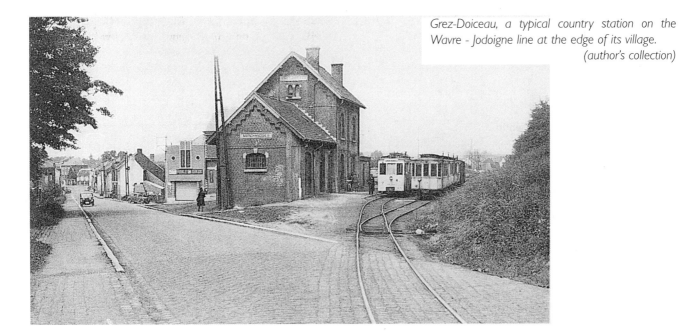

Grez-Doiceau, a typical country station on the Wavre - Jodoigne line at the edge of its village.
(author's collection)

In Bruxelles in the 1930s there were contrasts: the modern image as portrayed by one of the new Standard power cars with a train of purpose-built trailers in Allée Verte (SNCV)

And what can only be described as a lash-up. Fairly primitive multiple units for shuttles from Gare du Nord, composed of modernised 4-w cars of the Manage (9287-335) series with similar, trolley-pole fitted trailers (SNCV)

Capital	Section	Date
13/6	Ninove (Burchtdam) - Quai de la Dendre	31 Dec 1933
13/6	Anderlecht - Bon Air/Goedelucht	23 Dec 1928
	Bon Air - Itterbeek	15 May 1929
16	la Roue - Lennick-St-Quentin	28 Dec 1931
	Lennick-St-Quentin - Leerbeek	27 Mar 1932
18	Gros Tilleul - Schapenstraat and	27 Oct 1932
	Schapenstraat - Strombeek (Batavia)	1 Mar 1935
61	Batavia - Meise (junction)	25 Apr 1935
74	Braine-l' Alleud - Mont-St-Jean	18 Oct 1930
	Mont-St-Jean - Lasne	2 Nov 1931
	Lasne - Rixensart (station)	2 Oct 1932
	Rixensart - Wavre (station)	9 Apr 1933
120	Bruxelles - Zellik (Trois Rois)	3 Sep 1935
	Zellik (Trois Rois - Molen)	1 Oct 1936
	Molen - Asse/Assche - Aalst	25 Jul 1937
191	Zuen/Zuun - Leeuw-St-Pierre - Hal	16 Feb 1931

authorised as **Capital 203 BRUXELLES (Centenaire) - LONDERZEEL** on 27 December 1937. To work this latter service, the SNCV Cureghem works rapidly "knocked up" a four-wheeled electric locomotive (10293) using a spare Nivelles truck and an old Groenendael - Overyssche trailer body (C 2005) as the basis. The SNCV also initiated several through routes for the exhibition, as follows:

letter	colours	details
Ex	Green/red	Midi - Anderlecht - Molenbeek - Expo
Ex	Green/white	Scheut - Molenbeek - Expo
Ex	n/k	Chaussée de Ninove - Molenbeek - Expo
A	Pink/Pink	Midi - Expo

At about this time, it also acquired a series of fine steel-bodied four-wheeled motor cars from Braine-le-Comte (10111-25) to work the suburban traffic up from Gare du Nord and ran through-trams from all over the place. The 101xx series must also have been a pleasant change for the customers because Cureghem, worried about congestion at the cramped Nord terminus during the previous year, had put

While during WW2, 4-w cars and trailers also worked the Groep Leuven route to Sterrebeek. This is 9518 with an ex-steam trailer
(collection P Roovers.)

The other major work was another completely new electrified line running from Gros Tilleul, on Capital 18, through western Strombeek to Meise on Capital 61. It was intended to provide a direct route to Wolvertem and Londerzeel to replace the circuitous route via Grimbergen. Discussions for this had started in 1908, had been interrupted by the war and then revived afterwards in rather leisurely fashion. It was approved on 10 September 1928 and a short section was completed in 1932, but then there was a pause. What hurried matters on was a major cultural event, the 1935 World Exhibition, which was held on the Heysel plateau above Laeken. To serve this the cut-off was brought into use in April 1935 as a new route L, services on the Meise - Grimbergen link being reduced to a few shuttles and depot workings. At the same time, a third rail was laid in between Londerzeel SNCB and the exhibition site to enable direct transfer of exhibits and stores in standard-gauge wagons. When it became clear that this site would continue to be used for public events the third rail was made permanent, extended to Avenue de Meise and officially

together from stock parts a series of crude twin-car shuttle units (10037-40 and 9001"): these consisted of two short-wheelbase four-wheel cars permanently close-coupled and operable from either end of the set. They must have been successful even though a little spartan since they lasted a long time, being replaced by "N" class bogie cars from 1954-on.

* the 1939-45 war and after

The 1935 exhibition was certainly the highpoint of Bruxelles group development before the 1939-45 war, and the system was in very good shape when the pressures of that conflict were thrust upon it. The western and southern lines particularly played a vital part in providing cross-provincial links and in carrying food and fuel supplies to the capital. The group remained almost intact, the only losses on its main system being Hal - Leerbeek (closed 17 May 1943, reopened 31 July 1949), and removal of the third rail from most of the Londerzeel line at various times between 1940 and 1944. On the other hand, after another "false alarm" about electrification in 1939, Capital 106, the Nivelles - Virginal cluster, was chopped

Meanwhile the SNCV had been engaged in considerable parallel development to the east of Bruxelles city. As noted above, the lines on this side of Bruxelles were always considered as part of the Leuven group, and the first one was under consideration as early as 1885. This, **Capital 32 (BRUXELLES - HAECHT)**, was a proposal for a largely roadside line from Bruxelles to Haecht/Haacht some 20km to the northeast and, after some hesitation, was authorised on 17 November 1888. It cut across a triangle of standard-gauge railways, so did not compete directly but, even so, progress was slow. The first section, opened on 1 August 1889, was a purely

at the TB's request on 1 July 1908 (Rue Eenens - Schaerbeek station) and 3 June 1912 (St-Marie - Rue Eenens - St-Croix), at which time the operating length was 6.40km electric and 20.80km steam; the inner (Bruxelles) end of the Haecht route as far as Dieghem/Diegem (Lo) followed on 13 June 1914. It was proposed to electrify the whole route but war temporarily stopped the project. Apparently urban workings were for some years operated by the TB using ex BIB metre gauge equipment.

At St-Josse-ten-Noode (Pl.St Josse), about halfway between Rue Eenens and St-Croix, SNCV Capital 32 was eventually

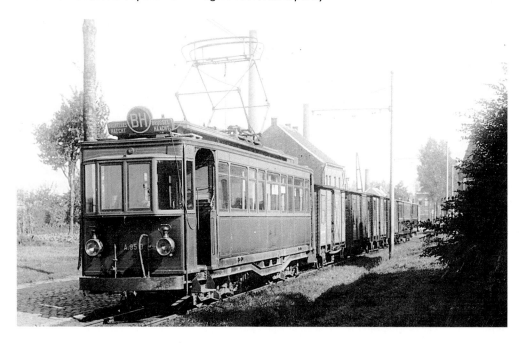

The "standard" view of a Titanic power car on a mixed train on the Haacht line.

(SNCV)

suburban one, north from Pl St-Croix/H-Kruisplein just outside the old ramparts, to Rue Eenens/General Eenenstraat and thence west and south again to Eglise Sté-Marie/St-Mariakerk at Schaerbeek/Schaarbeek. A short branch, authorised on 30 January 1889, continued north from Rue Eenens to Schaerbeek standard-gauge station, being opened on 1 August 1890. The "main line" from Rue Eenens east to Haecht standard-gauge station, where the depot was situated, followed on 1 September 1890 and was extended to Haecht (dorp) on 3 December 1891. It ran first through the streets to the suburb of Haeren whence it continued along the roadside via Dieghem (Lo) to Haecht. Its operation was initially conceded to the *SA des CF à Voie Etroite de Bruxelles à Ixelles-Boendael (BIB)*, then running various urban tramways in the area but, in late 1889, was transferred to the BIB's successor, the *Tramways Bruxellois (TB)* by a royal authorisation of 13 October. It should be mentioned here that the TB and its predecessors also worked a tramline south from St-Croix toward Boitsfort and one from St-Josse to Tervueren.

The Haecht trains actually terminated at Eglise Sté.Marie, a freight spur to Schaerbeek station being authorised on 31 January 1899 and the (TB) urban steam trams terminating at Rue Eenens. The Haecht line was very soon transferred to the *CF Vicinaux (CFV)* at the TB's request; presumably the latter did not consider operating rural lines as one of its functions. The CFV took over on 1 February 1902 and had no cause to regret it; the line always had a heavy market-garden traffic into Bruxelles and, as the most direct route to Haecht, had a fair passenger traffic too. The original urban lines were electrified

linked to the next Leuven group line, **Capital 46 (BRUXELLES - STERREBEEK - VOSSEM)**. Capital 46 again had a complex early history, and for much the same reasons as its close neighbour. From 1883 on, there had been attempts to provide a tram from the St-Josse area to the municipal cemetery at Evere, some 3.5km to the east. First the *SA du Tramway Bruxelles - Evere* opened a standard gauge line in 1883 and then in 1888 the *SA des Tramways de l'Est de Bruxelles* took over. They did run the line for a short time but ceased operating in 1889, at which point they ran up against the SNCV, which had its own plans. Basically it wanted to build a two-pronged route out to Overyssche to the southeast; as we have seen, the SNCV was always trying desperately to get direct links between Bruxelles and either Overyssche or Groenendael but never actually succeeded in doing anything but link those two places together. What it finally obtained, on 17 February 1891, was authorisation for a metre-gauge line east from Evere to Sterrebeek. It then took over existing rights in the St-Josse (Pl Madou) - Evere tramway and proceeded to convert that to metre gauge and build the rest. The first section from Pl Madou over a steep gradient to Pl Dailly and on to the commune of Schaerbeek (Ave du Tir National/Schietbaan), was opened provisionally on 19 July 1891 to cope with crowds going to a festival, while definitive services started on 2 August 1891. The extension to Evere cemetery followed on 9 September that year and the main line carried on from a junction at Bon Coin, just short of the cemetery. It opened in two stages, to Woluwe-St-Etienne/St-Stevens-Woluwe on 13 September 1891 and on to Sterrebeek (11.3km) on 15 October 1892.

Operation of the whole system was initially conceded to the Ixelles - Boendael concern which ran it virtually as two separate lines: St-Josse - Evere Cemetery was electrified from 31 March 1897 to a total of 3.53 km and using cars very similar to SNCV No 1-24, while the steam trams normally ran in as far as Pl Dailly, terminating there to avoid the final gradient to St-Josse (Madou) which was virtually abandoned. It was not particularly profitable but was extended on 21 July 1897 to Vossem (authorised 12 January 1897). As with Bruxelles - Haecht, operation passed to the TB, as heirs of the BIB, in 1900 and to the CFV on 1 February 1902. Once again the CFV did not regret it, the line becoming one of those that regularly paid a second dividend. At Vossem, also, it met **Capital 76 (LOUVAIN - TERVUEREN)** which was a result of development back at Leuven/Louvain, where the SNCV had already set about opening up the east and north of the province.

This was achieved through **Capital 58 (LOUVAIN - THIELT NOTRE DAME - DIEST)** which had been talked about since 1887 but was not authorised until 29 August 1892. It ran northeastward from Leuven station, following the main road through Kessel Lo, Linden and St-Joris-Winge/Winghe-St-Georges, which was reached on 17 July 1893. The remaining stretch through Onze Lieve Vrouw Tielt/Thielt (Notre Dame), hereinafter Tielt for short, followed on 1 November 1893, though regular services did not start until 3 January 1894. It ended at the Louvense Poort of Diest since the town council did not want nasty smelly trains within their town. The line, connecting a wide area with Leuven. prospered and was soon paying second dividends with money to spare. The depot was near Diest, and operating length was 26.85km. It should be noted here that there were various schemes for extending into Diest centre but nothing was done until 1911. On 25 October 1911 a short spur was authorised, joining the existing terminus to Diest railway station and a line from Diest to Koursel; it was opened on 11 December 1912.

The provincial structure of systems springing from Bruxelles and Leuven was now becoming firmly established. The next Leuven group line to open, though not in Capital sequence, was actually that **Capital 76 (LOUVAIN - TERVUEREN/LEUVEN - TERVUREN)** mentioned above. This was a blessedly simple line, authorised on 20 February 1896 and running southwest from Leuven station over common track with Capital 44 and then along a main road to Vossem (where it soon met Capital 46) and finally to the Bruxelles suburb of Tervueren. It was officially opened throughout on 10 May 1897, though there are suggestions that regular services did not start until five days later.

It was followed chronologically by the first part of **Capital 72 (HAECHT - AERSCHOT - TIRLEMONT/HAACHT - AARSCHOT - TIENEN,)** an important member of the lateral strands in the web that made a near semicircle around the north, east and south east of the province. This long rambling line was authorised on 20 September 1895 but was beset by bridge-building troubles, so was constructed in two parts from the town of Aerschot, to the east of Haecht. According to local records, the southern section was opened southeast to Tielt on 15 September 1897 and extended south to Tienen on 21 January 1898. A bridge over the Dyle at Werchter, however, plus arguments about the exact route, delayed the Haecht branch until 3 December 1901. (The SNCV considered it was opened throughout on 15 June 1901; you can take your pick). It may be worth noting that at Werchter it eventually shared tracks with the Lier - Werchter line between the standard-gauge station and Rue de Tremeloo. As might be

expected from such a long route, it was not a great money-earner though it undoubtedly helped to develop its territory.

The "inner ring" of lines encircling Leuven was then completed by **Capital 80 (TERVUEREN - TIRLEMONT)/(TERVUREN - TIENEN)**, and that was a true link completing a circle of lines that had Leuven as their centre and Capitaux 44, 58 and 76 as the spokes; there was a proposal for a fourth spoke, 22.9km from Leuven northward to Aerschot but it never materialised, being stopped by World War I. Capital 80 was authorised on 11 March 1897 and opened in three stages. The first section, from Tienen SNCV to Beauvechain/Bevekom was completed on 16 June 1902 having a common section with Capital 44 into Hamme Mille. The line from Hamme Mille on to St-Joris-Weert /Weert-St-Georges (standard-gauge link) followed on 15 June 1904, but the final section, to meet Capitaux 46 and 76 at Vossem, was not completed until 3 April 1905. Its operating length of 38.98km presumably included common sections.

The last line conceded to the CFV, and thus officially in the Groupe de Louvain, was **Capital 78 (COURCELLES - INCOURT - GEMBLOUX)**, which tends to get ignored by historians just because it was long, complex and crossed provincial borders (ie in some ways it belongs to the "miscellaneous" antennae discussed at the end of this chapter). It started in 1890 as a proposal for a line from Gosselies, near Charleroi in Hainaut, northeast via Chastre to Incourt on the Wavre - Jodoigne route, with a branch southward from Incourt to Gembloux near the provincial border. After a certain amount of humming and hawing, the northern part, as far down as Tilly on the provincial borders, was authorised on 17 December 1896. The rest, plus an extension from Gosselies west to Courcelles, followed on 9 January 1899; presumably the Hainaut communes were somewhat chary of contributing, as well they might be considering the rural nature of the country it was to run through. Nevertheless the line was built, substantially if slowly, with quite imposing stations and a large workshop at Chastre that was to become one of the major repair bases of the Groupe de Louvain. The first section of main line from Incourt through Opprebais (Sart Risbart) to Chaumont-Gistoux was opened on 1 September 1900, and the Gembloux branch from Opprebais on 21 April 1902. Then the main line plodded steadily south, to Mellery village on 14 September 1903, on to Tilly on 30 May 1904, over the border to Mellet on 11 July 1904, to Gosselies on 29 August 1904, and finally to Courcelles on 17 October 1904. The line was generally worked piecemeal though it provided a link between the Brabant and Hainaut systems.

The last two lines in the Groupe conceded to the CFV were **Capital 83 (Waterloo - Mont-St.Jean and Capital 74 Braine'lAlleud - Wavre** which completed the outer strand of the web but they, as has already been noted, link more to Bruxelles than Leuven. (see section 8.2.2).

8.3.2. The Leuven urban system.

Thus by 1910 the Groupe de Louvain had assumed almost its final shape, with the exception of the Leuven town electric system which was to be built during the next two years. This was run by a nominally independent company but had close interworking over the inner portions of all three steam lines and was certainly regarded operationally as part of the Groupe. After the war it was fully assimilated but its early history is covered here because it formed a distinct entity.

Leuven town system, with a re-bodied car of series 9561-80 on route 2 in the Grote Markt.   (G Desbarax)

This was **Capital 177 (NOUVELLES LIGNES ELECTRIQUES DE LOUVAIN)**. Tramways in Leuven town dated from as far back as the early 1870s when a London-based concern enquired about laying down an "american railway" as early horse tramways were frequently called. On 29 September 1873 the *SA des Tramways de Louvain* obtained authorisation for and, on 4 April 1874, opened a horse line from the station along what was then Stationstraat (later Bondgenotenlaan) to the central Grote Markt and thence along Brusselstraat west to "Blauwe Hoek". The company failed in July 1895, but a standard-gauge horse tram was organised by a new *SA des Tramways de Louvain*, plying between station and Grote Markt only.

The town council was not satisfied and, from 1906-on, negotiated with the SNCV for a network of electrified lines. An authorisation of 25 December 1910 allowed electrification of the inner ends of existing steam tramways, but these circumnavigated the town to the south via the Naamse Poort; some 12km of new routes were therefore authorised also. These lines crossed the town east to west, from the station through Grote Markt to join the Vossem line (Capital 76) just short of Terbank near Heverlee; provided a semi-circular route to the northeast, from Grote Markt via Mechelse Poort and the canal to the station; and linked Grote Markt to the peripheral ex-steam lines, southwest along the Naamsestraat to the Naamse Poort and southeast along the Tiensestraat towards Tivoli and Korbeek Lo. The old steam lines were electrified as follows:

Capital 44   (Leuven - Jodoigne): to Heverlee Station
Capital 58   (Leuven - Diest): to Kessel Lo (depot)
Capital 76   (Leuven - Tervueren): to Heverlee Terbank via the
                  southern boulevards

The existing horse tram ceased operation from 16 April 1912. The new sections were brought into use between August and November 1912, as follows:

Stelplaats/depot (north of station) - Kessel Lo	9 Aug 1912
Stelplaats - Station - Grote Markt - Heverlee	10 Sep 1912
Grote Markt - Heverlee (Terbank)	1 Oct 1912
Grote Markt - Stapelhuizen - Station (via canal)	5 Nov 1912
Grote Markt - Tivoli	19 Nov 1912

By 1914 operation had settled down and consisted of four routes, apparently designated by letters:

* Heverlee - Kessel Lo
* Station - Grote Markt - Canal - Station
* Station - Grote Markt - Tivoli
* Station - Grote Markt - Terbank

There was, therefore, a frequent service between the station and town centre, replacing the former horse tram. There is some doubt about the exact concession arrangements. Official operators were the *SA des Tramways de Louvain (TL)*, but this would appear to have been a subsidiary of the CFV. Certainly the town lines were being operated in common with the other lines of Groupe de Louvain by 1914, using cars 9411-25 among others. Services appear to have remained stable from then until the SNCV took over the CFV's contracts, except that the Grote Markt - Tivoli link was closed at the end of 1916 and not reopened until 1920. (the further history of Leuven town will be found in context on pp.118 and 119).

8.3.3 The 1914-18 war and its aftermath

The 1914—18 war hit the Groupe de Louvain quite severely. With the exception of the Tivoli (Korbeek-Lo) line, closed but not lifted in December 1916, the Leuven town trams survived almost intact as did the links into Bruxelles and across into Limburg; they were too much needed for bringing vital supplies into the capital. Most of the remainder, however, fell prey to the occupier's demands and were closed during 1916-17, though all were reopened after the war. The full list is given here for convenience:

A train on the through Leuven-Bruxelles route comprising welded-body standard car and trailer   (E de Backer)

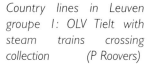

Country lines in Leuven groupe 1: OLV Tielt with steam trains crossing collection   (P Roovers)

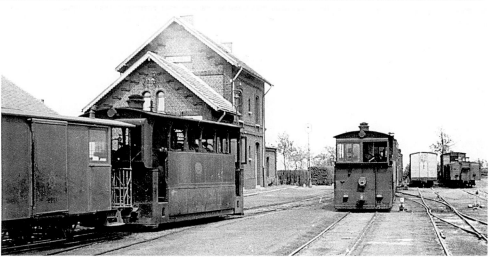

Table 8C: Leuven Group Lines Affected by World War I		
	Dates	
Capital Section	*closed*	*reopened*
44 Heverlee (stn) - Hamme Mille	Dec 1916	6 Apr 1920
72 Haecht - Werchter	Feb 1918	10 May 1920
Werchter - Aerschot	Feb 1918	12 Jul 1920
Aerschot - Tienen	Feb 1918	1 Oct 1920
74 Brain-l'Alleud - Wavre (all)	1916-17	
Braine-l'Alleud - Monument Gordon		1 Jun 1919
Monument-Gordon - Maransart		20 Mar 1920
Maransart - Lasne		1 Aug 1920
Lasne - Rixensart (stn)		1 Mar 1921
Rixensart - Wavre		9 Apr 1921
78 Courcelles - Incourt - Gembloux (all)	Aug 1915	
Incourt - Opprebais - Walhain		1 Oct 1920
Opprebais - Chastre		1 Oct 1920
Walhain - Gembloux		3 Mar 1921
Chastre - Courcelles (Motte)		1 Oct 1921
80 Beauvechain/Bevekom - Tienen/Tirlemont	Dec 1916	2 Jan 1920
106 Nivelles - Braine-l'Alleud - Virginal (all)	1916-17	
Braine-l'Alleud - Nivelles		9 Apr 1921
Bois-Seigneur-Isaac - Virginal		1 Nov 1921
branches from Virginal		16 Apr 1922
177 Leuven (Grote Markt) - Tivoli	Dec 1916	24 Jun 1920

Country lines : common sight was an autorail tracteur pulling wagons of agricultural produce, as here at Tienen (E de Backer)

8.3.4 SNCV Groupe de Louvain/Groep Leuven (Groupe 60), 1920-54

After the war the CFV was one of the early companies to surrender its leases and the SNCV took over control in 1920. The group was initially kept intact as an operating entity and the closed lines were slowly reopened as shown. As the SNCV took control in the whole province, however, some adjustments were made, Capitaux 74 and 83 being transferred to Bruxelles. The Leuven group was more fortunate than some in that it had good suburban traffic into Bruxelles and Leuven, plus a steady agricultural traffic in the rural regions. Hence its operating ratio (expenses as a percentage of receipts) stayed around or below the 100% mark all through this period. The country lines were steadily turned over to autorail operation, though this did not always imply infrequent services; some, for example Leuven - Diest and Leuven - Tienen via Hamme Mille, had 10-12 workings a day with almost hourly departures. Electrification was selective and concentrated on three routes: Bruxelles - Haecht; Bruxelles - Leuven and Leuven town. The only extensions were also to these three and they were minor.

Taking them in order: Bruxelles - Haecht had been earmarked for electrification in 1914 and services were already running from St Josse to Dieghem Lo, where a substation had been built. Work restarted as soon as money was available, and on 27 May 1924 services were extended to Haecht station. The line still had a considerable market-garden traffic into Bruxelles, and some heavy motor cars of the Titanic series were transferred from Petite Espinette specially to haul mixed and rush-hour trains on this section. A short extension at the Bruxelles end was authorised on 3 December 1929 (approved by Royal decree 2 May 1932 and opened on 7 May 1933), the town terminus being moved south from Eglise-Sté-Marie to Porte de Schaerbeek (St-Josse Rue Traversiere) where a large loop was put in. The line became designated as routes BH (to Haecht) and BD (to Dieghem) although by 1935 these were replaced by D (Diegem) and H (Haecht) with a D barré short working to Evere, and additional routes C to Campenhout and S to Steenokkerzeel. A feature of the new extension was that its dead-end terminus was on a very steep gradient. Accordingly, until a return loop was put in in 1954, trailers were always left at Eglise-Sté-Marie and the motor car went on alone to the terminus. This was all part of a general

rearrangement in the area, the line between Place - St Croix - St Josse - Evere which was the TB's route 5, being rationalised. The TB surrendered its SNCV concession and in 1934 was authorised to standard-gauge the route. In practice it was three-railed between Place St Josse and the Rue de Foyer Schaerbeekois at Evere so that SNCV trams could still reach Porte de Schaerbeek and have a service link to the Vossem line at St Josse. The SNCV then withdrew from Place St Croix and route 5 with effect from 22 February 1935.

* *Leuven town services again*

The next electrification was the development of Leuven town and suburban routes. This was done in two stages. On 25 April 1926, the Grote Markt - Tivoli line was extended through Korbeek Lo under an authorisation of 18 November 1925. A few months later, on 18 September 1926, a short branch was built off the Heverlee (station) route to Heverlee (Kantien) (same authorisation) and on 1 December 1927 the Terbank route was extended over existing track west to Bertem. There was a pause and then a second batch of extensions and electrifications in the 1930s. These comprised:

	Dates	
Section	authorised	opened
Extensions		
* Kessel Lo - Linden on existing track		1 Jan 1932
* Korbeek Lo - Louvenjoul (X-roads)		
	23 Jan 1933	14 Jul 1934
* Mechelse Poort - Herent	5 Oct 1936	5 Sep 1937
Electrification		
Naamse Poort - Tiense Poort		7 Apr 1935
New line:		
Leuvense steenweg - Beneden Kessel		
	20 Oct 1931	1 May 1940

The next major electrification project also concerned Leuven since it was the modernisation of Capitaux 46 and 76 in order to provide a fast through-route between Leuven and Bruxelles. The first section, from Evere to Sterrebeek, was electrified from 27 July 1930 to act as a Bruxelles suburban route, but further extension was painfully slow. It was started on 13 July 1934 by an equivalent extension at the Leuven end, from Bertem to Tervueren via Vossem but the final link, from Vossem to Sterrebeek, did not come into service until 22 May 1937. Initially and until 26 October 1940, the service was in two parts, passengers changing at Vossem. On that date, through service commenced as route B, the Vossem - Tervueren branch becoming an undesignated shuttle service connecting with the interurbans. Standard bogie cars were allocated to the route, which was the Leuven group's pride and joy. It used pantographs instead of the bow collectors of the town services and, until post-war SNCB electrifications, was the fastest public transport between the two cities.

At the Bruxelles end of the Louvain routes, meanwhile, the section from Pl St.Josse to Evere had been handed back by the TB and was operated by SNCV with its own stock between 1 August 1934 and 9 December 1941, then being sold to the TB and standard gauged; a fate that as we have seen also befell the route from Pl Sté Croix to Schaerbeek during 1934-35. A physical link between the Haecht line and the main Louvain system was maintained by third-railing Pl St Josse and Chaussée de Helmet at Evere. One other electrification is mentioned here since it concerns a line originally of the Leuven group. This was the Braine-l' Alleud - Wavre route, now firmly joined to Bruxelles via Waterloo and basically a Bruxelles outer-suburban line. It was electrified between 1931 and 1933; details will be found under Groupe de Bruxelles.

Meanwhile again, the Groupe de Louvain became Groupe 60 under the SNCV's reclassification scheme. During World War II, its lines formed vital links between the capital and the southern and eastern provinces, carrying vast quantities of foodstuffs and other supplies which could no longer travel by main line or by road. Its worst tragedy appears to have been a disastrous fire at Haecht depot on the night of 18/19 March 1937, which virtually destroyed five of the "Titanics" plus sundry other cars. The only line actually closed was Leuven route 4 (Stn - Grote Markt - Canal - Stn). Most of the Group's lines were rural however, and little further development was carried out after the war. The main change was the linking of Bruxelles to Mechelen (in Antwerpen province) via Haecht. On 15 May 1947, electrification was extended over existing track to Haecht village and then a new link was made northwards to Keerbergen (Grand Veneur) on the former Mechelen - Aerschot line. It was authorised on 10 November 1948 and brought into use on 1 June 1949 (some sources give 29 April 1949). It was served by standard bogie cars working through from Bruxelles to Mechelen.

That was undoubtedly the highpoint of the SNCV Groupe de Louvain. The following year closures started when the stretches from Wavre through Incourt to Chastre (parts of Capitaux 14 and 78) were closed to passengers on 30 September 1950. Chastre - Mellet was transferred to Hainaut, which had already taken over the southern portion on electrification. The section of Capital 80 from Tienen to Beauvechain lost its passenger service on 6 October 1951. Then it was the turn of Leuven town. Up to the war, Leuven routes mostly radiated from the station with the exception of Kessel-Lo - Kantien but in the late 1940s they were briefly reorganised as through routes, as under: (/ = barré)

No.	Route	closed
1	Linden - Station - Grote Markt - Heverlee (Kantien)	21 Mar 1953
1/	Kessel-Lo - Heverlee	21 Mar 1953
2	Beneden - Tervurense Poort (cut back from Bertem)	13 Feb 1952
3	Louvenjoul - Grote Markt - Herent	14 Aug 1952
3/	Bretonse Hoeve - Herent	14 Aug 1952

They closed quite suddenly and were replaced by one-man buses. After that there were just the interurbans: route B to Bruxelles, which came in along the boulevards by the old steam route and returned via Grote Markt and Naamse Poort, and a new electrification from Fochplein out to Diest as route D. This, virtually the last fling for Leuven, was part of the big 1950s electrification schemes. Services opened to Tielt (route T) at the beginning of September 1952 and on to Diest (Vest) on 17 May 1953. Four months later a reluctant town council allowed it through to Diest mainline station on 21 September 1953. Meanwhile, out in the country, Capital 44, Leuven (Heverlee) - Jodoigne, closed to passengers from 8 March 1953 and to goods on 19 July 1953; Haecht - Tienen/Tirlemont lost its passenger service on 16 May 1953, Geldenaken/Jodoigne - Tienen followed on 1 July and, for the record, the southern part of Capital 78, Mellet - Chastre, went on 1 September the same year. Four months later, the Groupe de Louvain itself ceased to exist, having combined with the Groupe de Bruxelles to form the SNCV Groupe de Brubant. At the time of takeover, the electric routes from Bruxelles were as follows:

Letter   Route
Routes from Schaerbeek (Chaussée de Haecht)
A   - Melsbroek (Aerodrome)
D   - Diegem Lo (route BD before 1940)
H   - Diegem Lo - Haecht (route BH before 1940)
K   - Haecht - Keerbergen (opened 1 Jun 1949)
M   - Haecht - Keerbergen - Mechelen (opened 1 Jun 1949)

Routes from Saint-Josse-ten-Noode (Chaussée de Louvain)
B   - Vossem - Leuven
K   - Kraainem
S   - Sterrebeek
V   - Vossem
W   - Wezembeek

NOTES: The intermediate terminus for the Saint-Josse routes at Pl Dailly was used for non-electric workings, in particular wartime through-trains to Liége and, for a period in the early 1950s, an autorail service to Beauvechain and Tienen; this latter was worked by the streamlined bogie cars of series AR 291-6.but ran for only about a year, from Autumn 1954 to 2 October 1955 when it was cut back to Vossem.

8.4   Lines on the Brabant periphery and a detached line

As with all provinces there were some lines which crossed provincial boundaries and which can therefore be considered under two or more headings. Brabant, being in the centre of the country, was particularly susceptible to this and, under SNCV control especially, several lines were effectively split (cf Courcelles - Incourt - Gembloux; Aalst - Oordegem - Asse/Assche - Bruxelles). Five lines in particular need chronicling since they did not fit neatly into any Groupes during early years. They were:

Capita	Name	Auth km
*	*Links into Antwerpen province*	
147	Lier - Werchter (mainly in Antwerpen)	24.50
148	Mechelen - Aerschot (mainly in Brabant)	30.85
*	*Links into Liége and Limburg*	
129	Jodoigne - Tirlemont - St- Truiden	44.28
138	Diest - Koursel	19.85
*	*Detached line in Brabant*	
54	Sichem - Montaigu / Zichem - Scherpenheuvel	4.00

8.4.1　Links into Anwerpen Province

Capitaux 147/148 were always confusing. Before the 1914-18 war, the SNCV classed both as being "Brabant: Groupe de Tremeloo" since their operating HQ was in the latter town where they crossed. Both were ceded for operation to a specially formed, Leuven-based company, the *SA pour l'Exploitation des CF Vicinaux et Tramways (VT)*, established on 2 April 1908 for the usual 30-year term. After the war, when the VT gave up its concession in March 1923, both became part of

30 July 1920, and Lier - Schriek on 28 September 1921. Its further history was largely uneventful. Suffice here to say that Lier - Putte was closed on 22 February 1943 and never reopened. It was replaced by buses after the war, and on 15 December 1947 the same fate befell the remainder of the line.

Capital 148 (MECHELEN - AERSCHOT) , however, was definitely a Brabant line which penetrated Antwerpen province. Authorised on 20 January 1906, it was also metre gauge from the start and ran west from Aerschot through

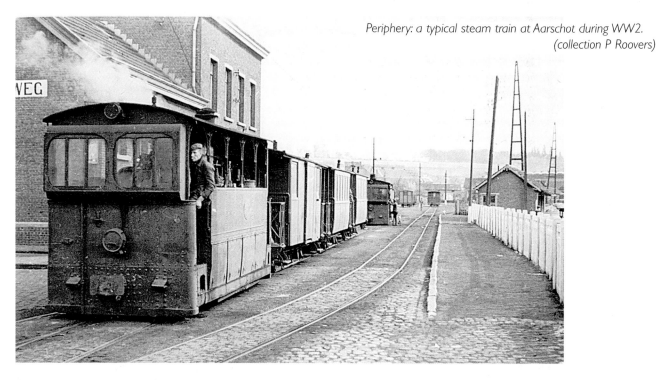

Periphery: a typical steam train at Aarschot during WW2.
(collection P Roovers)

SNCV Groep Antwerpen. On 1 March 1933, however, Capital 147 and the Rijmenam - Aerschot section of Capital 148 were transferred back to Louvain control since they were then unelectrified parts of otherwise electrified lines. While described in detail here, some notes on later history are also, therefore, incorporated into the Antwerpen chapter. Of interest is that both lines, being Brabant-based, had complications where they met the Antwerpen provincial system.

Capital 147 (LIER - WERCHTER) was in some ways the more straightforward of the two. First proposals were in 1900 but financial arguments delayed authorisation until 29 August 1905. The authority was specifically for a metre-gauge line starting from Lier/Lierre (Leuvense Poort) in Antwerpen province where it did not quite connect with other SNCV lines. Thence it ran south via Putte where it crossed the Antwerpen line from Mechelen to Heist-op-den-Berg and continued to the provincial frontier at Schriek. The Brabant portion ran on through Tremeloo/Tremeloo (depot) to connect with the Haecht - Aerschot line at Werchter; it was common with the latter between Werchter (Rue de Tremeloo) and Werchter station. It was opened in three stages, to Putte on 5 October 1908, on to Schriek on 1 December 1908 and finally to Werchter on 1 May 1909. The operating length was 25.01 km. For operating purposes it was classed as Brabant, but for finance as an Antwerpen venture, that province and its communes being the major contributors. It was, alas, never very profitable and so was an early victim of the 1914-18 war. It was closed and lifted throughout in August 1915 and was restored in leisurely fashion in two stages: Schriek - Tremelo on

Betekom, Tremelo and Keerbergen to cross the border and connect with the Mechelen - Heist line at Pasbrug on the eastern outskirts of Mechelen. There was initially some competition for the concession between the local *Kempische Stoomtram Mij (KSTM)* and the *Vicinaux et Tramways (VT)* concern which the latter won. The line was opened in stages, from Mechelen (Nekkerspoel) to the village of Rijmenam on 25 July 1908, on to Keerbergen on 1 May 1909, to Tremelo on 14 August 1909 and finally to Aerschot on 18 September 1910. At Mechelen, mixed gauge had to be laid on the 1067mm gauge line from Pasbrug inwards, and bridge works prevented access to Mechelen standard-gauge station until 22 June 1911; because of the small difference between 1000mm and 1067mm gauges, the mixed section had to be interlaced rather than third rail. At the other end, the line ran in over the Haecht - Aerschot - Tienen line from Betekom (Laakbrug) to Aerschot SNCV. Operating length was 29.39km. As with Capital 147, the line was closed and lifted during the war, from Pasbrug eastward, in July 1916 and was eventually reopened in two stages: Mechelen (Pasbrug) - Tremelo on 30 July 1920, and Tremelo - Aerschot on 18 July 1921.

In 1923 it was assimilated into the SNCV Groupe de Louvain. With their other lines it was modernised with autorails during the 1930s, and Mechelen - Rijmenam was electrified on 2 August 1931 as part of a plan to link with Bruxelles. The Keerbergen - Tremelo - Aerschot section (10.7km) was closed for good on 22 February 1943, requisitioned by the Germans; with it went the main SNCV Brabant - Antwerpen link. The section as such was not reopened, but after the war the rest became important when the link to Bruxelles was revived. This involved a new line from Haecht village north to Keerbergen (Grand Veneur) where it joined Capital 148. Authorised on 10 November 1948, it was completed on 1 June 1949 and electrified from the start. At the same time, the Rijmenam - Keerbergen section was electrified, so that 40km linked Bruxelles and Mechelen. Operation was given to the Groupe de Louvain but, when that amalgamated with Bruxelles in 1954, the line was transferred to Antwerpen control. Meanwhile, Tremelo town council had been agitating for reinstatement of "its" tramway. The original course had been obliterated by a wartime airfield, but a new link from Keerbergen was built and opened on 24 October 1949; it generally paralleled a road but for most of the route was on its own right-of-way. The intention was to electrify it. Indeed, Keerbergen workings from Mechelen carried the route letter T in anticipation of a pre-war intention to electrify to Tremelo, but this was never done and the link closed again on 3 October 1954. The new electric line did not last much longer, Keerbergen - Mechelen going on 1 June 1957 as part of a series of closures, while Haecht (station) - Keerbergen followed on 31 May 1958. Capital 148 was then dead.

8.4.2 Links into Liége & Limburg

Capitaux 129/138 were regarded as independent entities, each with its own operating HQ although both were ceded for operation to the big *SA de Transports Urbains et Vicinaux (TUV)* which ran tramways in various parts of the country. The TUV was a Bruxelles-based concern founded in March 1899 for the usual 30-year term. Discussions started in 1900 about **Capital 129 (JODOIGNE - TIRLEMONT - ST-TROND) /(GELDENAKEN - TIENEN - ST-TRUIDEN)**, examining various routes in the southeastern corner of Brabant. The final one was authorised on 20 November 1903 and consisted of a line from Jodoigne town square, where it met Capital 14, northeast through Esemael (standard-gauge connection), Overhespen and Orsmael, thence almost due east to St-Truiden/St-Trond on the provincial borders; a branch, authorised at the same time, went back from Overhespen to join existing lines at Tienen. The line served a mainly agricultural region and was opened in three sections; on 29 June 1907 from Tienen to St-Truiden; on 4 April 1908 from Jodoigne to Esemael and on to Overhespen on 15 October 1908. It was a straightforward rural tramway some 37.56km long which remained open during the First World War and was surrendered to the SNCV in late 1919 with other TUV concessions. It was then assimilated into the Groupe de Louvain and continued uneventfully as a steam and autorail-worked line until the 1950s. Passenger services were discontinued between Jodoigne and Overhespen on 30 June 1953, and on the remainder on 2 October 1954. The line remained in use for freight, at least in part, for some years, being discontinued from St. Truiden to Halle-Booienhoven on 19 April 1957, the track being lifted two years later. Jodoigne - Pietrain closed to goods from 1 June 1960 and the remainder officially from 2 May 1962 although effectively abandoned from the end of the 1961 beetroot season.

Capital 138 (DIEST - KOURSEL) was also allocated to the TUV and was effectively a straight extension of the Leuven - Diest route though worked as a separate entity. It was authorised on 28 November 1904 (SNCV: some sources say 28 April) and ran northeast from Diest to cross and recross the provincial borders before reaching Beringen in Limburg, where it met Capital 88 from Hasselt to Leopoldsburg. It

continued northeast to Koersel. The line was built from the Koersel end, Koersel - Beringen - Schaffen (just northeast of Diest) being opened on 28 October 1907 and extended to a junction with Capital 58 at Diest Vest (Leuvense Poort) on 11 January 1908. The common section into Diest standard-gauge station followed on 11 November 1912. The Beringen - Koersel spur was closed and lifted during World War I, being reopened afterwards. The line was taken back from the TUV in 1919, was "motorised" during the 1930s and survived the 1939-45 war intact, but Diest - Beringen was closed to passengers on 8 June 1952. Beringen - Koersel lasted a little longer as part of the reorganised Capital 88 from Hasselt, but closed to passengers on 25 April 1954 and to goods on 21 October 1954.

8.4.3 A detached line wholly in Brabant

Capital 54 (ZICHEM - SCHERPENHEUVEL/ MONTAIGU) was the only result of an 1885 plan to join Zichem, up in the northeast of Brabant, via Montaigu to Tienen/Tirlemont. The section from Zichem south to Montaigu was applied for by the SNCV in 1888, and the Capital was subscribed but the *CF Grand Central Beige (GCB)* was, unusually, a large shareholder. The line, when authorised on 4 January 1892, was therefore not surprisingly built to the standard gauge. It was opened on 10 January 1894 with the GCB supplying all equipment and working it simply as one of its branches. It was therefore agreed that it would be sensible to transfer the concession to the GCB in its entirety and this was done by purchase from 1 June 1898, ratified by Royal decree on 8 September 1898. The official handing over was on 1 July 1898, and the line then passes out of SNCV history, though for some years it was marked on their maps as a CF Vicinal owned and operated by a private company.

8.5 Brabant: SNCV Groupe de Brabant (Groupe 70), 1954-78

The new Groupe de Brabant, formed on 1 January 1954, had its headquarters in Bruxelles where the main Cureghem works was situated, and took over all the lines of the Groupe de Louvain, except for Bruxelles - Haecht - Mechelen which passed to the Antwerpen group. It started positively by opening a service link at Laeken between the Wemmel and Grimbergen routes (authorised 15 November 1953) and by producing, for the Société, the magnificent type 'S' semi-streamlined tramcars, successors to the "Standard" bogie cars, but was soon in the position of having to continue closing country lines. The first one, or rather its Brabant portion, Diest - Beringen, closed to all traffic on 12 July 1954, being lifted almost immediately. On 30 June 1954 the first electrified spur, from Vossem (Quatre Vents/Vier Winden) to Tervueren, closed and on 2 October 1954 the line from Tienen to St -Truiden (Capital 129) lost its passenger service; most of it remained in seasonal use for sugar-beet traffic as did the track from Overhespen southwards as far as Noduwez, 6.75 km from Jodoigne; the Halle-Booienhoven - St-Truiden section was closed completely.

In 1955 the rot continued. On 11 April, the Diest town council managed to close the town section, from Vest to the standard-gauge station, which they had never liked and, on 12 June, Capital 58 was accordingly cut back from Diest (Vest) to Tielt; thus its electrification lasted less than three years. Goods traffic on the final section, from Assent to Diest, followed on 29 August, though Tielt - Assent struggled on until 17 March 1958. In 1955, too, the Bruxelles - coast link was broken by closure of Aalst - Oordegem on 1 October, and Kapellen - Tienen (13.8km) finally closed for goods on 29 September. 1956 saw only one closure, that of the Jodoigne - Incourt - Gembloux route (parts of Capitaux 14 and 78) on 2 September; the Opprebais - Gembloux section hung on for a few sugar-beet seasons and then closed to freight also on 1 June 1959. In 1957, too, only one line closed to passengers; on 21 April, the Hamme Mille - Vossem service, unsuccessful even when given through bogie autorails to Bruxelles, was replaced by a bus and the track cut back to Nethen; the remainder was kept for agricultural traffic to Tienen. The Asse/Assche - Aalst section of Capital 120, however, closed to goods on 29 July. In 1957, too, the Haecht line came back to Brabant's control when the Mechelen - Keerbergen portion, in Antwerpen province, closed to all traffic on 1 June, while the Ave du Boulevard terminus of the Bruxelles northern lines was given a new turning loop at Place Rogier, via Rue Zerezo and Rue du Progres, where the new "Nord" terminus was located.

1958 was a more eventful year. True, the closures continued slowly, the Haecht line being cut back from Keerbergen to Haecht station on 31 May, while, for off-peak services, the Bruxelles southern routes were experimentally cut back to Boulevard Jamar at Midi/Zuid station to ease congestion in Place Rouppe. On the other hand, 1958 was also the year of the great World Exhibition at Bruxelles. As in 1935, it was held on Heysel/Heizel plateau, but this time the preparations were much more elaborate and the SNCV took a full part. Besides taking a stand in the Belgian pavilion, with specially-sectioned type "N" car 10485 as the centrepiece, all the local services were augmented to feed into the Exhibition, through trains being run from as far away as Wavre. A special series of "S" cars (type "SE") was produced to upgrade service standards, and considerable modifications took place on the exhibition site itself. The Wemmel route ran along the southern boundary, serving the main stadium en route, but on the Humbeek route a completely new tram station, called Porte Benelux after the nearby entrance gate, was built in cutting at Place St-Lambert to serve the main entrance; it included loops, a turning circle and car storage sidings. Immediately to the north, the line plunged into a new tunnel beneath the exhibition grounds, inaugurated on 20 February 1957, with an underground halt at

8/20 The final fling for the rural lines was seasonal goods traffic. ART 122 with a beet train passes beneath the main line at Tienen. (E de Backer)

Ave de Meyse by a junction for the Londerzeel line before it emerged on its old route. The latter was realigned for a short distance, and a short-lived electrified spur was built on viaduct over the motorway to a loop terminus at the edge of the car park "C" by the main entrance. To complement all this, on 11 October 1957, the approaches to the Nord (Place Rogier) terminus were improved with reserved track along the Boulevard du Jubilee. In addition, several short-lived services were operated:

Route	Route details
Ex	Gare du Midi - Porte Benelux
A barré	Anderlecht - Porte Benelux
F barré	La Roue - Scheut - Porte Benelux
H barré	Nord - Porte Benelux
M barré	Dilbeek - Porte Benelux

At peak periods the services were greatly augmented, leading to a maximum of some 82 trams an hour in each direction along Avenue E Bockstael. In all some 6,750,000 passengers were carried during the exhibition, some day totals exceeding 120,000 and the final day totalling 140,621. The Bruxelles system was busily promoted, and the exhibition was undoubtedly a financial success for the SNCV and a demonstration of what even conventional light rail systems could achieve. Unfortunately it did not stop the closures of outlying branches. In 1959, four more went. Leerbeek - Enghien (outer end of Capital 16) closed on 25 February. it had had little strategic significance since the link to Mons was broken and elderly autorails offered no competition to other forms of transport. On 28 March, the other autorail line from Leerbeek to Ninove closed for the same reasons, and on 4 July the Braine-l'Alleud - Nivelles - Virginal branches (Capital 106) closed to all traffic. Lastly, out in the country, the Hamme Mille - Tienen stretch closed to passengers on 29 November, though the track was retained for sugar-beet traffic into Tienen refinery. This last closure was something of an oddity; passenger services had already been withdrawn once, in October 1951, but were reinstated at the beginning of 1959 owing to major road works in the area.

1960 saw only one major closure, the Haecht route from Porte de Schaerbeek being closed throughout on 16 April, but in 1961 the downward trend continued, though trams returned to Place Rouppe as their terminus from 3 February. On 17 February, however, route O (Pl Rouppe - Observatoire) was withdrawn, and on 19 May route B (the Bruxelles - Vossem - Leuven interurban) was replaced by buses running purely local workings; a journey time of only 20 minutes on the newly-electrified SNCB meant that the SNCV could not compete. On 30 September 1960, route Z (the short-working over Capital 191 toward Hal) was withdrawn although Z barré continued in use for passenger workings between Pl Rouppe and La Roue (Depot). The Hal trams also continued, but on 31 October 1961 the Grimbergen - Humbeek section of Capital 18 closed, disposing of northern route H except for depot workings which continued until 3 April 1967. 1961 was also the last sugar-beet season

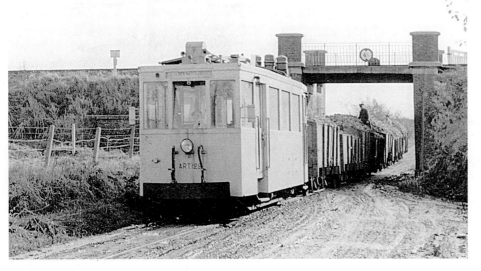

A common sight in the inmmediate post-war period - a standard car and trailer on the route to Hal *(the late G Desbarax)*

The long decline: the first electric lines to go were the inter provincial links such as that to Vlaanderen. No more would the trams trundle beside the canal at Aalst. *(B Y Williams)*

The 1958 Exposition saw a burst of activity with special workings common. This SE-type car is scheduled to go right across town to Zuun. *(E de Backer)*

The last Bruxelles lines were those to the North. An N type bogie car on the mixed gauge section in 1974 hotly pursued by a standard gauge STIB tram.
(author)

for the Tienen lines, with five autorail-tracteurs in use, though the stock was still there, huddled beneath the trees at Tienen SNCV, when the writer passed by in 1965. The last of the country lines, the electrified line from Leuven to Tielt, went on 31 March 1962, leaving only the Bruxelles suburban system, and the first real depredations on that were made the same year when the Aalst route was cut back to Hekelgem. After that it was all downhill as passenger traffic fell off, and road improvements made it both difficult and expensive to retain the trams.

A major landmark in the decline was the closure of the lines from Espinette Centrale to Monument Gordon and Braine l'Alleud (31 March 1964) followed by the Wavre section in two stages (24 & 28 June 1964) which removed route W (south) and finished sugar-beet transport via the SNCV; up to then a considerable tonnage had been delivered to the Wavre refinery by both electric and diesel traction, and the refinery owned its own steam locomotive analagous to the SNCV type 18. Route A (Place Rouppe - Bon Air - Itterbeek) closed on 16 May 1965, though the tracks were retained for stock transfer, and on 16 September 1966 there were three closures: Bruxelles Nord - Scheut short-workings went, and the two

linked lines from Bruxelles to Hal (Capital 191) and on from Hal to Leerbeek. Route Ni to Ninove was cut back to Eizeringen from 29 June 1968. Grimbergen - Meise followed the next day, and on 4 October 1968 Wolvertem - Londerzeel was closed to allow for road improvements. The following year, route R (Dilbeek - Rhode-St-Genese) was discontinued on 19 December 1969, involving total closure of Capital 47 from Vivier d'Oie onward, and on 20 February 1970 the remainder of Capital 47 went with the withdrawal of route V (Dilbeek - Place-St-Job). On the same date, the peak-hour trams to Eizeringen finally ceased, and on 20 June 1970 closure of the Wolvertem and Hekelgem routes meant that Capitaux 61 and 120 were finally dead. Closure of the last remnant of Capital 16 (Bruxelles - Leerbeek) on 1 September 1972 meant that only the Grimbergen and Wemmel lines with the Het Voor branch remained. They hung on until 31 July 1978, when all three were closed, thus bringing to an end over 90 years of SNCV rail passenger services in Brabant. A project to pass them to the STIB foundered for political reasons. The final blow was probably the decision to build a standard-gauge Metro. Remaining metre-gauge lines then became an inconvenience and so had to go.

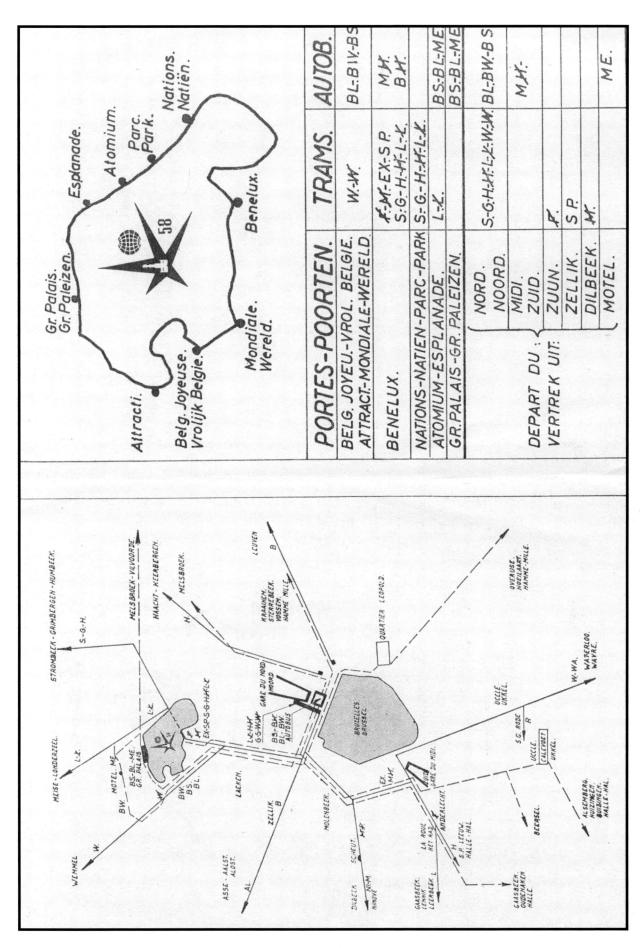

replica timetable leaflet for the 1958 exhibition workings. (SNCV)

Chapter 9: The SNCV in Hainaut Province

Note: because of the length & complexity of this chapter, the detailed section headings are at the appropriate points.

9.1   Hainault province: introduction

The SNCV in Hainaut has without doubt the most complex history of all the provincial systems. Hainaut is a long sprawling province situated in the centre-south of the country, firmly in the Walloon-speaking part and sandwiched between Brabant and the French frontier. It has always been the industrial heart of Belgium and was where the Belgian industrial revolution began. As a result it is densely populated, although with surprising tracts of agricultural countryside on the fringes of its big conurbations and down near the frontier, and is covered with the scars of heavy industry. Out to the west, abutting on Vlaanderen, is the old city of Tournai with its largely agricultural hinterland and then come the three interlinked conurbations centred on Mons, La Louvière and Charleroi; our Black Country is probably the nearest British equivalent. The land is, consequently, criss-crossed by standard-gauge railways and waterways.

Only one of the industrial areas, Charleroi, developed its own urban tramways company. Hence in the rest of Hainaut the SNCV gradually built up a dense network of urban and suburban passenger tramways, the majority of which were electrified sooner or later. Shifting needs and urban development often meant that the pattern of such services in later years did not correspond with the original concessions and, indeed, a drastic fusing of Capitaux was carried out in 1948. The result for the historian is a constant barrage of local place names, dates and service numbers and the reader will need to make constant reference to maps. Administration was, from the 1930s, united under a common SNCV Groupe du Hainaut (Groupe 30) but prior to that four separate groups were involved: Ath (Tournai), Mons-Borinage, Centre (La Louvière), and Charleroi, and these kept considerable operational independence even after the fusion. The chapter is, therefore, based on these divisions, with links where needed.

9.2.   The SNCV in the Tournai Area 1898 - 1954 (Map ref C-6)

9.2.1   Introduction to the Tournaisis
9.2.2   Groupe d'Ath 1898-1919 (TUV)
9.2.3   SNCV Groupe de Tournai to 1919-1954

    *   elecrification in and around Tournai
    *   Tournei urban services
    *   the end of the SNCV tramways in the Tournaisis

9.2.1   Tournaisis : introduction

The western part of Hainaut province was largely occupied by the ancient city of Tournai and its hinterland, decently separated from the main industrial conurbations. The SNCV lines there also seemed to be effectively separate from the rest and are therefore treated here as a whole. They never attracted

Tournai. — Rue Royale vers la Gare

Few views of the SNCV in Tournai town seem to exist. Here a Braine le Comte car traverses the Rue Royale with the railway station in the background.

(commercial card/collection Paul de Backer)

the publicity acquired by other portions of the system, so available information is much more sparse. The first minor rail transport in the area was actually a privately owned horse tram between Peruwelz and Bonsecours on the French frontier. This was opened on 30 May 1880 and lasted until the outbreak of war in August 1914; even then the track remained largely in situ until 1923-24. The SNCV came into the picture fairly late, not opening its first line until 1898, and then the tramways were mainly rural; the only urban network - if it could be so called - was in Tournai itself and was really the result of electrifying portions of existing routes already conceded to the main operator, the *SA des Transports Urbains et Vicinaux.*

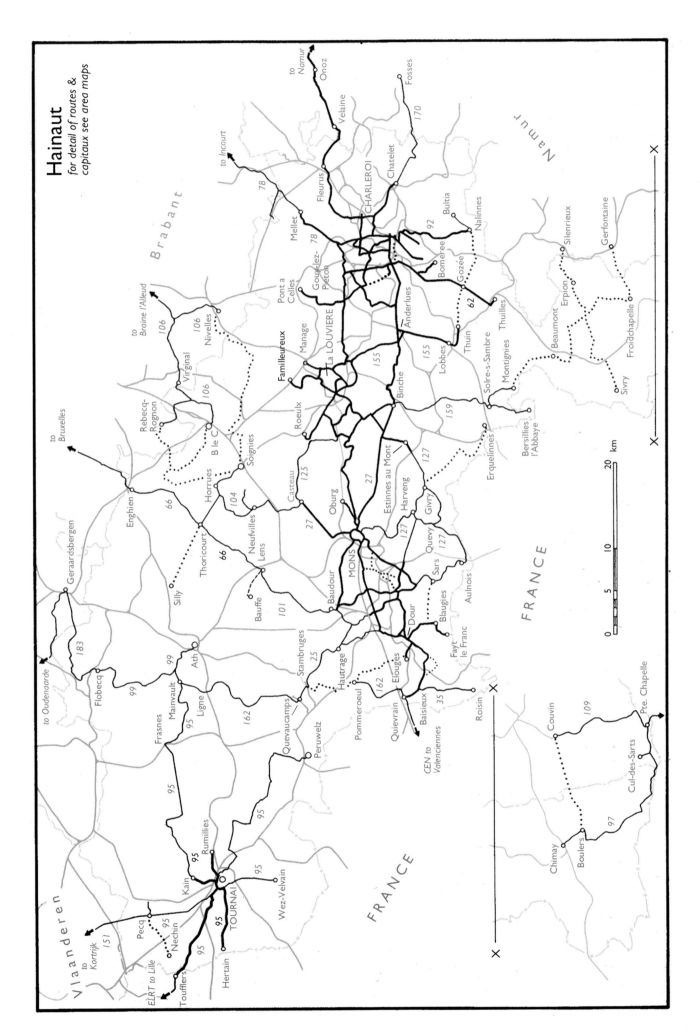

Hainaut
for detail of routes &
capitaux see area maps

Brabant

Namur

FRANCE

Vlaanderen

TOURNAI

MONS

CHARLEROI

La LOUVIERE

to Namur

to Incourt

to Braine l'Alleud

to Bruxelles

to Oudenaarde

to Kortrijk

km

20

10

5

0

Onoz

Fosses

170

Velaine

Fleurus

Chatelet

Mellet

78

78

92

Bultia

Bome'ree

Nalinnes

Gouy-lez-
Pieton

Pont a
Celles

Gozee

62

Anderlues

Thuin

Thuilles

Silenrieux

Gerfontaine

Manage

Familleureux

155

Lobbes

Solre-s-Sambre

Montignies

Beaumont

Erpion

Froidchapelle

Virginal

106

Nivelles

106

Roeulx

Binche

155

159

Sivry

Rebecq-
Rognon

106

B le C

Soignies

Casteau

125

Oburg

27

Estinnes au Mont

Harveng

127

Bersillies
l'Abbaye

Erquelinnes

127

Horrues

104

Neufvilles

27

Givry

Quevy

127

Enghien

66

Thoricourt

Lens

Baudour

MONS

127

Sars

Aulnois

Geraardsbergen

66

Silly

Bauffe

101

Dour

Blaugies

Fayt
le Franc

183

Flobecq

99

Mainvault

Ath

25

Stambruges

Hautrage

Elouges

162

Roisin

Frasnes

99

Ligne

162

Quevaucamps

Peruwelz

Pommeroeul

Quievrain

Baisieux

35

95

95

95

CEN to
Valenciennes

Rumillies

Kain

95

Wez-Velvain

151

Pecq

95

Nechin

Touffliers

95

ELRT to Lille

95

95

Hertain

FRANCE

Couvin

109

Pte. Chapelle

Cul-des-Sarts

Chimay

97

Bouiers

Lille - Roubaix - Tourcoing (ELRT) at Touffleurs on 1 October 1906. The lines were actually linked during World War 1, when the German army put in a connection. Finally a short extension from Peruwelz village to the Etat station was authorised on 15 March 1909 - and probably opened simultaneously.

The next batch of extensions started when a line authorised on 30 October 1910 was opened west to Hertain (9.163km) near the French frontier. It would appear that, in order to provide market trains with access to Tournai town centre, the line was taken from its entry point along the Chaussée de Lille through the town to skirt the Grand Place and cross the River Escaut via the Pont de Fer (iron bridge). There it joined an existing depot link and followed it to the mainline station; a link was also put in along the outer boulevard to join the existing branch from Templeuve. It was opened on 25 June 1911. In 1911 also, three more lines were proposed: one, to run

9.2.2 Groupe d'Ath, 1898-1919 (TUV)

Capital	Name	Auth km
95	Lignes de la Banlieue de Tournai	135.80
99	Ath - Flobecq	17.70
162	Mainvault - Pommeroeul - Quiévrain	35.68
183	Flobecq - Grammont/Geraardsbergen	15.96

Certainly the first major system in the district was SNCV **Capital 95 (LIGNES DE LA BANLIEUE DE TOURNAI)**. This was originally authorised on 12 November 1898 as three lines totalling 61.9km. They all started at Tournai standard-gauge station on the north edge of the city, going east, west and south. All were conceded for operation to the *SA des Transports Urbains et Vicinaux (TUV)* formed in 1889. Tournai - Kain - Quartes - Frasnes - Mainvault - Ath was the first line. This left westward but almost immediately turned north over the main railway line and ran first north, then generally eastward to the country town of Ath which was a fairly important standard-gauge junction. A detached section between Quartes and Frasnes was the first part to open, on 24 September 1900 for goods only at the request of the Frasnes sugar refinery, but it closed again on 15 December 1900 at the end of the beet harvest. The line then opened for all traffic from Tournai through to Frasnes (22.391km) on 12 September 1901 and on to Ath via Mainvault on 24 December 1903.

Meanwhile a link had been built round Tournai's north and west peripheral boulevards to a common depot by the north bank of the River Escaut which flows right through the city centre. Once across the river, the tracks swung west and then northwest to reach Templeuve (9.892km) by the French frontier; the route was opened in stages on 14 March and 12 September 1901. It was closely followed by a line east from the standard-gauge station which curved round the eastern ring and then headed southeast toward Peruwelz (37km). It reached Fontenoy (24.05km) by 15 October 1902 and Peruwelz (Village) itself on 1 May 1903. The Templeuve line was extended to the French border at Nechin (la Festingue) on 23 April 1905 and to a near-junction with the French *Tramways Electriques de*

south for 12.30km to Wez-Velvain, was delayed by difficulties over the exact route, but the other two were duly authorised. They were:

* firstly, a branch east to Rumillies, authorised on 29 April 1911. It was regarded as an extension of the Peruwelz line which it followed to the eastern outskirts of Tournai before diving under the standard gauge and breaking away on its own. It involved 3.445km of new track with a total route length from Tournai station of 4km.

* a more serious 12.50km line diverging from the Touffliers route and running northwards to Pecq on the provincial border with Vlaanderen, where it was intended to connect

with a line of Capital 151 south from Kortrijk to give a through link. It was authorised on 30 September 1911. A branch was also planned from Pecq westward to Nechin on the French frontier.

Unfortunately war came before any of these lines could be completed. The Pecq -Nechin branch was never constructed, and the others had to wait until the 1920s. The war also put paid to initial electrification plans for Tournai urban services. Meanwhile all of Capital 95, possibly bar a short stretch of the Hertain line to Orcq, was closed by war damage, Tournai being effectively in the rear battle zone on the German side. Some of the lines appear to have been used at times by the Germans, a physical link with the ELRT at Toufflers being put in during 1915, although it was little used.

While all these lines were being considered, further development was taking place up in the northeast corner of the group, from Ath and Mainvault. First was **Capital 99 (ATH - FLOBECQ)**, always considered an integral part of the Tournai system and operated by the same concessionaire. Authorised on 3 June 1899, its common portion with Capital 95 from Ath to Oeudeghien near Mainvault, was opened on 24 December 1903 and the remainder in two stages, from Oeudeghien to Lahamaide on 30 June 1904 and on to Flobecq on 1 October 1906; it was merged into **Capital 95 LIGNES de la BANLIEUE DE TOURNAI** on 11 January 1913. It ran almost due north from its junction near Mainvault, Flobecq being a standard-gauge connection near the provincial border, and the line undoubtedly being planned from the start as part of a future interprovincial link. Indeed the link line, **Capital 183 (FLOBECQ - GRAMMONT/VLOESBERG - GERAARDSBERGEN)**, was actually authorised as early as 24 November 1908; it was, however, held up by various legal problems and was still unbuilt when the 1914-18 war broke out. Ath - Flobecq was closed and lifted in that conflict so the link was temporarily in abeyance.

There remains one further outlier, **Capital 162 (MAINVAULT - POMMEREUL - QUIEVRAIN)**. This was a long rambling line south from Mainvault intended to go through Ligne, Quévaucamps and Pommereul to join Capital 35 at Quiévrain. The convoluted history of this and its associated Capital 186 are dealt with under Mons-Borinage but it is mentioned here because it was conceded to the TUV and because the northern portion to Quévaucamps came into the SNCV Groupe de Tournai after the war. For the present, suffice to note that as **Capital 162 (MAINVAULT - QUIÉVRAIN)** it was initially authorised on 11 May 1908 and built from both ends, although it was never finished. The northern section was opened to Quévaucamps (18.17km) on 31 January 1916 but apparently closed again soon after by German orders. It reopened, extended to Grandglise for a junction with the Mons-Borinage lines, on 28 October 1923. In general, while the Tournai - Peruwelz route remained open during the war, services over the remainder steadily deteriorated, trains first becoming mixed and then passenger traffic being abandoned altogether. The lines were severely damaged during the Allies' final offensive in 1918.

9.2.3 SNCV Groupe de Tournai, 1919-1956

After the war the TUV was one of the first companies to surrender its concessions, at the end of 1919. The SNCV took over and painfully rebuilt the system, in stages. The Peruwelz line appears to have remained open. The final restorations were:

section	reopened
Tournai - Frasnes	Oct 1919
Tournai - Hertain	1 Oct 1920
Ath - Flobecq	30 Apr 1921
Mainvault - Quévaucamps - Grandglise	28 Oct 1923
Tournai - Pecq (Pont de l'Escaut)	28 Oct 1923
Pecq (Pont - Village)	11 Jan 1934
Tournai - Rumillies	14 Jul 1929
Tournai - Wez	30 Aug 1930

And down on the Quévaucamps line, ART106 with a mixed train is ready to depart from Bliquy   *(JW Smith)*

The German-built extension to Touffleurs (Douane) was taken over by the SNCV and opened as such on 15 December 1926. These restorations required considerable bridge reconstruction and, although most bridges were repaired by 1921, the tracks at Tournai along the Pont de Fer and across Grand'Place did not reopen until September 1925. The group also gained the completely new line of **Capital 183 (FLOBECQ - GRAMMONT)** which was finally built south from Grammont/Geraardsbergen and opened in two stages: Grammont - Everbeek on 27 August 1927 and Everbeek - Flobecq on 6 October 1929. The section between Grammont and the locality of Goefferdingen (1.39km) was built as three-rail mixed gauge to serve local industries.

* Tournai urban services

Returning to Capital 95 as the stem line, the passenger traffic on most routes was not particularly heavy, although a fair tonnage of freight, sugar beet in particular, was transhipped at the various interchange points. Tournai itself never had a coherent urban network authorised as such but nonetheless the SNCV decided to embark on a programme of electrification which effectively provided urban services. The first services, from Tournai (Grand'Place) to Kain (Gare) and to Hertain (Terminus) operated from 10 September 1932, with a cross-town line from Tournai station to the Cimetière du Sud following on 31 December 1932 (authorised retrospectively on 26 July 1933). Maps and recollections are not entirely clear, but it appears to have run south from the station over existing track, then crossed the Escaut to circumnavigate the cathedral and Grand'Place, whence it traversed Rue St-Martin to cross the Wez line and terminate in a dead-end spur. Electric services were organised as shown below and it is not clear what then was the status of the original town-centre line, though it appears to have remained in existence. At about the same time the Tournai - Wez route was turned over to autorails.

Table 9A: Tournai electric services in the 1930s
(Initially these were designated by letters, replaced by route numbers in 1934)

No/letter	Route	Opened
1 (T)	Tournai Gare - Templeuve - Touffleurs	9 Jan 1933
1 barré	Tournai - Templeuve	9 Jan 1933?
2? K	Tournai (Cimetière) - Kain (Gare)	31 Dec 1932
3 (K)	Tournai (cimetière) - Kain (Trinite)	14 May 1933
4 (H)	Tournai (Gare) - Hertain (Terminus)	10 Sep 1932
?5 (O)	Orcq - Tournai - Rumillies	4 Feb 1934?
6 (R)	Tournai (Gare) - Rumillies (Terminus)	9 Jan 1934

The numbers 2 and 5 were apparently initially reserved for Pecq and Peruwelz but no more electrification was undertaken; rather as at Hasselt, there was really not enough traffic to justify it. Even the busiest suburban line, to Toufflers, had only twelve daily trains on average, Hertain having eight and Rumillies only six; non-electrified lines got standard diesel autorails although these, unusually, had to be fitted with pantographs to enable them to operate signalling and points over the electrified sections.

Came the second war and, on 10 May 1940, the German invasion. In the fighting, the Pont de Fer and other bridges were blown, the Kain - Cimetière route being closed at once and the 1933 track subsequently abandoned; the same fate befell Pecq village to station (officially abandoned 1944). After the war, the remainder continued and, during the building of a new motor road through the city of Tournai in 1948, provision is said to have been made for track to be laid in it. If so, commonsense prevailed and the route was never completed. Indeed Tournai was one of the first major groups to abandon electrification, the remaining routes closing on 27 April 1952. The overhead equipment and some cars were reclaimed for service elsewhere, though it was only in the last years that a few modern bogie vehicles had been provided for the Toufflers route; the others were mainly Braine-le-Comte four-wheelers.

* the end of SNCV services in the Tournaisis

The former electric routes remained open for diesel-hauled freight, Tournai having rebuilt many of its autorails to tractors in 1949-50 to replace its five remaining steam locomotives. Oddly, passenger services on the non-electrified lines outlasted their more modern cousins, although not for long. Tournai - Wez - Velvain closed on 26 April 1952. Tournai - Pecq lost its autorails on 17 May 1953; Tournai - Peruwelz followed on 23 August 1953; while Tournai - Ath followed on 9 August 1954. They remained open for goods a short while longer and for "strategic purposes" (ie inter-group stock transfers) but all finally had closed to all traffic by the end of 1954 as follows:

25 Mar 1954	Tournai - Touffleurs
	Tournai - Rumillies
	Tournai - Wez - Velvain
	Tournai - Hertain
21 Oct 1954	Tournai - Peruwelz
22 Oct 1954	Tournai - Pecq

The other lines in the Groupe did not last much longer. Mainvault - Grandglise and Ath - Flobecq were replaced by buses at the same time on 9 August 1954 and Flobecq - Grammont followed on 30 September 1956 for passengers and on 17 March 1958 for goods, bringing SNCV rail transport in the Tournai region to an end.

9.3 Hainaut: Mons-Borinage 1889-1939

9.3.1 Introduction to the Mons-Borinage area

The heavily industrialised area around Mons in the west of Hainaut is not particularly easy to chronicle. The SNCV used a variety of concessionaires so the conventional "groupes" are not clear-cut; there were limited experiments with ac electric traction which caused some confusion. It is conventional for tramway historians to treat the Mons system of the SNCV geographically, dividing it into Mons itself; the complex of lines in the region to its south west, known as the Borinage: the scattered lines which are usually described as "on the periphery". At the same time, however, there was also a definite chronological sequence in which the "country" systems to the north and east of Mons city came first from 1887 up to about 1906, the city being served only tangentially, so to speak; there followed the largely urban systems in the Borinage between 1906 and the mid 1920s during which time isolated lines were also linked into a more coherent network; finally there was the period up to the 1939-45 war which saw major links to other parts of the Hainaut system, development of the major electrification schemes and final unification under the Groupe du Hainaut. The major industrial emphasis of the region was in the Borinage, and the local adjectival labels: Montois for the inhabitants of Mons and its northern and eastern suburbs, Boraines for those of the Borinage, clearly show the local divisions. The SNCV developments, too, were initially quite separate from each other and joined up comparatively late; they were slightly complicated by a state-run tramway which will be dealt with first.

9.3.2 The Mons - Boussu Tramway

Mons never had a municipal tramway of its own but did have the odd episode of the "Mons - Boussu"; for just as Liége had its Liége - Seraing routes, so for many years the Borinage had its own "interurban" in the shape of a metre-gauge line run by the state railways, at that time the *CF de l'Etat Belge*. Its origins lay in a very early SNCV proposal for a tramway west from Mons station along a direct road to the busy industrial township of Boussu with a suggestion for eventually extending to Quiévrain on the French border. The proposed line paralleled an existing railway and, as sometimes happened, the state refused the SNCV application on the grounds of unnecessary competition. The need was still there, however, and, in an inspired (?) judgement, the concession was promptly given to the main line railway company. The latter rather lackadaisically commissioned the big Electricité et Hydraulique group to build the line, and the consequence was that a metre-gauge electric tramway opened on 24 August 1899 with cars and trailers almost identical to contemporary SNCV vehicles, using the same 500 volts dc with trolley-pole collection and passing within yards of several SNCV junctions without a single physical connection or, indeed, timetable acknowledgement of the Vicinal's existence.

Nonetheless, the Mons - Boussu line had several odd features in its 10.745km. It started on the "wrong" side of the Etat lines at Mons by the level-crossing with the road to Jemappes to avoid actually crossing the standard-gauge railway, and was laid in the street for its whole length. For most of its route it was double track but the tracks were interlaced

through the narrow streets of Jemappes itself, with one passing loop, and again on the approach to Boussu terminus - where the line stopped, almost touching the SNCV's 1896 route to Fayt-le-Franc. The line had a total of 20 intermediate halts, the depot and administrative offices being almost exactly half-way along in the yard of Quaregnon Etat station. Here and at Hornu crossroads where, from 1906-7, it was crossed by SNCV single-phase ac electric lines, there was complex isolating gear to separate the differing electrical systems. Needless to say, the competing lines otherwise ignored each other. Indeed the Mons - Boussu trams were painted blue to distinguish them from the common green of the SNCV.

The line served a continuous row of industrial communities at Jemappes, Quaregonon, Hornu and Boussu and from the very beginning its traffic was heavy. With the main line parallelling it for freight, the tramway was always purely a passenger line, tram-trains running initially on a 30-minute headway with a 15-minute service at peak periods. Trains were composed of a 1st/2nd class motor car towing a 2nd class trailer and traffic was so heavy that, from August 1902, services were increased to a standard 15-minute headway except in late evening. This required purchase of four more motor cars in 1905 to supplement the original stock of 12 motors and 12 trailers; two large bogie cars - inevitably later called "Titanics" by the staff - followed in 1911 but were not liked because of their Titanic-like propensity to founder (ie to derail at the slightest opportunity) although this attribution was presumably retrospective since the Titanic did not founder until 1912!

Along came the 1914-18 war, and the line was largely taken over by the Germans who promptly connected it up to the SNCV at Boussu and built the long-projected extension to Quiévrain on down the main road, thus enabling through traffic to be worked to the battle zone in France over the SNCV and the French *CF Economiques du Nord (CEN)*. Traffic comprised supplies up and wounded back, the link proving extremely useful. It was, of course, removed completely when the war finished, ("nothing to do with us") although the cars retained a flavour of wartime in being painted khaki immediately after the war - presumably there was spare military paint lying around! Alas, the Etat could not abstain from all contact with its rival; the material was so war-weary that four cars of the SNCV

Typical of the pre-electric lines around Mons. A steam train pauses at Riezes, on the line to Ghlin. (commercial card/author's collection)

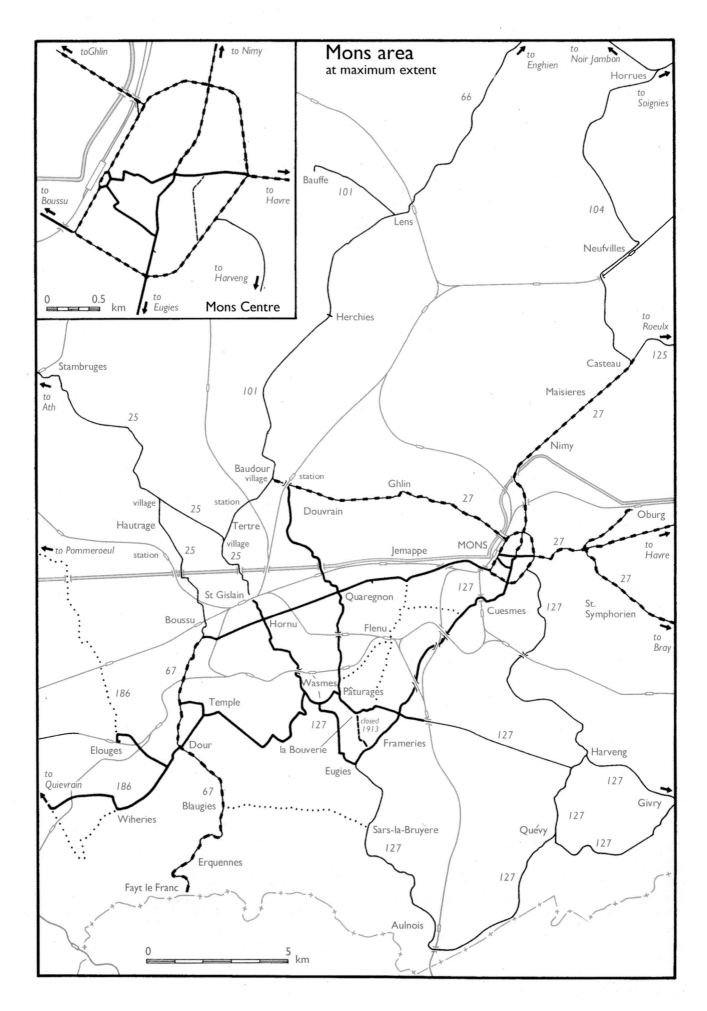

Mons area
at maximum extent

to Ghlin

to Nimy

to Enghien

to Noir Jambon

Horrues

to Soignies

to Boussu

to Havre

to Harveng

to Eugies

Mons Centre

0   0.5   km

66

Bauffe

101

Lens

104

Neufvilles

Herchies

to Roeulx

125

Stambruges

Casteau

to Ath

25

Maisieres

27

101

Nimy

Baudour

village

station

Ghlin

27

village

station

Douvrain

Oburg

Hautrage

25

Tertre

village

25

Jemappe

MONS

27

to Havre

to Pommeroeul

station

25

St Gislain

Quaregnon

27

127

Cuesmes

127

St.

Symphorien

Boussu

Hornu

Flenu

127

67

Wasmes

Pâturages

186

Temple

127

closed

1913

Framilies

127

Harveng

Elouges

Dour

la Bouverie

Frameries

to Quievrain

186

67

Eugies

127

to Bray

Blaugies

Givry

Wiheries

Sars-la-Bruyere

127

Quévy

127

127

Erquennes

127

Fayt le Franc

127

Aulnois

0   5   km

951x series had to be borrowed to maintain the service until eight new "Tashkent"-type cars were delivered in 1921. These rejuvenated the services, but the Etat clearly did not consider its tramway worthy of much attention. When the SNCB took over all mainline railways in 1926 it appears to have taken one horrified look at the state of its minor possession, and immediately opened negotiations to have it taken over by the SNCV. The latter agreed that Mons - Boussu would fit well into its local services and took it over by Royal decree on 1 July 1928, authorisation being given retrospectively as **Capital 197 MONS - BOUSSU** on 29 April 1929, and just as promptly condemned most of the existing stock, supplying its own. At the same time it used existing SNCV substations to provide current, thus enabling it to scrap the obsolete generating station at Quaregnon, although the depot was retained. 1929 saw physical links put in at Boussu, Hornu, Quaregnon and Mons, and in 1931 the line was fully integrated, electrification being extended from Boussu over the SNCV line to Fayt-le-Franc. Thus Mons - Boussu became "just another SNCV tramway" and its subsequent history will be found in the appropriate place

9.3.3 The SNCV I: Groupe de Mons 1888 - 1919

Capital	Name	Auth km
25	St-Ghislain - Hautrage et Extensions	32.20
27	Lignes Vicinaux de la Banlieue de Mons	51.70
66	Lens - Enghien - Soignies	19.11
67	Boussu a la Frontière vers Bavay	15.57
101	Baudour - Lens - Bauffe	13.90
104	Casteau - Ch ND de Louvignies et Neufvilles	17.26
125	Casteau - Bracquegnies	12.00

Most maps of the Mons area give the impression of a dense network of interconnected tramways but initially the reality was quite different; for a good twenty years, from 1888 to 1906, SNCV transport around Mons consisted of scattered, separated lines and systems, mainly rural and rarely interconnecting. All were operated by one local company the *SA des CFV Montois (CFVM)*, which ran them until the financial position after World War I forced the company to surrender its concessions in November 1919.

Capital 25 (ST-GHISLAIN - HAUTRAGE ET EXTENSIONS), to the west of Mons city, was the first system planned in the area, though the second actually to be opened. Its main line ran through another batch of industrial settlements, from St-Ghislain through Tertre village and north-west to Hautrage, with a branch from Hautrage (Etat) south to the Mons - Condé canal at Boussu It was authorised on 29 August 1887 and the main line was opened on 1 May 1888, its depot being at St.Ghislain. Originally an isolated line running through a heavily industrialised district and serving a chain of dreary mining settlements, it quickly grew various short branches to tap the freight traffic. First was a 3km line northwest from Hautrage authorised on 16 June 1890 and opened to Stambruges (Chemin de Bruyères, 2km), on 30 April 1891, a 1km spur to Villerot - probably authorised retrospectively on 16 June 1891 - being added almost immediately on 7 June 1891 and a section around Hautrage Etat station being four-railed for convenience. Then a branch, authorised on 14 December 1891, struck east from Tertre village to its Etat station with interchange sidings and thence to Baudour village (opened from Tertre Bifurcation to Etat on 24 August 1891 and on to Baudour on 2 July 1892). The inevitable Baudour station branch was authorised on 19 June 1893 and

opened on 19 December 1893, another short spur reaching from Baudour to le-Trieu-du-Haut-Coron on 16 April 1896.

Of these, only the sections between St-Ghislain - Hautrage and St-Ghislain - Baudour had passenger services, the major traffic being industrial products. Indeed, for these latter, a long goods-only branch as mentioned above was built south under the original authorisation from Hautrage Etat station to Boussu (Canal) in 1897 with a connection to the already existing line to Fayt-le-Franc (Capital 74: Boussu à la Frontière vers Bavay). Lastly, the traffic on the Baudour station spur grew so heavy that it was mixed-gauged in 1907 using four-rail track, in which form it outlasted the rest of the system. All this time the system, now a total of 30.24km long, had no direct links with Mons, its St-Ghislain terminus being on the north side of the standard-gauge, although a link northeastward via the little town of Lens in 1902 gave it access to Bruxelles! Otherwise it remained separate until 1 December 1915 when a link was provided via Capital 27 at Baudour (see below). Like other systems, however, it was closed in part during the 1914-18 war, the Tertre - Stambruges line being closed and lifted, but was restored to use piecemeal by February 1919.

In the meantime, way back on 18 November 1887, another small system had been authorised to the north and east of Mons itself. This, **Capital 27 (LIGNES VICINAUX DE LA BANLIEUE DE MONS)**, comprised three lines:

*   MAISIÈRES - MONS - ST-SYMPHORIEN, authorised on 18 November 1887, ran from Maisières, to the north of Mons city, southward via Nimy village and along the Nimy road to reach Mons (Grand Place) and thence turned west via the Grand'Rue and Rue des Capucins to reach Mons main line station. From there it took a circuitous course round the south of the city to a halt at Chemin d'Obourg and then up across fields to reach the Binche road to the south east, thus avoiding a steep climb by the direct route. It terminated just to the east of the mining village of St-Symphorien at an important phosphate works which provided much of its traffic. The section

'S' class in the street at Quiévrain   *(Paul de Backer)*

from St-Symphorien to Nimy opened first, on 17 December 1887, followed six days later by the remainder (the SNCV ignored the short hiatus in its reports!). Effectively it was worked in two sections, the northern stretch to Maisières being concerned mainly with commuter traffic and the eastern part depending heavily on freight. The depot for the line was at Mons Bassin, with a service link to the station and in 1888 a ring line (presumably for the freight traffic) was created using the Boulevards Britannique, Etats Unis and Italie; this was probably the local extension in Mons authorised on 27 February 1888. Finally a more substantial extension, authorised on 28 February 1889, was built from the northern terminus of Maisières northeastward to Casteau and opened on 8 June 1890.

* MONS - GHLIN. Authorised on 28 February 1889 like the Casteau branch and opened on 8 June 1889, this line ran almost due west from Mons Etat station through what was then agricultural countryside to the village of Ghlin, a quiet rural branch of which one Belgian historian commented "the most memorable thing about it was the extension to Baudour which, from 1 December 1915, joined the St-Ghislain network to that of Mons." - and which was lifted again in 1917.

* MONS - HAVRE came late. Authorised under the same capital, it was opened only on 6 December 1910 and was a straightforward steam-worked branch turning east by the Obourg road off the St-Symphorien line at a point where it left Mons. Entirely roadside and just 4km long, it ran along the roadside through pleasant wooded country to end at the big village of Havre; it was apparently worked as a separate route from Mons station.

All these three lines shared the same concessionaire and the same main depot, at Mons (Bassin) to the north of the standard-gauge station. All suffered whole or partial closure during the 1914-18 war, only Mons - Maisières - Casteau and Mons - Ghlin remaining intact. All were reopened in stages, to Baudour in February 1919, to Havre in June 1920 and to St-Symphorien in August 1920.

The next line actually to be opened in the area was **Capital 67 (BOUSSU A LA FRONTIÈRE VERS BAVAY)**, authorised on 20 June 1895 under the above vague title. It was isolated when opened on 14 July 1896, linkage to the rest of the system coming only a year later when the goods-only branch from Hautrage reached Boussu (Canal). The line started at Boussu (Canal), turned south to traverse that town via its square and mainline station, where the depot was situated, and then ran south on its own right-of-way through what was, at the time, mainly pleasant countryside. In the 14.73km actually built, it served the communities of Dour, Petit-Dour, Blaugies (whence a branch, never built, was planned eastward to Sars-la-Bruyère), Erquennes, Athis and Fayt-le-Franc, to end in the classic manner "in a field in the commune of Erquennes", where there was a secondary depot. This was presumably on the assumption that a French company would construct a cross-border link from Bavay but it was never built.

The northern part of Capital 67 saw fairly heavy coal traffic; the southern part was mainly agricultural since it ran through a very rural district - "diablement joli" was one contemporary and slightly wry description. As with other rural lines it was closed and at least partially lifted, from Dour southward, during the 1914-18 war; the Boussu - Dour section was reopened in 1919, the rest following on 6 December 1920.

Before Capital 67 in authorisation but after it in practice came **Capital 66 (LENS - ENGHIEN - SOIGNIES)** and its associated later links (Capitaux 101/104/125). Again, when

In the Borinage 1: A bustling scene at Frameries.
(collection Paul de Backer)

authorised on 29 December 1894, it was as an isolated line some distance due north of Mons, running northeast from the country town of Lens, not to be confused with the French mining town of that name. It reached Graty village, north east of the equally small village of Thoricourt, on 7 April 1898 and Enghien town, on the border of Brabant, on 1 October 1898. In the meanwhile, a branch from the oddly-named Noir Jambon (black ham), in the hamlet of Thoricourt, had been opened south eastward to Horrues and Soignies on 25 July 1898, mainly to serve quarries in the area. Operation was ceded to the CFVM and there was then an arc of track to the north of Mons.

Very soon the main line of Capital 66 was linked to Baudour by **Capital 101 (BAUDOUR - LENS - BAUFFE)**. Bauffe was actually a village to the northwest of Lens, the branch between the two, authorised on 12 July 1899, being the first part opened on 25 September 1899. It was followed by the "main" line northeast from Baudour to Lens, authorised on 15 January 1900 and opened on 28 January 1902 (official date 1 October 1899), which put the western Borinage in touch with Bruxelles long before it was linked to Mons itself. Meanwhile, showing a nice regard for commercial needs, the SNCV had authorised on 26 August 1900, and on 14 September 1901 had opened, a detached section of **Capital 104 (CASTEAU - CHAUSSÉE NOTRE-DAME-DE-LOUVIGNIES)** to join Neufvilles quarries to their standard-gauge station. The rest of that line was authorised on 31 January 1901 and construction followed in two stages: north from Neufvilles to the Soignies branch of Capital 66 at Horrues (Ch Notre-Dame-de-Louvignies) on 4 August 1903 and south from Neufvilles

station to Casteau on 23 February 1904. At Casteau the line met first the existing route from Mons via Maisières and then, within a couple of years, the main line of **Capital 125 (CASTEAU - BRACQUEGNIES)**. This latter, authorised on 11 April 1903, meandered eastward through Thieusies (opened 28 June 1906) and Roeulx (28 November 1906) to meet the lines of the Groupe du Centre at Bracquegnies on 22 October 1907. The lines were all operated by the CFVM and were soon interworked where this made sense. They were mainly rural and not particularly profitable. The sole extension project, from Noir Jambon west to Silly (8.07km) authorised in 1912 as an extension of Capital 66, remained stillborn. Like other lines of this group they suffered in the war; Baudour - Lens was put out of use by war damage, the Bauffe branch, Horrues - Soignies and the Neufvilles quarry line were all

lifted, being restored piecemeal during 1919. To bring the total system up to date: Mons - Havre had been built in 1910 as a dead-end branch, and in 1915 the western system had been linked to Mons via Baudour and Ghlin. Various lines had been wholly or partly lifted in the war but all were restored by 1924.

9.3.4 The SNCV 2: Urban networks in the Borinage area

Capital	Name	Auth km
127	Lignes Vicinales du Borinage	65.55

The SNCV intrusions into this geographical area were rather more complex than the earlier Mons area lines and can be divided into two linked parts: The compact urban electrified system to southwest of the city centre usually known as the "monophasé", and the network of, originally steam-worked, lines which connected to it.

The Monophasé system was the first SNCV development into the heavily built-up and industrial area to the southwest and south of Mons, known as the Borinage. This comprised a closely packed network of linked, grimy industrial communities to the immediate southwest of Mons centre, and a more sparsely scattered patchwork of industrial villages toward the French frontier to the south. The area was no stranger to rail transport, already having a dense web of standard-gauge lines and, indeed, having had some of the first colliery tramways in the country; the earliest of these dated from the 1830s and linked their industries to the extensive canal network. It is, therefore, rather surprising that the SNCV waited so long before entering the scene; the reason is probably that

Scenes in the Borinage 2: Frameries Grande Rue with a typical two-trolley 4-w car in green livery
(collection Paul de Backer)

the difficult terrain and urban environment needed electric trams and the SNCV made its first tentative experiments with electrification only in the early 1890s. The first exploratory plans were made in 1897 and 1898, finally envisaging four routes centred on Quevy, down near the French frontier: from Mons centre south to Quevy direct; from Quaregnon in the industrial heart of the Borinage south and east to Quévy via Aulnois; from Quevy east to Estinnes; and from the mining township of La Bouverie southeast to Harveng on the Mons - Quevy line. Authorisation for these lines was finally granted under **Capital 127 (LIGNES VICINALES DU BORINAGE)** on 17 June and 20 July 1903, together with two short lines, from Eugies to St-Ghislain and from Wasmes, on that line, to Pâturages on the Quaregnon route. In practice the system was built quite differently, mainly because of the mode of traction finally adopted, with consequent complications.

The SNCV, like several other companies at this time, was flirting with single-phase ac supply, a system which seemed to combine cheapness with the ability to take supplies direct from commercial generating companies rather than having to construct one's own supply network. Since the SNCV envisaged a 130km electric network, comprising Capitaux 25, 27, 67 (from Boussu to Dour) and 127, this appeared very tempting, and ambitious plans were laid accordingly. Fortunately, since the single-phase ac system (or monophasé as it was known locally) never realised its full potential, caution prevailed and the SNCV decided to start with only 20km of lines serving the most heavily populated areas, and then to see what happened. It cannily agreed with the big *Societé Intercommunale Belge d' Electricité (SIBE)* of Pâturages, for the latter both to furnish current and to build and equip the system on the understanding that, if it did not work well, the SIBE was mandated to convert it to direct current. The SIBE in turn subcontracted the *Union Elektrizitats Gesellschaft (UEG)* of Berlin, a leading advocate of ac traction, to construct and equip the tramways using 6.6kV supply at 40Hz, transformed to single-phase 600 volt supply through a series of small substations. The UEG in turn produced rolling stock very similar to previous SNCV cars, their main visual peculiarity being the two side-by-side trolley poles necessitated by an electrical system with two contact wires. This was intended to avoid interference with buried telephone lines and also to minimise complications of track maintenance.

All this led to a restructuring of individual lines within those authorised by the Capital (see map 34). Initially, a small self-contained group of lines was built within the Borinage and with a near contact to other SNCV lines only at St-Ghislain. The first route was Quaregnon - Pâturages - Wasmes - Eugies, opened as an electric line on 6 April 1905 and followed on 11 June 1905 by a link from Wasmes via Hornu to St-Ghislain Etat station, where the standard-gauge railway separated it from the SNCV steam line to Hautrage. A line from Pâturages to Frameries Nord-Belge station, with a branch from Frameries (Quatre-Pavés) to Eugies was opened on 10 February 1906, and on 1 May 1907 the system was completed by a short-cut linking these two lines, from La Bouverie (rue Ferrer) to La Bouverie (Couteaux). The ac system then comprised some 20 km of route with depot at Eugies and with five substations - at Hornu, Wasmes, Quaregnon, Frameries and Eugies. It crossed the Mons - Boussu dc tramway in two places, at Quaregnon and Hornu, but was not physically connected. Services on the system, once complete, were organised as follows:

Route	Headway
Quaregnon - Frameries (station)	30 min
Frameries (4 Pavés) - Eugies - Wasmes - St-Ghislain	30 min
Eugies - La Bouverie (cut-off) - Pâturages	2 hr
Pâturages - Wasmes shuttle	15 min

There were some short workings, and extra services ran at weekends and holidays; the services were initially not numbered, simply displaying small headboards with their principal destinations. The system was operated directly by the SNCV from its opening. In practice this remained the total monophasé system with the sole addition, in 1914 of the 6.5km route from Mons to Frameries.

So much for the monophasé . While this was going on, the SNCV was also building the more rural extremities of the authorised lines. Pending evaluation of the single-phase system, these were built as steam tramways with an infrequent service, and operation was temporarily granted to the local company, the *CFVM*. First was the straightforward extension from Frameries station eastward to Harveng, opened on 15 May 1907 and followed a year later on 1 May 1908 by the original north-south line from Mons through Harveng to Quévy. Quévy indeed soon became a considerable junction; on 10 August 1909 was opened the line east from there via Givry to Haulchin (actually the station of Estinnes-au-Mont where it met a newly-opened

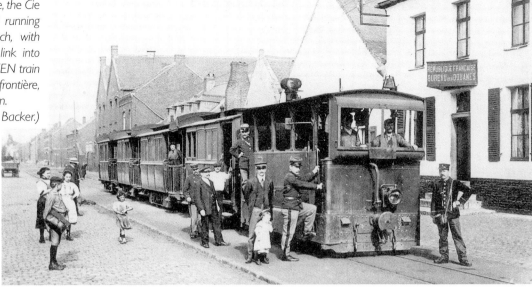

branch of the Réseau du Centre, from La Louvière) and on 1 March 1910 the long rambling line from Eugies via Aulnois followed. The Lignes du Borinage thus at last had direct, if tortuous, links right into Mons centre and also provided an equally tortuous connection towards Charleroi. Passengers naturally had to change at the steam/electric junction points, and the rural lines appear to have been run as separate entities.

The SNCV went some way toward rationalising this situation when it took over the whole system in 1911, although a tentative UEG plan for high-voltage ac electrification of Frameries - Harveng, dating from 1906, was not proceeded with as it would have required dual-supply equipment for interchange with the urban lines. The SNCV, however, did put forward tentative plans for extending the existing electrified system, proposing a line from Mons (Grand Place) to Frameries (Quatre Pavés); a link from Wasmes west to Dour with a branch from Warquignies to Petit-Dour; and a network of short lines linking Jemappes and Cuesmes with Flenu, Pâturages, La Bouverie and Frameries. On the rural sections, steam-worked branches were suggested from Sars-la-Bruyère, on the Aulnois line, west to Blaugies, and from Harveng southeast via Givry to Erquelinnes on the French border with a link en route into France. Of all these only the section from Mons to Frameries was built immediately, in stages between 1911 and 1915, while of the others only Harveng - Givry saw the light of day in original form. The Mons - Frameries line was initially built as intended, though a delay in constructing a viaduct at Cuesmes (Etat-Belge) meant that, when opened on 31 March 1912, it was worked piecemeal by "benzo-electric" cars 9426-8. Only on 9 July 1914 was the single-phase system put through from Frameries to Mons (Ave de Berlaimont) with an hourly service, and the outbreak of war delayed extension to the Grand Place until 3 December 1915. The single-phase system then totalled some 26.5 km, the cut-off at La Bouverie having been closed in 1913 as unnecessary.

Alas, no sooner opened than closed. Mons - Frameries, Eugies - Quevy - Estinnes, and Frameries - Harveng were all taken out of service during the war and not restored until October 1921 by which time the CFVM had surrendered its concessions. When they did reopen, the electrified lines were cut back from Frameries station to Quatre Pavés, and services were reorganised into three routes, each with a 30-minute service:

*   Mons - Frameries - Pâturages,
*   St-Ghislain - Wasmes - Pâturages - Quaregnon,
*   Wasmes - Eugies - Frameries.

The reconstruction, and assumption of direct control, gave the SNCV a chance to review its holdings in Capital 127. The steam-worked lines remained much the same, the long-projected extension from Harveng reaching Givry on 20 July 1924 and going no further. The electric lines, however, had to submit to a more drastic upheaval: the single-phase system was in trouble, not so much for inherent defects as because SIBE was finding it difficult to provide a reliable electricity supply. In addition, the standard SNCV 600-volt dc system had by now been fully established, and the Societé envisaged a rapid extension of its electrified routes to link with La Louvière and Charleroi. It therefore decided to convert the existing Mons system to 600 volts dc in stages, and this was done during 1921. Fifteen "Tashkent" cars originating in a cancelled export order (9615-22/29-35) were brought in to provide a "float" of stock, and the existing cars were withdrawn in batches for refitting with dc controllers and GE249 motors. The second overhead wire was left in situ for a time, but was then removed to allow the remaining wire to be aligned centrally; this permitted bow collectors and, later, pantographs to be fitted in place of trolley poles. Wasmes substation was equipped as a rectifier station, the others being abandoned, and services were once more altered to provide two routes from Mons via Frameries (to Pâturages, and to Wasmes via Eugies) plus the St-Ghislain - Quaregnon line, this being the position in the mid-1920s. It may be worth noting, too, that the region saw its first essay into railcars since the Benzos, when Mons-Quevy was provided with two railbuses in the shape of AR 11-12, heavy single-ended vehicles ordered through Franco-Belge and built by the German firms of Bussing and Uerdingen.

9.3.5 Peripheral lines along the French border

capital	title	auth Km
35	*Quiévrain - Roisin et à la Frontière*	11.70
162	*Mainvault - Pommeroeul - Quiévrain*	35.68
186	*Dour - Pommeroeul - Quiévrain*	23.00

Inevitably there were the usual detached lines around the periphery. The first of these lines, **Capital 35 (QUIÉVRAIN**

- ROISIN ET A LA FRONTIÈRE) was authorised as early as 28 February 1889 and was always the "odd man out" among the Mons systems. Originally an isolated line, it lay right against the French frontier to the west of Mons and was conceded initially to the French *CF Economiques du Nord* (app 5), which also ran the suburban tram network around nearby Valenciennes. This met the Belgian frontier at the railway district of Blanc Misseron and the first part of Capital 35 to open, on 15 March 1890, was a 1.28km extension of this CEN branch to Quiévrain standard-gauge station. The main line south to Baisieux and Roisin, 10.43km long, opened on 10 November 1890, a quiet country backwater with its depot at Roisin. Matters remained thus until 1911 when, possibly in anticipation of Capital 162, the Quiévrain - Roisin concession was transferred to the TUV, which already ran most lines in the Tournaisis - a clear indication that the line was then being thought of as within the influence of Tournai rather than Mons. The frontier link stayed with the CEN and was even electrified by them in 1914 when they electrified the Valenciennes system. It therefore escaped the fate of the remainder, which closed during the war and reopened only in December 1919. Its future history and the complications of its links with Capital 162 and Mons are described later.

To this period also belongs the confusing story of **Capital 162 (MAINVAULT - POMMEROEUL - QUIÉVRAIN)**. It was originally conceived as a complex of lines serving the essentially rural area to the west and north of the Borinage proper, and was envisaged as having three branches. The first was a long, north - south artery from Mainvault on the Tournai system, through Quévaucamps, Grandglise and Pommeroeul to Quiévrain, where it was to connect with the existing Capital 35 to Roisin. It was authorised on 11 May 1908, and construction started from both ends, apparently under direct SNCV control. The northern section was actually opened to Quévaucamps on 31 January 1916 and on to Grandglise, as part of post-war plans, on 28 October 1923 while the southern section came up as far as Montroeul-s-Haine and thence to Pommeroeul (Canal) by 14 April 1922, after which there was silence, though many of the intervening earthworks were complete. The other two lines were finally authorised on 13 April 1912 apparently separately as **Capital 186 (DOUR - POMMEROEUL - QUIÉVRAIN)** (23 km) but were not even started, probably because of the war. They were to have linked Pommeroeul to Elouges and Dour, and Dour to Quiévrain direct; possibly failure to construct the Dour - Wasmes section of Capital 127 also contributed. Thus the only results were the northern section transferred to Tournai group and the section to Quiévrain taken over by the TUV. It should be noted that a connection was later put in from Dour in the 1950s, but it was on a different route and financed by a different Capital.

9.3.6 SNCV: Developments from 1924-1939

By the end of 1924, the SNCV was in full control of all its lines in the Mons area. Although most of the extensions planned before World War I were abandoned, with the exception of Harveng- Givry, a fairly cautious programme of linking up with neighbouring systems was begun. 12 November 1923 saw a steam-worked extension from St -Symphorien east to Bray (Etat station), giving a direct link to La Louvière and Charleroi, while to the west a short spur from Stambruges into Grandglise in 1925 brought the Mainvault line back into the fold with a rather rambling connection to Tournai. In addition, as already noted, the SNCB Mons - Boussu tramway was taken over in 1928 as

Capital 197, and by the end of that decade the group's services had been reorganised yet again. In 1929, just before the big electrifications, the electric lines were running as shown below,

route	headway
Mons - Boussu (ex SNCB)	15 min
Mons - Pâturages (Pl. St.Pierre)	30 min
Frameries - Pâturages (short workings)	15 min*
Mons - Eugies - Wasmes (rue de Maubeuge)	30 min
St.Ghislain - Wasmes - Quaregnon	30 min/15 min*
* rush hours only	

The steam lines were given some interworking to rationalise connections. Thus there was a Mons - Estinnes service via Harveng and Givry; Frameries - Harveng trains were extended to Quevy; the northwest lines were focussed on St-Ghislain with through services to Quévaucamps (handover to the Tournai group) and Lens, while operation of the Lens group of lines was centred on Soignies.

As elsewhere in Belgium, the year 1930 was probably the climacteric, for it saw a wholesale programme of electrification with further extensions. First to benefit was the Mons - Maisières route, electrified on 14 August 1930 and utilising existing stock from the Borinage system. The line to St.Symphorien and Bray followed on 24 December. At the same time, route letters were introduced, the situation at the end of 1930 being:

letter	route
B	Mons - Boussu
C	Mons - Bray (in anticipation of extension to Charleroi)
E	Mons - Eugies - Wasmes
M	Mons - Maisières
P	Mons - Pâturages
S	St.Ghislain - Wasmes
W	Wasmes - St.Ghislain

The Bray line's branch to Havre, operated as a separate route, was electrified on 1 September 1931 and about the same time the line from Mons to Ghlin (20 October 1931) and on to Baudour (19 December 1931) was electrified together with the stretches from Boussu through Dour (7 February 1931) to Fayt-le-Franc (31 October 1931). The Maisières - Casteau extension followed on 1 May 1932.

As part of all this rearrangement, three short new sections were put in at Mons itself. An east-west line from the station through the Grand Place was created by two short links, from Place de la Gare to Rue des Capucins and from Grand Place to rue de la Biche. It was supplemented in 1934 by a parallel route along the rues des Cleres, du Chapitre and de la Houssière, while a cutoff along the Binche road replaced the old steam line detour via the Roeulx road - electric trams could climb steeper gradients! At the same time the system of route letters was extended (see Table 9B). One should note also several fairly short but important links put in during the 1930s under the appropriate Capitaux. Down on the Bray route (Capital 27), Bray and Binche were, as anticipated, linked on 15 February 1931 to give a direct electric line to Charleroi, this involving a short section of new track between Bray (Barrière) and Binche. At Havre, successive extensions brought the terminus from Château to Place Communale on 1 September 1931 and to Gare (standard gauge station) by 1932; to Maurage (Place) by 12 August 1933 and on to Maurage (Etincelles) by 1 July 1934. A connection from Bracquegnies linked it to the Centre lines on 1 August 1936 with a direct service to La Louvière.

Meanwhile, a short spur off the Maurage line, to the Mons suburb of Obourg, opened on 31 August 1935 giving Obourg a direct link into Mons centre.

To support all these extensions, there was naturally an increase in stock. On the electrified lines the four-wheeled cars of series 9920-39 were soon followed by "Standard" bogie cars fitted with pantographs. On the steam-worked lines, autorails were introduced from 1930 onward, starting with experimental use of AR 4 and followed in 1932 by the big Bussing single-enders, AR 11-12. Standard autorails were introduced generally from 1933-on, some thirty three being in service by 1939. Thus, by the end of 1936, when the Groupe was subsumed into Groupe du Hainaut, it was in full expansion. The route lettering was extended steadily and eventually, under Groupe du Hainaut, changed to route numbers. There were various changes but the table below probably reflects the general position in the mid 1930s, showing the original letter designations and the equivalent numbers.

Table 9B: A snapshot of Mons area services in the 1930s

Route	codes	Route details
A	15	Mons - Casteau (from 1 May 1932)
B	6	Mons - Boussu
C	90	Mons - Bray (route MC from 15 Feb 1931)
D	7	Mons - Boussu - Dour
E	2	Mons - Eugies - Wasmes
F	8	Mons - Boussu —Fayt-le-Franc
G	10	Mons - Ghlin
H		Mons - Havre (to 31 Aug 1935)
L	17*	Mons - Maurage
M	14	Mons - Maisières (later to Casteau)
MC	90	Mons - Charleroi (from 15 Feb 1931)
N	13	Mons - Nimy
O	16	Mons - Obourg (from 31 Aug 1935)
P	1	Mons - Frameries —Pâturages
R	11	Ghlin - Baudour
S	4	St-Ghislain - Wasmes - Ouaregnon
W	4	reverse working of S

NOTE:
* quickly replaced by through service 31.

In the remaining years up to World War II, further new electrically-worked extensions were constructed in the Borinage proper. On 10 April 1937, a short section to Boussu (Temple) lengthened route 6. Later the same year, on 15 September 1937, that route was again extended to Dour (Trichères) thus bringing about, though by a different route, a link suggested forty years earlier. The following year saw another east-west link off this line, from Trichères first to Warquignies (garage) on 1 February 1938 and then on to Wasmes (Rue Royale) on 1 March 1938. Physical junction with the original Borinage network at Wasmes, however, was delayed by the war until 1 April 1941, at which date a new route 2 from Mons via Eugies to Dour replaced the short-working route 9 from Boussu (Temple). Meanwhile, the final pre-war extension had been opened on 1 August 1938 from Quaregnon SNCB north to Baudour via a connection with the Ghlin line at Douvrain. A route 5 was then created, running in a big semi-circle from St Ghislain to Baudour via Wasmes, Pâturages and Quaregnon.

9.4.1 Introduction

The clusters of lines in the centre of Hainaut, between Moms and the Charleroi area, were initially regarded as a separate entity although they were basically a hotch-potch. The overall allocation of Capitaux was essentially as shown below.

Capital	Name	Auth km
43	Lignes du Centre I	43.52
89	Binche - Bracquegnies et La Louvière - Estinnes	22.52
124	Mariemont - Chapelle lez Herlaimont	3.00
145	Haine St.Pierre - La Louvière - Familleureux	n/k
155	Carnières - Thuin*	13.00
157	Chapelle-lez-Herlaimont - Anderlues*	16.52
159	Binche à Beaumont et à Bersillies-l'Abbaye	32.93
167	(Binche -) Leval - Anderlues*	10.30

NOTE: * part of Lignes du Centre II.

Sometimes associated with these is Capital 125 Casteau - Braquegnies which linked with the Mons group; it is described under Mons because of its original concessionaire.

East of Mons and in the industrial heart of the industrial Hainaut lies that complex of towns whose names are especially evocative to railway historians: La Louvière, Haine-St-Pierre, Familleureux, La Hestre, Manage, all giving title to railway stock builders known the length and breadth of Europe. Their SNCV history is as complex as the region for, although only four main Capitaux were involved, all took a long time a-building and got tangled up at various points, both with each other and with antennae from Mons and Charleroi. It must be remembered that, even though it all looks extensive on a map, we are dealing here with a small densely-populated area; from Binche to La Louvière is only about 11 km, and from Bracquegnies across to Morlanwelz is scarcely longer. It seems sensible, therefore, to try and sort out the early history by systems; those which criss-crossed the area of La Louvière with lines and those which served the surrounding country - and the heart of all these was that network of lines known as the Lignes du Centre I with its more rural extensions collectively called Lignes du Centre II.

9.4.2 Lignes du Centre I (Capital 43)

Capital	Name	Auth km
43	Lignes du Centre I	43.52
124	Mariemont - Chapelle lez Herlaimont	3.00km*
145	Haine St.Pierre - La Louvière - Familleureux	n/k*

* these two were later assimilated into Capital 43

The first batch of lines in the district were those known collectively as **Capital 43 (LIGNES DU CENTRE I)**. As at Mons, the SNCV came early to La Louvière, but it served the urban centres from the start and was only the second SNCV system to be electrified. Discussions started in 1888, and the first authorisation for a network of urban lines in and around

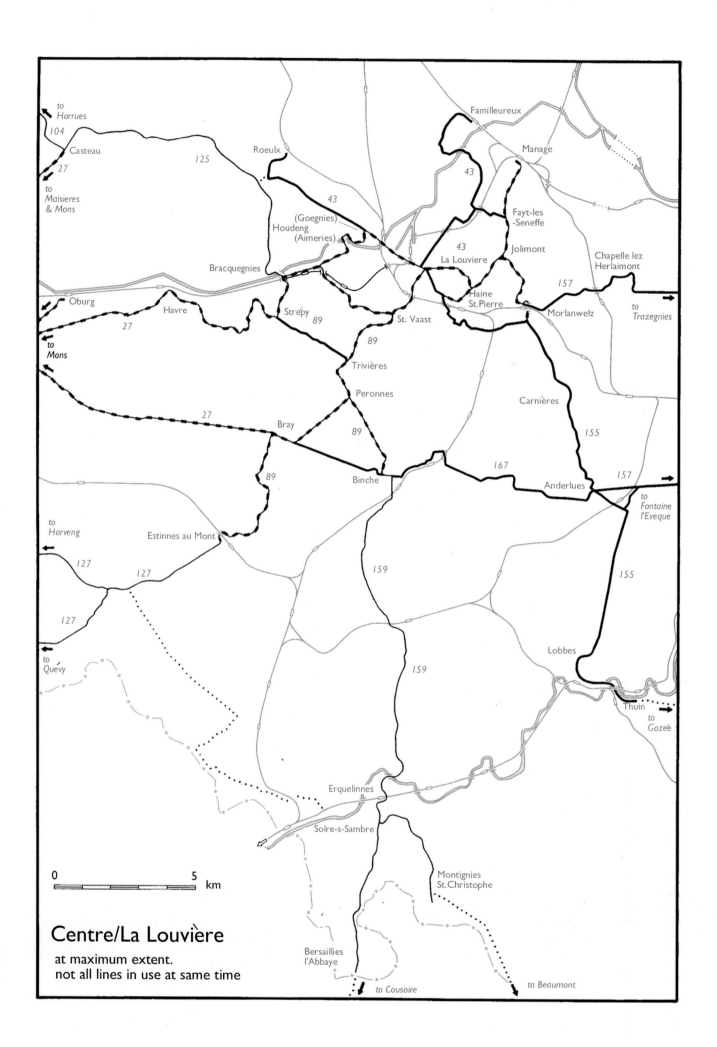

to
Horrues

104

Casteau

27

to
Maisieres
& Mons

125

Roeulx

43

Familleureux

Manage

43

Fayt-les
-Seneffe

Jolimont

Chapelle lez
Herlaimont

157

to
Trazegnies

(Goegnies)
Houdeng
(Aimeries)

43

La Louviere

Bracquegnies

Haine
St.Pierre

Morlanwelz

Oburg

Havre

27

Strépy 89

St. Vaast

89

Trivières

Peronnes

Carnières

155

to
Mons

27

Bray

89

Binche

89

167

Anderlues

157

to
Fontaine
l'Eveque

to
Harveng

127

Estinnes au Mont

159

127

127

Lobbes

155

to
Quévy

159

Thuin

to
Gozeé

Erquelinnes

Solre-s-Sambre

Montignies
St.Christophe

0   5 km

Centre/La Louvière

at maximum extent.
not all lines in use at same time

Bersaillies
l'Abbaye

to Cousoire

to Beaumont

A remembrance of the Centre: Rue Hamoir, looking towards Manage, with a standard bogie car on doubletrack. (commercial card. collection Paul de Backer.)

the area of La Louvière was granted on 28 July 1890 followed by extension orders on 11 April 1892 and 23 May 1893. Construction was quick, the first routes being opened on 20 October 1891 with operation, as for all lines in this Capital, being granted to the SA des CF Vicinaux du Centre (CFVC).

These first routes effectively criss-crossed the major population centres. They consisted of five main sections. First was a line south from Manage (Chaussée de Nivelles) through the eastern fringes of La Louvière, then turning west via the town centre to the suburb of Houdeng where it terminated at Houdeng-Aimeries; a problem of bridging the Canal du Centre temporarily prevented any extension towards Bracquegnies, which was the final goal. Off this line to the east, branches ran from Jolimont to the large village of Morlanwelz and from Pont Brognies south to Haine-St-Pierre with its heavy industry. The routes were mainly roadside, except just south of Manage and between Jolimont and Pont Brognies, where they detoured on their own right-of-way to avoid heavy gradients; and through Mariemont woods on the Morlanwelz branch. The complex was steam-operated with a depot at La Louvière, and appears to have been worked initially as a north-south line from Manage to Haine-St-Pierre and an east-west one from Houdeng to Morlanwelz. It was purely passenger-carrying and the traffic exceeded expectations, so much so that extra stock had to be provided and an hourly service was run. On 11 June 1895 it was extended to Bracquegnies using a massive swing bridge over the Canal du Centre.

The success of this first line encouraged the SNCV to develop further and, consequent on its initial trials in Brabant, to suggest full-scale electrification. Its initial requirements frightened off prospective builders, but rapid adjustments were made; as a result in June 1896, the Union Elektrizitats Gesellschaft (UEG) of Berlin was appointed as main contractor to electrify existing lines and equip any future ones. The 500-volt dc overhead wire system already used at Petite Espinette was

adopted, using trolley-pole collection and almost identical motor cars; a generating station was established at La Louvière depot

Existing lines were converted first, being operated as electric routes in two stages from 7 December and 14 December 1898 with an improved service. Over the next few years, various minor extensions of these original lines were built, most importantly from Morlanwelz (Place) south to Carnières authorised on 22 July 1897 and opened on 26 May 1900 and, as a separate route, east from Mariemont station on the Morlanwelz branch as far as Chapelle-lez-Herlaimont (3km). Technically this latter was authorised as **Capital 124 (MARIEMONT - CHAPELLE LEZ HERLAIMONT)** on 28 December 1902 and opened on 28 June 1903; it was actually the trunk section for an SNCV project to extend eastwards, but was frustrated for the time by local opposition and was assimilated into Capital 43 from 30 January 1905. Lastly, a short extension in Manage itself brought the terminus from the Nivelles Road level crossing up to the standard-gauge station from 27 April 1904. All lines were electrically worked from the start and traffic was so heavy that in 1907 short lengths of track at Mariemont and between Jolimont and La Louvière were doubled.

Meanwhile there was slow progress on a further extension often considered as a separate line. Starting from Houdeng on the Bracquegnies route, it was electrified from new and ran northwestward to that quarter of Houdeng-Aimeries known as Pont-du-Sart; it was authorised on 22 July 1897 and opened 14 December 1898. A further short extension of 2km or so to Roeulx centre was authorised on 22 June 1905 and opened on 24 February 1906 bringing the total length to some 3.4km, and a final stretch was authorised on 4 August 1910 and opened on 6 October 1911, winding through the streets below Roeulx castle to end up at the standard-gauge station. It took over twelve years to open about 4km of line, but then Roeulx was always unlucky in its tramways. A project for linking Roeulx station with Braine-le-Comte via Henripont was found to be dubiously viable and promptly dropped, and even a later short link to the Mons system was never used although the track was put in. The existing route was operated mainly as a shuttle from La Louvière and trams normally stopped in the centre of town; they reached the station only during rush hours; at weekends and holidays they didn't even reach La Louvière, terminating at Houdeng where passengers had to change.

To return to 1907, however, that year saw the last of the Centre I lines started. This also had a quickly-dropped scheme for a link to Braine-le-Comte from its northern end but was planned mainly as a crosstown link from Familleureux in the north, through La Louvière to Haine-St-Pierre and thence eastward via Hayettes to Morlanwelz. La Louvière - Haine-St.Pierre was authorised on 8 July 1905 and La Louvière - Familleureux on 12 May 1906 both as a nominally separate **Capital 145 (HAINE ST PIERRE - LA LOUVIÈRE - FAMILLEUREUX)**; they were in practice built piecemeal. The Haine-St-Pierre to La Louvière (Centre) part opened as a shuttle service on 30 March 1907, and was followed on 14 August 1907 by a section northward as far as La Croyère, but the final few km proved a real struggle: La Croyère - Pont-au-Thiriau on 22 February 1908; Pont-au-Thiriau to Bois-d'Haine on 25 April 1908; Bois-d'Haine to Familleureux only on 13 March 1910 - by which time the scheme had been assimilated into Capital 43 from 10 July 1908. In 1910, also, a short cross line from La Croyère to Fayt-lez-Seneffe on the Manage route was opened (authorised 7 August 1909 and opened 1 December 1910) and just before World War 1 the SNCV actually managed a junction with existing lines at Haine-St-Pierre. As for the Morlanwelz section which was authorised on 15 May 1912, well, that was delayed by a complicated bridging problem at Hayettes and, what with the war and one thing and another, it did not get opened until 1933. Otherwise Centre I was complete and, with only minor adjustments, was handed over to the SNCV in 1922 when the concessionaire withdrew.

9.4.3 Lignes du Centre II
(Capitaux 155, 157, 167)

capital	Route	auth km
155	Carnières - Thuin	13.00
157	Chapelle-lez-Herlaimont - Anderlues	16.52
167	(Binche -) Leval - Anderlues	10.30

Although not next in chronological sequence, the Lignes du Centre II were so closely linked with their predecessors that they must be dealt with here. They were actually authorised in 1906 as three separate Capitaux, all of which were under direct SNCV control from new and were planned as electric lines. Breaking with SNCV tradition, current was to be provided at industrial voltage by a commercial undertaking, and transformed and rectified to 500 volts dc through two substations: at Anderlues and at Trazegnies on Capital 157. In due course, the operating voltage rose over the years to 600.

In practice the group was built as a whole, the various discontinuities coming more from physical problems than defects in the financing. The first section was on **Capital 157 (ANDERLUES DEPOT - FONTAINE-L'EVEQUE)**, east from Chapelle-lez-Herlaimont to Trazegnies standard-gauge station; it was officially opened on 1 August 1908, though not put into public service until a week later. Eventually to be very important as part of an east-west link, the line currently turned south to reach Fontaine-l'Eveque station, though problems with Trazegnies viaduct delayed its opening until 6 December

1910. By that time the section of **Capital 155 (Carnières - Thuin)** south from Carnières to Anderlues Etat station (6.03km) had been opened on 1 October 1910, quickly followed by the remainder of Capital 157 on 1 November 1910. The Anderlues (Depot - Station) link was not finished until 10 May 1911, again owing to bridging works over the standard gauge. This last link completed what was in effect a huge circular route including some parts of the Centre I layout. Thus Centre II trams started from Mariemont station, where connection was made with trams from La Louvière, and terminated on the same line at Morlanwelz SNCV (or vice versa). In between, they ran through a series of densely-populated townships, and passenger traffic was high.

Meanwhile, to complete the story, the next section of Capital 155, from Anderlues south to Lobbes was opened on 11 April 1914, though the final part to Thuin had to wait until 1930 owing to the war and legal troubles. A long-talked-of extension from Thuin to Nalinnes (15.5km) never saw the light of day. On the other hand, **Capital 167 ((BINCHE -) LEVAL - ANDERLUES)** was completed on 4 May 1915 and worked as a shuttle from Anderlues (Monument) as far as Leval-Trahegnies (la Madeleine). No Centre I or Centre II lines suffered during World War I but it did delay the inevitable link from Leval-Trahegnies west to Binche, which was not completed until 3 July 1926.

9.4.4 Groupe du Centre: connecting lines

capital	route	auth km
89	Binche - Bracquegnies et La Louvière - Estinnes	22.5
159	Binche à Beaumont et à Bersillies-l'Abbaye	32.93

1903, meanwhile, saw the first real penetration of the Groupe du Centre into the surrounding countryside. **Capital 89 (BINCHE - BRACQUEGNIES ET LA LOUVIÈRE - ESTINNES-AU-MONT)**, was authorised in 1896 for the construction of a network of largely rural tramways to be centred on the town of Binche, some 10km south of La Louvière, and to be steam-worked. Negotiations had indeed been going on since 1892, but work did not start until 1900, and even after that the arguments continued; it appears the communes concerned did not altogether share the SNCV's enthusiasm. The first section was opened on 21 February 1903. It ran north from Binche on its own right-of-way through rather bleak country to meet industry at St-Vaast and then swing northwest to Bois-du-Luc (12 km); legal hitches delayed the completion to Bracquegnies until 21 May 1903.

Operation of this and associated lines was ceded to the specially-formed SA pour l' Exploitation de la Ligne Vicinale de Binche - Bracquegnies et Extensions (BB) and the main depot was halfway along it at Trivières. Subsequent extensions pushed the line from St-Vaast north into La Louvière on 16 May 1907, though it made no physical connection with the electrified lines; more importantly, the long projected branch southwest from Peronnes to Estinnes-au-Mont was specifically authorised in 1906 and opened through Bray to Estinnes-au-Val on 1 September 1908. The uphill spur to Estinnes-au-Mont standard-gauge station followed on 1 August 1909, and the first link to the Groupe de Mons was thereby established (with the line from Quevy). Further improvements were contemplated almost immediately. Two short extensions, from Bracquegnies to Havre and from Trivières across to the "Havre project" at Strepy were authorised on 27 November 1911, though nothing was actually done, and on 22 May 1911 the direct line La

Louvière - St-Vaast - Trivières - Peronnes - Binche was electrified using standard 500 volts dc with trolley-pole collection. Cars of the 9353-8 series, built by the local firm of Ateliers du Roeulx, were used with matching trailers. This thus became the main line, the St- Vaast - Bracquegnies line, when electrified on 8 March 1913, being treated as a shuttle. Matters stayed thus throughout World War I, all lines remaining intact. They were surrendered to SNCV control in 1921.

Meanwhile, back in the early 1900s, the possibility of yet another rambling line had been tentatively explored. This eventually emerged as **Capital 159 (BINCHE A BEAUMONT ET A BERSILLIES-L'ABBAYE)**, authorised on 9 February 1907. It was planned as a steam-worked line south from Binche to Solre-s-Sambre and on southeast to Beaumont, with a branch from Solre to Bersillies-l' Abbaye near the French frontier; there was also talk of a short cross-border link into Cousoire in France, but it never materialised. Indeed the whole line had a rather frustrating early history and appears never to have left SNCV control. Work started in 1908 and the section between Merbes-le-Chateau, just north of Solre, and Vellereille-les-Brayeux, just south of Binche, was actually ready by 1910, but modification of an awkward bridge at Binche delayed the opening until 18 May 1912. The sections south to Bersillies and from Solre (depot) as far as the little village of Montignies-St-Christophe were opened some two years later on 3 March 1914, (SNCV: some sources say 3 April) giving a total of 23.66km built; earthworks on the remainder were well advanced when, during the war, the Germans ordered the whole line to be closed and lifted. In practice it appears that Binche - Solre-s-Sambre remained open and that the other lines were reopened piecemeal in September 1921, but neither the Montignies - Beaumont section nor the French link were revived. The line was exclusively rural with very light traffic. Nothing came either of the associated **Capital 180 (SIVRY - BEAUMONT -SILENRIEUX)**, a complex of three branches authorised in 1912, and planned to extend south and east from Beaumont to a total length of 31.70km.

9.4.5 SNCV Groupe du Centre, 1921-1939

By autumn 1921, the *SNCV's Groupe du Centre* was operating all lines previously described. Apart from a service

link between the Binche and Centre I lines at La Louvière in 1925, electrification of the Leval - Bracquegnies - Binche line on 3 July 1926 and a connection to Charleroi via Fontaine-l'Eveque on 30 June 1929, there was little real change until the 1930s electrifications. Then Lobbes - Thuin was electrified from 17 May 1930, and the route from Peronnes to Bray was electrified from 31 December 1930 as part of a through link (La Louvière - Peronnes - Bray - Mons) and was followed on 15 October 1931 by the branch from Bray to Estinnes-au-Mont. Lastly, a new link Morlanwelz - Hayettes - Haine St.Pierre followed on 1 July 1933, electrified from the start. From 1 July 1931, too, the group's services were reorganised as shown in Table 9C. The numberings were theoretically allocated to particular Capitaux but soon got mixed up.

Table 9C: Centre Routes in 1931

No	Route details
1	Bracquegnies - La Louvière - Mariemont - Morlanwelz
2	Manage - Haine-St-Pierre - La Louvière - Familleureux
3	Manage - Haine-St-Pierre - La Louvière - Fayt
5	Houdeng-Goegnies - Roeulx
	(combined with new route 4 in 1933)
6	La Louvière - St-Vaast - Peronnes - Binche
7	St-Vaast - Bracquegnies
8	Peronnes - Bray - Estinnes-au-Mont
9	Mariemont - Trazegnies - Fontaine-l'Eveque
	(to 30 Jun 1933)
10	Anderlues Jonction - Thuin

Route number 4 was allocated to a link from Morlanwelz through Hayettes and Haine-St.Pierre to La Louvière which came into operation from 1 July 1933. It was then combined with route 5 and renumbered 9, the latter being subsumed in a new route 11 as below.

11	Bracquegnies - La Louvière - Mariemont - Trazegnies - Fontaine-l'Eveque (from 1 Jul 1933)

Routeings were getting more complex all the time as the Centre was joined to its neighbours and patterns of route designation changed accordingly (see below). First, two lines penetrated the Centre: Mons route C (Mons - La Louvière via Bray and Peronnes); Charleroi route 78 (Charleroi - Fontaine-l'Eveque - Binche, from 30 June 1929). A second link from

Lamahide, down in the south was an equally typical village halt, here with a standard railcar in later days.

(JW Smith)

Chastre — Gare du Vicinal

In the centre & east there were also country lines at the edges. Chastre, on the line to Incourt in Brabant, is a typical large SNCV country station.
(author's collection)

And there were rural bits: Nalinnes sidings right down near the end of the long railcar line from Charleroi to Bultia
(P van Campenhoudt)

Table 9D: Centre Routes after 1937

Route.	Route details
30	Anderlues - Jolimont - La Louvière - Bracquegnies
31	Charleroi (R Turenne) - Anderlues - La Louvière - Bracquegnies
32	Manage - Jolimont - Haine-St-Pierre - La Louvière - Familleureux
33	Manage - Jolimont - Haine-St-Pierre - La Louvière - Fayt - Manage
34	Roeulx - La Louvière - Morlanwelz - Carnières
35	Manage - Fayt - La Louvière - Haine-St-Pierre - Jolimont - Fayt - Manage
36	La Louvière - Trivières - Binche
37	La Louvière - St-Vaast - Bois-du-Luc
38	(La Louvière -) Peronnes - Bray - Estinnes-au-Mont 39 Manage - Jolimont - La Louvière - La Croyère
40	Trivières - Strepy

Charleroi was established on 25 September 1932 by a new line from Courcelles to Trazegnies (route 61, altered to route 80 when the direct line via Roux was opened on 1 December 1933). It was extended to Bracquegnies in 1935, replacing existing route 11. Lastly, on 1 August 1936, another link to Mons was established from Bracquegnies via Strepy with an end-on junction to Capital 27 at Maurage (Etincelles), while 1 July 1937 saw the eventual opening, as an electric line, of the Trivières - Strepy branch of Capital 89. That was basically the position when war broke out in 1939, by which time, as related on page 148, the whole Hainaut system had a "rationalised" system of routes in which the Centre was allocated numbers 30 - 40 A typical snapshot of the position in 1937 is given in table 9D

9.5   Hainaut: Groupe de Charleroi

Capital	Name	Auth km
9	*Charleroi - Mont-s-Marchienne*	*4.31*
10	*Charleroi - Lodelinsart (St-Antoine)*	*3.50*
11	*Charleroi - Montigny-le-Tilleul*	*8.72*
40	*Lodelinsart (Bonnaire) - Chatelet*	*?8.13*
62	*Montigny-le-Tilleul - Thuillies*	*11.36*
92	*Charleroi - Nalinnes et Embrt vers Marcinelle*	*18.40*
39	*Charleroi - Jumet (Heigne)**	*3.00*
170	*Chatelet - Fosse*	*15.37*
196	*Trazegnies (station) - Courcelles (Motte)*	*?*
198	*Gilly - Ransart (Masses Darbois)*	*2.75*
202	*Marchienne-au-Pont (Stn) - Courcelles (Trieux)*	
	Souvret - Roux (Plomcot)	*?*

NOTE:
* *subsumed into Capital 10 before opening but also used for lines between Jumet and Gosselies.*

9.5.1. Introduction to Charleroi area

The original Charleroi system was, as one Belgian commentator has remarked, a "compact enough little system" but its history is anything but compact. Nowhere else did the SNCV become so embroiled with the local urban tramway concessionaires or enter into such complex cross-leasing or running-power arrangements. Only the first period of its history is, more or less, simple and that may have been partly because of the terrain.

"Charleroi" as an area is really a complex of interlinked mining and industrial towns of which the township of Charleroi itself, spread along the River Sambre, is but one - though somewhat unusual in that mines sprout from the middle of the urban area. It is surrounded by neighbours: Jumet, Lodelinsart, Roux, Mont-s-Marchienne, Marchienne-au-Pont, to name only the nearest, have much the same relationship to their administrative centre as Harborne or Hall Green have to the city of Birmingham. This complex that is Charleroi lies on very hilly ground, especially in its northwest quarter, and so initially the steam-worked lines of the SNCV struck out to the south and east over easier country. The SNCV was not the first light railway builder in the region in any case, the grandly named *Societé de CF Vicinaux Belges (CFVB)* having been active since 1882. By 1887 the CFVB was running not only urban lines but a suburban network extending to Gilly in the northeast and to Montigny-s-Sambre and Couillet to the south-east. It was into this existing standard-gauge system that the SNCV, between 1887 and 1918, inserted its comprehensive network of metre-gauge lines. Because of the situation - and the involvement of several concessionaires - there was no such thing as a formal operating Groupe de Charleroi to begin with and the development is probably best taken chronologically.

9.5.2   Developments to 1923

Of the lines listed at the start of this section, Capitaux 9, 10 and 11 were opened on the same day, 3 June 1887, thus being some of the SNCV's earliest urban routes and were initially steam-worked; the next two were in practice extensions of them, so may be taken in conjunction. **Capital 9 (CHARLEROI - MONT-S-MARCHIENNE)**, authorised on 22 December 1886, was a straightforward passenger tramway starting from near the mainline Gare du Sud on the southern bank of the river and running southwest through industrial suburbs. Authorised to reach the Gadin district of Mont-s-Marchienne, it terminated for the time being at the town square (3.22km). **Capital 10 (CHARLEROI - LODELINSART)**, authorised on 17 January 1887, started from the town prison in Charleroi Centre, north of the river and headed north up the Rue de Bruxelles through equally urban surroundings to Lodelinsart (St-Antoine). **Capital 11 (CHARLEROI - MONTIGNY-LE-TILLEUL)**, authorised on 28 February 1887, headed west from the local prison and then on south via Marchienne-au-Pont to terminate at the suburban town of Montigny-le-Tilleul; a short branch of 1.4km at Marchienne, mainly for goods traffic, was put in during the 1890s as part of the original authorisation. All these lines were conceded for operation to the *SA des Railways Economiques de Liége-Seraing (LS)*, a prolific operator of trams in all parts of Belgium. It was clear early on that all the above routes would need extending and this was soon done though, oddly enough, by creating new Capitaux in most cases; presumably "new" communes were involved in the financing. Thus, under **Capital 40 (LODELINSART - CHATELET)**, a line diverged from Capital 10 at Lodelinsart (Bonnaire as then spelt), first east to Gilly (Haies) and then southeast. Authorised on 28 May 1890, it was opened in two stages, to Chatelineau on 1 July 1891 and on to Chatelet (Pl.St.Roch) itself on 11 August 1891 (the SNCV officially declared the whole thing open on the earlier date). Two years later **Capital 62 (MONTIGNY-LE-TILLEUL - THUILLIES)** was authorised on 28 May 1893, running southwest through agricultural country from a junction with Capital 11 to the village of Thuillies; it was officially opened throughout on 14 January 1895 but apparently actually in two stages, from Montigny to Gozée (Place) on 14 January 1895 and Gozée - Thuilles on 1 April 1895 (a bridge problem?). Like the others, operation of these was formally conceded to the LS and they were all-purpose lines carrying both passengers and goods.

Passenger traffic on all the inner lines, however, was intense, and they were electrified almost simultaneously in 1901 using the, by-then standard, 600 volts dc, generated by the SNCV and fed through trolley-poles - changed to bow collectors in 1912. The Mont-s-Marchienne line was done on 28 March 1901; the route from Charleroi (Viaduc) to Lodelinsart (St-Antoine), and the Montigny branch on 30 May the same year. At first Viaduc was the inner terminus but the line on to Charleroi (Boulevard Janson) was also opened at the end of May and that soon became the new terminus. The Chatelet line followed on 1 June 1901, but the Thuillies branch remained steam-worked.

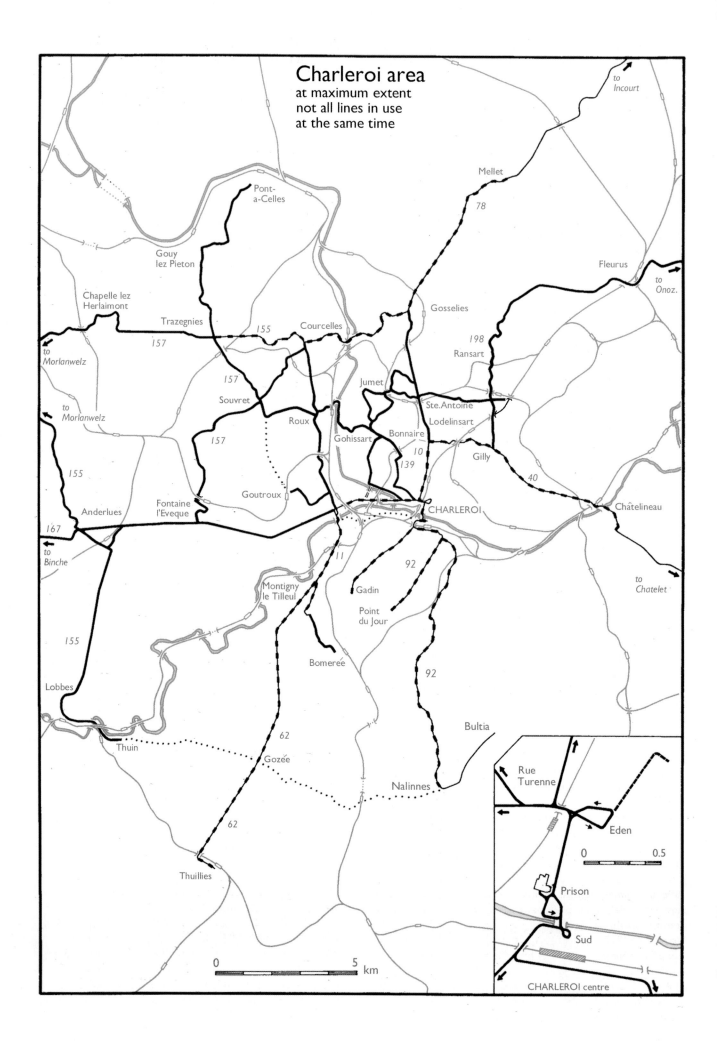

Charleroi area

at maximum extent
not all lines in use
at the same time

to Incourt

Mellet

78

Fleurus

to Onoz.

Pont-a-Celles

Gouy
lez Pieton

Gosselies

198

Chapelle lez
Herlaimont

Ransart

Trazegnies

Courcelles

155

157

157

Jumet

Ste.Antoine

Souvret

Lodelinsart

to
Morlanwelz

Roux

157

Bonnaire

to
Morlanwelz

Gohissart

10

Gilly

139

155

40

Goutroux

Anderlues

Fontaine
l'Eveque

CHARLEROI

Châtelineau

167

to
Binche

11

92

to
Chatelet

Gadin

Montigny
le Tilleul

Point
du Jour

155

92

Bomereé

Lobbes

Bultia

62

Thuin

Gozée

Nalinnes

62

Thuillies

0   5 km

CHARLEROI centre

Rue
Turenne

Eden

0   0.5

Prison

Sud

The other lines and extensions of the group came at intervals and not necessarily in number order. The final major extension to south and east was first, being **Capital 92 (CHARLEROI - NALINNES AVEC EMBRANCHEMENT VERS MARCINELLE)**. It was, in practice, somewhat complex. Authorised in 1900(?) the initial line started from the Gare du Sud, turning soon off the Mont-s-Marchienne route and stretching east into the Marcinelle district where it split, southeast to Marchinelle (Hauchies) and south west to Marcinelle (Cherbois). The inner sections were apparently opened in stages, as under:

Marcinelle (Pont Vilette - Rue Allard)	28 Mar 1901
Marcinelle (Rue Allard - Hauchies)	4 Apr 1901
Marcinelle (Hauchies - Haies) branch	29 Jun 1902
Marcinelle (Eglise - Vieille Place)	4 Apr 1901
(in two stages)	May 1903
Marcinelle (Vieille Place - Ferme Bal)	28 Jul 1903

As can be seen the inner routes, when opened in April 1901, were initially steam-worked but were soon extended to the edge of Marcinelle on 29 June 1902 and to La Ferme Bal (official date: 28 July 1903) respectively, being electrified from these dates. Meanwhile the main line had been extended south to Nalinnes (Centre) on 31 October 1902 using steam traction and thence northeast to "a place known as Bultia" (another green-field site no doubt) on 1 September 1904. With hindsight it would seem this last 3km extension was always rather an embarrassment. Finally, a short extension southwest from La Ferme Bal brought it to Le Point-du-Jour in the township of Mont-s-Marchienne once again, on 1 August 1907. This latter section was electrified from new. All this would have been comparatively simple if it had not been for the confusions in concessions that are not entirely clear even now. While busily building its lines, the SNCV appears to have operated them either directly or through short-term leases to the LS. The latter was also involved in taking over various urban tramways in Charleroi and in converting two of them to metre gauge; to operate these acquisitions it formed a subsidiary company, *Tramways Electriques du Pays de Charleroi et Extensions (TEPC)* in October 1904. The TEPC in turn then agreed to operate all SNCV lines in the area from the end of 1904. This agreement was intended to obviate unnecessary competition and extended at times to interworking; from 1918 to 1923, for example, the TEPC's own route 4 (Charleroi Sud - Chatelineau station) used SNCV tracks from Gilly.

Meanwhile traffic increased steadily, and various small additions and improvements were made to the inner city system. Notably, Capital 139 was used to finance the first Jumet loop (Premiere Boucle de Jumet) which eventually ran from Charleroi centre on the Marchienne-au-Pont line north west to the Gohyssart quartet and then round east and south through the industrial suburb of Jumet back to Lodelinsart (St-Antoine). Initially promoted as **Capital 139 (CHARLEROI - JUMET (HEIGNE)**, the stem line was opened on 15 May 1906 and immediately assimilated into Capital 10, but the final 3km from Heigne to St-Antoine, along with a spur to new depot/workshops at Jumet, was not opened until 30 November 1912. This was part of the works which created the "loop", Lodelinsart - Jumet (Chaussée de Gilly) being opened on 12 August 1912 and Jumet (Chaussée de Gilly - Heigne) on 11 April 1913. Meanwhile in Charleroi a new dead-end spur to Sud station was brought into use on 28 July 1908 and the Mont-s-Marchienne line was doubled in 1910, forerunner of

several more double-track sections. Also in 1910, the in-town terminus of these lines was improved by the installation of a large loop terminus at Rue Turenne, supplementing the existing spur at Boulevard Janson.

Probably because of its built-up catchment area and extensive electrification, the Charleroi system did not suffer any closures during the 1914-18 war. Indeed, in two stages on 19 June and 3 July 1915, Capital 10/139 was extended north from Jumet (Brulotte) via Jumet (Carosse) to reach Gosselies (Calvaire) on the northern edge of the conurbation, a total length of some 20.90km. Here it met up with the existing inter-provincial line from Courcelles through Gosselies to Mellet, Chastre and Incourt (Capital 78) at this time operated by the CFV and allocated to Brabant (see ch 8). Immediately following the war, too, **Capital 198 (GILLY - RANSART)** was used to build a branch from the Chatelet line at Gilly, northward to Ransart (Darbois), opened on 16 December 1918.

Came the dawn. ...or rather, the aftermath of war. As with several other companies, the TEPC had, since 1917, been running on short-term leases and finally surrendered its SNCV concessions late in 1923, though in this case it was to concentrate on running its own tramway system. The two concerns remained on reasonable terms, and in the 1930s the SNCV even helped to re-establish TEPC route 4 with the loan of three ex Mons - Boussu Tashkent-type cars and their crews. In the meantime, the SNCV took control of its own lines through the *SNCV Groupe de Charleroi* and began again to expand its empire. In particular **Capital 170 (CHATELET - FOSSES)**, already briefly opened in 1915 and then closed by the Germans, was resuscitated and brought into use. This was a rural line running east into Namur province, originally authorised on 15 April 1904.

9.5.3 SNCV Groupe de Charleroi to 1939

The 1920s and 1930s, moreover, saw considerable extension and electrification of existing routes, mainly under the umbrellas of existing Capitaux and, although to some extent they overlap the formation of Groupe du Hainaut, they are recorded here for continuity. On the Nalinnes line, electrification was extended first to La Bruyère on 1 December 1921 and then on to Nalinnes (Centre) by 20 April 1925 ; this involved closure of the final spur to Bultia from that date, no doubt much to the SNCV's relief. To be fair, the Bultia spur was intended only as the first stretch of further extensions which never materialised. A succession of electrifications and new links followed during the late 1920s and up to 1939. They are summarised below so far as can be determined, although local sources do not always agree with official records.

The last one completed what was then known as the second Jumet loopline (Deuxieme Boucle de Jumet). In addition one non-electrified line, Montgniy - Thuillies, was improved by being operated with autorails from 1 January 1934. All this involved some new Capitaux, later assimilated into others; These were **Capital 196 (TRAZEGNIES - COURCELLES)** authorised on 26 March 1929, **Capital 198 (GILLY - RANSART)** authorised retrospectively to Diarbois on 22 July 1930 and to Place on 29 July 1937, and **Capital 202 (MARCHIENNE-AU-PONT - COURCELLES - SOUVRET - ROUX)** authorised to Courcelles (Trieux) on 17 September 1934 and on to Roux (Plomcot) on 4 April 1939.

reorganisation were a wholesale restructuring of services in 1936 which allocated route numbers as follows:

1-29 Mons-Borinage
30-40 Centre
41-92 Charleroi

The prides of the system were route 90 which ran through from Charleroi to Mons via Anderlues and Binche, and the associated route 31 from Charleroi to Bracquegnies via La Louvière. In Charleroi itself, the concentration of routes meant that there were no less than four town termini during the 1930s. Gare du Sud served the Marcinelle, Nalinnes and Mont-s-Marchienne services; Boulevard Janson looked after the Montigny line and Rue Turenne was used by the other western lines. Prison coped with the northern routes until 1939 when a new bridge over the River Sambre allowed them to be extended to a developed Gare du Sud site. Alas this arrangement did not survive destruction of the bridge during the 1940 invasion.

A more typical later scene. Mons central railway station with an S-class car waiting (WJK Davies)

9.6 Hainaut: SNCV Groupe du Hainaut: 1937 to 1991.

9.6.1 Formation and development of Groupe du Hainaut

Up to the early 1930s, the Hainaut lines, as we have seen, were divided into four different working groups. Tournai, Mons-Borinage, Centre and Charleroi. As the physical links between these developed, however, the need arose for some coordination and in 1936-37 the administrative *SNCV Groupe du Hainaut* was set up to oversee the region. The individual groups remained in being for both financial and operating reasons - indeed Tournai continued to distance itself from the rest - but central administration allowed more flexible working and interchange of stock when required. The first fruits of this

Because of its largely electrified and passenger-carrying nature, the Groupe du Hainaut escaped comparatively lightly from the depredations of World War II. Only two lines in the Mons system, Frameries - Harveng - Givry and Soignies - Horrues, were actually dismantled, in 1943, though they closed for good. In the Centre, apparently only Solre - Montignies-St-Christophe was closed, equally definitively, on 5 April 1943. Charleroi escaped entirely, though ten four-wheel cars, 9830-9, were requisitioned by the Germans. Otherwise the system saw a great increase in traffic, being favoured with a good allocation of standard bogie motor cars including most of the, then new, welded-steel variety. There was even a very short new link at Anderlues (1 November 1941) to provide a direct route for east-west trams. There were various minor route adjustments

148

And another (formerly an N-class) at the later terminus in Quiévrain.(WJK Davies)

during the period, but by 1945 the electric services had settled down more or less into the pattern shown in Tables 9C, 9E and 9F. The autorail-worked services, turned over to steam traction during the war, were restored during 1945 and 1946.

9.6.2 Hainaut postwar history

The immediate postwar period saw yet more improvements. Most of the big SNCV development programme was stillborn after the disastrous financial year of 1946-47, but Hainaut was favoured. A complete restructuring of the financial basis was carried through from 30 December 1948, whereby the former disparate Capitaux were fused into three large ones: Mons-Borinage, Groupe du Centre and Groupe de Charleroi. As part of the readjustment, Quévaucamps - Mainvault was hived off to Tournai, and Casteau - Bracquegnies (Capital 125), always a border line, was combined with old Capitaux 43 (Centre I) and 89 (Binche - Bracquegnies) in the new Centre. The former Centre II lines and Binche - Beaumont were transferred to the control of Charleroi. A minor casualty of the changes was the short stretch between Bracquegnies and Bois-du-Luc, the passenger service being withdrawn and Bois-du-Luc being served by a new direct route 37 from La Louvière via St-Vaast.

Simultaneously with these adjustments, the Hainaut system actually constructed several quite substantial new lines. First was the long-projected Borinage line west from Dour to Wiheries (11 September 1948) and on to Quiévrain (30 October 1949), with a branch to Elouges opened on 15 October 1950; the Quiévrain - Roisin line (Capital 35) was partly electrified north from the junction at Baisieux. This, though on a partly different route and under Mons-Borinage Capital, effectively brought to fruition all but one section of the old Capital 186, through services being provided from Mons centre. It was followed on 15 September 1952 by electrification of an existing route from St-Ghislain to Baudour via Tertre, a route which was at the same time finally linked to the southern lines by a new bridge over the SNCB at St-Ghislain.

In the Centre there was little change, but on the fringes of the Centre and Charleroi several new electric lines materialised. First were two spurs opened on 15 January 1949, one running north from Trazegnies to Gouy-lez-Pieton and the other from Roux to Souvret, this providing a direct route from Charleroi to Trazegnies and Gouy (route 42). Various other extensions of service included Ransart (Diarbois to Bois) on 14 October 1950; Heppignies to Wangenies on 18 May 1952; and a new alignment from Dampremy (Pont du Canal) to La Docherie as late as July 1955. Meanwhile The Gouy line was slowly and painfully extended first to the Chensee district on 18 May 1952 and thence to the outskirts of Pont-a-Celles town. A further short spur took it into Pont-a-Celles centre (Rue de Courcelles) on 1 June 1956, and to Pont-a-Celles (Moulin) on 1 July? at a time when elsewhere the tram was in full retreat. In the same area, meanwhile, Souvret had been linked by a line northeast to Courcelles (Trieux) on 27 August 1952 (local sources differ, giving extension of services to Courcelles Centre on 23 August and to Trieux on 10 November). Both agree on a link to a junction with the Gosselies line on 1 October 1952.

Several other electrifications and extensions were projected but did not materialise. The electrification projects were, for the record: Roeulx - Casteau over existing lines (a physical link was put in at Roeulx but never used) and Binche - Bersillies l'Abbaye. New projects included a spur to the SNCB station at Pont-a-Celles; Goutroux - Souvret; Marchiennes-au-Pont - Mont-s-Marchienne direct; Thuin - Nalinnes. These would certainly have eliminated some circuitous services but in the event all that was done was to reorganise terminal arrangements at Rue Turenne. A completely new tram station (Eden) was laid out on the eastern face of the Turenne loop, the dead-end spurs to Boulevard Janson and Gare du Sud being discontinued although Gare du Sud continued as a terminus in its own right. Later, in 1968, northern area trams serving the Sud station were cut back to the north side of the river where they terminated beside the old prison; a turning circle was put in there.

There was, nonetheless, one further major extension in the Charleroi area which is something of a saga on its own. This was the long interurban link from Charleroi (Ransart) to Namur. Namur group already had an electrified line west to Onoz and a diesel-worked extension across the provincial border to Fleurus, where it met route 7 of the Charleroi urban system (*TEPC, now Societé des Transports Intercommunaux de Charleroi or STIC*). From 1950 onwards, SNCV Charleroi slowly built an electrified line from its end, from Ransart north to Heppignies (18 August 1951); from Heppignies on to Wangenies in June 1952, and through to Fleurus on 17 May 1953. running a shuttle service as the line extended and meanwhile electrifying the Fleurus - Onoz section. The first tram made its triumphal through journey to Namur SNCB station on 1 July 1953, just in time to be greeted by the news that Namur was closing its last tram routes. So keen was Namur to get rid of its trams that the new line found itself distinctly unwelcome, and a virtual feud sprang up. First Namur insisted that the station area was needed for other purposes and discontinued its own service to Onoz; Charleroi cut the service back 100 metres to a new terminus from 29 August 1955. Then Namur pointed out it was stupid to maintain a substation just to service a single route; Charleroi promptly dispatched a mobile substation to the Namur end to ensure current supply. It was a brave rearguard action but the result, alas, was inevitable. The service was cut in two at Onoz because the route was interrupted by SNCB electrification in summer 1957, then cut back to Velaine on 1 January 1959, save for a few school trips, and finally back to Ransart on 26 May 1963, by which time trams were in retreat over the whole province. Table 9F shows the general pattern of services during this period.

But that was later. In the early post-war years, it is worth noting that the SNCV put a good deal of effort into the Hainaut lines. Services were integrated, the express links between the groups formed by routes 82, 90, and the shorter workings of 31 and 92, being some of the finest interurbans in Europe. Modern efficient stock was provided; first the local modifications of standard cars, especially from Eugies works, and then the fine series of single-ended motors and matching trailers known as the "Braine le Comte" bogie cars. These, in turn, were followed by PCC-cars for urban workings and the splendid "S" type for the interurbans. Service 90, especially, was a magnificent ride along the whole spine of Hainaut province.

Nonetheless, even such measures could not save the area entirely from the rising tide of road motor transport and even "new" lines often had a life of less than ten years. From 1950 onwards, even while new construction continued, the first closures were taking place. Initially it was, of course, the outlying autorail-worked lines that went. Chatelet - Fosse, never very profitable, had been cut back to Presles on 14 October 1943, and had gone entirely by 1950. The same year saw Casteau - Horrues - Noir Jambon (Capital 104 plus part of 66) close to passengers on 20 March 1950, and by 1953 the rot had really set in, though some lines hung on a few more years for goods. On 1 August 1953, passenger services were withdrawn from Binche - Bersillies (Capital 159) and on 30 August 1954 it closed entirely. On 23 August 1953 Quévy - Aulnois - Eugies of the Borinage group lost its passenger service, and on 1 March 1954 autorails stopped running from St-Ghislain to Quévaucamps, entailing closure of the Tertre - Quévaucamps section. North of Quévaucamps the service went very soon after, in the foundering of the Tournaisis lines. Very soon afterwards, autorail services were withdrawn between St-Ghislain and Enghien, with consequent closure of the lines north of Baudour (1 August 1954), while on 23 May 1954 Roisin - Quiévrain - Montreuil followed. The Quiévrain - frontier spur had been closed during the war, though parts were still in situ in the late 1950s and goods traffic on the system lasted to 12 March 1955.

All those closures, however, were quiet rural lines and were expected. From 1955 it was the turn of the electric lines. For

A much more typical recollection: Charleroi Eden in the rain, with a Braine-le-Comte bogie set on the left and S types on the right   *(WJK Davies)*

the historian, these pose something of a problem for, not only had the Capitaux been altered, but the routes as then running bore little correspondence to the originals. It is simplest, therefore, to take each of the three major groups in turn to see how they shrank.

9.6.3 Mons/Borinage closures

This was the first group to suffer, route 16 being withdrawn on 28 May 1955 with closure of the short spur to Obourg. The year 1956 saw only one closure, but a significant one: a new urban bus service in Mons entailed getting rid of the north-south links through the town and also those between station and town centre, thus causing the remaining routes to take circuitous routes round north and south (18 March 1956). Routes 10, to Ghlin and 13 to Nimy, were replaced by buses at this time. Two years later, on 1 June 1958, the last autorail service, from Mons to Quevy and Aulnois, was withdrawn and from then on decline was steady, as shown below.

Section	date closed
Mons - Maisières - Casteau	31 May 1959
Mons - Ghlin - Baudour	31 May 1959
St-Ghislain - Tertre - Baudour	29 May 1960
Mons - Havre - Maurage (link to Centre)	20 Aug 1962
Pâturages - Quaregnon - Baudour (Douvrain)	26 May 1963

Wasmes - St-Ghislain	2 Jul 1966
Wasmes - Boussu (Temple)	2 Jul 1966
Dour - Fayt-le-Franc	2 Jul 1966
Dour - Elouges	2 Jul 1966
Wiheries - Quiévrain	2 Jul 1966
Baudour goods lines incl mixed gauge	26 Jun 1968
Mons - Quaregnon - Boussu - Dour- Wiheries	15 Mar 1970
Mons - Wasmes via Pâturages	15 Mar 1970

Finally, on 2 June 1973, the last urban service, route 2 from Mons Centre to Frameries, Eugies and Wasmes, was withdrawn and the long interurban route 90 was cut back to Binche, entailing the closure of all Mons urban links and the Mons - St-Symphorien - Bray route. (Route 2 had, in any case been run as an extension of route 90 since 1972 so the change was not unexpected). On that date, trams had left Mons and its hinterland entirely.

9.6.4 Centre closures

First to go was the autorail line from Casteau to Bracquegnies (Capital 125) which lost its passenger service on 28 August 1955, though it remained open for goods traffic until the end of July 1957. Otherwise the Centre survived intact until 1959 when the Carnières - Roeulx service (route 34) was withdrawn on 31 August 1959, leading to dismantling of the

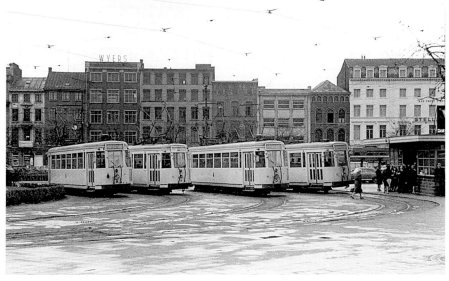

And an equally rainy but even busier Sud terminus   *(WJK Davies)*

The first of the rebuilt SM Class at Jumet works   *(SNCV)*

Table 9F: Electric services in Charleroi area, ca 1953

No.	Route details
41	Charleroi (Turenne) - Goyhssart - Roux - Souvret - Trazegnies
42	as 41 but extended to Pont-a-Celles
43	Charleroi (Turenne) - Gohyssart
44	Charleroi (Turenne) - Gohyssart via Docherie
50	Charleroi (Sud) - Nalinnes
51	Charleroi (Sud) - Marcinelle (Haies) to 1952
52	Charleroi (Sud) - Marcinelle (la Bruyère)
53	Charleroi (Sud) - Marcinelle (Centre)
54	Ransart (Bois) - Gilly - Lodelinsart - Charleroi (Sud) - Point-du-Jour
55	Reverse working of 54
56	Charleroi (Turenne) - Gilly (Haies) - Chatelineau - Chatelet
59*	Charleroi (Sud) - Jumet (depot)
60	Charleroi (Sud) - Jumet - Gosselies - Mellet
61	Charleroi (Sud) - Jumet - Gosselies - Courcelles - Souvret - Roux - Gohyssart - Charleroi
62	Charleroi (Sud) - Jumet - Gosselies
63	Charleroi (Sud) - Jumet - Gosselies - Courcelles - Souvret - Fontaine-l'Eveque
64	As 63 but returning direct via Souvret
65	Deuxieme Boucle de Jumet (clockwise)
66	Deuxieme Boucle de Jumet (counter clockwise)
67	Charleroi (Eden) - Jumet - Ransart - Fleurus - Onoz - Namur
68	Charleroi (Eden) - Jumet - Ransart (Place)
69	Charleroi (Eden) - Wanfercee-Baulet
70**	Charleroi (Sud) - Mont-s-Marchienne (Place)
71	Charleroi (Sud) - Mont-s-Marchienne (Gadin)
72	
73	Charleroi (Turenne) - Gozée
74	Charleroi (Turenne) - Montigny - Bomerée
75	Charleroi (Turenne) - Montigny - Thuillies
76	Charleroi (Turenne) - Montigny - Bois-au-Prince
77	Fontaine-l'Eveque - Souvret
78	Charleroi - Binche
79	Fontaine-l'Eveque - Souvret - Trazegnies - Pont-a-Celles
80	Charleroi (Turenne) - Courcelles - Trazegnies - La Louvière - Maurage
81	Charleroi (Sud) - Marchienne-au-Pont - Goutroux
82	Charleroi (Turenne) - Courcelles - Trazegnies - La Louvière - Maurage - Mons
83	Marchienne-au-Pont - Docherie - Gohyssart
84*	Charleroi - Courcelles - Trazegnies (depot)
85	Premiere Boucle de Jumet (via Docherie; clockwise)
86	Premiere Boucle de Jumet (via Docherie; counter clockwise)
89*	Charleroi - Anderlues (depot)
90	Charleroi - Anderlues - Binche - Mons
91	Anderlues - Thuin
92	Charleroi - Anderlues - Thuin

NOTES:
* depot workings;
** peak hours only.

Houdeng - Roeulx section. On 1 January 1962, the Trivières - Strepy link went completely, followed on 1 April 1962 by the La Louvière - Bois-du-Luc service and subsequent lifting of the St-Vaast - Bracquegnies stretch. On 1 July 1962, services to Estinnes were withdrawn, the lines southwest from Peronnes being dismantled, and the following month saw services in the direction of Mons cut back to Maurage. Lastly, on 27 July 1971, (La Croyère - Familleureux) and 28 May 1972 (La Louvière - La Croyère - Fayt - Manage, and Jolimont - Fayt), the original northern lines were closed and lifted. The remainder stayed intact and was integrated with the remaining Charleroi routes.

9.6.5 Charleroi closures

At their peak, about 1953, the electrified routes under the control of Charleroi were: as in Table 9F

However, the closure of Ransart - Namur, already mentioned, was a symptom of the decline in Charleroi. As in the Centre, routes rather than Capitaux were closed. On 1 February 1957 the first line of all, to Marchienne and Gadin, was replaced by buses, followed on 29 October 1957 by total closure of the Gosselies - Mellet section. Route 70 (Marcinelle - Mont-s-Marchienne) went on 6 April 1959 and route 74 (Montigny - Bomerée) on 1 July 1962. Then there was a long pause until, on 5 February 1967, Trazegnies - Gouy - Pont-à-Celles, one of the most recent lines, closed, leading to discontinuance of route 79. On 28 May 1967, route 56 (Charleroi - Chatelet) was withdrawn with total closure of the track between Gilly and Chatelet. At the very beginning of 1968, route 81 to Goutroux followed with closure of its terminal spur, and on 1 March 1968 the last vestiges of Capital 40 disappeared with the abandonment of route 68 and closure of lines from Lodelinsart to Ransart.

The long line to Nalinnes closed on the same day, with withdrawal of routes 45, 50 and 52, and the branch to Point du Jour (route 53). On that day too, route 84 from Marchienne-au-Pont to Souvret was withdrawn, though the tracks remained, while on 26 May 1968 withdrawal of services 74, 75 and 76 caused abandonment of the old line to Montignies and Thuillies with the Bomerée branch. From 8 August 1968, Charleroi Sud was again replaced by Prison as a terminus, to allow for work on the proposed metro system. That, however, proved to be the last in Charleroi's series of closures for some years. The remaining system was compact, heavily trafficked and, in the hilly narrow streets of the district, offered a service which buses could not easily give, Hearteningly, in the early 1970s, the SNCV and the local authorities decided to capitalise on its existence, to give the region of Charleroi a

modern light transit system. Plans were made for what was to be effectively a light metro serving Charleroi centre and stretching out to connect with the SNCV links into La Louvière. Colour section shows the proposals.

Unfortunately all did not go according to plan. The scheme involved some 53km of new or upgraded line in subway, on viaduct or on reserved track, and the first section, a stretch across the river which once more took trams to Sud Station, was completed in 1976. After that, unfortunately, development slowed quite drastically, since the inception of work coincided with a world-wide recession. The older industrial areas were worst hit, and Charleroi is certainly an old industrial area; hence the projected traffic never materialised. Between 1980 and 1983, the existing works were extended northward, first to Piges station above the Bruxelles road and then to a temporary terminal at Beaux Arts with a new link to the existing Gosselies route in the Chaussée de Bruxelles itself, and with links to the Roux and Anderlues routes at Dampremy and Providence respectively. These works in turn led to the closure of the former Eden terminus on 12 June 1983. At the time the first edition of this history was written, one could reasonably state "The Fontaine-l'Eveque route is being steadily upgraded and 1985 should see extension eastward from Beaux Arts to Gilly and Châtelet, and it now seems certain that the SNCV will work those new routes. The route north to Jumet is also in prospect to relieve the Bruxelles road but it is uncertain how much further work will be done." In practice very little transpired. Meanwhile, regrettably, several more urban routes closed during 1982-84, including the Jumet loops and route 92. True, the "country" routes out towards the north and west were to some extent upgraded with heavy rail and new catenary - being totally relaid in many cases. A new series of articulated cars was introduced with a marked increase in speed and comfort while most surviving type "S" cars were drastically rebuilt. The list of closures below shows how quickly the situation changed for the SNCV lines between 1985 and 1988. With the exception of route 63 the November 1986 closures were advertised as being temporary suspensions of service, awaiting upgrading of the track but despite earlier intentions, the opposite happened: less than two years later the route to Trazegnies also closed, another 'temporary' measure.

So, on New Year's Eve of 1990, the final day of the Vicinal as an operating company, there was just one tramline left: Charleroi-Anderlues-La Louvière and this did not long survive the changeover. At the time there already were rumours about the closure of Binche-La Louvière, whilst the promises of further Metro Legàre expansion seemed vague.

153

Table 9G: Closures 1985-88

route Section

41	Roux (Marais) - Trazegnies (Ecoles)	2 Jun 1985
41	Gohyssart - Roux (Marais)	14 Apr 1985
30/1	Anderlues (Jonction) - Mariemont - Braquegnies - Maurage	1 Nov 1986
80	Trazegnies - Mariemont - La Louvière - Braquegnies - Maurage	1 Nov 1986
63	Courcelles (Trieux) - Souvret - Fontaine l'Eveque	1 Nov 1986
41	Charleroi (Beaux Arts) - Gohyssart	1 Mar 1988
80	Charleroi - Gosselies - Courcelles - Trazegnies	5 Apr 1988

Following the 1984 closures, route numbers were reassigned, giving a multiple of numbers for just a few lines, but the ultimate was reached in November 1986 when 13 route numbers were in use for three lines! Charleroi area services in November 1986 were as follows:.

Table 9G: Charleroi routes at 1986

no.	Colour	Description
41	Yellow	Charleroi-Gohyssart
55	Red	Courcelles(Trieux)-Gosselies(Faubourgs) (schooldays, one trip each way)
57	Green	Charleroi-Gosselies-Courcelles(Trieux) (one trip on schooldays)
58	Yellow	Trazegnies(Ecoles)-Courcelles-Gosselies- Jumet(Depot) (late evening depot workings)
59	Brown	Charleroi-Gosselies-Courcelles- Trazegnies(Ecoles) (basic service, weekdays, no bus connection at Trazegnies)
61	Yellow	Charleroi-Jumet(Depot) (late evening depot workings)
62	Red	Charleroi-Gosselies(Faubourgs) (one trip on schooldays, plus one late evening working)
80	Blue	Charleroi-Gosselies-Courcelles- Trazegnies(Ecoles) (basic service, weekdays, bus connection to Maurage)
81	Black	Charleroi-Gosselies-Courcelles- Trazegnies(Ecoles) (basic service, weekends, bus connection to racquegnies)
82	Orange	Charleroi-Gosselies-Courcelles- Trazegnies(Ecoles) (basic service, all week, bus connection to La Louvière)
89	Blue	Charleroi(Beaux Arts)-Anderlues(Jonction)
90	Brown	Charleroi-Anderlues-Binche-La Louvière
93	Yellow	La Louvière-Binche-Anderlues(Jonction) (saturday morning markets plus school workings)

Notes:

The bi-colour codes were replaced by blinds with a single colour. With the exception of route 89, all Charleroi routes had their terminus at Charleroi (Sud) and ran via Beaux Arts.

Routes 41, 89, 90, 93 were operated with BN cars, the others with SM and SJ cars. Only numbers 41, 89, 90, 93 appeared on BN binds, while 93 did not appear on the SM and SJ blinds.

The colours given for routes 89 and 90 are those on the BN blinds. These two routes did appear on SM and SJ blinds with colours green(89) and blue(90), but these were never used. Remarkably the SM/SJ blinds also included workings west of Trazegnies, which of course never existed.

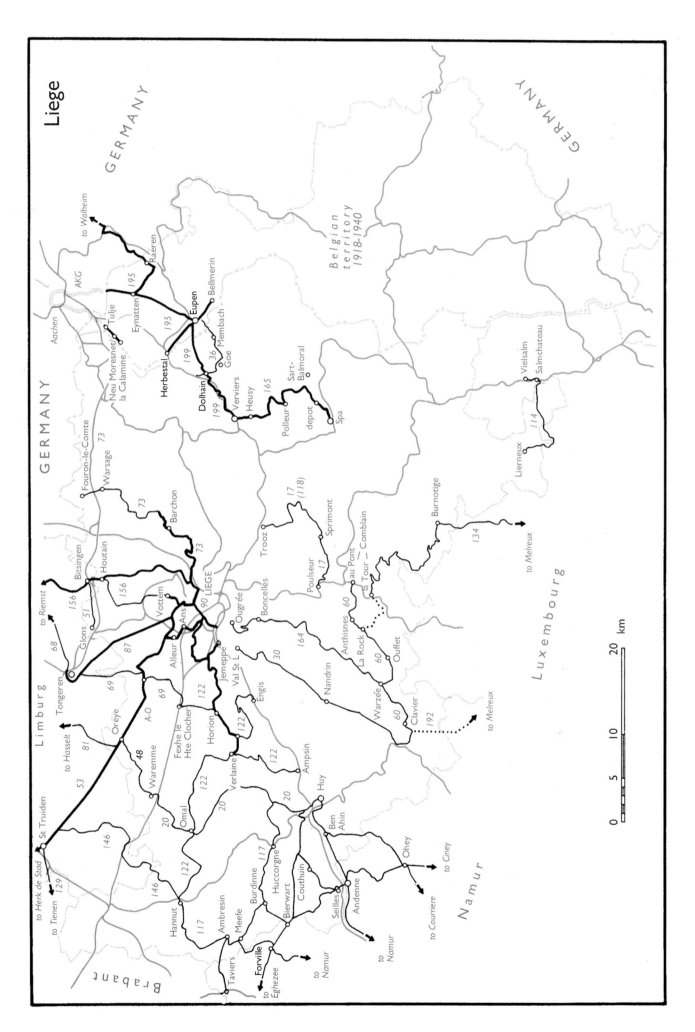

Liege

Chapter 10: SNCV in Liége and Limburg Provinces

10.1 Liége-Limburg: Introduction

The history of the SNCV operation in Liége and Limburg provinces causes something of a problem. In most ways the two were as different as chalk from cheese; Limburg was Flemish, generally poor and looking to the Netherlands and the north, while Liége was largely French-speaking, prosperous and looking to south and east. The major portions of their rail systems were equally distinct but, along the provincial boundaries and along the border with Namur they were almost inextricably tangled. Even in early days the private operating Groupes of Waremme, Liége and Andenne (Namur) crossed and recrossed the boundaries; as for the SNCV, though the operating groups were quite distinct in the 1920s and 1930s, administratively, it combined the two into *Groupe 50 (LIÉGE - LIMBURG)* This must have been more expedient than natural for, as the railways died, the groups were again split in 1965 - but that is another story.

Fortunately the inter-provincial split-up of lines after 1918 more or less followed the pattern of the original reseaux. The systems of the former *Limburgsche Stoom Tramweg Mij (LSTM)* and the *SA Belge-Neerlandaise de Transports et Travaux (BNTT)* became the poorly-endowed Groep Limburg with headquarters at Hasselt. The rest, in general, went into the Groupe de Liége, although the affair was complicated by the fact that two big concessionaires were kept on until 1929. These were the *CF d'Ans - Oreye (AO)*, which ran one of the few private railways and had also taken over the extensive Groupe de Waremme to the west of Liége, and the Namur-based *Societé Mosane pour l'Exploitation des CF Vicinaux (MOSANE)*

which ran the equally extensive network radiating from Huy and Hannut along the western borders. It seems best, therefore, to treat the two provinces separately and to cross-refer where needed.

First, a brief word on the geography. Liége city lies astride the Meuse river, that vital artery of transport and historical corridor for invaders. Southward, the land rises first to the plateau of the Condroz and then shades upward into the foothills of the Ardennes. Westward, it is rolling agricultural country around the Meuse valley, and northward it flattens into the Limburg plain. In the 19th century, Limburg province, grouped round its major centres of Tongeren/Tongres, Maaseik and Hasselt, was a poor agricultural region, sparsely populated and not very profitable for light railways, though with strong cross-frontier links with the Netherlands. During the early 20th century, discovery of large coal reserves to the northeast of Hasselt in the region known as the Campine led to some industrialisation, but it seems always to have been somewhat half-hearted, at least from the SNCV's point of view. Groep Limburg was always poor and, if a cross-border line did get electrified, it invariably disappeared into the grasp of the richer province "down south".

10.2 Lines attributed to Liége Province

10.2.1 SNCV in Liége province: Introduction

The main SNCV network in Liége province can best be considered as several separate systems, some of which were later connected by internal links in Liége city. To the west and northwest of that city, the systems ran into or connected with lines in Namur and Limburg, and their original allocation is sometimes unclear. The SNCV did acknowledge three nominal operating groupes: the major ones of Liége and Waremme and the small detached Groupe de Clavier, though Waremme originally appears to have had at least two major operators as well as the SNCV itself. Basically, Liége provincial lines comprised:

* *Groupe de Liége*: Urban tramways in the city of Liége, together with three connected lines stretching out north and east (Capitaux 90, 73, 87, 156, though the last was regarded as a Limburg operation until the fusion of Liége and Limburg Groupes).

* *Groupe de Waremme*: A cluster of lines to the west (Capitaux 20, 48, 53, 117, 122, 146) linking mainly with Limburg province but also connected to central Liége by the city tramways and by a private light railway, the *CF d'Ans - Oreye (AO)*. To complicate matters, Capitaux 53 and 146 were almost entirely in Limburg but operated by a Liége company, while Capital 117 straddled the three provinces and is best dealt with under Namur.

* Three isolated clusters to the south and east of Liége city, including the *Groupe de Clavier*, having no physical links either between themselves or to those mentioned above, and whose history is so self-contained that they are dealt with individually.

The SNCV's Liége urban system really arose almost by accident, coming into being as the inner ends of the country lines were linked and electrified so it was never as distinct as that of, say, Mechelen. Liége city itself also had private operators distinct from the SNCV - the CF d'Ans - Oreye already mentioned, the CF Economiques de Liége - Seraing, the municipal tramways (see app 6).

10.2.2 Groupe de Liége (Liége area lines), 1898-1919 including SNCV Liége urban system

Capital	Name	Auth km
73	Liége - Barchon - Fouron-le-Comte	30.70
87	Liége - Wihogne - Vottem - Tongeren	22.68
90	Liége - Tilleur - St-Gilles - Hollogne - Ans	16.96*

* this last effectively formed the core of the electrified urban routes.

The operating Groupe de Liége appears to have been the responsibility of a single concessionaire, the *SA pour l'Exploitation du CFV de Liége - Barchon et Extensions (LB)*, founded on 9 May 1898. This concern started with Capital 73, acquired the rights to Capital 87 and probably, it being SNCV policy, also effectively took over the urban system which linked the two. This latter system, Capital 90, was officially conceded to a separate company, the *SA des Tramways Interurbains (TI)* which, as at Leuven, was probably a holding company for the municipal interests. It linked the Groupe to the other lines penetrating the Liegois: to Capital 122 of the Groupe de Waremme; and to the privately owned Ans - Oreye railway.

As we have seen, by the last years of the 19th century, Liége city had its own standard-gauge tramway system stretching out to all quarters, together with the busy standard-gauge interurban line of the *Railways Economiques de Liége-Seraing (LS)* running east-west along the north bank of the river. In addition light railways were slowly encroaching from all points of the compass, and by 1903 they had a ring of termini in the outer suburbs. Gradients were too steep to allow steam working inwards of these, and between 1901 and 1907 the SNCV built a network of connecting, electrically-worked lines through the city centre and suburbs. To some extent they competed with the existing town tramways, especially as the SNCV quickly extended its electrification along the inner portions of most of its rural lines and ran an urban and suburban network which eventually comprised nine routes.

The first line of this Groupe came comparatively late. **Capital 73 (LIÉGE - BARCHON - FOURON-LE-COMTE)** was originally authorised in 1895 as Liége - Barchon, with an operating length of 13.74km. Its original operator was actually the *Compagnie du CF de Liége - Maestricht et Extensions* founded in Bruxelles on 31 March 1860 to operate regional railways. It was opened on 14 July 1898, was worked by standard steam tram locomotives and stock, and had a fairly heavy freight traffic; the Liége terminus was at Quai des Pêcheurs on the south bank of the river. In 1899 the Liége - Maestricht company failed and this concession was taken on by the LB. During SNCV expansion in the area in 1905-7, the

Liége. — Quai des Pêcheurs, Tram de Liége-Barchon.

Liége. Quai des Pêcheurs terminus with a Liége - Barchon train in steam days   (SNCV)

The easiest way to sort out a considerable confusion is to start with the city of Liége itself. One of Belgium's major cities, it lies in a deep river valley, extending up steep hills to the north and west, and sprawling along both sides of the River Meuse in its once great industrial suburbs of Seraing, Ougrée and Jemeppe. To the south lies the high Condroz plateau, and to the east hilly wooded country stretching towards the German frontier. The area is rich in industry and has considerable mineral resources.

line was extended northeast from Barchon via Blegny, Dalhem and Warsage (mainline connection) to the frontier town of Fouron-le-Comte/'s Gravenvoeren; it was opened in three stages, to Blegny on 22 December 1906 (never acknowledged officially in reports but noted in the local press); to Dalhem on 14 August 1907; and to Fouron-le-Comte on 21 March 1908. It then had a length of some 30.50km. At the inner end, urban development about the same time resulted in a short section to the suburb of Jupille being electrified and linked to the SNCV town system at Place St-Lambert on 1 May 1910, via a mixed-gauge river crossing in common with the Liége tramways. Steam trains to the country still terminated at Quai

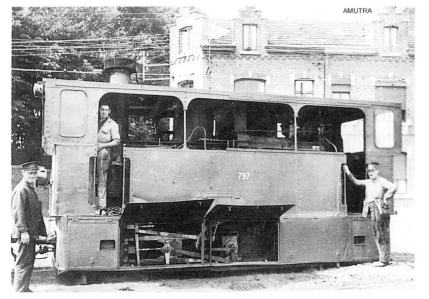

The Ans - Oreye was fairly shy but this is AO No 5, later taken over by the SNCV as 797. (AMUTRA)

des Pêcheurs and all trains terminated there from 6 August 1914 when the bridge was wrecked, and remained a separate operation until the SNCV reclaimed the concession. During World War I, two sections were closed and temporarily lifted: Warsage - Fouron-le-Comte in December 1915 and Jupille - Warsage in November 1917.

The next system was also a suburban and rural link. **Capital 87 (LIÉGE - WIHOGNE - VOTTEM - TONGEREN)**, which served the area north of Liége city, had been talked about since 1893 when a proposal to link Othée and Wihogne with Liége had been turned down for the usual reasons; in this case, competition on the Liége - Othée sector. Rethinking produced a two-branched system running northwest from Liége via Wihogne to the market town of Tongeren, with a short branch northeast from the Sté-Walburge district of Liége to suburban Vottem. The first portion, from Liége (Rue de l'Academie/Rue J de Bois) below the citadel, up to Wihogne was authorised on 4 February 1898+; it opened on 5 August 1899 and was followed very reluctantly by Wihogne - Vreren on 24 October 1905 and Vreren - Tongeren on 21 July 1908; (both were authorised on 20 February 1906+). Meanwhile, in Liége city, it was twice extended, to Rue de Campine on 18 January 1900 and to Place Rocheporte on 1 May 1900. The Vottem branch had been authorised on 1 September 1901 and opened on 19 September 1903, while some electrification of the inner sections had taken place as under:

Section electrified	Date
Rue de l'Academie - Rocourt* (depot)	14 Aug 1901
Sté-Walburge - Vottem (from new)	19 Sep 1903
Rocourt (depot - Etat station)	24 Oct 1905

NOTE: * Electrified from new. At different times the SNCV spelt this Rocour and Rocourt.

On 6 July 1907, the system was linked to Capital 90 (qv) at Place St-Lambert by a short new electrified stretch, and the SNCV electric trams were then assimilated into the city routes. At this time the electrified sections totalled 8.46km and the steam services, which terminated at Rocourt, 14.13km.

During this period, too, Liége gained the urban and suburban network of **Capital 90 (LIÉGE - TILLEUR - ST-**

GILLES - HOLLOGNE-AUX-PIERRES - ANS) Capital 90 allowed for three connected lines, electrified from the start and built between 1901 and 1907 (see map 159). They were:

* Liége (Place St-Lambert) - St-Gilles - Tilleur, a purely urban line opened in two stages on 9 May 1901 to Grace Perou which was the junction for Tilleur, and 6 July 1901 on to Tilleur.

* St-Gilles - Grace-Berleur (16 May 1903) - Hollogne-aux-Pierres (12 December 1905); at Hollogne it later connected with a long steam-worked line, Capital 122, which arrived from Verlaine in 1911.

* A spur off the Hollogne line, from Montegnée northwards up the hill to Ans (11 July 1907) where it ran in over mixed gauge with the *Tramways Urbains de Liége et Extensions (TULE)* to connect with the Ans - Oreye; the depot was at St-Gilles. The Ans line branched off the Tilleur route at Bons Buveurs, some sources having it as opening to Ans (Bolsée) on 12 December 1905 and to Ans (Plateau) on 11 November 1907. In Liége, an extension inward to Place St.Lambert connecting Capitaux 87 and 90 was opened on 16 July 1907. Note that the mixed gauge section at Ans was not SNCV owned.

Traffic on the urban lines grew to such an extent that, in 1911-12, the tracks of Capital 90 plus Capital 87 to Rocourt and to Sté-Walburge-Cimetière were doubled. The group as a whole remained intact during World War I and was handed to the SNCV after the 1914-18 war when the LB & TI surrendered their leases. (different sources give 1920 & 1922)

10.2.3. Groupe de Waremme (West Liégeois), 1888-1929

The other main cluster in the Liégeois was the so-called Groupe de Waremme comprising the following lines:

Capital	Name	Auth km
20	Huy - Waremme	25.85
48	Waremme - Oreye	10.04
53	St-Truiden - Oreye	16.44
117	Hannut - Huccorgne - Vinalmont- Burdinne - Huy	55.43
122	Hannut - Jemeppe-s-Meuse et Embrts	72.70
146	St-Truiden - Hannut	25.80

Associated with this group and joining it to the Liége system at Ans was the privately owned *CF d'Ans - Oreye* (later part of Capital 53). Impinging on it at various points, and mainly allocated to Liége for financial purposes, was Capital 117 which operationally became part of the Andenne group in Namur province and was later split between the SNCV groups see Chapter 11). This tangled cluster of lines in the west Liégeois was classed as a single groupe by the SNCV prior to 1918, though it was originally the responsibility of more than one concessionaire; it is possible the companies were associated in some way but probably one was in effect taken over by the other before World War I.

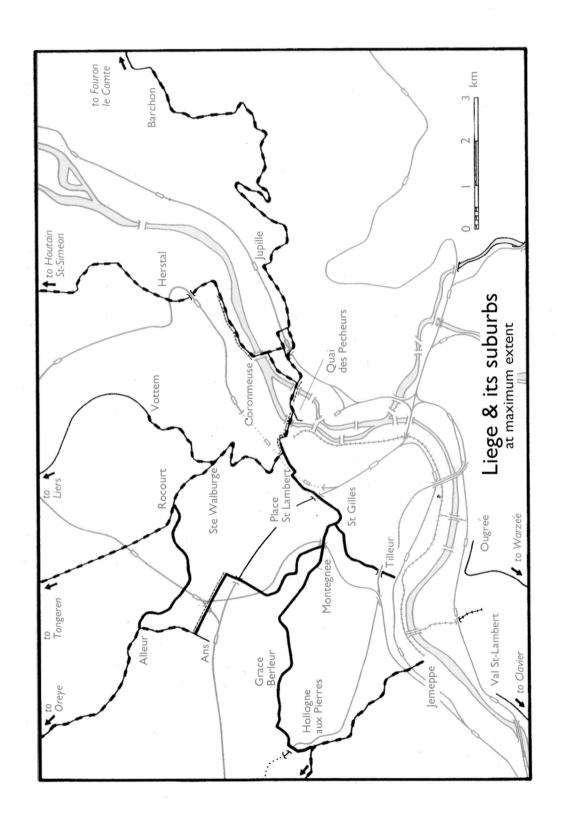

Liège & its suburbs
at maximum extent

to Fouron le Comte

Barchon

to Houtain St-Simeon

Herstal

Jupille

Vottem

Coronmeuse

Quai des Pecheurs

to Liers

Rocourt

Ste Walburge

Place St-Lambert

St Gilles

to Tongeren

to Oreye

Alleur

Ans

Grace Berleur

Montegnee

Tilleur

Ougree

to Warzee

Hollogne aux Pierres

Jemeppe

Val St-Lambert

to Clavier

0   1   2   3   km

The "trunk line", if there was such a thing, was **Capital 20 (HUY - WAREMME)** running from the Namur provincial town of Huy northward to Waremme on the Liége - Bruxelles railway line. Authorised on 21 July 1887 and opened on 6 May 1888, it was a simple country branch with operation ceded to the specially-formed *SA d'Exploitation du CFV de Huy - Waremme et Extensions (HW)*. At the outset it was an isolated line as was the next one, from Ans near Liége, to Oreye.

The *CF d'Ans - Oreye*, though metre gauge and built to SNCV standards, was one of the very few privately-promoted light railways in Belgium under the Act of 1875. Negotiation started before the SNCV was formed, and it appears to have been originally granted, on 30 June 1888, to a firm calling itself the *Sté d'Entreprise Genéralé de Travaux* formed at Tilleur by a M. Seputchre in 1889 and reconstituted as the *SA du CF d'Ans - Oreye et Extensions (AO)* in 1892. The line, running northwest from Ans along the main road, was opened on 1 June 1890. It had its own rolling stock including seven locomotives of types analogous to SNCV classes and, in its early years, also borrowed three locomotives (16, 29 and 40) from the SNCV.

These two lines were very soon joined by **Capital 48 (WAREMME - OREYE)**, whose operation was granted to the Huy - Waremme company. It was authorised on 16 June 1891, opened from Waremme town northeastward to Oreye outskirts (Porte de Liége) on 15 October 1892 and extended to Waremme (Etat) station on 5 August 1894. As originally built it had the dubious distinction of not making physical connection with its neighbours at either end. The final link into Oreye Etat station and a junction with the AO was authorised on 11 April 1893 and opened in April 1894, but the equivalent at Waremme seems to have taken longer. Indeed the Huy - Waremme company was specifically compensated for having to operate two separate lines, and it appears that a junction was not made until some time in 1912.

Long before then, however, yet another line had reached Oreye, this time from the provincial boundary to the northwest. **Capital 53 (ST-TRUIDEN - OREYE)** was authorised on 27 December 1891, being opened for goods on 24 October 1892 and for passengers on 26 November 1892; operation was ceded to the AO and the main depot was at Oreye, which was fast becoming a major SNCV junction; the "cross" was completed in October 1900 by Capital 81 coming in from Hasselt in Limburg. Again the line was straightforward, following the main Liége - St-Truiden road all the way and being worked integrally with the AO. The SNCV sometimes classed both these last two lines among their Limburg possessions.

To complete the picture of this group of lines, it is sensible to take out of sequence here **Capital 146 (ST-TRUIDEN - HANNUT)** This, though almost entirely in Limburg province, was ceded for operation to the AO, so was considered operationally as a Liége line until after World War I. It ran due south from St-Truiden, wandering over the countryside via Jeuk and Montenaken to the town of Hannut, which was also fast becoming a major SNCV junction. Authorised on 27 September 1905, it was opened in two stages, from Hannut to Montenaken on 24 December 1909 and on to St-Truiden on 9 March 1911; the operating total was 26.20km, including its links at both ends. At St-Truiden it ran in over Capital 53, from a junction at Brustem. Along with Waremme - Oreye and the Huy - Omal portion of Capital 20, it was closed and lifted during World War I, in September 1916.

Last and least known, perhaps, among the Waremme Groupe lines was **Capital 122 (HANNUT - JEMEPPE-S-MEUSE ET EMBRANCHEMENT VERS FEXHE-LE-HAUT-CLOCHER)** This had a very long gestation period, being initially authorised in 1904 and not completed until the 1920s. It started life as a line from Hannut, by the Limburg border, east via Omal, Verlaine, St-Georges and Horion to Jemeppe-s-Meuse just west of Liége city, with a branch from Horion to Fexhe. It was opened in sections, but this is one of the few areas in which local historians disagree with the SNCV. The available SNCV dates are: 1 June, 1 July, 18 July, & 11 October 1905; 19 March & 22 September 1906; 21 July 1908 but without note of exact sections. The (usually reliable) local historians say it was as follows:

Haneffe - Horion	2 Oct 1905
Verlaine - Hannut	11 Nov 1905
Omal - Haneffe	1 Jul 1906
Mons - Horion - Fexhe	18 Jul 1906
Hannut - Omal	22 Sep 1906
Jemeppe - Mons	21 Jul 1908

(Jemeppe - Mons and the later section Ampsin - Villers were four-rail mixed gauge)

At Hannut it connected with Capitaux 117 and 146, while en route it met Capital 20 (Huy - Waremme) at Omal, Capital 69 from Tongeren at Fexhe and the then-new Liége urban system at Hollogne-aux-Pierres near Jemeppe. In 1908 The length was then 47.70km and operation was ceded to the AO.

Two more branches were authorised in 1910, from Verlaine south to Ampsin (11 km), and from St-Georges to Engis (12.34 km), both termini being on the Namur - Liége railway. The Engis branch was apparently opened on 25 June 1913, but the Verlaine - Ampsin section, delayed by arguments about mixed gauge, was still under construction when war broke out in 1914. Its rails and fittings were requisitioned by the Germans and it was not completed until the early 1920s (1921 and 1 February 1923 have been given variously). Apart from the Engis branch, which was treated similarly, in general the groupe appears to have otherwise survived the war reasonably intact, only two other sections, from Huy to Omal (Capital 20) and Waremme - Oreye (Capital 48) being closed and lifted, in August and June 1917 respectively.

10.2.4 SNCV lines in the Liége area, 1920-1961

Since these groupes were so intertwined it makes sense to continue their history here. As noted above, the connected lines of the former Waremme and Liége groups survived the war reasonably intact and the Liége-Barchon company surrendered its leases in the Groupe de Liége soon after war ended. The AO company, however, continued to operate its own line and to hang on to its SNCV concessions. According to local records, closed sections were reopened as shown below:

Capital	Section	Date reopened
20	Huy - Omal	1 Oct 1920
48	Waremme - Oreye	5 Oct 1919
73	Liége (Quai des Pêcheurs - Pl St.Lambert)	12 Aug 1919
	Jupille - Dalhem	12 Aug 1921
	Dalhem - Fouron-le-Comte	1 Mar 1922
146	Mielen - Jeuk (standard-gauge connection)	15 Oct 1920
	Mielen - Brustem	24 Oct 1921
	Jeuk - Hannut	20 Dec 1921

A standard train of the Liége area after electrification (E de Backer)

The newly-formed SNCV Groupe de Liége-Limburg proceeded fairly cautiously with development, doing little until the late 1920s. The AO finally gave up on 1 January 1928, handing back its leases and selling its trunk line to the SNCV together with all usable equipment. The St.Truiden - Oreye stretch was authorised retrospectively under Capital 53 on 11 September 1929 and the whole line was then assimilated into Capital 53; this gave the latter a total length of 36.22km, and seems to have stimulated electrification. First, at the Liége end, it was extended over the AO as far as Alleur on 1 December 1930 and on to Oreye on 2 August 1931. On Capital 87, Rocourt - Tongeren followed on 14 August 1932 (local records or 1 November 1932 (SNCV official). There was then a pause until 1936 when a new line was put in from Alleur to Rocourt (2 February 1936), on the route of an abandoned colliery railway, giving a direct link into Place St-Lambert; to complement this, Oreye - St-Truiden was electrified from 15 June 1936 and through services were initiated. Meanwhile a section of the Jemeppe - Verlaine line as far as Mons-Crotteux was electrified on 7 May 1933, being worked as part of the network of town routes with which it connected at Hollogne, and Mons - Horion was electrified on 17 December 1936.

The urban routes had route letters initially (eg R for Rocourt; T for Tilleur) but by 1939 they had been extended and numbered as shown in Table 10A. The country routes were unnumbered but had coloured destination plaques as listed.

1938 saw the electrification from Liége of the southern part of Capital 156 (see Limburg for early history), the section between Coronmeuse and Bitsingen/Bassenge being assimilated into the Liége electric network from 4 April 1938 and extended to Place St.Lambert, while electrification was started on the Liége - Barchon route. A setback was destruction (again!) of the Meuse bridge in May 1940 which meant that Barchon trams had to use Quai des Pêcheurs as terminus from 11 May 1940 to 18 December 1947. However, the initial stage of electrification, to Bellaire, was brought into use on 15 July 1940, and extended to Barchon in two stages

Table 10A: Liége urban and country routes, 1939

a) Urban network

No	Route details
50	Place St-Lambert - Rocourt
51	Place St-Lambert - Vottem
52	Place St-Lambert - Sté-Walburge
53	Place St-Lambert - Grace-Berleur - Jemeppe
55	Place St-Lambert - Grace-Berleur - Hollogne
56	Place St-Lambert - Grace-Berleur
57	Tilleur - Place St-Lambert - Jupille
58	Place St-Lambert - Montegnée - Alleur
59	Jemeppe - Mons-Crotteux
60	Place St-Lambert - Jupille
61	Tilleur - Place St-Lambert - Bressoux
62	Place St-Lambert - Herstal
63	Place St-Lambert - Coronmeuse

two short workings were added during the war

| 65 | Liége - Othée |
| 66 | Liége - Juprelle |

b) Liége electrified country routes 1939

colour	route details
Brown	Jemeppe - Verlain
Blue	Liége - Tongeren
Red	Liége - Oreye
Red	Liége - St.Truiden
Yellow	Liége - Riemst

(Bellaire - Saive 21 April 1941; Saive - Barchon 22 November 1943 - or "by 22 October 1943" according to local sources). There were three minor closures to balance all this, Verlaine - Ampsin and St.Georges - Engis losing their passenger services from 4 April 1932 and Horion - Fexhe from 19 July 1936 but otherwise life was quiet. Indeed, passenger services were restored to Fexhe and Engis (the latter only for a few months) in summer 1940. The system as a whole appears to have suffered very little in the war, totally losing only Verlaine - Ampsin from Capital 122 on 10 November 1942, and the stretch between Dalhem and Fouron-le-Comte on 24 May 1943 (SNCV) or 15 December 1942 (local). On the other hand Horion - Verlaine was electrified from 14 February 1944.

After the war, however, decline set in, especially on the periphery. There was one further electrification, between Barchon and Blegny, on 25 December 1947 but Hannut - Haneffe in Capital 122 and Horion - Fexhe (again) closed to passengers on 1 February 1948, and Huy - Waremme followed on 10 June 1949. Verlain - Haneffe closed "during 1950". Capital 156 remained whole until 16 August 1949, when it lost the non-electric stretch from Riemst to Zutendaal. The similarly non-electric stub of Capital 73 from Blegny to Dalhem is noted by some sources as following on 3 October 1948, although the line from Dalhem to Warsage was actually relaid, for goods only, from 28 June 1952, to serve the Argenteau colliery at Trembleur. It was the only SNCV operation to use transporter wagons and operation was transferred to the collieries from 8 October 1960, using ex-SNCV equipment. Coal traffic ceased on 31 March 1980, although a preservation group worked spasmodic tourist services for some years thereafter.

Meanwhile, St-Truiden - Hannut closed to passengers in May 1950, although for goods it died hard; section after section was lopped in the ensuing years but the last bit, from Trognée to Hannut, did not close until 17 March 1958, and much had happened in between. The official list of goods closures is given below although in many cases they were merely nominal by that time.

Yernawe - Engis	19 Mar 1950
Hannut - Viemme	3 Jan 1952
Huy - Hollogne-s-Geer	3 Jan 1952
Yernawe - Verlain	15 Dec 1952
Viemme - Verlaine	14 Apr 1955
Horion - Fexhe	3 Jan 1956
St.Truiden - Trognée	3 Aug 1956
Oreye - St.Truiden	7 Jan 1957
Hollogne-s-Geer - Waremme	29 Jul 1957
Trognée - Hannut	11 Mar 1958
Blegny - Dalhem	17 Mar 1958
Waremme - Oreye	1 Jun 1959

So far as the electrified system was concerned, at the beginning of the 1950s, the Liége electric routes were as shown in Table 10B, with route numbers where allocated and closure dates:

The real decline started in 1953, when passenger services over the Waremme - Oreye line ceased on 17 May. 1954 saw final closure of the Liers branch on 21 October and the first of the electric lines, Liége - Vottem, on 12 December. On 2 October 1955 the electric service to Barchon and Blegny was discontinued, together, apparently, with the autorail service on to Dalhem and the following year Oreye - St-Truiden went, on

---

Table 10B: Liége routes, ca 1950

Main urban routes

No/col		Route details	
50	rd/bl	Pl St-Lambert - Rocourt	18 Dec 1955
51	bl/rd	Pl St-Lambert - Sté-Walburge -Vottem	11 Dec 1954
52	rd/bl	Place St-Lambert - Sté-Walburge	18 Dec 195
53	rd/gr	Place St-Lambert - Jemeppe	13 Jul 1960
56	rd/gr	Place St-Lambert - Grace-Berleur	31 Jul 1960
58	gr/rd	Place St-Lambert - Montegnée - Ans - Alleur	7 Oct 1956
60	rd/bla	Place St-Lambert - Jupille	2 Oct 1955
61	rd/gr	Place St-Lambert - Tilleur	2 Aug 1961
62	or/bn	Place St-Lambert -Herstal	1 Sep 1955

urban short workings

colours	route
gr/rd	Pl St Lambert - Bons Buveurs
gr/rd	Pl St Lambert - Montegnée
rd/gr	Pl St Lambert - Hollogne
rd/bla	Pl St Lambert - Bellaire
rd/bla	Pl St Lambert - Saive
rd/blu	Pl St Lambert - Rocourt (Stade)

Country routes and short workings ca 1950

colours	route
red	Jemeppe - Verlaine
or/bn	Liége - Bassenge/Bitsingen - Riemst
rd/bla	Liége - Barchon - Blegny
red	Liége - Rocourt - Alleur - Oreye - St-Truiden
blu	Liége - Rocourt - Tongeren

---

25 October 1956 as did the goods service on the Horion - Fexhe branch. The Liége town route from Montegnée to Ans and Alleur also appears to have gone in 1956; at least it was lifted by 1957. Additionally, from 31 January 1957, the Liége end of Capital 156 (Riemst) was cut back to Place Coronmeuse because of a weak bridge at Pont Bressoux. From 22 July 1958 this route was reduced to peak-hour workings and these were discontinued entirely from 30 June 1959, together with the Liége - Riemst line which closed entirely; it had been restricted to peak hours from 27 July the previous year. It was followed by Verlaine - Jemeppe on 14 September and by Oreye - Rocourt on 20 December, the goods services on all these branches being discontinued as noted above. On 1 August 1960, Liége urban services 53 and 56, to Grace-Berleur and Jemeppe, were discontinued, officially "to allow road works", but they never reopened. Finally, in 1961, the goods line from Trembleur to Warsage was officially sold to the colliery on 12 February 1961, and the last Liégeois line, from Rocourt to Tongeren, closed to all traffic on 23 December 1961. There remained in the province only the remnants of Capital 17 which hung on until 1965.

10.2.5. Liége (Condroz) Groupe de Clavier

Capital	Name	Auth km
30	Clavier - Val-St-Lambert	25.03
60	Clavier - Comblain-au-Pont	29.85
164	Warzée - Ougrée	28.70

This system was the third of the original operating groupes but was always separate and is therefore taken on its own. It consisted originally of three separate Capitaux built at different times and based on the small town of Clavier, on the hilly wooded plateau of the Condroz, some 30 km southwest of

Liège. It was typical of those rural SNCV systems which plodded on year after year, carrying all types of traffic for the small communities they served.

The trunk line was **Capital 30 (CLAVIER - VAL-ST-LAMBERT)** running north and then northeast from Clavier's standard-gauge station to the Liége outer suburban village of Val-St-Lambert. The SNCV obtained authorisation in two stages on 16 April 1888 and 8 January 1890, allocating the concession to the newly formed *SA pour l'Exploitation des CF Regionaux en Belgique (CFRB)*. This was an amalgamation between the *Kempische Stoomtram Mij (KSTM)* and the local *Société Baclat et Leclerc (BL)*, and it opened the line throughout on 22 January 1890. The line started northward from Clavier alongside the standard gauge and then turned northeast over the Condroz, mainly on its own right-of-way. It served a scattering of small villages, of which the most important were Nandrin (whose station was at Quatre-Bras crossroads some 2km away) and St-Severin, both of which had station buildings. At St-Severin it rejoined the road and, after crossing the main "Route du Condroz", descended through deep woods to its terminus at Val-St-Lambert's Nord-Belge station. A further depot was situated in Villencourt wood, about 2 km south of Val, and there were no less than 40 sidings along the route, serving small factories, farms and forestry operations. The line prospered; in 1890 the SNCV actually applied for a 2.7km extension to central Seraing which would have competed with other transport and was therefore refused, as was a project for a 22.4km transverse route from Huy to Warzée via Tinlot on the existing line. In 1893 the concession was taken over by the locally formed *SA du Condroz pour l'Exploitation des CF Vicinaux (Cond)* and matters remained stable until after the 1914-18 war.

Meanwhile, on 23 February 1893, the SNCV obtained authorisation for another line eastward from Clavier, over the Condroz plateau and down into the Ourthe valley at a village called Comblain-au-Pont on the Liège - Marche line of the CF de l'Etat Belge. Like the Val-St-Lambert line, **Capital 60 (CLAVIER - COMBLAIN-AU-PONT)** was largely rural, partly roadside and partly on its own right-of-way, but had several peculiarities. The main depot was at Warzée , some 6km east of Clavier, the first stretch through there to Ouffet (13.08km) being opened on 1 October 1894. A 4km extension to Anthisnes followed on 10 May 1895, a further 7.10km to Comblain (Ecole) being opened on 2 January 1896. Even while the line was being built, however, on 18 July 1893, the SNCV had received authorisation for a 2.60km extension to the mainline station at Comblain, and this was opened on 8 January 1898; the delay was due to bridging problems at the River Ourthe. The concession was sublet to the Condroz company; as with Capital 30, only the most important stations had buildings, though a sub-depot was provided at Comblain. The Comblain line was one of those which eventually had mixed-gauge sections, in this case the 13.60km from Comblain to Ouffet which was four-railed between 1905 and 1907 to serve local industry, being operated as such from 12 February 1907; traffic was worked by metre-gauge locomotives with match-wagons. The line was profitable but the 1914-18 war, alas, brought disruption; all traffic was stopped at the end of September 1917, some 27.184km of track being lifted that autumn (this presumably including sidings).

The last line of the three, **Capital 164 (WARZÉE - OUGRÉE)** had a slightly more complex early history. The original scheme submitted by SNCV in 1901 allowed for a 28.70km line from Warzée north across the Condroz to the Liége suburb of Ougrée-Seraing, but disputes at the northern

end continued for six years before the SNCV got fed up. In 1910 it asked for and received authorisation for a line from Warzée to Boncelles village, some 20.18km in all, on the understanding that it might be extended later. Even so the line, probably the most hilly and difficult of the group, was not opened until 15 May 1914, operation being granted to *"M Collard, Ingenieur, de Liége"* who submitted the lowest tender. Alas he was not left in peace for long; war intervened, the Germans closing the line in July 1916, after which they lifted the Warzée - Boncelles section in August 1916. There was nothing else to dismantle since the line had no buildings apart from a share in Warzée depot.

It should be mentioned that these three lines might well have been joined by a fourth; in 1908 the SNCV applied for a 30km route south from Clavier via Somme-Leuze to Melreux in Province Luxembourg, with a branch from Somme-Leuze to Marche as a link to their Ardennes system. Authorisation was granted on 04 November 1913 as **Capital 192 CLAVIER - SOMME-LEUZE - MELREUX and SOMME-LEUZE - MARCHE**, but after the war nothing more was done.

As with other systems, the aftermath of the 1914-18 war effectively bankrupted both concessionaires, who surrendered their leases late in 1919. The SNCV then organised the complex into its Groupe de Clavier, with a line controller at Clavier and main workshops at Warzée depot. The Comblain line was reopened in three stages, as listed:

*	Comblain - Anthisnes	12 May 1920
*	Anthisnes - Ouffet	20 May 1921
*	Offet - Clavier	30 Oct 1921

It was followed on 13 April 1921 by the branch to Boncelles, which was extended to the Haut-Pré district of Ougrée-Seraing, a total of 28.7km, on 21 May 1925. A bid was made in 1921 for a further extension to Kinkempois (4.50km) which would have connected with the Nord Belge and greatly increased traffic; it was refused, as was a more modest link to a transhipment point at Seraing (Beguines) in 1933. Equally, two other extension plans came to nothing. The first, in 1922, would have linked La Rock, west of Anthisnes on the Comblain branch, and Comblain-la-Tour, the northern terminus of an extensive Ardennes line from Melreux. The other, in 1936, was a revival of the 1908 plan for a line from Clavier to Melreux. Considerable earthworks were actually constructed, but the project was cut short by World War II and never restarted.

By 1936, anyway, all the Groupe's lines, which by now came under the SNCV Liége-Limburg group, were suffering from road competition. Introduction of standard four-wheeled autorails in that year postponed disaster - though the fact that four cars could cover virtually all passenger services shows how trade had given way to private transport and to the SNCV buses that replaced many trains between Warzée and Comblain. Indeed the Clavier - Comblain service was reduced to market days only from 1 May 1936 and the rail service between Boncelles and Ougrée was withdrawn in late 1938, both, however being restored in 1940 under wartime pressures. The war also virtually closed the Comblain line when the Ourthe bridge was blown up in May 1940, and the metre-gauge tracks were lifted from Comblain as far as Ouffet at the beginning of 1943. Thus, even after repairs, services on this line from September 1941 were limited to Clavier - Ouffet (passenger and freight) and to standard-gauge freight over the remainder; the latter was worked by SNCV locomotives coming light from the nearby Poulseur depot when needed.

Elsewhere on the system there was a temporary surge of both goods and passenger traffic, but after the war's end services diminished rapidly. All the Ougrée - Warzée line, together with passenger services between Clavier and Ouffet, was closed on 8 December 1947, metre-gauge goods workings surviving until 1949 when they were cut back to Ochain. Goods workings between Ochain and Ouffet followed on 9 January 1950. The last passenger service, to Val-St-Lambert, was withdrawn on 4 October 1952, and goods between Val and Nandrin followed on 21 June 1953 "owing to modernisation of the Route du Condroz"; the 14.5km concerned were lifted in 1954. Of the remainder, the standard-gauge goods workings to Ouffet lasted until 29 July 1957, except for a spur at Comblain which lasted until 13 October that year. The remainder closed to all traffic on 17 March 1958, leaving the countryside to SNCV buses and lorries working from the old Warzée depot.

In conclusion, two peculiarities must be mentioned. Firstly, there was the one-man autorail service to Ougrée during the 1930s; the rear entrance of each car was locked, a notice advising passengers to take their tickets from the driver. Secondly, there was the "radio train" operated on summer Sundays between 1935 and 1939. In principle this started from Ougrée, making a complete return trip over the whole complex of lines, with a visit to Comblain grottoes thrown in, and with loudspeaker music relayed to each coach from a gramophone in the van. There were numerous beer stops, and the train was deservedly popular with the Liégeois , the evening return to Val being, it was said, "very merry indeed".

10.2.6 Liége: Lines on the German border around Verviers and Eupen

Capital	Name	Auth km
36	Dolhain - Goe - Membach (frontière)(- Eupen)	*8.91
165	Spa - Verviers	16.8
195	Lignes d'Eupen	?
199	Verviers - Dolhain - Eupen (et Embrs)	14.00
NOTE:*	length on Belgian territory.	

Liége province had one odd anomaly, the apparently interconnected, but otherwise isolated, group of lines around Verviers to the southeast of Liége which was in reality three separate systems: a standard-gauge steam-worked line from Dolhain, on a mainline railway, through Goe to the then German frontier at Membach, with a German extension to Eupen; the well-known Spa - Verviers tram; a collection of electric lines around Eupen which "came over" to the SNCV as part of the spoils of war after the 1914-18 conflict. To these was added in the 1930s a completely new electrified link from Eupen to the eastern end of Verviers town. In spite of their physical proximity and the fact that the two metre-gauge systems had separate connections to an independent tramway network in Verviers, there were no regular service links, and they are best taken as separate entities. One might also add, as an outlier of this group, the odd little isolated section to the north in the pre-1914 neutral territory of La Calamine; this came into Belgium with the Eupen area after World War I; though physically linked to Eupen via Aachen while Eupen was German, it became a detached section of the Vicinal in due course.

Capital 36 (DOLHAIN - EUPEN), officially Dolhain - Bethane (frontière), was the first line in the area and one of only three standard-gauge railways operated by the SNCV. Its history is somewhat tortuous. It was, to start with, an international line, crossing the then German frontier at Membach and with its German portion ceded to the *Eupener Kleinbahn Gesellschaft*, who in turn ceded operation to the SNCV and its subsidiaries; The line, 9.2km in total, ran from Dolhain in a curve south and then east through the small town of Goe to Bethane and thence via the nearby frontier at Membach into a terminus in the southern part of Eupen town. It was mainly roadside, and the first section, 4.3km to Goe (Bethane), was authorised on 18 May 1889 but the SNCV could not find a concessionaire willing to take it on. It had,

lines in the east 1: A goods train on the standard gauge line from Dolhain to Goe with Type 10 locomotive 805.

(Paul de Backer)

lines in the east 2: Balmoral hotel on the Spa - Verviers with an early electric car.
(author's collection)

Spa - Verviers: a "boat" tourist car in later years, after being enclosed.
(SNCV)

Lines in the east 3: Eynatten, on the ex-Aachen system, with a typical car.
(author's collection.)

desbarax

Eupen, with ex-Aachen car 9682 (G Desbarax)

truncated by destruction of a bridge. Wartime pressures actually benefited the line to some extent; a daily passenger service (to Eupen in the morning and return in the evening) was instituted from 19 February 1942 and, following bridge repairs, goods services over the whole line were resumed from 16 April 1942. The allied advances in 1944, however, caused final stoppage to passengers in September 1944 and cutting back of goods services; After World War II, even goods traffic declined, and on 1 June 1959 the line was accordingly cut back first to Membach and then to Goe for purely local industrial traffic. This stub lingered on until 15 March 1963, when it was closed to all traffic

Capital 165 (SPA - VERVIERS) was fundamentally a simple tramway, carrying only passengers and parcels, but nonetheless was one of the best-known SNCV routes. It had a complex history, being originally authorised on 3 May 1907 as Spa - Heusy (a locality about 2km south of Verviers town). Its route was what can only be called a switchback. In the course of its 17km across the grain of the wooded and hilly region south of Verviers, it scrambled down into and climbed out of no less than three valleys; gradients included a short stretch of nearly 8 per cent (1 in 13) and nearly 2.5km of 5 per cent (1 in 20) with four curves down to 40m radius. For most of its course it followed the road, deviating only where terrain made this impossible and at the entrance to Spa terminus. Its outer reaches tapped the tourist health resort of Spa (which gives spas their title) and the nearby prestigious district called Balmoral. Its inner end entered the Verviers suburbs on the north side of the Hoegne river, terminating in a loop at Heusy where it made end-on connection with the local tramways company, the *Tramways Vervietois (TV)*. Apart from its electricity substation at Tiege and the Sart (Balmoral) depot there were few buildings. Polleur alone had a proper station. Shelters were erected at four of the more important halts; otherwise, as on so many rural SNCV lines, the local cafe benefited.

The line was built by the SNCV and opened in sections. The first 2km or so, from Spa to Balmoral (Bois de Spa), were opened with electric traction on 3 August 1909, a temporary depot being provided until the permanent one, a few hundred metres further on in the woods, was reached. Thence construction was pushed on toward Heusy, a twice-daily steam-hauled service actually being operated between Tiege and Heusy in 1910-11 before the electrification was completed; this was presumably mainly for the benefit of workmen from Verviers although photographs show open toastrack trailers. Officially electric operation was extended from Bois de Spa to Tiege (Charmille) on 6 October 1909, to the Tiege substation on 28 August 1910 and on to Heusy on 20 May 1911, all operated by the SNCV itself. With the line complete, it then ceded operation to the TV, who took control on 4 January 1912, extending the service over their own route 3 to the town centre at Place Verte on 4 April of that year. It was always worked by SNCV stock, including early cars of the Petite Espinette type (M 31-47 series). The outbreak of war and the German advance in August 1914 interrupted services, but they were restarted on 24 August 1914 on orders from the occupying power since the line provided an alternative route

perforce, to operate the line itself from its opening on 4 July 1891, while extending the railway to Bethane (Pont) which was reached on 1 May 1896. It was further extended, to Membach (gare) on 2 September and to Membach (frontière) on 1 October 1896. The *SA des Railways Economiques de Liége-Seraing (LS)* then accepted the concession and also agreed to operate the final portion into Eupen, opened on 1 June 1897 although a short portion was not completed until 1 August 1904. At this period the line was completely isolated from other SNCV possessions. Operation passed to the *SA Liégeoise du CFV Chimay - Couvin (CC)* in 1912 and affairs continued thus until well into World War I; the German section was closed in 1917 but the whole line came into Belgian territory as a result of frontier readjustments after World War I. The SNCV took over direct control in 1919, reopening Membach - Eupen from 22 November 1919 but passenger traffic never prospered, and was withdrawn from 30 April 1926. The construction of the metre-gauge electric line between Verviers and Eupen would have rendered it redundant anyway.

The German invasion of 1940 quite naturally resulted in another modification. The redrawn frontier meant that all the line from Bethane bridge (3.5km) was now in Germany and from 5 June 1941 the *Aachener Kleinbahn Gesellschaft (AKG)* operated the whole line under a provisional agreement with SNCV. Goods services were resumed throughout from 19 June 1941 but in December of that year the Dolhain end was to the mainline railway. It was much used for local troop movement and especially for transporting wounded to the many hospitals and convalescent homes set up around Spa. To help with this traffic, the Germans extended the service over TV route 5 (Pre - Javais) to the mainline station of Verviers Est.

So useful was the line that in 1918 the Germans even planned to double the track, but eventually just ran an intensive service on the existing line. From 5 March 1918, Spa was put under an interdict as a security precaution since the German GHQ was in the armoured cellars of the nearby Chateau de Neubois. Civilian travellers could go no further than Polleur bridge and, on 28 July, the line was entirely requisitioned by the military. On 29 July, the staff refused duty and were imprisoned at Liége. The tramway continued somehow, even "acquiring" the direct TV line from Verviers Est station to Place Verte while the TV got diverted via their old route 5.

On 21 August 1918, the line reverted to civilian control. There were various minor incidents up to the armistice, but matters then reverted to normal until the TV surrendered its concession on 1 March 1920. The terminus, perforce, reverted to Heusy, where passengers had to change, save for a short period in 1920-1 when they ran through to Verviers (Harmonie). In 1929, a new agreement was made with the TV whereby SNCV cars ran in to the then-new Verviers Centrale SNCB station; a second track was laid between Vieuxtemps and the terminus at Place de la Victoire so that clashes between the two organisations would not occur. Services were extended from 15 May 1930 and continued up to closure despite occasional SNCV/TV friction.

There were always problems with cars on the Spa route, the hilly tortuous nature restricting it to short wheelbase four-wheelers with only one trailer - though a former "benzo-electric" bogie car, 9408, was tried unsuccessfully. In 1936 the SNCV so far accepted the position as to rebody some of the old 9159-68 series. These rebuilds were unique on the SNCV, having bulbous semi-open bodies designed for tourist traffic and were officially the "Panoramiques". Always flippantly known locally as "the boats" because their short wheelbase and top-heavy bodies made them pitch and roll, these cars were later fully enclosed and ran most services up to the end.

Meanwhile, the 1939-45 war broke out. The line appears to have functioned fairly normally, apart from a further spate of ambulance trams in 1944, until the von Runstedt offensive in December of that year. The personnel, however, had numerous complications to contend with, among them running the Verviers - Dolhain stub of the former electric line to Eupen (see below) in addition to their own. The British military authorities stopped all services for a short time early in 1945, and the line never recovered. Traffic fell off steadily and, on 30 June 1952, the line was closed completely, its main claim to fame being the highest tramway summit in Belgium at the time (a mere 370m, at Arbespine). The SNCV replaced it with buses for a while, but in 1971 withdrew even these. It was hoped to sell the suburban section from Heusy to Cheval Blanc but agreement could not be reached with the TV, and in 1958 this last remnant was lifted.

10.2.7 The Eupen system & lines in the Vierlandespunkt

As noted above, following the 1914-18 war, Belgium gained territory in the Eupen region, the German frontier being moved back northeast beyond the small town of Eynatten to Kopfchen.

Included in this area were several metre-gauge electric tramways, opened between 1906 and 1910 as part of the *Aachener Kleinbahn Gesellschaft (AKG)* system (see app 5). From early 1919 they were taken over and initially worked by the Belgian military government using ex-Aachen stock. When the region was handed over to civilian control, the lines and stock were, in turn, handed over to the *SNCV Groupe de Liége-Limburg* with effect from 23 March 1923. They were typical German small-town tramways, comprising three routes based on Eupen and a cut-back branch off the former line from Eupen to Aachen. The Aachen line was now broken at the frontier at Kopfchen, the original line to Eupen Bahnhof having been opened on 19 July 1906, together with a longer branch from Eynatten through Raeren to Walheim (12.3km), opened in two stages, to Raeren on 19 July 1906 and on to Walheim on 31 October 1907. Walheim stayed in Germany and Raeren became the branch terminus from Eynatten where there had been a depot since 1906. On 10 July 1910, the Eupen route was linked to the standard gauge station from Eupen Rathaus (town hall) (0.5km), followed on 2 September 1910 by a 2.6km branch from the Rathaus southeast to Bellmerin, and on 2 December of the same year the 4.7km branch northwest to the mainline railway at Herbestal completed the system. Under Vicinal operation, the focus of this system became Eupen Rathaus, with a depot a short way along the Herbestal branch. With it came four bogie and five two-axle cars of typical German design which were taken into SNCV stock as 9683-87 and 9678-82. For some time, at least, the AKG German-language signs and timetables were retained and the SNCV in this region was indeed known as the *National Kleinbahn Gesellschaft*

There was also an outlier of this system. Northeast of Herbestal and west of Aachen, the frontiers of Belgium, Germany and the Netherlands meet at the Dreilandespunkt (three countries point). This was originally known as the Vierlandespunkt (four countries point) since also meeting at this point and to the south of it was a small triangle of neutral territory which, in practice, had been managed jointly by Belgium and Germany from 1816 to 1914. There was a small cluster of villages in its south, including La Calamine, Neu Moresnet, and Altenberg or Preussisch Moresnet, and all except La Calamine were served by the last 0.5km of a 5km route of the AKG terminating at Neu Moresnet (Altenberg in the AKG timetables). This route opened on 27 March 1907. Though the area was originally called Moresnet, Moresnet village is over 1km into Belgium to the west of the neutral territory, and the most appropriate name is the Belgian title of La Calamine, a corruption of Galmei or zinc, a zinc mine being the reason for it all in the first place.

Came the peace and, in 1919-20, the Belgian military government with its frontier adjustments which incorporated the neutral territory and Eupen district into Belgium and moved the border to cross the Moresnet tram route at Tullje (sometimes spelt Tulje), leaving 1.2km of its outer end in Belgium. This was effectively cut off from other Belgian tramways and was apparently operated by the military government or by the SNCV under contract using a couple of Tashkent cars provided by the SNCV. This was not satisfactory and, under some pressure, the *Aachener Kleinbahn Gesellschaft* once again started through operation on 29 March 1923 under a 20-year concession. In 1924 it agreed to work the line as an integral part of its own system. The SNCV thriftily reclaimed its cars but continued to show the line on its system maps.

In January 1931, the SNCV was authorised to add a further electrified route, from Eupen back through Dolhain, where it crossed Capital 36, and on to Verviers where it terminated just short of the TV depot at Renoupré; cars could continue over TV tracks to the town centre at Place des Martyrs. A new depot for this was built at Eupen, Eynatten thereafter serving only the truncated stub of the Walheim branch which had been cut back to Raeren in 1916 and not reopened. Opened on 15 May 1933, the new line was purely passenger-carrying and was worked mainly by "Standard" bogie cars. It may be worth noting that the TV had also been interested in such a line as an extension of its own system, but the legislature decided in favour of the SNCV. There was no through connection to the Spa line, apart from TV rails, the systems even using different forms of current collection: trolley on Spa - Verviers and bow on Verviers - Eupen. Of minor interest is that there was still a notional connection to Aachen at Kopfchen but traffic was discouraged for political reasons.

The situation was once again shattered by war. In May 1940 the Germans occupied Belgium and reclaimed their former territories together with the lines from Eupen, which closed briefly on 10 May. They were more-or-less gratefully received by their former owners, the AKG, which reopened them from 1 July 1940, restoring the through Aachen - Eupen service; the AKG in turn acquired some SNCV vehicles to add to reclaimed cars and incorporated the routes into its own system, renumbering them as shown below:

No	Route details
14	Aachen Westbhf - Kopfchen
24	Aachen Theater - Eupen Rathaus
27	Aachen Hbf - Neu Moresnet
34	Eynatten - Raeren
44	Eupen Rathaus - Herbestal
54	Eupen Rathaus - Bellmerin
64	Eupen Rathaus - Dolhain (Baelen)

As to the SNCV line proper, it was cut back to Dolhain (Haut Fourneau), initially owing to destruction of a viaduct, but was later allowed to operate up to the frontier at Baelen. The cut-back route had to be operated by a mixture of rolling stock from Spa and Liége, which was transferred first to the TV depot at Renoupré and then to a temporary shed hastily erected at Dolhain. Four cars were allocated permanently to

this service since they had to be fitted with bow collectors instead of trolley poles; this feature also caused annoyance when they had to return to Balmoral for overhaul, since a trolley-equipped car had to haul them from Renoupré onwards. Apart from this, the shortened line appears to have had an uneventful war until 11 September 1944 when services were officially suspended. The most noteworthy item recorded against it was a special journey on the eve of liberation, when the retreating Germans commandeered two cars, one each from Verviers - Spa and the TV, forcing the drivers to take their troops as far as Eupen; the main oddity of that was the fact that both conductors had to travel the whole way on the fenders, guiding the trolley poles along the incompatible contact wire. It is said that normal service was then resumed, only to be interrupted once more during the German Ardennes offensive in December; the cars were hurriedly evacuated to Balmoral.

After 1945 the frontier was once more adjusted to Kopfchen but things were never quite the same, including the running numbers of the cars returned from Aachen, at least one retaining its ASEAG fleet number for reasons unknown. The link from Eynatten to the frontier, the short branch to Raeren, and the now-isolated Neu Moresnet section, had closed during the fighting in September 1944 and were not reopened, while the link from Eupen to Eynatten town according to local sources closed on 2 October 1951 (SNCV gives 20 December 1951 as the official closure date for all routes). It was followed on 13 April 1953 by the branches to Herbestal and Bellmerin, bringing about final withdrawal of the German cars, the best of which returned to Aachen. Finally, Eupen - Verviers was officially closed to all traffic on 20 February 1956 although in practice heavy snow had caused services to be suspended from 17 February; note that the Eupen terminus had been moved from Rathaus to Polizeiamt in Spring 1954.

10.2.8 Liége Province: detached lines

Capital	Name	Auth km
17	Poulseur - Sprimont	8.50
118	Sprimont - Trooz	13.69

This, the first SNCV tramway in Liége province, was one of only three standard-gauge railways worked by the SNCV, and in general had an uneventful history; its main claim to fame was that, for reasons given below, it continued working with steam into the 1960s, becoming the last SNCV line to do so on a commercial basis.

Detached line: a steam train of the standard gauge Poulseur-Sprimont-Trooz branch in passenger-carrying days
(collection E de Backer)

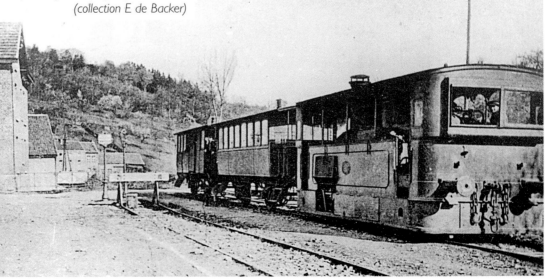

Capital 17 (POULSEUR - SPRIMONT) originally comprised a single track from the mainline station of Poulseur, on the Liège - Jemelle railway, to the small town of Sprimont, and was intended mainly to serve the many stone quarries in that area. The route, authorised on 21 May 1887, ran mostly through a narrow rocky valley, road, rail and river being clustered together with numerous sharp curves; the headquarters and depot were alongside Poulseur mainline station and were the only substantial buildings. Operation was ceded to the *SA pour l'Exploitation de Railways Vicinaux (RV)* an otherwise unknown operator, the initial 7.70km being opened on 9 December 1887. In 1888, short extensions at Sprimont appear to have taken the length to 8.50km, with passenger services starting on 1 March and in 1906-8 a further 13.69km was added under **Capital 118 (SPRIMONT - TROOZ)** to connect with the Liége - Spa railway at Trooz. It was opened in three stages, to Louveigne on 1 September 1906, to Trooz

The Poulseur - Sprimont section was one of the few lines to carry on with steam into the 1960s. Here a short train is made up at Sprimont quarries as late as 1965.   *(WJKD)*

(Viaduc) on 24 January 1907 and on to Trooz (Etat Station) on 22 January 1908. Operation then passed to the local *SA du Vicinal Poulseur - Sprimont - Trooz (PST)* of Poulseur; operating length was given as 22.19km, including one of the SNCV's few tunnels. In World War 1 the Trooz extension was closed and lifted in December 1917 and not reopened until 24 March 1921 after the SNCV took over control in 1920. The extension was never very profitable, lost its passenger services from 18 February 1936 and closed completely from 6 December 1937. The remainder stayed open for passengers until September 1944 and for stone traffic thereafter; indeed a big Dutch order for dyke-building purposes kept traffic running until 30 April 1965, when the line finally closed. Locomotives were always 0-6-0 Tram bicabines of the 8xx series, and standard SNCV four-wheeled stock was used for internal purposes; one brake/third coach remained in use as a "caboose" until the end. It is worth noting that, from time to time, Poulseur depot also provided motive power for the nearby mixed-gauge route from Comblain-au-Pont to Ouffet (Capital 60), locomotives being sent up from Poulseur depot when required.

10.3 Liége-Limburg: Limburg Province

10.3.1 Introduction

In the late 19th century, Limburg, up in the north eastern corner of Belgium, was a rural province, flattish except in its very southern parts, and with strong links to the Dutch province of Limburg to its north and east. Its secondary lines developed accordingly, long straggling, not very profitable tramways which made frequent cross-border connections, and which joined the country districts to major market centres such as Hasselt, the provincial capital; Maaseik and Lanaken, near the Dutch border; Tongeren in the south. They were largely the concern of local companies, and after the first twenty years there was little development except where the province abutted on Liége. Even after 1918, the only real development was around Hasselt where exploitation of the Campine coalfields to the east and north led to some half-hearted expansion and a small amount of electrification. The latter was quite the least successful of all SNCV initiatives of the period; the Hasselt suburban routes lasted less than ten years as electrified lines and the extensions were never completely finished.

At its most extensive, the Limburg system can best be visualised as a huge irregular circle with antennae stretching out in all directions, except to the northwest which was never really served by the SNCV at all. The "circle", never operated as such, extended from Hasselt north to Leopoldsburg and east to Maaseik, thence south to Lanaken, southwest to Tongeren and back northwest to Hasselt. In later years, three branches intruded inside it to meet up at Genk; in 1912 Genk was a big village, but by 1927 it had become a thriving mining town of some 40,000 inhabitants. Initially and up to 1920, the province was dominated by two companies which formed the operating Groupes of Tongeren and Hasselt, with the single lines from Koersel and Molenbeersel entrusted to small operators. To serve their empires, the big companies had works at Hasselt, Bree and Bilsen (Limburgsche Stoomtramweg Mij or LSTM) and at Lanaken (Liége - Seraing or LS).

10.3.2. Groep Hasselt, 1887-1920

Capital	Name	Auth km
24	Leopoldsburg - Bree - Maaseik	44.21
81	Hasselt - Oreye	29.80
86	Hasselt - Herk-de-Stad - Halen	18.10
88*	Hasselt - Leopoldsburg	30.47
96	Maaseik - Kessenich	7.80
108	Tongeren - Kortessem	12.56
156	Genk - Liége - Vottem	60.05
168	Herk-de-Stad - St-Truiden (transferred to Capital 86)	16.10

NOTE: Capital 88 was later used to cover a deviation between Zonhoven and Beringen

The biggest, and least profitable, part of the Limburg system was that ceded for operation to the *Limburgsche Stoomtram Mij (LSTM)*, formed at Bree in December 1887 and initially known as Groep Bree. It started with the province's first line and spread out all round the provincial capital of Hasselt, with routes running almost entirely through farming areas and tiny villages. Not until after World War I was there any industrial development, and by then the company had given up.

through Trekschuren to Kortessem and then swinging sharply southwest to Oreye in Liége province, where it linked to Capitaux 48 and 53. It was authorised on 7 June 1897+ and opened in two stages: from Hasselt to Borgloon on 1 September 1899 and on to Oreye on 15 November 1900. Its length was 30.17km, with small depots at Hasselt, Kortessem and Oreye. The section from Kortessem to Oreye was closed by the Germans in April 1917 and not reopened until 12 January 1920.

Train at the military camp at Beverlo near Leopoldsburg.
(author's collection)

A typical steam train at Herk de Stad. *(E de Backer collection)*

Capital 24 (LEOPOLDSBURG - BREE - MAASEIK) was the first line in Limburg, built mainly to open up the north of Limburg. It ran due east from Leopoldsburg and was authorised and opened in two stages: Leopoldsburg - Bree, authorised on 19 August 1887 and opened 9 January 1888 and Bree - Maaseik, authorised on 28 February 1889 and opened on 1 May 1890. A short extension to Leopoldsburg Canal, authorised on 3 July 1890, followed quickly. The main depot was at Bree with sub-sheds at each end and, after a poor start, the line paid its way. There was even talk of a branch from Bree north to Hammant in 1911 though it was never built, while from 1899-on there was considerable exchange of traffic at both ends; with Capital 88 at Leopoldsburg and Capitaux 82, 96 and 130 at Maaseik. The line remained intact during World War I.

Capital 81 (HASSELT - OREYE) was the next line, ten years later. It initiated the group of routes from Hasselt town. Again it was a straightforward country line running southeast

It was followed quickly by **Capital 86 (HASSELT - HERK-DE-STAD - HALEN)**, which headed west from Hasselt to the village of Herk-de-Stad, from where an extension (frequently omitted from later SNCV maps) continued to Halen on the Brabant border. Authorised in two stages, from Hasselt to Herk on 25 January 1898 and on to Halen on 28 October 1903, it was opened to Herk on 1 July 1900 and on to Halen on 7 August 1905. Plans for a branch from Herk to Beringen were refused. It was not, alas, a profitable venture, though it usually paid first dividends. It later took over **Capital 168, (ST-TRUIDEN - HERK-DE-STAD)** which was authorised on 21 August 1909, opened as an extension on 15 May 1913 and was worked by the LSTM. Both lines were closed during World War I as shown below:

Section	closed	reopened
Hasselt - Herk-de-Stad	Apr 1917	12 Dec 1920
Herk-de-Stad - Halen	Aug 1915	Apr 1921
Herk-de-Stad - St-Truiden	Mar 1917	Apr 1921

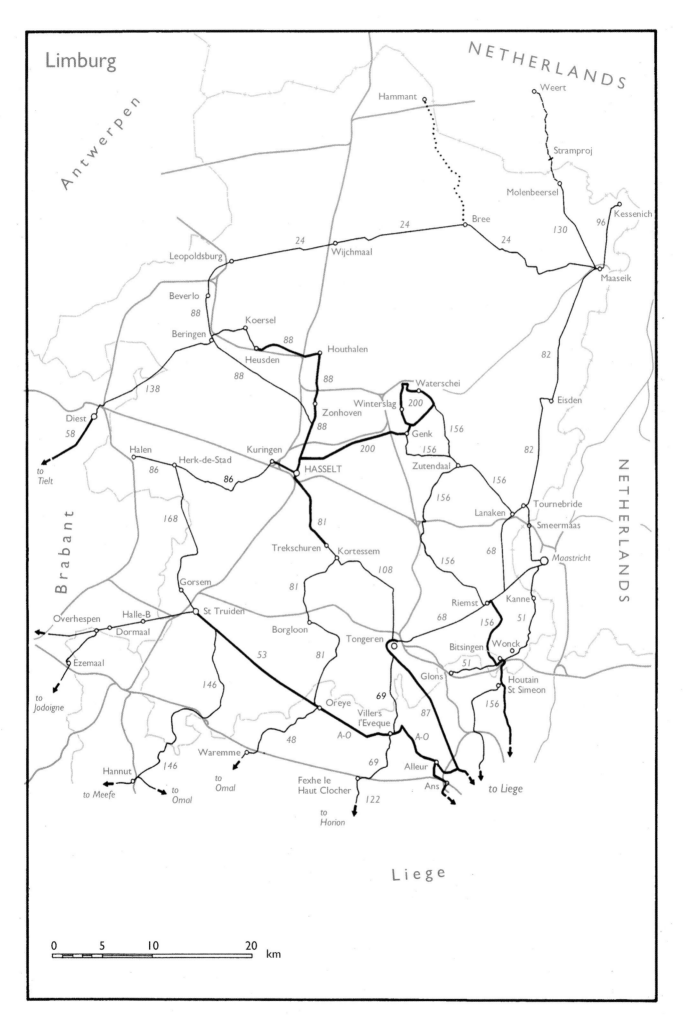

Limburg

NETHERLANDS

Antwerpen

Brabant

NETHERLANDS

Liege

Weert
Stramproj
Molenbeersel
Kessenich
Hammant
Bree
Maaseik
24
24
24
130
96
82
Eisden
82
Leopoldsburg
Wijchmaal
Beverlo
88
Koersel
Beringen
88
Heusden
Houthalen
88
88
Waterschei
138
Winterslag
200
Zonhoven
88
Genk
156
Diest
Kuringen
200
156
58
Halen
Zutendaal
156
to
Tielt
Herk-de-Stad
86
HASSELT
156
86
Lanaken
Tournebride
156
Smeermaas
81
168
Trekschuren
Kortessem
68
Maastricht
108
156
Gorsem
81
Riemst
Kanne
St Truiden
68
156
51
Overhespen
Halle-B
Borgloon
81
Tongeren
Bitsingen
Wonck
Dormaal
53
Glons
51
Houtain
St Simeon
Ezemaal
146
51
156
to
Jodoigne
Oreye
69
Villers
l'Eveque
87
48
A-O
A-O
Waremme
69
Alleur
to Liege
Hannut
146
Fexhe le
Haut Clocher
Ans
to Meefe
to
Omal
to
Omal
122
to
Horion

0 5 10 20 km

The next concession in this group was **Capital 88 (HASSELT - LEOPOLDSBURG).** This had been proposed as long ago as 1886, but authorisation was refused because of possible competition with the railways. After extensive route alterations, it was finally authorised on 25 January 1898 and opened throughout on 1 September 1899. It had a common section to Beverlo just south of Leopoldsburg where it connected with the line to Maaseik. The main depot was at Leopoldsburg, and operating length was 29.58km. The Hasselt - Beringen section was closed and lifted in February 1918 by the Germans, being restored to use on 15 August 1919.

The other LSTM lines were basically offshoots of the main system. **Capital 96 (MAASEIK - KESSENICH)** was a straightforward branch northeast to the Dutch frontier where it met but did not physically connect with the Dutch *Centrale Limburgsche Spoorweg Mij*, though this was also metre gauge. Authorised on 7 December 1898, it was officially opened on 1 May 1900 and had its depot at Maaseik which it shared with other lines. It was closed and lifted in August 1915, not being restored until April 1921. **Capital 108 (TONGEREN - KORTESSEM)** provided a link line connecting Hasselt with the Liége group but was intended mainly as a rural line providing access for local farms with refineries at Oreye and beyond. It ran northwest from Tongeren SNCV, to Kortessem where it met Capital 81, was authorised on 8 May 1901, opened on 28 October 1904, and had a length of 13.67km. The depot was at Kortessem. It remained intact during World War I.

Of this group there remains one late-comer, not generally considered as being within the LSTM empire. **Capital 156 (GENK - LIÉGE - VOTTEM)** was a complex system with a complex history, mainly because construction was interrupted by the war. It was originally authorised on 27 October 1906 as a line south from Genk Village, running via Bilzen, Riemst (where it met the Tongeren - Lanaken line), Bitsingen/Bassenge (crossing with Glons - Kanne) to cross the provincial border near Houtain-St-Simeon. From there branches were to run southwest via Liers to Vottem (junction with Capital 87) and south through Herstal to Liége centre. The Genk - Bitsingen portion was opened on 23 May 1910 and the Bitsingen - Liers stretch on 8 March 1911, a total of 44.52km. Operation was put out to tender and allocated to the LSTM as "offering the best terms available", though these were pretty hard! It appears that a section between Riemst and Val Meer had been operated since 2 November 1909 purely for sugar beet traffic. The Vottem - Liége branch was officially opened as far as Herstal on the eastern outskirts of Liége on 8 June 1914, but there it met the usual bridging problems and was overtaken by the war and shut again from 5 August to some time in October. During the war the sections from Bitsingen to Liers and Houtain to Herstal were closed on 23 April 1918 and Bilzen - Bitsingen followed in May; the tracks were lifted. The line was reopened throughout on 8 August 1920 and extension started once more. To complete the saga, Liers - Vottem opened on 21 January 1924; the line from Herstal to Liége (Coronmeuse), authorised on 18 November 1925 to overcome problems of admission to Liége, opened on 1 February 1927. Almost contemporaneously with electrification of Bitsingen - Liége (24 April 1938) it was extended across the river via Bressoux to Place St-Lambert on 4 April 1938. By this time the Houtain - Liers - Vottem branch had already closed to passengers on 31 January 1936, though it remained in use for coal traffic from the Campine fields. Liers - Vottem was closed and lifted in 1951, Liers - Houtain following three years later (two dates are quoted: 21 October and 30 November 1954).

10.3.3 Groep Tongeren, 1891-1919

Capital	Name	Auth km
51	*Glons - Kanne (- Maastricht)*	16.01
68	*Tongeren - Lanaken - Vroenhoven (- Maastricht)*	25.80
69	*Tongeren - Fexhe-le-Haut-Clocher*	19.02
82	*Maaseik - Lanaken - Grens (- Maastricht)*	26.40

NOTE: The cross-border Tongeren - Liége line, Capital 87, which might logically come under this grouping, was ceded to the *CFV de Liége - Barchon (LB)* and therefore attributed to Liége province.

This group of lines, with operating headquarters at Lanaken and head office at Tongeren, was ceded from the start for operation to the local *Liége - Seraing (LS)* company formed at Liége in 1881. The LS tended to operate its acquisitions directly at first, and then to hive them off to various subsidiaries specially formed for the purpose; this group was no exception, being passed in 1911 to the *SA Belge-Neerlandaise de Transports et Travaux (BNTT)*, formed that year. The transfer may have been connected with the group's cross-border activities. With the exception of a single line wandering south from the market town of Tongeren, the group was an eminently logical one since all

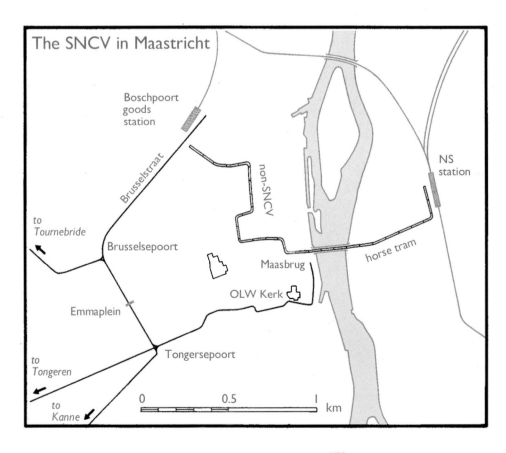

The SNCV in Maastricht

Boschpoort goods station

Brusselstraat

to Tournebride

Brusselsepoort

non-SNCV

Maasbrug

OLW Kerk

Emmaplein

horse tram

NS station

Tongersepoort

to Tongeren

0   0.5   1 km

to Kanne

three of its major routes crossed the border to end up in the Dutch city of Maastricht. Strictly speaking, the sections in the Netherlands were built to the order of Maastricht municipality and then ceded to the SNCV, but in practice the system was operated as a whole.

Capital 51 (GLONS - KANNE (- MAASTRICHT) was the first line in the group, being authorised on 24 August 1891. From Glons SNCV it ran roughly northeast through Boirs (3km), Bitsingen/Bassenge (where it later met Capital 156), and on through poor countryside to the frontier at the little town of Kanne, a total of 15.88km opened on 1 September 1893. It was extended through to Maastricht on 14 January 1894, running via the Tongerse Poort and Brusselse Poort to the standard-gauge Boschpoort goods station in the northwest of the town; passenger trams terminated at Tongerse Poort until 1909 (see below). The main traffic was chalk and lime to the cement works near Maastricht, much cargo being discharged into canal barges just short of that town; indeed a short goods-only branch to quarries near Boirs was opened on 1 June 1912 and this provided much of the traffic. The line seems to have had an uneventful if not very profitable career up to 1914 when it was abruptly affected by closure of its cross-border links on the outbreak of war. With its main traffic gone, the remainder was closed and lifted in two stages, from Wonck to Kanne in September 1915 and from Glons to Wonck in May 1918; the sections were not reopened until 25 October 1920 and sometime in February 1921 respectively.

Capital 68 (TONGEREN - LANAKEN) and **Capital 82 (MAASEIK - LANAKEN)** were built almost simultaneously, and in effect formed a continuous line, with two spurs into Maastricht. The line from Tongeren was authorised on 8 July 1895 and opened on 15 May 1897. It ran northeast over flattish country to Riemst and then turned north to Lanaken. A cross-border branch from Riemst to Maastricht via Vroenhoven Grens was not opened until 1 May 1909; it connected into the line from Kanne just southwest of Maastricht (Tongerse Poort) and was then extended round the south of Maastricht to a terminus by the river at Onze Lieve Vrouwekade near the Maas river bridge. The extension opened for goods on 5 April 1909 and for passengers on 1 May 1909. It should be noted that this stretch was comparatively short-lived, being cut back in 1924 to the Tongerse Poort and diverted to Emmaplein, near the Brusselse Poort.

Capital 82 (MASSEIK - LANAKEN - GRENS - (MAASTRICHT) was actually built out from Maastricht, running northwest via the frontier at Smeermaas to Lanaken (Tournebride), with a link into Lanaken town. Then it ran north along the frontier to Maaseik in the northeast corner of Limburg. It was authorised on 13 June 1897 and opened in two stages, from Maastricht to Eisden (in early days spelt Eijsden) on 7 January 1898 and on to Maaseik on 15 June 1898. Both lines were surprisingly profitable, paying second dividends up to the outbreak of war, when they lost their Maastricht links. Both survived the war otherwise intact except for the short section between Tournebride and Smeermaas; this was closed in March 1916 and not reopened until 31 March 1919. The quoted distances for these lines are dubious since it is not clear how far the cross-border spurs are taken into account; there were approximately 6km of route on the Dutch side.

Odd-line-out of the Groep was **Capital 69 (TONGEREN - FEXHE-LE-HAUT-CLOCHER)**. This was a simple line running due south from Tongeren for 19.11km via Villers-l'Eveque to its sleepy little terminus with the resounding name in Liége province. There it later connected with Capital 122 (qv). Authorised on 20 July 1895, and opened on 15 May 1897, it was extended from Fexhe to Fexhe Etat station on 4 October 1899 and, in reports, was often classed as a Liége line. It was not particularly profitable, but survived the 1914-18 war intact

10.3.4 Other lines in Limburg province prior to 1920

Capital	Name	Auth km
130	Maaseik - Molenbeersel	11.90
138	Diest - Koersel (see Brabant)	19.42

These two lines were worked by separate companies. **Capital 130 (MAASEIK - MOLENBEERSEL - WEERT)** was actually an international route. Authorised on 14 December 1903, it ran north to the frontier at Molenbeersel village (11.16km; depot) and thence across the Dutch frontier via Stramproij to the Dutch town of Weert; the Dutch portion, 8.7km long, was built by the two councils concerned and leased to the SNCV. It was opened on 18 January 1910 and worked as a whole until 1914 when the link was broken by the outbreak of war. There is some evidence of goods traffic between Weert and Maaseik during the early part of the war and, unusually, the Stramproij and Weert councils continued to work their portion using three locomotives on loan from the SNCV until the link was remade in 1918. The operating company for the whole of its independent career was the *NM tot Uitbating van den Buurtspoorweg Maaseik - Weert en Uitbreiding (MW)* founded on 12 April 1906 with HQ at Weert. It surrendered its concession in 1925, the line then becoming part of SNCV Groep Limburg.

Capital 138 (DIEST - KOERSEL) was a cross-border line and its history will be found under Brabant.

10.3.5 SNCV in Limburg province, 1920-1958

Although the LSTM had been granted a new 12-year lease as recently as 1917, the two major concessionaires in Limburg were amongst the first private companies to surrender their lease under the law of November 1919, and the SNCV accordingly found itself reluctantly running the Limburg system. Prospects were not bright; the province was poor and sparsely populated, while the prevailing goods traffic - mainly chalk, sand and lime with some sugar-beet in season - did not pay well. Nevertheless the Groep, with its Limburg head-quarters at Hasselt, faithfully restored to life all those lines which had been closed during the war. They were reopened as shown below:

Capital	Sections	Reopening date
51	Kanne - Maastricht	31 Mar 1919
	Glons - Boirs	25 Oct 1920
	Boirs - Kanne	Feb 1921
81	Kortessem - Oreye	12 Jan 1920
82	Smeermaas - Tournebride	30 Sep 1919
86	Hasselt - Herk-de-Stad	12 Dec 1920
	Herk-de-Stad - Halen	Apr 1921
	Herk-de-Stad - St-Truiden	Apr 1921
88	Hasselt - Beringen	15 Aug 1919
96	Maaseik - Kessenich	Apr 1921
156	all closed sections	8 Aug 1920

To try and reduce costs for the heavy mineral traffic on Glons - Kanne, the SNCV acquired two magnificent Garratt

locomotives in 1929, though it must be noted that this "modernisation" was very much an exception. At this date the province did not boast a single electrified line, and of its 68 steam locomotives some 53 were of the elderly Type 4; there were only five modern Type 18s in the whole Groep. Fortunately, or possibly because of this, Hasselt works proved to be one of the most imaginative and inventive on the system. At this period the SNCV was not officially permitted to construct its own equipment but, working very much on a shoestring, Hasselt somehow "rebuilt" a number of redundant four-wheel trailers into double-ended autorails in the 1920s. It has recently become clear that very little of the original vehicle structure was reused, probably only the main body ossature if truth be known - certainly trailer underframes marked with the same stock numbers were noted serving various other functions years later. They were not entirely successful, but sufficiently for SNCV Cureghem first to complete some 16 further chassis and then for SNCV to use the design as a basis for comparative trials and later series of cars. Fired with its own enthusiasm, the works later even converted an elderly bogie coach (although that was an oddity) and after World War 2 designed and built a very useful series of modern bogie railcars (AR 291-96).

In other respects, the Groep suffered heavily. Capital 156 was completed to Liége (Place Coronmeuse) on 1 February 1927 but there was little further development. Even its share in the 1930s electrifications was small and half-hearted. Rocourt - Tongeren was electrified from 14 August 1932 but otherwise it centred round Hasselt where a single new line, electric from the start and authorised on 24 October 1933, was built eastward to Genk and thence in a huge loop through the "new" mining communities of Waterschei and Winterslag back to Genk again; this was to serve the then-developing Campine coalfield and was opened on 20 September 1936. A non-electric link for the coal traffic, relic of much wider schemes, was also authorised in 1931 between Zutendaal, on Capital 156, and Lanaken, being opened in 1934 and linked to a goods branch of Capital 156 running north to the Andre Dumont mine near As. It was later connected into the Waterschei loop and was originally goods-only, save for a financially-disastrous three-month trial in 1936 of four autorail services each way daily; they finished abruptly on 17 June 1936. In the early thirties, too, the inner portions of the three existing steam lines from Hasselt were electrified as far as Trekschuren (Capital 81); Kuringen (Capital 86) and Zonhoven

(Capital 88), an urban and suburban service operating from 17 April 1932. With between 12 and 18 journeys daily on each line, it was also a financial encumbrance from the start, proving completely uneconomic owing to lack of patronage.

The same lack of patronage, partly because of the sparse population, caused Limburg to start closing complete lines earlier than anywhere else. The Dutch portion of Capital 130 from Molenbeersel to Weert was closed on 23 July 1934; the Houtain - Liers - Vottem branch of Capital 156 lost its passenger service on 31 January 1936, and on 31 December 1937 the two short lines from Maaseik, to Molenbeersel (Capital 130) and to Kessenich (Capital 96) followed. There was a slight improvement the following year, when the southern portion of Capital 156 from Liége to Houtain-St-Simeon, was extended to Place St-Lambert and electrified, but this was really a Liége suburban line. (The same applies to the post-war electrification on to Riemst on 16 August 1948).

Then came the war, which disrupted all links into the Netherlands to some extent. Preliminary flooding around the main Belgian defence line at Eben Emael cut the eastern section of Capital 51 from Bitsingen/Bassenge onwards, and on 10 May 1940 the German invasion followed. Several lines promptly closed because of frontier complications, including the Maastricht links via Tournebride and Smeermaas. Others closed because of war damage, including Glons - Boirs and Bitsingen - Kanne which were lifted in 1941 as was Lanaken - Smeermaas. The other main victim was Capital 69 (Tongeren - Fexhe), which closed officially to passengers on 10 May 1940, though a few market-day trains are said to have worked through until 15 May 1942. The northern section, from Villers l'Eveque to Tongeren, was then assimilated into Capital 68 (Tongeren - Lanaken) and was used intensively for sugar beet traffic destined for Tienen refinery. This was initially transhipped to the SNCB at a special yard near Tongeren goods station until the SNCB Tongeren - Tienen route closed in 1953. From then until 1959, the SNCV yard at Villers (Villers-Traversée) took over, passing traffic through to refineries at Oreye and Crisnée as well as Tienen and it is recorded that in season traffic was so heavy that trains were stacked up waiting at various stations and yards all the way beck to Tongeren; all varieties of motive power were pressed into service at such times, including steam locomotives, autorail-tracteurs, electric locomotive 10329 and cars 9880/1. The Villers-l'Eveque - Fexhe section remained in situ and officially in use for goods traffic until 3 August 1956, Villers - Tongeren following on 20 December 1959 at the end of the beet season.

The uneconomic electric routes from Hasselt to Trekschuren and Kuringen were also discontinued from 10 May 1940; one feels it was something of an excuse for closing these since the steam services remained. The other lines that closed were, as one might expect, those linked to the Dutch frontier. Glons - Kanne and its extension finally and officially closed to all traffic on 10 April 1943 save for a short portion between Boirs and Bitsingen; the Vroenhoven - Maastricht spur of Capital 68 and the Tournebride - Smeermaas line, which had been reinstated during the early part of 1943 for goods traffic, followed on 17 July 1943. On Capital 156, the Genk - Zutendaal link was lifted during the war, traffic apparently being transferred to the line north from Zutendaal to Waterschei in the heart of the coalfield. According to post-war timetables, an autorail passenger service was later run over this line, both to Bilzen on Capital 156, where it connected with services to Riemst and Bitsingen and through to Lanaken over the goods line; there were five or six services daily in each case but they probably did not last long. The section between Zutendaal (Wit Paard) and Riemst was closed completely from 16 August 1948, passenger services to Lanaken being discontinued in late 1949 or 1950, while the goods line was closed in 1952 and lifted the following year.

Meanwhile there were surprising extensions. On 22 February 1940 a deviation of Capital 88 was authorised to run north from Zonhoven to Houthalen, then west and south in a sweeping semicircle to regain existing tracks at Koersel. This was to serve new developments in the coalfield, and the first stage was opened to Houthalen on 20 October 1941; it was electrified on 1 February 1944 with surplus equipment from the Hasselt routes. Moreover, after the war, it was gradually extended with autorails, first to Zolder (1 December 1946), then to Heusden (Cite) on 15 September 1947 and finally to a link with Capital 138 at Koersel on 3 October 1948. The through services to Beringen appear to have been transferred to this route, the direct link between Zonhoven and Leopoldsburg being marked as lifted by May 1950, though a spur north from Beringen village to Beringen (Mijn) was incorporated in the "new" system.

About 1950, the surviving electric routes from Hasselt were as follows

No.	Colour	Route
*1	red	Hasselkt - Genk via Winterslag, Zwartberg and Waterschei
*1	red	Genk - Winterslag, Zwartberg, Waterschei - Genk
2	blue	Hasselt - Houthalen - Heusden
2	blue	Hasselt - Houthalen - Beringen Mijn

*These two above routes also worked in the reverse circular direction

For a short time after the war, a real effort was made to promote surviving services. In particular the Tongeren - Lanaken - Maaseik line was given increased frequency of service, modern bogie autorails of the 29X series (constructed

On the country section 1: Bogie autorails were used. This is one of the AR28X series near Maasiek   (JW Smith)

by Hasselt Works, naturally) and even an automatic signalling system. Until about 1950, this line also retained an important goods traffic to and from Lanaken where it was transferred to and from barges on the Meuse/Maas river. Alas it was not to last. From 1 September 1954 buses took over all but school workings and those ceased at Christmas 1954.

By that time, several other lines had closed to passengers also Capital 86 (Hasselt - Halen) and its extension to St-Truiden closed on 25 January 1948; the last spur of Capital 51 from Boirs went in March the same year. Leopoldsburg -Bree - Maaseik (Capital 24) followed the same August, with total closure of most of its route, and the Zutendaal - Riemst route, as noted, went in August. Hasselt - Oreye (Capital 81) and Tongeren - Kortessem (Capital 108) followed on 17 December 1949. Lastly, Vroenhoven to the Dutch frontier went officially on 4 January 1950, although it seems unlikely that much had run over it since the war; one source states that lifting commenced in August 1949, so the SNCV date may be a retrospective authorisation. Oddly, almost as a dying reflex, some minor electrification was still taking place on Capital 88. It was extended from Houthalen to Zolder on 27 June 1952 and on to Heusden on 19 August 1952, though the final link to Koersel remained diesel. It was but a final flicker, however, for the whole remaining Limburg system closed over the next few years, as shown below.

Capital	Section	Passenger	Goods
88/138	Heusden - Koersel - Beringen		
		25 Apr 1954	21 Oct 1954
82	Maaseik - Lanaken	Nov 1954	4 May 1955
68	Tongeren - Lanaken	24 Dec 1954	4 May 1955
88	Hasselt - Zonhoven - Heusden		
		21 May 1955	—
	Hasselt - Genk and the loop		
		31 Jan 1958	21 Oct 1954
24	Wychmaal - Bree(goods only)		29 Aug 1955

With the closure of these routes, SNCV rail transport in Limburg was effectively extinct, except for the electrified section of Capital 156 operated from Liége.

Chapter 11: SNCV in Namur and Luxembourg Provinces

11.1 Namur and Luxembourg: General Introduction

The two provinces of Namur/Namen and Luxembourg occupy most of the southeast of Belgium, with the eastern end of Hainaut and Charleroi to the west and with Liége and Limburg to the north east. They were always thought of by the SNCV after 1918 as one operating group (Groupe 40), probably mainly because of the limited number of lines and the lack of any particular focus in Luxembourg province. That is not to say that the lines which did exist were small; the distances in Luxembourg alone would have swallowed up any other single province. Yet the Luxembourg lines were thinly spread, especially in the high region of the Belgian Ardennes, and really need to be considered historically as separate entities.

From Namur, perched around the rocky confluence of the Sambre and Meuse rivers, the hills rise south and southeast in forested waves toward France and the Duchy of Luxembourg. Namur itself is one of the great cities of Belgium, strategically placed to act as a fortress against incursions from the east and, hence, having a violent history. Its immediate hinterland has been fought over again and again and, in the 19th century , consisted mainly of agricultural countryside dotted with small market towns like Andenne, Eghezée and Huy, and of semi-resorts like Wepion and Profondeville along the Meuse river. The south of the province, and all of Luxembourg, consisted basically of wooded hills with many scattered communities difficult of access over the poor roads of the period but with an increasing tourist trade.

Hence it is not surprising that, apart from a small group of lines round Andenne which looked more to Liége than to Namur, the SNCV's early forays in the area were almost entirely in the rural Ardennes. No less than five separated lines or clusters of lines were in existence by 1892, and it is a commentary on the poverty of the area that two of them were among the four consistent loss-makers of the period. The main suburban complex around Namur city came later, between 1892 and 1905 for the most part, with an urban electric network following in 1907-12 to bind it together. The first decade of the 20th century also saw steady development throughout the Ardennes, both of isolated lines and of lines physically linked to existing routes. One has to put it that way, because most of the lines were long. Hence lines might share a common terminus and even a common operator, but were usually worked as separate entities. It must have been a frustrating business trying to make something of lines where one needed 90 minutes to cover 20km, and that with a maximum load of only five or six vehicles.

The Ardennes lines also had their own distinct flavour. More than any other SNCV routes, they tended to use their own rights-of-way, wandering off to follow the ever-changing contours, winding round forested slopes and up craggy river valleys. Here was the home of that odd Belgian feature, the "horizontal station" - complete sets of sidings laid out in grassy clearings, crammed in season with wagons loading timber but with not a building in sight. They served crag-dominated old fortress towns like Dinant and Bouillon, upland resorts like La Roche, tourist sites like the Grottes de Han. All round the periphery they poked rambling branches into neighbouring countries, meeting up in hill-town squares with the French CFD des Ardennes or the Duchy of Luxembourg's CF Cantonaux. There is no real coherent "whole" to the history of the Ardennes lines, and they will, therefore, be treated as individuals under the SNCV's original operating groups' definition. The major concessionaires in the early days were the mainline CF du Nord (CN) and its subsidiary, the *Societé Mosane (MOSANE)*; the *SA pour l' Exploitation de Tramways dans le Luxembourg Belge (TLB)*; *SA des CF Regionaux en Belgique (CFRB)*; and the *CF Provinciaux (CFP)*, the last of which was a big operator elsewhere. The complete story of concessions in the two provinces is very complicated, owing partly to the loss-making nature of some lines, and the writer has not been able to sort it out completely. Certainly there were lines where the SNCV itself had to assume direct control for short periods "faute de mieux", and several lines were so long in building that the SNCV never got around to allocating a concession before World War I began. Long-serving or not, however, the concessionaires all surrendered their leases after World War I except for the *CF pour l'Exploitation du CFV de Rochefort - Grottes de Han - Wellin et Extensions (RGW)*, which had the profitable tourist line to Grottes de Han, and which hung on to most of its system right up to 1955. Even after the SNCV died, it managed to talk the powers that be into letting it have a new lease for the summer-only Grottes de Han branch, and still runs it at the time of writing with the only ex-SNCV diesel autorails in regular service.

In general, the two provinces suffered badly in World War I, many lines being closed and lifted; even though all were restored, little further development took place. The provinces became the SNCV Groupe de Namur - Luxembourg but its lines had too little traffic. There was virtually no electrification before World War II, except around Namur city itself where some of the suburban services were modernised. Post war, apart from completion of these, the only new electrification the provinces saw was initiated by Hainaut just as Namur was closing everything down. A partly new line from Charleroi via Fleurus and Onoz gave an inter-provincial connection from 1953 but, in the face of Namur's lack of interest, it retreated to the provincial boundary only six years later.

Instead, the Ardennes lines in particular were dieselised or partly so; small lines such as Bourcy - Houffalize often were issued with only one autorail so that steam had to be substituted whenever the car was under repair. The SNCV did make an attempt after 1945 to develop tourist travel, bringing in bogie autorails for the Melreux and Marche systems and running "radio trains" with commentary relayed to the trailers. Inevitably, the deficits were too great and, one after another, the long lines closed to passengers. Freight, mainly timber, kept some open until the end of the 1950s, but now only two detached lengths survive. The Tramway Touristique de l'Aisne operates part of the old Melreux - Manhay stretch, and the Han - Grottes de Han line continues as the last non-electric narrow gauge route in passenger service. Around Namur, even the suburban electrifications closed in the early 1950s, and the country lines went at the same time. It is fair to say that the tramways did their job, linking remote areas to civilisation, but that they were never justified in purely financial terms. As soon as roads were improved, buses and lorries could do the job much better and more cheaply. Because of their nature, this chapter follows through each cluster of lines in detail, as shown below:

Operating groups	Capitaux
Namur province	
Groupe d'Andenne++	3, 15,52,63,91,117,131,194
Groupe de Namur++	50, 56,71,123,140
Groupe de Wellin+	49,112,144
Groupe de Petite Chapelle	97, 109
Detached lines;	
* Florennes - Dinant	116
* Olloy - Oignies	160
* Gedinne - Bohan - Alle-s-Semois	161
Luxembourg province	
Groupe d'Arlon	45,94,143,149
Groupe de Melreux	4, 134
Groupe de Poix	5, 34, 93, 135
Detached lines:	
* Houfallize - Bourcy	26
* Lierneux - Vielsalm	114
* Etalle -Villers-devant-Orval	141
* Marbehan - Sté-Cecile	163

Notes: ++ Groupes later largely combined under one concessionaire. + Groupe held by concessionaire until 1955.

11.2 Namur Province

11.2.1 Groupe d'Andenne, 1886 - 1929

Capital	Name	Auth Km.
3	Andenne - Eghezée	19.70
15	Jambes - Samson - Andenne - Huy	31.62
52	Andenne - Sorée - Ciney	30.51
63	Eghezée - St-Denis-Bovesse	16.63
91	Namur - Forville - Meefe	25.67
117	Hannut - Huccorgne - Vinalmont et Burdinne - Huy	55.43
131	Courrière - Ben-Ahin	24.50

Acquired after 1918

194	Taviers - Ambresin*	?

Authorised but not built

63	St-Denis Bovesse - Sausin (extension)	4.80
?	Ohey - Havelange	15.90
189?	Namêche - Assesse - Evrehailles	29.50
*	name originally spelt Embresin	

The first line in Namur province was a simple one. **Capital 3 (ANDENNE - EGHEZEE)** started from the Nord-Belge station at the small industrial town of Andenne, some 19 km east of Namur on the River Meuse, and ran northward via Seilles, Bierwart and Forville to Eghezée, a market town on the provincial border. It was authorised on 27 March 1886, and opened throughout on 18 October 1886 with an operational length of 19.90km. Concessionaire for this and the other Groupe lines was the big *Cie des CF du Nord (CN)*, which ran the neighbouring main lines as the Nord-Belge, and Capital 3 was notable mainly as the start of quite a complex network. It had a largely agricultural route with much seasonal sugar-beet traffic, and its profitability improved steadily.

It was soon joined by the first section of **Capital 15 (JAMBES - SAMSON - ANDENNE - HUY)**, originally just a 13.80km line from Andenne west along the Meuse valley to Samson with a link to the coalmines at Gives. This section was authorised on 10 May 1887 and opened on 8 October 1887. A line east from Andenne to Huy was authorised on 22 March 1888, and ten years later, on 1 May 1897, the 8.52km from Andenne to Huy (Collegiale) was actually completed, meeting the existing network stretching out from Liége via Waremme. Indeed Liége was really the focus for the Andenne lines until a link was put in to Namur in 1914. On 20 January 1914, a 9.05km extension joined Samson westward to the Namur suburb of Jambes on the east bank of the Meuse; here it met a branch of the Namur electric system (qv) over which trains could reach Namur mainline station.

The line had a heavy coal and stone traffic to both ends and also to branches running north and south from Andenne, for on 31 August 1913 **Capital 52 (ANDENNE - SORÉE)** was authorised, being opened on 3 October 1893. It was initially 13.91km long, running due south from Andenne via Coutisse and the spread-out village of Ohey and was later extended a further 16.60km to Ciney on the Namur - Marloie railway. The extension was authorised in 1910 and was listed as "to be built" in 1911 but was not completed until after the 1914-18 war: the final 5.8km from Emptinne to Ciney did not open until 1927, thus completing a cross with Andenne as its centre. Ciney might well have had two SNCV routes since the standard-gauge line from Yvoir was originally allocated to the SNCV as **Capital 42 (YVOIR - CINEY)** on 16 June 1893 but later reallocated to the *CF de l'Etat Beige*.

The Andenne lines proper were complemented by several extensions and "attachments". First was **Capital 63 (EGHEZÉE - ST-DENIS-BOVESSE)**, authorised on 19 April 1894, which ran 16.552km south-west from Eghezée via the village of Meux to a junction on the Namur - Bruxelles railway. Opened on 20 September 1895 for goods and on 1 October 1895 for passengers, this was an unexciting rural line, save for repeated attempts to extend still further to Sausin on another SNCV route from Namur to Onoz. Proposals started in 1884, and on 24 February 1914 the extension was actually approved, but it was never built. Then came an offshoot of the Eghezée route. **Capital 91 (NAMUR - FORVILLE -**

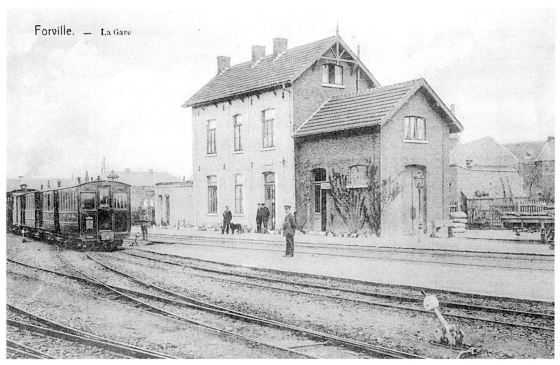

Forville station, in the Andenne Group. Note the bogie coach at rear of the train.
(Commercial card/collection E de Backer)

MEEFE) was initially authorised in 1899 as Namur - Forville (17.59km) and opened as such on 15 May 1902. It ran northeast from a connection with the Namur lines just north of Namur standard-gauge station, going across country via Champion and Franc-Waret to Forville on Capital 3. In 1912-13 it was extended 7.00km to Meeffe on Capital 117. The extension (authorised 9 June 1912) was, as often happened, complicated by road works, in this case at Hemptinne. It reached Meeffe in two further stages, to Hemptinne town on 8 December 1912 and on to the junction on 26 January 1913.

The third "attachment" to be opened was **Capital 131 (COURRIÈRE - BEN-AHIN)**, a 24.45km line which left the Andenne - Huy route at Ben-Ahin and ran first southwest and then roughly parallel through a junction with Capital 52 at Ohey and on to Courrière on the Namur - Ciney railway. It was ceded to the CN as usual and opened in four stages, probably as shown below:

* Courrière - Gesves: 6 May 1907
* Gesves - Ohey: 15 January 1908
* Ohey - Perwez: 1 October 1908
* Perwez - Ben-Ahin: 30 June 1909

These are SNCV dates; some local sources give Courrière - Ohey as 6 May 1907 and Ohey - Ben-Ahin as 2 June 1908. There were plans to take it further but they never got past the drawing-board stage, neither did subsequent thoughts of a connection southeast from Ohey toward Havelange or, for that matter, a planned line wandering south from Namêche, on the Andenne - Samson route, through Gesves on Capital 131, to Evrehailles near Yvoir. The first war stopped them.

Last in time and geographically belonging more to Liége province than to Namur, was the complex of lines described under **Capital 117 (HANNUT - HUCCORGNE - VINALMONT et BURDINNE - HUY)**. Presumably they were originally grouped under the Andenne label because the CN was picked as the concessionaire, but they took so long in

building that the matter became academic. The first short section, from Vinalmont standard-gauge station to Roua quarries, actually came into use in 1905 for goods traffic. A stretch from Hannut to Thisnes opened on 20 April 1908, and the major section from Acosse through Burdinne to Bierwart on Capital 3 and on to Heron followed on 1 October and 8 November 1908; the intermediate link between Acosse and Thisnes did not come into general use until 20 May 1909. The branch east from Burdinne opened as far as Huccorgne (Route de Burdinne) on 5 October 1909, while the Heron line had been extended to Couthuin from 20 May with the intention of reaching Huy or, rather, of joining Capital 20 at Statte just north of Huy. Reading between the lines, the SNCV was having local legal troubles, since it was three years before the Huy branch was completed by a section from Moha (Raperie) to Huy town on 9 June 1912, a further cross-link from Couthin to Seilles on Capital 3 being opened on 1 February 1913. The penultimate spur from Huccorgne (Route de Burdinne) to Huccorgne station (1.60km) and then on to Roua and Vinalmont was not completed until 1915, meeting the existing Huy - Waremme route. Total length was some 59.90km and it is not clear when or if operation was handed over to the concessionaires; just how they operated such a cat's cradle of richochetting branches is not clear either! In any case, virtually the whole Groupe d'Andenne was closed and lifted during the 1914-18 war in 1917-18. Only Andenne - Sorée for some reason escaped the purge.

The end of the 1914-18 war saw the Andenne group in something of a turmoil. Its own lines were largely destroyed; on the other hand, since 1 January 1913, it had been assimilated with the Namur group (qv) under the control of the *Societé Mosane pour l' Exploitation des CF Vicinaux (MOSANE)*, a wholly-owned subsidiary of the Cie du Nord, and this was determined to keep going - even though its leases were effectively extended only from year to year. The SNCV slowly restored the affected sections during 1919-22, as recorded below:

Capital	Section	Date
3	Andenne - Bierwart	7 Sep 1919
	Bierwart - Forville	21 Sep 1919
	Forville - Eghezée	7 Mar 1920
15	Andenne - Huy	8 Jun 1921
	Andenne - Jambes	2 Jul 1921
63	Eghezée - St Germain	10 Oct 1920
	St Germain - St.Denis-Bovesse	10 Sep 1927?
117	Hannut - Embresin	22 Nov 1919
	Burdinne - Bierwart	1 May 1920
	Embresin - Burdinne	20 May 1920
	Bierwart - Moha	1 Oct 1920
	Moha - Statte	1 Apr 1921
	Couthin - Wanze	24 Aug 1921
	Burdinne - Huccorgne	17 Jan 1922
13	Courrière - Ben Ahin	1 Nov 1921

Of the other lines, **Capital 91 Namur - Forville - Meeffe** was restored "by December 1919". Although Capital 63 as noted was restored as far as St.Germain on 10 October 1920, it apparently reopened to St-Denis itself only on 10

In the country: Ohey, with a typical local train.   (Author's collection.)

September 1927. The same year saw completion of the final section of Capital 52, from Emptinne to Ciney. A minor oddity was that the SNCV did take over the derelict roadbed of a former 720-mm gauge line from Taviers to Embresin (see Chapter 12), being authorised to do so on 16 August 1923, initially under **Capital 194 (TAVIERS - EMBRESIN)**. It was treated as an extension of Capital 117. The SNCV rebuilt it to metre gauge opening it for goods during the 1925 sugar-beet season, and for public traffic on 1 January 1926. It had a three-rail mixed gauge section between Noville and Boneffe.

11.2.2: The Andenne lines under the SNCV, 1929-1960

The Andenne Group was so distinct that it seems sensible to continue its later history here. The MOSANE finally had to give up its contract at the 15-year breakpoint on 31 December 1928, the SNCV insisting on taking over, though, with the exception of the "main line" from Namur through Andenne to Huy,

the system was scarcely profitable. The Hannut - Burdinne - Vinalmont stretch actually passed to the control of the SNCV Groupe de Liége, but for reasons that will become clear its history is continued here! Otherwise the main change was that, from some time in 1937, the Huy - Andenne - Jambes services ran through to Namur SNCB station as Namur route 10.

World War II caused considerable problems for the lines of the former Andenne group. Operationally still largely distinct from the Namur area lines, it had its main base and workshops at Andenne town and was running a complicated network of services over the wandering routes of Capitaux 3, 15, 91 and 117. Passenger traffic on Taviers - Ambresin (as it was by now) ceased after the invasion in 1940. The central section of Capital 117 from Meeffe to Burdinne and on to Roua near Vinalmont was closed and lifted late in 1942, effectively disrupting services. At the same time the Eghezée - St-Denis route was cut back 4km to the village of Meux, and Couthuin - Seilles (Tramaka) was also closed, on 1 December 1942. In addition, the two extremities of Capital 131, from Ben-Ahin to Perwez and from Courrière to Gesves, followed on 10 March 1943, leaving just two short stubs to be operated from the centre point at Ohey.

None of the lifted lines was reinstated after the war, but the remaining lines were more-or-less dieselised and lasted a few more years. The services had, of course, to be worked on a different pattern because of the gaps and, to assist in this, the Hannut - Meeffe section, presumably including Taviers - Ambresin, was handed back to Namur's control at the beginning of 1946. Henceforward, Forville in effect became the hub of the system, one service running Namur - Forville - Meeffe - Hannut while the others were:

Ambresin station with a typical train after the SNCV metre-gauged the "tram Zaman" (see Ch12)   (author's collection/SNCV)

* Forville - Eghezée - Meux
* Forville - Bierwart - Statte
* Forville - Bierwart - Seilles - Andenne

It would appear that Burdinne was served by sorties off the "main line" from Bierwart, though these lasted only until 14 March 1948; the passenger service to Meux closed on the same date while the detached stub from Roua to Vinalmont had already gone on 1 February 1948. The writer has not been able to find out exactly what happened to the Taviers - Ambresin passenger service; it does not appear in early post-war timetables and may not have been reinstated, though the line remained open for goods.

The decision of Namur province in the early 1950s to run down its rail services was soon reflected in sweeping closures. First to lose its passenger service was Andenne - Sorée - Ciney on 18 May 1952, and it was quickly followed on 17 May 1953 by the long line from Namur through Jambes, Sclayn and Andenne to Huy. This latter actually had an hourly service but could not survive the amputation of its Namur link; a parallel bus route was instituted at the end of the year. The remainder went on 1 July 1955 (Huy - Forville) and on 2 October 1955 (Andenne - Forville; Namur - Forville - Meeffe - Hannut) although various portions remained in use for goods traffic. For the record, the official goods closure dates are shown in the accompanying table.

Section	Closure date
Roua - Vinalmont	3 Dec 1951
Jambes - Sclayn	31 Dec 1953
Coutisse - Ohey	1 Jun 1955
Ohey - Perwez	29 Sep 1955
Moha - Wanze	1 Oct 1955
Taviers - Franquenée	6 Jan 1957
Ohey - Gesves	1 Mar 1958
Meux - Eghezée	17 Mar 1958
Francquenee - Ambresin	13 Oct 1958
Bierwart - Burdinne	1 Jun 1959
Andenne - Seilles - Forville	1 Jun 1959
Sclayn - Andenne	1 Oct 1959
Eghezée - Forville	1 Dec 1959
Andenne - Andennelle	1 Dec 1959
Bierwart - Statte	1 Jun 1960
Franc-Waret - Hannut	1 Jun 1960

NOTE: Obviously these are only "official" dates, since by then there was really only seasonal agricultural traffic.

11.2.3 Namur: Groupe de Namur (Namur area lines), 1891-1929

Capital	Name	Auth Km.
50*	Namur - Malonne - St-Gérard et	
	Embrt vers Wepion	35.40
56*	Namur - Spy - Onoz	14.49
71	Onoz - Fleurus	11.80
123	Lesves - Warnant	15.60
140*	Lignes Electriques de Namur	23.86

NOTE: * amalgamated into single Capital 50 (Onoz - Namur - St-Gérard - Profondeville et Extensions).

The second major system in Namur province was that around the provincial capital itself. Namur is another of those Belgian cities perched on crags round a river's banks, in this case the confluence of the Sambre and Meuse; its massive if antiquated Citadelle crowned a rocky bluff on the west side of the Meuse and, even by the late 19th century, its grounds were a well-known place of recreation.

The lines radiating from Namur are, to some extent, confusing in that one Capital was extended bit by bit until it included not only its own two lines but also a third, with a further branch at its end, and also the tangle of urban routes which joined them all. There was also one line into Namur, **Capital 91 (NAMUR - FORVILLE - MEEFE)**, which belonged to the Andenne group and has already been described under that heading. Finally an urban system developed in Namur itself which will be taken separately.

The first line in the Namur area was **Capital 50 (originally NAMUR (PORT - MALONNE - ST-GÉRARD)**. As such it was authorised in two sections: Namur - Malonne on 13 August 1891 and Malonne - St-Gérard on 19 May 1893. The first part was Namur (Port) to Malonne (Port), an 11.32km line running round the edge of Namur town from the quays to the mainline station and thence southwest to a terminus by the canal at Malonne (Port) where its depot was situated. It was opened on 25 January 1892 and was extended first to Malonne (Malpas) (2.05km) on 13 May 1893 and then on to Malonne (Insepre) (1.32km) on 15 June 1893. The 16.80km on to St-Gérard took another two years: to Bois de Villers (3.42km) on 9 September 1893, on to Lesveon 6 January 1895, and finally to St-Gérard itself and a standard-gauge connection on 19 May 1895.

By this time a second branch had been authorised, from Namur station south along the Meuse to the semi-resort of Wepion (authorised 19 February 1894 and opened 19 May 1895; 6.80km). The whole complex, by this time sporting a title long enough to embarrass any letter writer, was ceded for operation to the *SA pour l'Exploitation de CF Regionaux en Belgique (CFRB)*, as was the next concession, **Capital 56 (NAMUR - SPY - ONOZ)**. This was a 15.20km line running due west along roads through the small towns of Temploux and Spy to a terminus and depot at Onoz near the provincial border with Hainaut. It was authorised on 3 May 1892 and opened throughout on 15 October 1893, except for the final kilometre into Namur. This was authorised in 1897 but delayed until 11 June 1899 by problems with a standard-gauge crossing at St-Servais. This line was soon assimilated into Capital 50 which then became **Capital 50 (ONOZ - NAMUR - ST-GÉRARD - WEPION)**. (for the serious-minded, it is worth noting that, here as elsewhere, where capitaux were combined, the SNCV often recorded only the major opening dates of each section; the intermediate dates are from local sources).

There was then a distinct pause until **Capital 71 (ONOZ - FLEURUS)** was opened in 1898 in two stages on 1 August (Onoz - Fleurus (Ecole Moyenne) and 8 October (on to Fleurus Gare). Like some other end-on branches, very little information has come to light. It was a simple country roadside branch west from Onoz through Velaine to the Hainaut village of Fleurus, talked of since 1894 and originally intended to be longer, apparently run as a separate entity though conceded to the CFRB. At Fleurus, in due course, it met route 7 of the Charleroi (TEPC) tramways.

Meanwhile, the main Capital 50 continued to swallow lines rather like a complacent python. It soon extended its Wepion branch 4km further south via Fooz to the river-bank town of Profondeville, (SNCV quotes 1 January 1905 but other sources suggest 7 July 1906 which may have been a final short extension) and over the next few years it also took in **Capital 140 (LIGNES ELECTRIQUES DE NAMUR)**, initiated in 1908. Furthermore it apparently changed its concessionaire,

The village square at Spy on the Namur-Onoz route: the train includes one of the long
De Rechter radial axle cars   (commercial card/author's collection)

Namur suburban: Profondeville with an electric car.   (Author's collection)

the whole Namur group being reallocated about 1908 to the *SA pour l' Exploitation des CFV de Namur et Extensions (NE)*.

Before going into the Namur urban system, however, mention must be made of one further country line. This was **Capital 123 (LESVES - WARNANT)**, granted from new to the NE. It was 17.20km long, leaving the St-Gérard route about halfway between that town and Malonne, and running southeast via Bioul (opened 5 December 1908) to a standard- gauge link at Warnant (1 April 1909). Again it was an ordinary semi-rural line and does not appear to have had through workings to Namur.

11.2.4. Namur urban network: inception & development (Map ref C-7)

Namur city over the next few years acquired a considerable urban and suburban electrified network, initially under **Capital 140 (LIGNES ELECTRIQUES DE NAMUR)**, soon assimilated into Capital 50. The concession arrangements are not entirely clear, but it appears the electric routes at least were, from 1 January 1913, allocated to the *MOSANE* which also

took over the neighbouring Andenne group from that date. During 1909-10, the Onoz line was electrified as far as Belgrade in the Namur western suburbs and the Wepion branch as far as the suburb of Les Plantes. New lines were built through the town and out to Faubourg St-Nicolas to the east, on the north bank of the Meuse. Another new spur went to St-Servais off the Onoz line and, from Salzinnes district on the St-Gérard route, a line climbed via Hayettes to reach the Citadelle from the west side. There appear to have been four main routes, totalling 23.28km of electric lines, and opened in five stages between 30 January 1909 and 1 June 1910. The routes were:

* La Plante - station - St-Servais
* Place d'Armes (in town centre) - station - Citadelle via Hayettes
* Faubourg St-Nicolas - Hayettes
* Jambes - station - Belgrade, with short workings to St-Servais.

The depot was at Salzinnes, and a spur across the Meuse to Jambes allowed connection with the Andenne group lines from

Namur station square, with steam and electric trams.
(Commercial card/E de Backer collection)

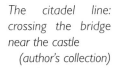

The citadel line: crossing the bridge near the castle
(author's collection)

Rebuilt 4-w car (Salzinnes Works) in the street, Namur.
(the late G Desbarax)

1914 through Capital 15. In 1911-12, electrification was extended from Salzinnes depot to Malonne, and a tourist route was promoted to descend the steep crag to the east of the Citadelle by the Route Merveilleuse. This hairpin descent is, indeed, wonderful but, since the city had not yet built it, the 3km line down to La Plante was naturally somewhat delayed - until after war broke out and stopped all work on it.

The system suffered to a minor degree in the 1914-18 war, the Lesve - Warnant branch being closed and lifted, the Jambes bridge being blown and a total of 8.153km being lifted from Capital 50 between Lesve and St-Gérard, but it was restored during 1919-20. Some references suggest that the outer section of the Onoz line was also lifted; if so, it was quickly restored. The MOSANE combined the two Groupes and carried on until the end of 1928 when the SNCV took control. The Citadelle line was reopened in 1921 and a relieving route through the town was opened later between Place d' Arrnes and Rue Brabant; this allowed one-way working in the town centre.

11.2.5 Namur area under the SNCV, 1929-1960

The SNCV Groupe de Namur-Luxembourg took over the existing Groupe de Namur on 1 January 1929 but continued to run its systems very much in the same self-contained way. The Profondeville line was electrified in 1935 and the line from Belgrade to Onoz was electrified during 1937, Although the Jambes bridge was again temporarily destroyed in 1944 and the Warnant branch was briefly cut back to Bioul, the system did not suffer unduly during World War II. the St-Gérard line was electrified in two stages during 1947 and at its peak the combined system was running ten routes, plus short workings, as shown below. The only non-electric route was Namur - Andenne - Huy which was autorail-worked with an hourly service; note that the Warnant and Fleurus branches were not included.

Table 11A: Namur route list at maximum (1949)

No	Route details (\ = barré)
1	Namur station - Wepion - Fool
2	La Plante - Namur station - St-Servais
3	Place d' Armes - Namur station - Citadelle via Hayettes
3\	Namur - Sallinnes - Hayettes
4	Malonne - Profondeville
5	Faubourg St-Nicolas - Namur station - Hayettes
5\	Rue Brabant - Namur station
6	Namur station - Lesve - St-Gérard
6\	Namur station - Malonne (Malpas)
7	Namur station - circuit de la Citadelle (counterclockwise, tourist season only)
8	Jambes - Namur station - Belgrade
8\	Jambes - Namur station - St-Servais
9	Place d' Armes - Namur station - Belgrade - Onoz
10	Namur - Andenne - Huy (autorail service)

The peak years did not last long. Following the satisfactory results obtained at Brugge with one-man buses, it was decided to transfer all Namur urban services to the road. Sections were replaced by bus routes from the dates shown in the following list.

Section	Date closed
Faubourg St-Nicolas - Namur station - Hayettes - Citadelle	10 Mar 1952
(St-Servais -) Namur station - Profondeville	18 May 1952
Belgrade - Namur station - Jambes	15 Dec 1952

The suburban lines, both electric and diesel, remained in use for a short time but several of their services were discontinued on 17 May 1953. On that date the complete St-Gérard route closed to passengers, as did the Warnant branch between Lesve and Bioul; because of poor roads, the outer stub to Warnant retained its service temporarily. Goods services on these lines also ceased from 15 October 1953 (St-Gérard) and 12 July 1954 (Lesve - Bioul), while the tourist route round the Citadelle closed after the 1953 summer season, on 13 September. The Onoz line and its extension to Fleurus, ironically, were temporarily saved by incorporation into a new through electric service from Charleroi from 17 May 1953 (route 67, see Chapter 9). The Namur group was not to be baulked by such a scheme for long, however. Its own goods traffic out to Temploux was discontinued from 29 August 1955, and for "traffic reasons" the Namur terminus of route 67 was cut back to Rue du Vicinal. The through link lasted until 1 January 1959, when its terminus was cut back to the provincial border at Velaine, officially because of complications with SNCV electrification at Onoz. The last part of the Fleurus branch died on 26 May 1963 when the stub of route 67 closed, but by then it was no concern of Namur. That group's last Namur provincial line went in 1960 when the outer portion of Capital 123 from Bioul to Warnant closed, on 31 August 1960 for passengers, and on 31 October 1960 for goods.

11.2.6 Namur: Groupe de Wellin, 1894 onwards

Capital	Name	Auth km
49	Grupont - Wellin	13.76
112	Rochefort - Wellin - Graide	40.10
144	Han-s-Lesse - Grottes de Han	3.80

The last major groupe in Namur province, the so-called Groupe de Wellin was, historically, unusual in that its concessionaire held on to it right up to the system's closure in 1955 and, even up to the finish of SNCV, a small part was still in private hands. The system, isolated from other SNCV lines but connected to the standard gauge at all three of its major termini, sprawled awkwardly across the boundary of Namur and Luxembourg provinces. For accounting purposes, Grupont - Wellin was classed as being in Luxembourg; the remainder was in Namur. Operationally, however, the system was typical of the Ardennes, serving a hilly region of country towns and villages but with a substantial tourist traffic to one of the "sights" of Belgium, the renowned Grottes de Han. These caves were formed where the River Lesse suddenly plunges underground to cut through spectacular limestone caverns and emerges almost 2 km further west; they have, since the mid-19th century, been a very popular attraction.

The first line of the groupe, however, was **Capital 49 (GRUPONT - WELLIN)**, purely a country tramway connecting the central town of Wellin eastward to the standard gauge. It was authorised on 21 June 1891 and opened throughout on 1 February 1894 with a length of 13.66km. Operation was ceded to the SA pour l'Exploitation des CF Regionaux en Belgique (CFRB) which ran it until the 15-year breakpoint. By that time the line had been joined by a longer route, **Capital 112 (ROCHEFORT - WELLIN - GRAIDE),** authorised in two portions, from Rochefort to Wellin on 5 July 1901 and on to Graide on 17 September 1904, and running southwest from the hill town of Rochefort via Han-s-Lesse village to Wellin (opened 14 February 1904; 14.40km). It was extended to the main railway line at Graide, a total of 25.70km of which 2km were in common with Capital 49 to a junction at Chanly and opened in two parts - from Chanly to Daverdisse on 25 June 1908 and on to Graide on 14 August 1908. The concessionaire for this new line was the newly formed SA pour *l'Exploitation du CFV Rochefort - Grottes de Han - Wellin et Extensions (RGW)*, which also took over the Grupont branch from 1 January 1909. At Rochefort it started on the far side of the town square from the Etat station; at Graide it occupied the station forecourt. From both junctions came a substantial tourist traffic.

Most of this traffic headed towards Han-s-Lesse where, since 1 June 1906, **Capital 144 (HAN-s-LESSE - GROTTES DE HAN)** left from the shadow of Han's huge church to run its 3.80km up to the Grottes - or, more specifically, to "Les Seconds Rochers de Faule". Authorised on 8 July 1905, this branch was more than it seemed. The nearest point to the cave entrance was about two-thirds of the way up, but the line continued beyond, giving its passengers both thrills and views as it climbed tortuously round massive outcrops (premiers and seconds rochers) to reach its final terminus, whence passengers walked sharply downhill to the Grottes. It was provided with special observation coaches, including a so-called "royal" coach, and worked during the tourist season only, traffic being one-way (from Han to the Grottes).

Nonetheless the system was very profitable and, even though the Germans lifted Rochefort - Wellin in July 1916, together with Wellin - Graide and the Grottes line in September of that year, they were restored quite quickly so that the Grottes line could function for the summer season of 1920. The official reopening dates were:

*	Rochefort - Wellin	23 May 1920
*	Han-s-Lesse - Grottes	13 Jun 1920
*	Chanly - Porcheresse	20 Jul 1921
*	Porcheresse - Graide	3 Oct 1921

After World War 1, the SNCV gradually adopted a policy of taking over lines as their concessions fell due but, for some reason, it omitted to do so in this case. As noted above, the RGW renegotiated its concession and kept the lines for another 35 years or so. The SNCV provided several of its rare bogie coaches (steam trailers) and some autorails, but otherwise appears to have given little support. That disadvantage of being a lone concessionaire was also felt by the coastal SELVOP, priority for new equipment tending to go to the SNCV's own operations.

Apart from the Grupont - Chanly section, closed on 9 November 1943 and not reopened until 15 May 1949, the remaining system escaped closure or serious damage during the 1939-45 war, but by the early 1950s was distinctly run down. The last section between Graide and Daverdisse was closed to passengers by 1950 and the final 8km were lifted by 1952, though goods appear still to have been carried from Chanly to Gembes. In 1955, when the concession became due, the SNCV took over the "main lines", closing them to passengers on 1 September 1955 and substituting buses. The section from Chanly to Grupont closed completely, but the remainder stayed open for freight until 29 July 1957, though cut back to Halma on 9 January 1956. The Grottes de Han line, however, was receded to the same

Groupe de Wellin: Graide station and train on the Rochefort - Wellin - Graide system (Author's collection)

the street at Han-s-Lesse with a railcar waiting to depart for the Grottes de Han
(author's collection)

The Grottes de Han. Steam tram at the view point of the Seconds Rochers de Faule
(commercial card collection E de Backer)

operator, the RGW, though it now started in splendid isolation in Han square and the title was shortened accordingly as sections closed. Further autorails plus some ex-Oostende open trailers and, it is reported, some from Melreux were drafted in, and the line continued to operate, mainly for coach parties.

By the mid-1960s, coach operators were getting restive over the duration of a Grottes visit and, to avoid complications, the SNCV agreed to shorten and streamline the journey. On 29 March 1968, it opened a 1.70km diversion, branching from the original track about half-way along, and curving through woods to end by the upper entrance to the caverns, with a new depot there. This, alas, lost the panoramic section along cliff edges, though the potential horror of a vast car park by the Grottes was also removed. The "new" line is 3.282km long but much quicker to traverse, and it cuts out a long walk for visitors. Since 1968 the stock has been further reinforced and now includes "Standard" bogie trailers from a batch built by Cureghem works. The auto-rails are now ageing, and at the time of writing a project for electrification is being considered.

11.2.7 Namur: Groupe de Petite-Chapelle, 1904-1919

Capital	Name	Auth km
97	*Chimay - Petite-Chapelle - Cul-des-Sarts*	27.16
109	*Couvin - Petite-Chapelle - Le Bruly*	16.00
173	*Couvin - Bourlers (not built)*	14.20

Down on the French border, where Namur and Hainaut meet, was a small separate group of lines, largely rural but with one industrial section. They formed the pre-1918 Groupe de Petite-Chapelle which was allocated operationally to Namur, though financially one line belonged to each province - and the bus replacements were totally run by Hainaut. They are grouped here with Namur for convenience.

The first part actually authorised, in 1898, was **Capital 109 (COUVIN - PETITE-CHAPELLE - LE BRULY)** intended to run from the market town of Couvin, terminus of a standard-gauge railway from Mariembourg. It went due south to Le Bruly village, thence to Petite-Chapelle and on to the French frontier at a location within Le Bruly commune

Gpe de Clavier: a typical timber train at Chimay, with an ART in charge.
(Paul de Backer)

sometimes known as Hiraumont. There it was expected to link up with the Le Tremblois - Rocroi branch of the French *CFD des Ardennes (CFDA)*, already opened and extending north to the frontier. There were immediate complications! Specifically to discourage its use by possible invaders, the CFDA had been built to the non-standard gauge of 800mm, and some time was wasted investigating whether a third rail could be laid through to Couvin. In the event, the CFDA decided to change all its lines to metre gauge and accept the consequences. Hence the Couvin - Petite-Chapelle route, opened on 1 December 1904, was finally linked with the CFDA a year later on 17 December 1905, with a total working length of 15.39km. Operation was ceded to the *SA Liégeoise du CFV de Chimay - Couvin et Extensions (CC)*, and traffic was certainly exchanged with the CFDA, although there is no evidence that passenger trains worked through.

Meanwhile, on 16 January 1899, **Capital 97 (CHIMAY - PETITE-CHAPELLE - CUL-DES-SARTS)** had been authorised in the adjacent province of Hainaut from Chimay, on the railway line from Dinant into France. It was to run south and then east to join Capital 109 at Petite-Chapelle with a subsequent spur en route to the small village of Cul-des-Sarts (authorised 2 February 1903). The first section, from Chimay to Forges (ca 4km), was mixed gauge to serve industrial premises and was opened on in two stages, from Chimay to Bourleurs on 25 April 1903 and on to Forges on 13 September 1903. Thence the line appears to have been extended almost station by station in four stages between 13 September 1903 and 1 December 1904. Detailed dates are quoted as: Forges - Regniowelz (provincial border) on 15 November 1903 and on to Cul-des-Sarts on 1 May 1904; to a place in Petite-Chapelle on 3 October 1904 and the final link to the newly opened Capital 109 from Couvin on 1 December 1904). As with many country lines, sections were opened as soon as completed, clearly in order to get some revenue. A short reversing spur was put in to Cul-des-Sarts village, and on 17 December 1905 the line was finally linked to its neighbour. As with Capital 109 it was operated by the CC.

The SNCV then proposed to complicate the situation further by promoting, in 1911, **Capital 173 (COUVIN - BOURLERS)**. This was an east-west link spanning the provincial border and running from Couvin to Bourlers about 3km south of Chimay, but the 1914-18 war intervened before it could be built. The Germans immediately severed the cross-frontier link and, in 1917-18, closed and lifted the entire network. The CC was one of the first to use the law of November 1919, surrendering its concession early in 1920, and the SNCV restored the lines piecemeal during 1921-22. The cross-border link was restored in April 1922 following reconstruction of the CFDA branch, but Capital 173 was never built. A bus concession was acquired instead.

The later history of the system appears to have been comparatively uneventful. It was not seriously incommoded by World War II except that cross-border links ceased for the duration in 1940 because Belgium was officially neutral. It eventually acquired first diesel autorails and then autorail-tracteurs to replace its ageing steam locomotives; several ARTs were specially fitted with mixed-gauge buffing and coupling gear. Passenger services effectively worked out of Cul-des-Sarts, that to Couvin lasting until 1 June 1953, and the Chimay link being replaced by buses from 23 May 1954. The Couvin - Petite Chapelle line closed entirely as far as Le Bruly on 29 August 1955 and the Le Bruly - Cul section closed on 1 November 1959. The remainder to Chimay lasted until 1 June 1960, probably because of the standard-gauge traffic at its northern end.

11.2.8 Namur: Detached lines in Namur province

Capital	Name	Auth km
116	*Dinant - Florennes*	25.08
160	*Olloy - Oignies*	10.00
161	*Gedinne - Bohan - Alle-s-Semois*	36.20

In the south and southeast of Namur province were three isolated lines, two of which seem to have worked out their lives without anyone taking very much interest; the third was one of those hesitant frontier-crossers that got all tangled up with the wars. All were in fairly rugged country and none were particularly profitable.

Detached lines: Dinant station on the Dinant - Florennes line south of Namur. *(Author's collection/SNCV)*

The first chronologically was **Capital 116 (DINANT - FLORENNES),** authorised on 6 March 1902 and opened from the old walled town of Dinant west to a standard-gauge junction at Florennes (Est) on 16 September 1905, a total of 23.74km. It was ceded for operation to the local *SA Messieurs Janssens et Surny (J&S)* on 23 March 1904, and never claimed to be anything other than a strictly local light railway. A short extension to Florennes town centre was opened in 1911 (1.076km), but the whole line was inevitably lifted in World War I, being restored to use by the SNCV afterwards in 1921. It was duly dieselised in the 1930s and survived the 1939-45 war, except that its western end was cut back to Rosée and the track lifted due to construction of a Luftwaffe base at Florennes. The remainder closed to all traffic on 20 July 1947.

If Capital 116 was quiet, Capital **160 (OLLOY - OIGNIES)** was almost moribund from the start. It lay in a bight of Namur province just east of the Groupe de Petite-Chapelle and was a simple north-south branch from Olloy village via its standard-gauge station south to the village of Oignies; with its 72 major curves, including two that were virtually right-angle bends, its crews may not have thought it so simple! Authorised on 21 September 1907, it was opened throughout on 25 March 1911 but the SNCV was unable to find a concessionaire; it therefore had to run the line itself.

During World War I, the line was closed and lifted in August 1915, not being reopened until 21 June 1921. It appears thereafter to have had an uneventful history, although with the slight complication that, while it was in Namur, it was run and maintained by the Hainaut group from Forges depot. It survived into the mid-1950s before its final closure to passengers on 22 May 1954. It was closed to goods on 8 February 1956 and lifted shortly after. It must have been a very basic railway since at the start it had but two locomotives and ten staff. An interesting sidelight is that its former bridge over the SNCB at Olloy now runs over the amateur-run standard-gauge CF des Trois Vallées.

The third detached line, **Capital 161 (GEDINNE - BOHAN - ALLE-S-SEMOIS)** was different. Situated in a hilly region of Namur province, trapped between France and the province of Luxembourg, it was authorised in 1910. Work started from its standard-gauge junction at Gedinne in 1910 with a contract date of mid-1912 for the first section, which was not actually opened until 16 June 1913. This ran south to the small town of Vresse, from which it was extended westward to Membre on 28 July 1913, a total of 24.94km. From Vresse a short branch continued south to Alle-s-Semois, almost within spitting distance of the Pussemange line, though land wrangles delayed its opening until 27 July 1914. West from

The square at Anthée, on the Florennes line, with a typical rural steam tram   (author's collection)

Gedinne - Alle s Semois: In the woods - timber traffic was always important down here   (commercial card/SNCV)

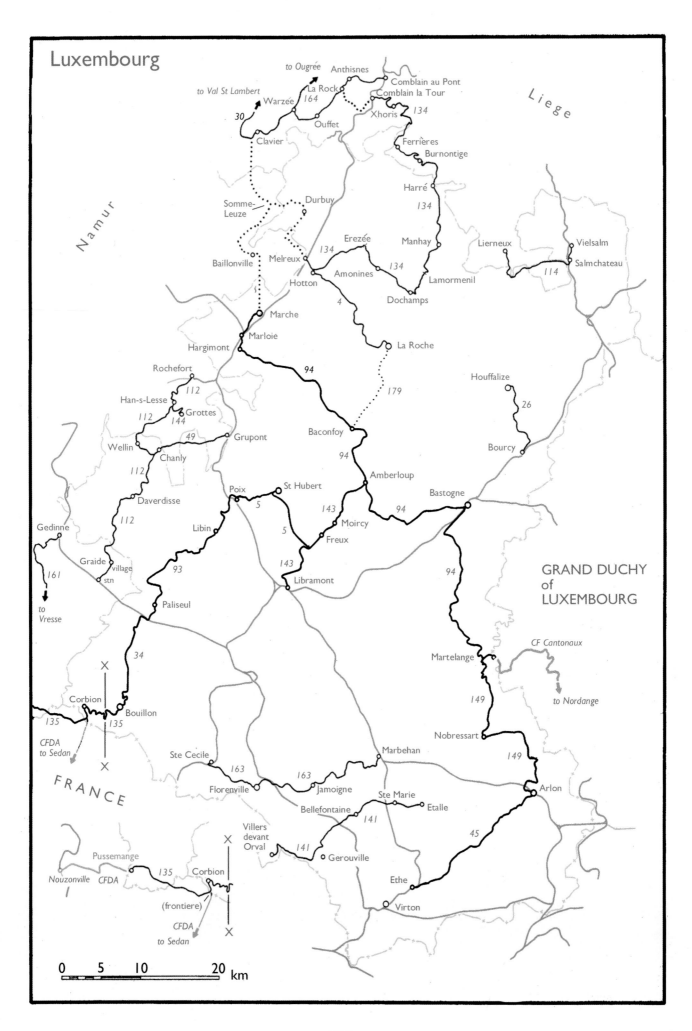

Luxembourg

to Ougrée
Anthisnes
to Val St Lambert
La Rock
164
Comblain au Pont
Comblain la Tour
Warzée
30
Ouffet
Xhoris
134
Clavier
Ferrières
Burnontige

L i e g e

Harré

134

Durbuy
Somme-
Leuze
Erezée
Manhay
Lierneux
Vielsalm

Baillonville
Melreux
134
Salmchateau
114

N a m u r

Hotton
Amonines
134
Lamormenil

Marche
4
Dochamps

Marloie
La Roche

Hargimont
94

Rochefort
Houffalize
112
26

Han-s-Lesse
112
Grottes
144
Baconfoy
Bourcy

49
Grupont
94

Wellin
Chanly
Amberloup
Bastogne

112
St Hubert

Daverdisse
Poix
143
94

112
5
Moircy

Gedinne
Libin
Freux

5

161
Graide
93
143
Libramont
GRAND DUCHY
of
LUXEMBOURG

village
stn

to
Vresse
Paliseul
CF Cantonaux

94

34
Martelange

to Nordange

Corbion
149

135
Bouillon
135
Nobressart

CFDA
to Sedan
Ste Cecile
Marbehan
149

163
Arlon

Florenville
163
Jamoigne
Ste Marie

F R A N C E
Bellefontaine
Etalle
141

Villers
devant
Orval
141
Gerouville
45

Pussemange
135
Corbion
Ethe

Nouzonville
CFDA
Virton

(frontiere)

CFDA
to Sedan

0   5   10   20 km

Membre, a planned extension to Bohan and across the border into France was well advanced when war broke out and all work stopped. Furthermore, the Germans requisitioned the stockpiled rails and fittings, compounding this by lifting the completed track back to Vresse and down to Alle-s-Semois. After the war the SNCV was in no hurry to do much about restoring it. The concessionaire was local, the *SA des CFV de la Semois (CFVS)*, which had stepped in when the big CF Regionaux en Belgique (CFRB) withdrew its bid, and which was still in existence in 1920 but gave up the following year.

The lines from Vresse were reopened in 1921, but the 2km Bohan extension needed a tricky double crossing of the Semois involving two bridges and a tunnel. Consequently it was not completed until 15 May 1935, and the link on to the French frontier near Sorendal came as late as 17 October 1938. Still, 3km into France, it did finally make contact with the *French CFD des Ardennes*, and passengers appear to have been exchanged until all cross-border connections were broken on outbreak of war in 1939. This one was never reopened, the terminus being cut back first to Bohan village and then to Vresse in May 1940 as the Semois bridges erupted in jagged chunks before the German advance. Gedinne - Vresse struggled on for passengers until 14 May 1950 and the odd ART-hauled goods working carried on for several more years. Bohan tunnel, at 230m the longest and least-used of all SNCV tunnels, was used for growing mushrooms. The Alle-s-Semois branch closed to goods on 21 October 1954 and the "main line" followed soon after, on 4 May 1955.

11.3 Province Luxembourg

11.3.1 Luxembourg: Groupe d'Arlon, to 1920

Capital	Name	Auth km
45	Arlon - Ethe	22.08
94	Marche - Bastogne - Martelange	81.41
149	Arlon - Martelange	30.31

Physically connected to this group was:

143	Libramont - Amberloup	20.30

Three lines forming, in effect, one long chain, this group provided one of the longest connected runs on the SNCV. The first component was **Capital 45 (ARLON - ETHE)** across

the southern tip of Luxembourg province. It was authorised on 10 November 1890 and opened throughout on 1 August 1892. It ran from Arlon railway station southwest to another standard-gauge connection at Ethe, where the depot was situated, and there was a tenuous project - never realised - to extend it further via Virton to the French frontier. As it was, with an operating length of 24.83km, operation was ceded to the *CF Regionaux en Belgique (CFRB)* but the line was never profitable. Indeed to start with it was one of the four big loss-makers, and even in the years just prior to the 1914-18 war it only just met its first dividend. Hence the CFRB gave up at the 15-year breakpoint and the line was run directly by the SNCV until 1910 when the *SA de CF Provinciaux (CFP)*, by then running the other components, was persuaded to take it on.

The next line in the chain was the northernmost one. **Capital 94 (MARCHE - BASTOGNE - MARTELANGE)** headed southwest from Marche, alongside the Liége - Rochefort railway, through Marloie to Hargimont where it swung away southeast. Thence it plunged into the high Ardennes, running via Baconfoy (whence a projected branch from La Roche would have joined, had it been built) and through Amberloup to the strategic hill town of Bastogne. Here it crossed a standard-gauge railway and turned due south along the frontier to end at Martelange. Martelange was an odd place, a border town which had two stations about a hundred metres apart and on different sides of the frontier but each with a link to a common industrial site; the "other" station was that of the Duchy of Luxembourg's *CF Cantonaux* line to Nordange (app 5). Goods traffic was exchanged, but there were apparently no through workings. The line was opened in five stages between 15 December 1900 and 25 July 1903, with a final belated sixth portion on 11 January 1906. It was 81.27km long and appears to have been ceded originally to *Monsieur Renken of Marloie*, who also ran the neighbouring Groupe de Poix. Presumably he found his Poix group of lines enough to handle since by 1911 the Arlon lines were in the hands of the *CF Provinciaux*.

Last, but by no means least, the chain was completed by **Capital 149 (ARLON - MARTELANGE)**. The line was authorised in 1905 and opened in two stages, from Arlon to Nobressart on 1 February 1910, and from Nobressart to

Marche, a typical rural junction station in the Ardennes
(SNCV/commercial card)

then the long rambling route through Erézee, Manhay and Xhoris to Comblain must be typical of the complicated ones. Even its prehistory is complex. It stemmed from a very early proposal in 1885 for a west-east route from Marenne through Hotton and Manhay to Lierneux and on to a standard-gauge junction at Vielsalm. The government said no, so the western terminus was changed to Melreux, on the mainline railway. Even so, the section from Manhay to Lierneux was for some reason not acceptable and, after some discussion, the SNCV gave in. The Lierneux - Vielsalm section (Capital 114) was built as a detached line, and the Manhay one was diverted northwest

Paliseul junction with standard gauge station in the background   (E de Backer collection commercial card)

over rugged country until it reached the same main line again at Comblain-la-Tour, about four times the distance by the direct standard-gauge route. The whole line, at over 60km, was authorised in sections as work progressed and, somewhat naturally, it was both built and worked piecemeal from both ends. The list below shows just how laborious construction was, the "ends" meeting at the little town of Manhay in the heart of nowhere. Presumably, like other long lines, the SNCV opened it in sections to try and get at least some revenue.

Section	Date opened
Southern part	
Melreux - Hotton - Soy	13 Jun 1908
Soy - Fisenne	20 Aug 1908
Fisenne - Erezée(Pont)	19 Oct 1908
Erezée - Amonines	15 Sep 1909
Amonines - Forge-a-l'Aplé	26 Feb 1910
Forge-a-l'Aplé - Dochamps (Village)	21 May 1910
Dochamps - Manhay (depot)	25 Feb 1911
Northern part	
Combiain-la-Tour - Xhoris (Village)	28 Aug 1909
Xhoris (Village - St-Roch)	9 Nov 1909
Xhoris (St-Roch) - Ferrierès (Ferot)	10 Mar 1910
Ferrierès (Ferot - Village)	26 Mar 1910
Ferrierès (Village) - Burnontige	1 Feb 1912
Burnontige - Harre - Manhay (depot)	15 Sep 1912

Total working length including the common section with Capital 4 at Melreux was 64.175km. The main depot was at Manhay with a sub-shed at Melreux, and operation, somewhat thankfully one imagines, was handed over to the local *CF Vicinaux des Ardennes*, promoted by one Monsieur Melotte of Liége. The poor chap didn't really have much of a chance. War broke out soon after, and in March 1918 the southern part up to Harre was lifted along with the La Roche route. The SNCV consequently got the line back on their hands as soon as the 1919 law permitted, and conscientiously restored the whole route between 1919 and 1921. Known dates are as shown:

section	date
Harre - Manhay	17 Oct 1919
Manhay - Dochamps	19 Jul 1920
Dochamps - Soy	20 May 1921
Soy - Hotton	Jul 1921

Traffic was never very heavy, timber and local stores being the freight staples, but the line had autorails from 1934-on. Even so, passenger totals were so poor that the service was actually suspended in 1939 and was saved only by the war. Hence it is

not surprising that the various proposed links from Comblain and Melreux to the Clavier group of lines never came to fruition, though work was certainly started on the latter.

The line appears to have worked throughout the 1939-45 war, although with bridge problems at the western end, and afterwards the SNCV tried to promote tourist traffic; it even drafted in bogie autorails of the AR 28x series with rebuilt De Rechter coaches as loudspeaker-fitted trailers so that passengers could have primitive "muzak" and a running commentary. It did not succeed, and the northern section from Manhay was closed to passengers on 22 March 1948; the rest followed on 11 April 1954. The Werbomont - Comblain stretch was closed completely in 1955, but the remainder saw occasional freight trains until some years later. Werbomont - Manhay finally closed from 13 October 1958, Manhay - Melreux following on 1 November 1959. Ardennes roads were not generally capable of coping with the timber traffic but, once they were improved, the narrow gauge was finished, at least commercially. Most of it was lifted in the early 1960s but the AMUTRA negotiated for a lease of the scenic part from Erezée bridge through Dochamps and up a wooded hill to Lamormenil and on over a lifted section to Cranhay; the lease was signed on 1 April 1965. The total length was rather ambitious for a small group but part opened in 1965 as the Tramway Touristique de l' Aisne (TTA) and is still functioning. It has had to refurbish the track completely and, since the country sections had no building to speak of, has had to build its own stations and a new depot at Blier

11.3.3 Luxembourg: Groupe de Poix

Capital	Name	Auth km
5	Poix - St-Hubert - Freux	17.06
34	Paliseul - Bouillon	15.24
93	Poix - Paliseul	28.17
135	Bouillon - Corbion - Pussemange - Frontière	22.35

The Poix group was in reality a chain of lines which eventually started from Freux, on the SNCV's Amberloup - Libramont branch and headed generally southwest to reach and cross the French frontier. Theoretically one could, presumably, have used it as a final link in a sprawling network which reached Marche to the north and Ethe to the far south, but in practice even traversing its whole length took patience.

Most exchanges took place at Corbion, here seen with French (CFD des Ardennes) and Belgian trains celebrating.   *(Author's collection)*

The "trunk" line, **Capital 5 (POIX - ST-HUBERT)** as it originally was, was one of the SNCV's earliest ventures, authorised on 27 March 1886. It was a very short spur from the double-barrelled standard-gauge station of Poix-St-Hubert, east and south to St-Hubert village where the depot was. It was 6.23km long, opened on 1 October 1886 and ceded to a small local operator, the *SA pour l'Exploitation de Tramways dans le Luxembourg Beige (TLB)*. It was not profitable, rarely meeting even the whole of its first dividend. At the 15-year breakpoint, the concession was reallocated to a *Monsieur Renkin of Marloie*.

The second line, again initially isolated, was **Capital 34 (PALISEUL - BOUILLON)**, authorised on 18 December 1888 and running southwest from a standard-gauge junction at Paliseul into the hilly frontier area round Bouillon, where the depot was situated. It opened throughout on 12 October 1890 with an operating length of 15.30km. It was ceded for operation to the fairly big CFRB but, like Capital 5, it was not very profitable in spite of taking goods that had previously gone by canal. It had steep gradients, often over 2.5 per cent (1 in 40), and with a 1km climb that became as steep as 3.6 per cent (1 in 28) in places. It also had one of the few SNCV tunnels, under a spur of rock at Bouillon. The CFRB surrendered the lease on 30 June 1899, and the line was either run temporarily by the CFP or directly by the SNCV until the above mentioned *M Renkin* took over on 28 March 1900.

Quite logically, the next step was to join the two. **Capital 93 (POIX -PALISEUL)** some 28.19km long, did just that. Authorised in 1900, it was opened in three stages during 1903. (SNCV gives 15 February, 10 May and 1 October, but without indication of sections). It was initially ceded to the ubiquitous M Renkin who, one suspects, soon formed a proper limited company as happened elsewhere. Certainly by 1910-11, all three lines had passed to the specially formed SA pour *l'Exploitation du CFV de St-Hubert - Bouillon et Extensions (HB)* which was the final concessionaire. This concern also accepted, from new, **Capital 135 (BOUILLON - CORBION -**

but the line went further. This is Pussemange station, end of the line from Paliseul with an interesting clerestoried bogie coach.   (Author's collection)

195

PUSSEMANGE - FRONTIÈRE) which was to form the final link in the chain.

Authorised at various dates between 1903 and 1912, **Capital 135 (BOUILLON - CORBION - PUSSEMANGE - FRONTIÈRE)** was a much more complex system. It was originally Bouillon - Corbion (Frontière), a 9.40km line opened in two sections, to Corbion village on 31 October 1907 and on to the French frontier station on 24 July 1910. It is often referred to as the CF Bouillon - Sedan and was intended from the start to give a through connection to Sedan via a branch of the French *CFD des Ardennes* which was opened on the same date. In practice all traffic exchanges seem to have taken place at Corbion (Frontière) which was on French soil, and there were no through workings. Almost as soon as it was open, however, the SNCV proposed a 12.90km extension northwest through a salient of French territory to regain Belgian soil near the small town of Pussemange. From there a further cross-border connection would link it to yet another CFDA branch from Nouzonville to Gespunsart which had been opened on the 800mm gauge in 1896 and regauged in anticipation as early as 1902. As might be expected, negotiations over the complicated leasing arrangements took a long time, and it was not until after World War I that the link was finally put in; it was opened throughout on 1 May 1925.

World War I otherwise appears to have affected the system only partly. The French connection at Corbion went, of course, but the only SNCV section actually closed and lifted was that from Paliseul northeast to Libin, about three-quarters of the way to Poix. This was restored on 30 May 1919 and was followed soon after by a much delayed extension of Capital 5, from St-Hubert to the SNCV's Amberloup - Libramont line at Freux; it had been authorised before the war but not built.

As in other areas, the SNCV took over control in 1922, and the system was to some extent modernised with autorails in the 1930s, though it lost its Corbion connection when the

CFDA closed its branch in 1933. All lines survived the second war but closed during the next decade and a half. Details are given below:

	Closure dates	
Line	Passenger	Goods
St-Hubert - Freux	7 Oct 1951	12 Jul 1954
Paliseul - Bouillon	16 Jul 1955	1 Jun 1960
Bouillon - Pussemange	16 Jul 1955	1 Jun 1960
Poix - Paliseul	6 Jan 1956	
Paliseul - Maissin		17 Mar 1958
Poix - Smuid		Nov 1959
Poix - St-Hubert	1 Nov 1959	1 Nov 1959

11.3.4 Luxembourg: Detached lines

Capital	Name	Auth km
26	*Houffalize - Bourcy*	11.49
114	*Lierneux - Vielsalm*	15.25
141	*Etalle - Villers-devant-Orval*	31.20
163	*Marbehan - Sté-Cecile*	30.40

One of the "black sheep" of the Vicinal family, **Capital 26 (HOUFFALIZE - BOURCY)** was authorised on 31 August 1887 and opened two years later on 14 July 1889. Its birth was beset by arguments, the logical shorter route east from Houffalize to Tevigny being rejected because a line south would keep further from villages and "we don't want the damn thing frightening our cattle". Consequently the line, running from Houffalize south over picturesque but difficult country to the mainline railway at Bourcy, took a long time to build, and was consistently in deficit in its early years. A short-term contract, renewed in 1894, was agreed with the CFRB, which operated other lines in the area. Fortunately Houffalize was famous for its fairs, and these, together with the delightful countryside, brought rapidly in-creasing tourist traffic that, along with timber, made it more profitable. Like other country lines it was closed and lifted by the Germans in 1917-18 and restored after the war by the SNCV. The SNCV took control and its later

Detached lines : An aerial view of Houffalize village, terminus of the little line to Bourcy. (commercial card)

history is uneventful. Even in the 1939-45 war it was closed only for a few weeks during the 1944 Ardennes offensive, although it was shot up once or twice. It was one of the few lines not to be dieselised until the 1950s, receiving its first car (ART 64) in September 1950 and not being "fully dieselised" (ie getting another autorail) until June 1954. Four years later, in May 1958, it closed to passengers, and the spasmodic goods trains followed on 28 July 1959 (the SNCV official date of the last train was 1 June 1959). It was lifted during the next year.

Capital 114 (LIERNEUX - VIELSALM) was almost an afterthought. As already related, the SNCV had a grand project for an east-west route from west of Melreux to the province's eastern border. Although there was no direct railway competition, the vital link from Manhay to Lierneux was refused and the SNCV had to settle for a line north to Comblain. Nevertheless in 1900 it applied for, and received, a 14.60km detached section between Lierneux, Salmchateau and Vielsalm which it opened on 23 October 1904, possibly in the hope that it would facilitate further requests. Operation was conceded to the CFRB and, in the event, nothing more was done. Apart from the usual hiccups in World War II, traffic being restricted to the Salmchâteau - Lierneux stretch for some time after the war, the line appears to have pursued a largely uneventful career right up to its closure, to passengers on 28 September 1958 and to goods on 1 June 1959.

Capital 141 (ETALLE - VILLERS-DEVANT-ORVAL) was also, to some extent, a second-best; situated in the extreme southwest of Luxembourg province, it was originally proposed as a longer line starting at Habay. This was refused and, as authorised in 1903, it ran west from Etalle to cross the standard gauge near Sté-Marie, and thence ran southwest to a standard-gauge connection at Bellefontaine. From there it reached Gerouville on the French frontier and followed that frontier to its quaintly named terminus. The line was opened in two stages on 1 February 1908 and 9 December 1908. Operation was initially ceded on 22 December 1906 to the *MM Janssens et Surny (J&S)* who ran isolated lines else-where, and they apparently formed the local *SA pour l'Exploitation du CFV Etalle - Villers-devant-Orval*. It proved so unprofitable that in 1911 the lease fell through and the *CF Provinciaux* took over. The whole line was closed and lifted during the first war and not restored, under SNCV control, until about 1922. After that it had an eventful if depressed life, except for the usual hiccups during the 1944 fighting. Services were withdrawn soon after the war, the line being out of use by 1950.

The last detached line in this province was **Capital 163 (MARBEHAN - STE-CECILE)**, a few kilometres to the north of Capital 141 and running roughly parallel to it. The line was authorised in 1910 and the SNCV officially classed it in the Groupe de Namur - which suggests the Nord Beige or the CFV de Namur (NE) were marked as the eventual concessionaire. In the event, only the eastern section, from Marbehan to Jamoigne (Ch de Moyen) (12.56km) was opened prior to World War I, on 1 June 1911. A link to Jamoigne station followed in 1915 but the remaining 18km or so through a standard-gauge connection at Florenville to Sté-Cecile were still under construction when the Germans lifted all there was. The Sté-Cecile end of Capital 163 was completed after the war in 1921 and the rest restored. It was very much a local line, its main distinction being that the SNCV tried out its very first rail-buses (AR 1-2) there; they apparently worked well enough to run the passenger services until the line finally closed, which it apparently did either just before or during World War II; it was dismantled during that war and never reinstated.

And an atmospheric scene at Salmchateau on the line from Vielsalm.   *(author's collection)*

Branchon près Wasseiges
Viaduc du chemin fer Zaman 128 m. longueur.

Another view of a train on the viaduct (author's collection)

passengers had to sit with their knees interlocked. Luggage was carried on a collapsible "grid" hung by chains at one end of the vehicle, and is said to have been piled as high as the roof at times; what that did for the car's stability is best not thought of. The crews wore "a sort of uniform - bare feet, blue pantaloons, rust-coloured jumper and a kepi," and both they and the horses were apparently "characters". The mode of operation at peak periods was for all six (or seven) cars to be lined up against the hedge at Adinkerke waiting for the arrival of a train; they then filled up and set off, following each other on sight. At other times, presumably, normal tramway practice was followed.

The line was taken over by the Allied armies during World War I but reopened soon after. A contemporary photo shows an ex-WD Simplex tractor towing a short train of cross-bench trailers, but apparently this wore out and, after a short period of horse power, in 1920 the proprietor bought two small 0-4-0T steam locomotives of unknown origin; one was 'Adele', and the other 'Laura'. These lasted until 1928 when they were replaced by a Fordson-engined tractor. The latter is said to have been based on the old locomotive frames and the only photograph shows a machine reminiscent of a garden hut with a trailing bogie (some sources say there were two tractors but this may be confusion with the Simplex.) The trailers had by that time been at least partly rebodied since they were semi-opens without clerestories and of a vaguely fairground appearance. As related elsewhere, an agreement was reached on 4 October 1931 for the line to be replaced by a metre gauge SNCV electric line and the old tramway closed in August 1932.

which preceded it. This started as a horse-bus, or horse van to be more precise, in 1894 and was operated by Mme Terlinck, a local hotel proprietor. From 14 July 1901 the bus was replaced by a 600mm gauge horse tramway. The tramway started in Adinkerke station forecourt, turned out to a crossroads, almost immediately crossed on the level the Adinkerke - Dunkerque railway, and then went straight down the Avenue de la Mer through De Panne town to the seafront, where it terminated; en-route there were passing loops at Adinkerke (Markt), Adinkerke (Veurnestraat) and De Panne (St.Pieterskerk). At the seaside terminus were the stables and a wooden beach-hut which did duty as a station - and, on occasion, a left-luggage office, though the more usual routine was for travellers to leave their address with the tram crew, their bags eventually being deposited in the sand outside their front door.

The line was apparently built by a firm called Chapel et Pluntz, but later came into the control of one Van Neufville, believed to have been a hotelkeeper. It was 3.7km long, took 21 minutes to traverse and originally possessed six or seven one-man horse tramcars. These were neat but narrow bogie vehicles with end platforms and short clerestories. Seating was longitudinal; even so, the gangway was so narrow that

12.4   Other minor tramways

a)   *SA de Coxyde Plage (Westvlaanderen)*

Organised by the SA de Coxyde Plage which ran the local bathing beach, this single-track, metre-gauge horse tramway was 3km long and was opened on 24 July 1904 from Koksijde

The original horse tram en route from Adinkerke to De Panne
(author's collection)

ADELE 2: Adele herself, puffing along the roadside .(author.'s collection)

ADELE 3: Street scene at De Panne with original clerestoried cars (author's collection)

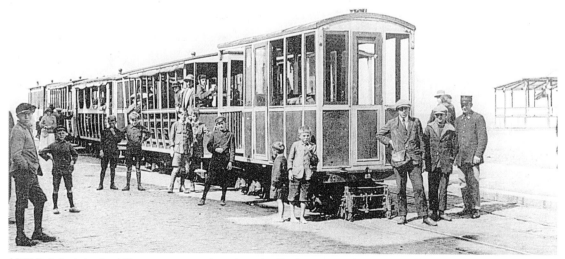

ADELE 4: And the final fling; reconstructed stock and a Fordson-engined tractor in 1932. (author's collection)

The Koksijde horse tram in its context at the beach terminus.
(commercial card/E de Backer collection)

St Idesbald Dunes with what appears to be a bogie tram.
(author's collectioncommercial card)

village where it met the SNCV, to the developing resort of Koksijde Bad. Operated by the Gemeente Koksijde (the local council), it appears to have been laid down the centre of an unpaved road, terminating at a dead-end on the beach approach. The only known car was a neat closed four-wheeler with four side windows and end platforms. The tramway was replaced by an SNCV branch line from 1 July 1909.

b)   SA du Tramway de St Idesbald (St-Idesbald - De Panne; Westvlaanderen)

This tramway, unusually, ran along the coast, from De Panne beach to the Hotel des Dunes at St-Idesbald. It was 600mm gauge and 1.7km long, being built by the development company, the SA de St-Idesbald, about 1910. Opened on 29 August 1910, it was effectively superseded by an SNCV line through to Koksijde from 1 July 1914 and actually closed on the outbreak of war, from 3 August of that year.

c)   SA du Tramway de Knocke-sur-Mer (Knokke; Westvlaanderen)

On 2 April 1904 the SA du Tramway de Knocke-s-Mer opened its line from Knokke village (Hotel de Bruges) to the beach at Bunnenplein, then known as Place Publique. It was 1.70km long, metre gauge, and was a more substantial affair than those mentioned above, having several one-horse cars.

The tram was, alas, too successful and the SNCV replaced it with an electric line from 29 June 1912.

d)   St-Mariaburg (Antwerpen)

Very little information is available about this short line apparently built in the early 1900s to serve a housing estate in St-Mariaburg, northeast of Antwerpen. It was 600mm gauge, roadside, steam hauled by small 0-4-0T locomotives with enclosed motion, and was privately owned (by the developers?). It ran from Ekeren station via St Mariaburg to the small hamlet of Kaart near Brasschat and is said to have been put out of business by the SNCV line in 1911. The track was lifted by the Germans in 1914-15.

e)   Peruwelz - Bonsecours horse tram.

This horse tram was opened on 30 May 1880 to serve pilgrims visiting the Basilique de Notre Dame at Bonsecours. It ran from Peruwelz main line station to Bonsecours (Grand'Rue) and had a length of 12.4km. The line was privately operated by *Mm F Delattre and E Pilverdier*. Public operation ceased in August 1914 but the line was used by the Germans to transport wounded soldiers during the 1914-18 war. It was not reopened after the war and the tracks were lifted in 1923-24.

Knokke beach with an elaborate tram (commercial card)

St Mariaburg in 60cm gauge days with an unidentified locomotive and genuine passengers .(commercial card.)

Back to Adele: A variant car en route crossing the Adinkerk road by the convent (author.s collection)

ADINKERKE. — *Couvent des Sœurs de St Vincent de Paul.*
Edit, Vve, Boeve et Enfants,

Appendix A: Summary of SNCV Concessions, by Capitaux.

Columns:

a. Capital No
b. Capital title
c. Province
d. Original authorised km
e. year authorised
f. year first section opened
g. original or major concenssionaire
h. Year reclaimed by SNCV
j. First section electrified
k. last section closed to passengers
l. last section closed to goods
m. major portion lifted

a	b	c	d	e	f	g	h	j	k	l	m
1	Antwerpen—Hoogstraten—Turnhout	Ant	53.25	1886	1885	AMDB	1921	1941*	1962	1960	1964
2	Oostende—Nieuwpoort—Veurne	Vla	36.95	1886	1885	SELVOP	1956	1927*	—	1952	
3	Andenne—Eghezee	Nam	9.70	1886	1886	MOSANE	1929	1955	1959	1967	1963
4	Melreux—La Roche	Lux	19.30	1886	1886	TLB	1921		1959	1959	1961
5	Poix—St-Hubert—Freux	Lux	17.06	1886	1886	StHB	1922		1953	1959	1955
6	Tielt—Aalter	Vla	18.06	1886	1886	CFP	1917			1953	
7	Oostende—Blankenberge—Heist	Vla	45.03	1886	1886	SELVOP	1956	1905	—	1952	
8	Gent—Zomergem—Ursel	Vla	21.13	1886	1887	ETG	1954	1930*	1959	1958	1960
9	Charleroi—Mont-sur-Marchienne	Hai	4.31	1886	1887	TEPC	1923	1901	1957	1962	
10	Charleroi—Lodelinsart (St-Antoine)	Hai	3.50	1887	1887	TEPC	1923	1901			
11	Charleroi—Montigny-le-Tilleul—Bomeree	Hai	11.36	1887	1887	TEPC	1923	1901	1968	1964	1959
12	Mechelen—Itegem—Westerlo—Turnhout	Ant	72.26	1887	1887	KSTM	1920	1932*	1957	1958	1970
1	Bruxelles—Schepdael—Ninove	Bra	15.88	1887	1887	VFB	1920	1910	1970	1960	1961
14	Wavre—Jodoigne	Bra	28.35	1887	1887	CFV	1920		1956	1960	1960
15	Jambes—Samson—Andenne—Huy	Nam	31.62	1887	1887	MOSANE	1929		1953	1959	
16	Bruxelles—Leerbeek—Enghien	Bra	30.90	1887	1888	VFB	1920	1909*	1972	1960	1972
17	Poulseur—Sprimont—Trooz (see 18)	Lie	21.99	1887	1887	PST	1920		1937	1965	1967
18	Bruxelles—Humbeek	Bra	21.50	1887	1889	VFB	1920	1909	1978	1960	1978
19	Gent—Zaffelare	Vla	16.50	1887	1888	TUV	1919	1930*	1957	1958	1958?
20	Huy—Waremme	Nam	25.85	1887	1889	AO	1929		1949	1957	1957
21	Twy du Nord d'Anvers (retrospective)	Ant	5.06	1887	1886	VA	1921	1908	1968	n/a	
22	Antwerpen—Brasschaat—Grens en Uitbr	Ant	38.81	1887	1887	VA	1921	1909	1968	n/a	1968
23	Antwerpen—Zandvliet—Lillo	Ant	38.61	1887	1887	VA	1921	1927	1961	n/a	1961
24	Leopoldsburg—Bree—Maseik	Lim	40.90	1888	1888	LSTM	1920		1948	1955	1952

a	b	c	d	e	f	g	h	j	k	l	m
25	St-Ghislain—Hautrage et Extns	Hai	32.20	1887	1891	CFVM	1919	1952*	1960	1968	1964
26	Houffalize—Bourcy	Lux	11.49	1887	1889	CFRB	1920?		1958	1959	1960
27	Banlieue de Mons (5 routes)	Hai	51.70	1887	1887	CFVM	1919	1930	1973	1960	1960
28	Deinze—Oudenaarde	Vla	19.00	1888	1888	TUV	1919		1943	1943	1943
29	Veurne—Ieper	Vla	36.89	1888	1889	ODI	1921		1952	1953	1954
30	Clavier—Val-St-Lambert	Lie	25.03	1888	1890	Cond	1919		1952	1958	1958
31	Antwerpen—Broechem—Oostmalle—Lier	Ant	37.99	1888	1889	AMDB	1921	1928*	1958	1959	1960
32	Bruxelles—Haecht	Bra	29.11	1888	1890	CFV	1920	1914	1960	1960	1961
33	Hooglede—Tielt	Vla	32.84	1888	1889	TH	1920		1952	1952	1953
34	Paliseul—Bouillon	Lux	15.24	1888	1890	StHB	1922		1955	1960	1961
35	Quievrain—Roisin et a la Frontiere	Hai	11.70	1889	1890	TUV	1919		1954	1955	1956
36	Dolhain—Goe–Membach (—Eupen)	Lie	8.91	1889	1891	CC	1919		1926	1963	1964
37	Brugge—Sluis—Heist	Vla	29.08	1889	1890	SELVOP	1956	1912	1957+	1952	1961
38	Gent—Wetteren—Hamme	Vla	37.50	1890	1891	TUV	1919	1931*	1958	1958	1961
39	Eeklo—Watervliet—Grens	Vla	15.80	1890	1891	CFP	1917		1950	1950	1951
40	Lodelinsart (Bonnaire)—Chatelet	Hai	8.10	1890	1891	TEPC	1923	1901	1967	n/a	1967
41	Kortrijk—Wervick—Menen	Vla	29.07	1890	1892	IC	1927	1932*	**1957**	**1957**	1957
42	Yvoir—Ciney	Nam	23.70	1890	Reallocated to CF de l'Etat Belge		1922	1898	1972	n/a	1972+
43	Lignes du Centre I (La Louviere)	Hai	43.52	1890	1891	CFVC	1922		1953	1953	1955
44	Louvain—Jodoigne	Bra	29.00	1890	1892	CFV	1920		1937	1937	1937
45	Arlon—Ethe	Lux	22.10	1890	1892	CFP	1920		1961	1958	1961
46	Bruxelles—Sterrebeek—Vossem	Bra	16.35	1891	1892	CFV	1920	1930	1970	1960	1970
47	Bruxelles—Petite Espinette—Waterloo	Bra	26.94	1891	1894*	BPE	1919	1894	1953	1959	1961
48	Waremme—Oreye	Lie	10.04	1891	1892	AO	1929		1955	1958	1958
49	Grupont—Wellin	Nam	13.76	1891	1894	RqW	1955		1953	1953	1955
50	Namur—Malonne—St-Gerard et Embrts	Nam	35.40	1891	1892	MOSANE	1929	1911	1948	1948	1948
51	Glons—Kanne	Lim	16.00	1891	1893	LSTM	1919		1952	1959	1953
52	Andenne—Soree—Ciney	Nam	30.51	1891	1893	MOSANE	1929		1956	1956	1957
53	St-Truiden—Oreye	Lie	16.44	1891	1892	AO	1929	1936	1959	1959	1961
	incorp Ans—Oreye (private)	Lie	18.32	1888	1890	AO	1929	1931			
54	Zichem—Montaigu	Bra	4.00	1892	1894	GCB to Grand Central Belge 1898			1949	1964	1967
55	Groenendael—Overyssche	Bra	6.40	1892	1894	CFP	1919		1959	1959	1961
56	Namur—Spy—Onoz	Nam	14.49	1892	1893	MOSANE	1929	1937	1949	1951	1952
57	Turnhout—Arendonk	Ant	5.39	1892	1894	AMDB	1921		1962	1960	1965
58	Louvain—Diest	Bra	30.08	1892	1893	CFV	1920	1952	1944	1944	1944
59	St-Niklaas—Kieldrecht—Doel	Vla	23.18	1892	1895	TUV	1919		1947	1958	1958
60	Clavier—Comblain-au-Pont	Lie	26.20	1893	1895	Cond	1919		1970	1960	1970
61	Grimbergen—Londerzeel	Bra	2.88	1893	1893	VFB	1919	1926	1936	1968	1968
62	Montigny-le-Tilleul—Thuillies	Hai	11.30	1893	1895	TEPC	1923		1948	1958	1958?
63	Eghezee—St-Denis-Bovesse	Nam	16.63	1894	1895	MOSANE	1929				
	extension: St-Denis—Sausin	Nam	4.80	1914		not built					
64	Turnhout—Mol—Westerlo—Zichem	Ant	56.77	1894	1895	AMDB	1921		1955	1958	1958
65	Brugge—Zwevezele	Vla	19.96	1894	1896	BS	1920	1913	1952	1952	1953
66	Lens—Enghien—Soignies	Hai	19.11	1894	1898	CFVM	1919		1954	1957	1960

a	b	c	d	e	f	g	h	j	k	l	m
67	Boussu a la frontiere vers Bavay	Hai	15.57	1895	1896	CFVM	1919	1931	1970	1958	1970
68	Tongeren—Lanaken—Vroenhoven—Grens	Lim	22.66	1895	1897	LSTM	1920		1954	1955	1955
69	Tongeren—Fexhe-le-Haut-Clocher	Lim	18.70	1895	1897	LSTM	1920		1940	1956	1957
70	Brasschaat—Brecht—Westerlo	Ant	52.00	1894	1896	AMDB	1921		1950	1951	1952
71	Onoz—Fleurus	Hai	11.80	1895?	1898	CFP	1920?	1953	1959	1953	1960
72	Haecht—Aerschot—Thielt—Tirlemont	Bra	48.01	1895	1897	CFV	1920		1953	1955	1960
73	Liege—Barchon—Fouron-le-Comte	Lie	30.74	1895	1898	LB	1920	1940*	1955	1958	1962
74	Braine l'Alleud—Wavre	Bra	21.61	1895	1898	CFV	1920	1931	1964	1964	1965
75	Ieper—Waasten—Nieuwkerke—Steenwerck	Vla	30.19	1895	1897	ODI	1920		1949	1951	1952
76	Louvain—Tervueren	Bra	17.22	1896	1897	CFV	1920		1934	1961	1961
77	Antwerpen—Boom—Mechelen—Duffel—Lier	Ant	40.48	1896	1900	KSTM	1920	1931	1966	1958	1968
78	Courcelles—Incourt—Gembloux	Bra	67.48	1896	1900	CFV	1920	1929*	1957	1959	1960
79	Gent—Merelbeke	Vla	7.43	1897	1898	ETG	1955	1900	1955		1958
80	Tervueren—Tirlemont	Bra	39.80	1897	1902	CFV	1920		1957	1961	1966
81	Hasselt—Oreye	Lim	29.80	1897	1900	LSTM	1919		1949		1952
82	Maaseik—Lanaken—Grens	Lim	26.40	1897	1898	BNTT	1919		1954	1955	1956
83	Waterloo—Mont-St-Jean	Bra	5.57	1897	1901	CFV	1920	1923	1964	1960	1965
84	Turnhout—Hoogstraten—Grens	Ant	42.31	1897	1899	AMDB	1921		1949	1949	1952
85	Aarsele—Kortrijk—Moeskroen—Menen	Vla	50.90	1897	1900	IC	1927	1932*	1963	1958	1964
86	Hasselt—Herk-de-Stad—Halen	Lim	18.10	1898	1900	LSTM	1920		1948		1949
87	Liege—Wihogne—Vottem—Tongeren	Lie	22.68	1898	1899	LB	1920	1901	1961	1957	1962
88	Hasselt—Leopoldsburg	Lim	30.47	1898	1899	LSTM	1920	1932*	1955	1954	1960
89	Binche—Bracquegnies et Extns	Hai	22.52	1898	1899	BB	1921	1911	1962	?	1966
90	Liege—Tilleur—Hollogne—Ans	Lie	16.96	1898	1903	TI	1920	1901	1960		1960
91	Namur—Forville—Meefe	Nam	25.67	1899	1902	MOSANE	1929		1955	1960	1961
92+	Charleroi—Nalinnes (—Marcinelle)	Hai	18.40			TEPC	1923	1907*	1968	?	1968
93	Poix—Paliseul	Lux	28.17	1900	1903	StHB	1922		1956	1959	1960
94	Marche—Bastogne—Martelange	Lux	81.41	1900?	1900	CFP	1920		1960	1960	1960
95	Banlieue de Tournai	Hai	135.80	1898	1901	TUV	1919	1933*	1954	1954	1958
96	Maaseik—Kessenich	Lim	7.80	1898	1900	LSTM	1920		1937	1937	1949
97	Chimay—Cul-des-Sarts—Petite Chapelle	Nam	27.16	1899	1903	CC	1919		1954	1960	1961
98	Aalter—Eekloo	Vla	12.64	1899	1900	CFP	1917		1949	1949	1950?
99	Ath—Flobecq	Hai	17.70			TUV	1919		1954		1960
100	Overmere—Lokeren—Zaffelare	Vla	20.70	1899	1901	TUV	1919		1942	1942	1943
101	Lens—Baudour—Bauffe	Hai	13.90	1899	1899	CFVM	1919		1954	1958	1960
102	Wetteren—Zottegem	Vla	20.50	1899	1903	CFP	1920		1955	1954	1958
103	Geraardsbergen—Oudenaarde	Vla	25.52	1899	1905	TUV	1919		1943	1943	1943
104	Casteau—Ch ND de Louvignies (Horrues)	Hai	17.26	1900	1901	CFVM	1919		1950	1958	1961
105	Itegem—Zandhoven	Ant	18.33	1900	1902	KSTM	1920		1951	1951	1952?
106+	Nivelles—Virginal etEmbr	Bra	39.08	1900	1903	SNCV	1903		1959	1958	1960
107	Diksmuide—Poperinge—Ieper	Vla	41.80	1901	1906	ODI	1920		1953	1953	1954
108	Tongeren—Kortessem	Lim	12.56	1901	1904	LSTM	1920		1949	1949	?
109	Couvin—Petite-Chapelle—Le Bruly	Nam	16.00	1898	1904	CC	1919		1954	1955	1956
110+	Hamme—Moerzeke—Baasrode Veer	Vla	36.31	1901	1904	TUV	1919	1931*	1959	1958	1961

a	b	c	d	e	f	g	h	j	k	l	m
111	Hal—Ninove	Bra	27.00	1901	1906	VFB	1919	1953*	1966	1960	1966
112	Rochefort—Wellin—Graide	Nam	40.10	1900	1904	RGW	1955		1955	1957	1958
113	Brugge—Knesselare—Ursel	Vla	20.47	1901	1904	NWV	1913		1953	1957	1957
114	Lierneux—Vielsalm	Lux	15.25	1900	1904	CFRB	1919		1958	1959	1962
115	Poperinge—Veurne—De Panne	Vla	46.18	1901	1901	ODI	1920	1929*	1954	1954	1956
116	Florennes—Dinant	Nam	25.08	1904	1905	J&S	1919?		1947	1947	1947?
117	Hannut—Vinalmont & Burdinne—Huy	Nam	55.43	1903	1908		??		1955	1960	1965
118	Sprimont—Trooz	Lie	13.69	see Capital 17							
119	Brugge—Middelburg—Aardenburg	Vla	21.90	1902	1904	NWV	1913	1913	1943	1943	1943
120	Assche—Aalst—Oordegem	Vla	25.70	1902	1904	CFP	1918	1936*	1970	1957	1970?
121	Ieper—Geluwe	Vla	17.71	1902	1905	IC	1927		1949	1949	1952
122	Hannut—Jemeppe-s-Meuse et Embr	Lie	72.70	1904	1905	AO	1928	1948?	1959	1959	1961
123	Lesve—Warnant	Nam	15.60 ?	1901		MOSANE	1929		1960	1960	1963
124											
125	Casteau—Bracquegnies	Hai	12.00	1903	1906	CFVM	1919		1955	1957	1957?
126	Gent—Lochristi	Vla	9.90	1903	1903	TUV	1919	1930	1957	1958	1961
127	Lignes du Borinage	Hai	65.55	1903	1905	SNCV	1903	1905*	1970	1966	1970
128	Gent—Merelbeke—Geraardsbergen	Vla	36.80	1903	1907	CFP	1920		1955	1955	1956
129	Jodoigne—Tirlemont—St-Truiden	Bra	44.28	1903	1907	TUV	1919		1954	1961	1967
130	Maaseik—Molenbeersel (—Weert)	Lim	11.90	1903	1910	MW	1925		1937	1937	c1943
131	Courriere—Ben-Ahin	Nam	24.45	1907	1907	MOSANE	1929		1943	1958	1959
132	Oostende—Dijksmuide	Vla	26.13	1904	1907	ODI	1920		1951	1951	1952
133	Turnhout—Poppel	Ant	21.64	1904	190x	AMDB	1921		1948	1951	1951
134	Comblain-la-Tour—Manhay—Melreux	Lux	61.50	1904	1908	CFVA	1919		1954	1959	1963
135	Bouillon—Corbion—Pussemange	Lux	21.30	1903	1907	StHB	1922		1955	1960	1964
136	Gent—Bassevelde	Vla	25.84	1904	1910	TUV	1919	1931*	1959	1958	1961
137	Brugge—Leke—Diksmuide	Vla	32.90	1904	1910	NWV	1919		1951	1951	1953
138	Diest—Koursel	Bra	19.85	1904	1908	TUV	1919		1954	1954	1955
139	Charleroi—Jumet—Lodelinsart	Hai		see Capital 10							
140	Lignes Electriques de Namur	Nam	23.28	1905?	1909	MOSANE	1929		1909	1952	1953
141	Etalle—Villers-devant-Orval	Lux	31.20	1905	1908	CFP	1920		—by 1950—		
142	Oostende—Westende (retrospective)	Vla	14.70	1897	1904	SELVOP	1956	1904			
143	Libramont—Amberloup	Lux	20.30	1910	1910	Ard	1920		1951	1959	1959
144	Han-sur-Lesse—Grottes-de-Han	Nam	5.40	1905	1906	RWG	1957				
145	La Louviere—Haine St.Pierre	Hai		1905							
146	St-Truiden—Hannut	Lie	25.50	1905	1911	AO	1929		1950	1958	1959
147	Lier—Werchter	Bra	24.50	1905	1908	VT	1923		1947	1943	1943
148	Mechelen—Aerschot	Bra	30.85	1906	1909	VT	1923	1949*	1957	1958	1959
149	Arlon—Martelange	Lux	30.31	1905	1910	CFP	1920		1952	1952	1953
150+	Roeselare—Diksmuide —Bixschoote	Vla	39.91	1906	1911	ODI	1920		1951	1951	1952
151	Kortrijk—Bellegem—Pecq	Vla	18.80	1905	1909	IC	1923		1953	1955	1958
152	Ardooie—Izegem	Vla	6.53	1906	1910	TH	1919		1952	1952	1952
153	Izegem—Wevelgem	Vla	13.95	1906	1911	IC	1927		1952	1952	1953
154	Aerschot—Westerlo	Ant	14.90	1906	1911	KSTM	1920		1953	1953	1955

207

a	b	c	d	e	f	g	h	j	k	l	m
155	**Carnieres—Thuin**	**Hai**	**13.00**	**1906**	**1911**	**CFVC**	**1921**	**1911**			
156	Genk—Liege—Vottem	Lim	62.77	1906	1910	LSTM	1920	1938*	1959	1955	1961
157	Chapelle-lez-Herlaimont—Anderlues	Hai	16.52	1908	1908	CFVC	1921	1908	1959	1958	1961
158	Gent—Nevele—Ruiselede	Vla	26.60	1907	1909	TUV	1919	1932*	1953	1954	1956
159	Binche—Beaumont—Bersillies-l'Abbaye	Hai	32.93	1907	1912	SNCV	new		1954	1956	1958
160	Olloy—Oignies	Nam	10.00	1910	1911	SNCV	new		1950	1955	1957
161	Gedinne—Bohan—Allers—Semois	Nam	36.20	1910	1913	CFVS	1921		1954	1958	1960
162	Mainvault—Pommereul—Quievrain	Hai	35.68	1908	1916	TUV	1919		1954		
163	Marbehan—Ste-Cecile	Lux	30.40	1910	1911	SNCV	new		during WorldWar II		
164	Warzee—Ougree	Lie	21.10	1914	1914	Coll	1919		1947	1947	?
165	Spa—Heusy (—Verviers)	Lie	16.80	1907	1909		1920	1909	1952	1952	?
166	Kortrijk—Berchem	Vla	24.30	1908	1912	IC	1927	1932*	1957	1958	1
167	Binche—Anderlues	Hai	10.30	1915	1915	CFVC	1920		1947	n/a	
168	St-Truiden—Herk-de-Stad	Lim	16.10	1909	1913	LSTM	1920	1915			
169	Soignies—Nivelles	Bra	29.16	not built							
170	Chatelet—Fosse	Hai	15.30	1904	1915	SNCV					
171	**Erpion—Froidchapelle—Fontaine**		**18.45**	**not built**							
172	Zottegem—Ninove	Vla	18.50	not built							
173	Couvin—Bourlers	Nam	14.20	not built							
174	Braine-le-Comte—Soignies/Rebecq-Rognon	Hai	23.00	not built							
175	Laeken—Wemmel	Bra	3.60	1910	1911	VFB	1919	1911	1978	1960	1978
176	Strombeek—Vilvoorde—Haecht	Bra	22.80	not built							
177	Lignes Electriques de Louvain	Bra	8.20	1910	1912	TL	1920	1912	1952	1952	
178	Lignes Electriques de Bruges	Vla	5.75	1910	1910	NWV	1919	1910	1951	1956	
179	La Roche—Baconfoy	Lux	22.30	1910?	not built						
180	Sivry—Beaumont—Silenrieux	Nam	31.70	191?	not built						
181	Hal—Braine-l'Alleud	Bra	19.90	1911	not built						
182	Deinze—Aalter	Vla	16.00	1911	not built						
183	Floesberg—Geraardsbergen	Vla	15.40	1906	1929	SNCV	new	1929	1956	1958	1960
184	Stadsdiensten van Mechelen	Ant	3.30	1911	1913	EN	1929	1913	1955	1956	
185	Moerbeke—Grens	Vla	5.70	1912	1919	ZVTM	1950		1940	1950	1950?
186	Dour—Pommeroeul—Quievrain	Hai	23.00	1912		not built under this concession					
187	Pecq—Lechin?	Vla		1912	not built						
188	Merelbeke—Zottegem	Vla		1913	not built						
189	Hanneche—Gesves—Eurhailles?	Lim		1913	not built?						
190	Leuven—Aerschot	Bra		1913	not built						
191	Bruxelles—Hal	Bra	19.70	1913	1914	VFB	1919	1914	1966	1960	1967?
192	Clavier—Melreux—Marche	Lie	n/k	1913	not built						
193	Koksijde—De Panne	Vla		1914	1914	SELVOP	1956	1929			
194	Taviers—Ambresin	Nam		1923	1925	SNCV	1925		1965		
195	Elektrische Lijnen van Eupen (ex AVG)	Lie		1924	1924	SNCV	1924		1958		
196	Trazegnies (station)—Courcelles (Motte)	Hai		1929	complex see ch 9						
197	Mons—Boussu	Hai	10.75	1929	taken over from Etat Belge. see Ch 9						
198	Gilly—Ransart	Hai	2.75	1918?	1918	TEPC	1923	1918			

a	b	c	d	e	f	g	h	j	k	l	m
199	Verviers—Dolhain—Eupen et embrts	Lie		1931	1933	SNCV	n/a	1933	1956	1956	1959
200	Hasselt—Genk	Lim		1933	1933	SNCV					
201	De Panne—Adinkerke	Vla		1933	1933	SNCV	1933	1933	1956	now rebuilt	
202	Courcelles - Marchienne-au-Pont	Hai		1934	complex see Ch 9						
203	Brussel—Londerzeel	Bra		1937	confirming Expo tracks. see ch 8						
204	a Mechelen trolleybus line										

Full titles of lengthy Capitaux
12	Mechelen—Itegem -Westerlo -Geel -Turnhout
92	Charleroi—Nalinnes avec Embr:vers Marcinelle
106	Nivelles—Braine-l'Alleud—Virginal et Embr
110	Hamme—Zwijndrecht—Moerzeke—Baasrode Veer
150	Roeselare —Woumen —Diksmuide —Bixschoote
202	Courcelles (Trieux) - Marchienne-au-Pont (station)
192	Clavier—Somme Leuze—Melreux & Somme Leuze—Marche

Appendix 2: Concessionary Companies of the SNCV with Abbreviations as used in the text

In the following list, companies are arranged in the order of their abbreviations since it is anticipated that readers will seek names from abbreviations rather than the contrary. Dates given are the years in which companies began and ended their association with the SNCV. Standard abbreviations for Societé Anonyme (SA) and its flemish equivalent Naamloze Maatschappij (NM) are used in the titles as appropriate

		Dates of Associn	
Abbr	**Company name, generally In full where space allows**	**Start**	**End**
AMDB	Antwerpsche Mij voor den Dienst van Buurtspoorwegen	1885	1921
AO	SA du Chemin de Fer d'Ans - Oreye	1888	1929
Ard	Societé Anonyme l'Ardennaise	1910	1921
BB	SA pour l'Exploitation du CF Vicinal Binche - Bracquegnies et Exts	1903	1921
BL	Societé en Nom Collectif Balat et Leclercq	1888	1889
BNTT	SA Belge-Neerlandaise de Transports et Travaux	1911	1919
BPE	SA pour l'Exploitation du CFV de Bruxelles à la Petite Espinette et Exts	1892	1919
BS	NM tot Uitbating van den Buurtspoorweg Brugge - Swevezeele	1896	1920
CC	SA Liegoise du Chemin de Fer Vicinal Chimay - Couvin et Exts	1905	1919
CEN	Cie Genéralé des Chemins de Fer Economiques du Nord	1890	1914
CFP	SA des Chemins de Fer Provinciaux	1900	1920
CFRB	SA pour l'Exploitation des Chemins de Fer Regionaux en Belgique	1889	1920
CFV	SA pour l'Exploitation des Chemins de Fer Vicinaux	1887	1920
CFVA	SA des Chemins de Fer Vicinaux des Ardennes	1912	1919
CFVC	SA des Chemins de Fer Vicinaux du Centre	1891	1922
CFVM	SA des Chemins de Fer Vicinaux Montois	1887	1919
CFVS	SA des Chemins de Fer Vicinaux de la Semois	1913	1921
CGE	Cie Genéralé de l'Electricité	1912	1914
CGVE	Cie Genéralé des Chemins de Fer de Voie Etroite	1886	1905
CMW	SA pour l'Exploitation du CFV Courtrai - Menin - Wervicq	1892	1899
CN	Cie des Chemins de Fer du Nord	1886	1913
Coll	M. Collard, Liége	1914	1919
Cond	SA pour l'Exploitation des Chemins de Fer Vicinaux du Condroz	1893	1919
EN	Cie de l'Electricité du Nord de la Belgique	1911	1929
ERB	SA pour l'Exploitation des Chemins de Fer Vicinaux en Belgique	1888	1893
ETG	Electrische Tramwegen van Gent	1899	1954
EW	SA en Nom Collectif du CF Vicinal d'Eecloo - Watervliet et Exts	1891	1901
GB	SA Intercommunale du Vicinal Gent - Bassevelde	1910	1911
GCB	Chemin de Fer Grand Central Belge	1886	1898
HB	SA pour l'Exploitation du CFV de St-Hubert - Bouillon et Extensions	1910	1922
Hein	Ir J. Heintz, Termonde	1891	1893
HW	SA d'Exploitation du Chemin de Fer Vicinal de Huy - Waremme et Extns	1887	1919?
IC	SA Intercommunale de Courtrai	1899	1927
J&S	SA Messieurs Janssens et Surny	1904	1919
KSTM	Kempische Stoomtram Maatschappij	1889	1920
LB	SA du Chemin de Fer Vicinal de Liége - Barchon et Exts	1898	1920
LR	SA La Ruche pour l'Exploitation de CF Vicinaux en Belgique	1894	1896
LS	SA des Railways Economiques de Liége - Seraing et Extensions	1885	1927
LSTM	Limburgsche Stoom Tramweg Maatschappij	1887	1920
MOSANE	SA Mosane pour l'Exploitation des Chemins de Fer Vicinaux	1913	1929
MW	NM tot Uitbating van den Buurtspoorweg Maaseik - Weert en Uitbreidingen	1910	1925
NE	SA pour l'Exploitation des CF Vicinaux de Namur et Extensions	1908	1913
NWV	NM tot Uitbating den Buurtspoorwegen van het Noorden van Westvlaanderen	1903	1920
OB	SA du Chemin de Fer Electrique d'Ostende - Blankenberghe et Exts	1905	1927
ODI	NM voor de Uitbating den Buurtspoorwegen van de Om trek Diksmuide - Yper	1910	1920

PST	SA du Vicinal Poulseur - Sprimont - Trooz	1908	1920
Renk	M. Renkin, Marloie	1900	1910
RGW	SA pour l'Exploitation du CFV Rochefort - Grottes de Han - Wellin	1908	1955
RV	SA pour l'Exploitation des Railways Vicinaux	1887	1908
SELVOP	SA pour l'Exploitation des Lignes Vicinaux d'Ostende et des Plages Beiges	1927	1956
SNKD	SA pour l'Exploitation du CFV St-Nicolas - Kieldrecht et Extns	1893	1908
TEOL	Tramways Electriques d'Ostende - Littoral (Cie North d'Ostende)		independent
TEPC	SA des Tramways Electriques du Pays de Charleroi et Extensions	1904	1923
TH	SA pour l'Exploitation du Chemin de Fer Vicinal de Thielt - Hooghlede	1889	1920
TI	Societé Anonyme des Tramways Interurbains	1901	1920
TL	Societé Anonyme des Tramways de Louvain	1912	1920
TLB	SA pour l'Exploitation de Tramways dans le Luxembourg Belge	1886	1919
TNA	SA des Tramways du Nord d'Anvers	1886	1893
TUV	SA des Tramways Urbains et Vicinaux	1889	1919
TV	Tramways Vervietois	1912	1920
VA	Societé Les Vicinaux Anversois	1908	1921
VDO	SA pour l'Exploitation du CFV Etalle - Villers-devant-Orval	1908	1911
VF	SA des Vicinaux en Flandres	1892	1911
VFB	SA pour l'Exploitation des Voies Ferrees en Belgique	1887	1919
VT	SA pour l'Exploitation des Chemins de Fer Vicinaux et Tramways	1908	1923
ZVTM	Zeeuwsch Vlaamsche Tramweg Maatschappij	1915	1950

Appendix 3: General statistics

3.1 Operating Ratios for the Critical Years

The ratio shown in this table is that of the operating cost expressed as a percentage of receipts; a ratio below 100 is favourable, and above 100 loss-making.

Year	Ratio	Year	Ratio	Year	Ratio
1921	100.77	1941	91.05	1966	101
1922	96.99	1942	88.57	1967	104
1923	97.88	1943	89.38	1968	105
1924	94.40	1944	96.75	1969	105
1925	90.68	1945	97.11	1970	117
1926	94.80	1946	98.36	1971	140
1927	93.87	1947	109.29	1972	157
1928	91.83	1948	108.30	1973	180
1929	92.36	1949	100.61	1974	190
1930	98.34	1950	96.18	1975	216
1931	102.23	1951	97.06	1976	231
1932	101.41	1952	97.51	1977	234
1933	99.44	1953	96.53	1978	
1934	99.37	1954	95.57	1979	238
1935	100.36	1955	95.70	1980	244
1936	97.45			1981	267
1937	98.35			1982	267
1938	100.84			1983	263
1939	100.52				
1940	94.18				

NOTE: It will be evident from the above data that the SNCV was in serious financial trouble after about 1970, being unable to meet deficits rising over 1000 million Francs by 1972. The consequence was the introduction of state subsidies. Less spectacular, but nevertheless significant, were earlier periods of difficulty caused by two world wars and the world depression of 1930-1.

Prior to dates shown, ratios fluctuated between about 60 and 75. Between 1955 and 1965, ratios were around the 100 level with fluctuations each side. Recent ratios were dominated by the motorbus data and really have little relevance after the mid 1970s; tramway data are thought to be slightly less favourable.

App 3.2 Evolution and Contraction of the Rail System

Years	Non Electric *km operated	Electric km operated
1885	60	
1890	838	
1895	1307	18
1900	1780	70
1905	2600	137
1910	3446	291
1915	3802	413
1902	3852	443
1925	3938	523
1930	3838	794
1935	3471	1290
1940	3333	1479
1945	3345	1466
1950	2708	1528
1955	1227	1278
1960	147	830
1965	19	557
1970		282
1975		216
1980		200
1983		186

NOTE: * indicates the figure excluding the remaining concessionary line (Han-s-Lesse - Grottes de Han). The length of this line was 3.7km to 1966 and 5.4km from 1967

Appendix 4: SNCV Infrastructure

SNCV track and infrastructure: general note

With such a span of time and so many different operating Groupes, any attempt to describe the infrastructure must be fraught with difficulty; whatever one says, there will be evidence to show that, somewhere, sometime, different principles applied. However the SNCV did lay down standards, at least in the early days, and they are of interest in showing the general quality of provision.

Standard cast iron halt sign. Typically the message would be in French on one side and Flemish on the other,

(JW Smith)

a) Permanent way

In general, the SNCV preferred to lay its lines alongside or on public roads wherever possible, although this was said to increase rather than decrease the cost in practice. The reasons for laying the lines thus were that much of the land was already publicly owned and that, by keeping to roads, the trams would serve local communities better. The

reason for the increase in cost was that, for roadside lines, the Societé, besides having to make a trackbed, was responsible for maintaining the road edge nearest its track; for lines in the road (chaussée/steenweg), it had to bear the cost of laying and maintaining the pavé (cobbles or road surface) immediately surrounding the rails - which were not to project above the surface.

"Standard" track initially consisted of flat-bottomed, or Vignoles, rails of 23kg/m weight resting on metal bearing-plates and fastened through them by dog-spikes to hardwood sleepers approximately 100mm deep by 200mm broad by 1.80m long. There were normally ten sleepers to a 9m length of rail, unequally spaced so that there was more support near the joint, and the rails were joined by angle-section fishplates. The track was bedded in 200mm of gravel or, more commonly, cinder ballast and then ballasted approximately to sleeper depth. Pointwork was on special sleepers, with a frog angle of 1:5, 1:6 or, where room allowed, 1:8; except in streets, points were normally worked by counterweighted levers and set for the through road. Street points were worked by a key operating a turner set between the rails.

All loops and sidings were supposed to have a horizontal marker board at each end to show limits of clearance for stock entering a loop or parked in it. The trackbed was to be separated from the road proper by a raised stone kerb, pierced at intervals to allow cross drainage, and properly maintained. Where track was to be laid in a paved road and stone setts were the normal surface, a special flat-bottomed rail weighing 31 kg/m was used rather than grooved tram rails. This was screwed or bolted to sleepers laid under the surface and had a spacer bar bolted or rivetted to one side to provide a channel for the wheel flanges and also to act in lieu of fish plates. It was, however, common practice to replace this bar with lengths of creosoted wood attached to the rails by heavy bolts and clips, the pavé itself then forming the outer edge of the flangeway. Another alternative, certainly used around Leuven, was the provision of special steel shoulder pieces.

Because of the necessarily sharp curves, down to 75m radius on free-standing track and sharper in towns, particular attention was paid to effective superelevation, with the centre line remaining at road height (ie the inner rail was dropped and the outer one raised). Where stations were required, the extra lines were normally to one side on their own ground but, in the case of passing loops and purely passenger termini, they often intruded on the pavé. However, it should be recollected that, even into the 1920s, many country roads were unpaved, or paved only at places where heavy wear was expected, such as factory entrances or town streets. Indeed the very names Chaussée or Steenweg were important as implying a fully-paved road.

After the 1914-8 war, with the development of motor traffic, increased weight of locomotives, and the onset of electrification with its higher speeds, standards of trackwork were raised. The same principles were employed, but roadside lines and lines on their own right-of-way were gradually reconditioned with 32kg/m Vignoles rails in 18m lengths. Rails laid in the roadway proper were increased to 49kg/m with deeper flangeways and, on very sharp curves of less than 50m radius, 51kg/m rail was used for extra stiffness. This was partly because, with the advent of tarmac surfaces, it was no longer so easy to relay street track. For the same reason, on electrified street lines, a change was gradually made to continuous welded rail while, on other lines, two out of every three (or in some cases three out of four) rails were long-welded to increase the effective rail lengths. At the same time, ballast was, at least in theory, upgraded to gravel or crushed stone, though this was certainly never done on some of the more rural routes. Since then, particularly with increases in asphalted roads, standards have been upgraded again and again until modern street track is prefabricated, on a continuous base and using very heavy rail.

An example of the later signalling on busy electric routes with double track changing to single. Lights were doubled at such points for added security. Above the signal are the lights controlling the level crossing in the distance. (SNCV)

b) Signalling and train operation

Since the SNCV deliberately chose to operate under tramway regulations, signalling in pre-electric days was kept to an absolute minimum. Trains were normally signalled away by the guard blowing a whistle (on SELVOP) or a specially designed horn (cornet) on most other lines. Standard stop signs were provided at stopping places. They were usually cast in iron and comprised a column topped by an ornamental plaque usually having the Flemish *Trein Stilstand* on one side and the French *Arrêt du Tram* on the other. With few exceptions, line signalling was confined to places where the Vicinal made flat crossings with standard-gauge railways or merged into mixed-gauge sections. Here, red-disk or square-board (carré) signals were provided,

equipped with red and green lamps for night use; in continental fashion, they showed "road clear" when the edge faced the driver - ie was almost invisible to him. They were normally supplemented by single-blade catch points - on the SNCV line, of course, since the standard gauge had priority. At some places where tracks merged to form mixed gauge, especially on the coastal lines, there were upper-quadrant latticed-arm semaphore signals showing "clear" when raised. There was also the usual complement of fixed warning signs, mostly in blue on a white background. They included, for example "A" (end of restriction); "F" (fluten in Flemish) or "S" (siffler in French), meaning whistle; "V" (slow down); and a rather special one on parts of the coast routes, showing "H" (you are three overhead masts away from a stop). It was possible to combine these where required. Speeds on non-electric lines in any case were limited to 30 km/h in the country and 10 km/h in towns.

On urban electric lines, ordinary tramway regulations applied, but on the long interurban routes automatic signalling with colour-light signals was later provided to speed up operation. A train approaching a single-line section actuated a contact on the overhead wire. If the section was occupied, the signal already showed red. If it was free, the signal at the loop end (normally extinguished) showed green, and at the same time signals for the entry from the facing direction to the far end of the section and behind the train showed red to bar access. Repeater signals at intervals along the section - which could be quite long - showed green to the oncoming train and red to the other direction so that, even if a car inadvertently entered an occupied section, it could not get far without another warning. A white light indicated the end-of-section and another contact on the overhead wire cleared all signal displays for the section just traversed. A supplementary relay determined priority in the event of trains simultaneously trying to enter each end of a section. The system was eventually applied to some 700km of line in 524 sections; the lines included, for example, the coast, with Knokke —Brugge, Bruxelles— Leuven, and the Kortrijk area where diesel autorails had to be fitted with dummy pantographs to enable them to operate the signals in town on their way in and out. A system similar to automatic signalling was used to initiate the operation of light signals at road crossings on electric lines where the Vicinal had right-of-way. Here, activation of an initial overhead contact set in operation flashing lights to stop road traffic and illuminated a double orange or yellow light facing along the railway to confirm to the driver that crossing lights were working. A second overhead contact on the other side of the road switched off all lamps as the train passed, confirming this to the driver by showing a single white light.

Apart from lines with such signalling, the country lines were run by timetable and train order. The train crew was normally responsible for such operations as setting down or picking up vehicles en route, and tickets were sold on the train, any other chores being delegated to local businesses which acted as agents. This saved the cost of employing commercial staff who might be occupied for only a few hours each day, and at the same time cemented relations with the local communities. The chef de train, in association with these agents, took care of the necessary paperwork. Where operational control had to be exercised - eg intermediate issue of train orders - a stationmaster would be employed purely for such purposes.

Vossem, a larger pattern of station with a typical SNCV water tower.
(SNCV/commercial card)

Pussemange, a border station showing a range of buildings including customs facilities; the standard station house and outbuildings are on the right of the picture.
(collection E de Backer)

Baconfoy, an intermediate station on a long rambling line, with added stock sheds and servicing facilities
(collection E de Backer)

Lasne, a typical small country station in Brabant. station building with accommodation above; small goods shed; toilet block with the characteristic continental pissoir screen.
(author's collection)

c) Buildings

On country routes, the SNCV had from the beginning adopted the above policy of using agents to handle commercial business at all but the most important stations. Even freight traffic was handled by this means and, consequently, many stations had no need of buildings or, at most, had a small shelter. All business was done via the local agent who often owned a nearby cafe or hotel which could double, profitably for him, as a waiting room. Where buildings were provided, however, they were often substantial two-storey structures, since they had to house the section or system operating headquarters or were associated with depots. All lines had one or more depots where the locomotives and stock were serviced. As a minimum, these would include a shed containing a wide

inspection pit, one or more carriage sheds, a lamp-room (most lines used acetylene or paraffin lamps) and a lockable coal store; coal brickettes, used everywhere but in towns, were "attractive" items for the local population and had to be locked away. There was invariably also a water tower or column, usually supplied by a hot-air pump.

Bigger depots, of which there was at least one on any substantial line, normally had multiple-road sheds (remises) and facilities to carry out at least running repairs, while each pre-1914 Groupe had one or more adequately-equipped workshops; these they needed since they were on a repairing lease, and so responsible for maintaining their stock - though the SNCV was by no means always pleased with the results! After the SNCV itself took over, each major Groupe had one or more really big workshops

Bouillon station, showing a typical cluttered yard with timber and agricultural items prominent. (author's collection)

216

A large depot in steam days. (late Ir Debot)

An example of the mobile power stations used when required to boost voltage. (WJKD)

217

The SNCV had a number of mixed gauge sections which it usually shunted with metre gauge equipment. This is a typical 4-rail yard at Mol with a metre gauge railcar equipped with dual-gauge buffing/coupling gear
(Paul de Backer

which were capable not only of undertaking major repairs but of building new equipment when required. The most ingenious of these were undoubtedly Hasselt (Limburg) and Destelbergen (Gent), while the most efficient was probably Cureghem (Bruxelles).

Building styles depended on the region, with tall, red-brick designs very common. One interesting feature of stations was the almost complete absence of the traditional light railway goods shed. With its widespread use of agents, the SNCV provided few facilities for storing heavy goods; these had to be loaded and unloaded directly by the customer. Some places had permanent ramps to assist in loading cattle or sugar-beet, and some movable wooden ramps were provided for occasional traffic. Otherwise the main provision was a parcels office where a station was manned anyway, and where its community was big enough for a "smalls" traffic.

d) Electricity supply
In the earliest days of electric working, the SNCV preferred to buy its electricity from outside firms and to convert it to operating voltage at strategically-placed substations. Policy on primary supply varied over the years, the Societé at times generating its own current, but the traction-supply voltage, initially 500 volts dc and later 600 volts dc, remained fairly constant. The number of substations naturally grew with the electrified system and, to save personnel, the SNCV in the 1930s became a pioneer in the use of automatic substations using mercury-arc rectifiers. The first was installed at Eizeringen in 1929 and, five years later, 50 out of the 71 existing substations were automatic. A number of mobile sub-stations was available for emergencies or when electric lines were being extended.

The overhead was of the normal tramway type, sometimes just a contact wire and sometimes with catenary suspension. Various types of current pick-up were employed, most common in the early years being trolley poles or bow collectors although pantographs later came into widespread use. In recent years replacements on both coastal and Hainaut systems involved modern heavier railway-type catenary suspension, with current collection by Faiveley-type single arm or new-pattern double arm pantographs.

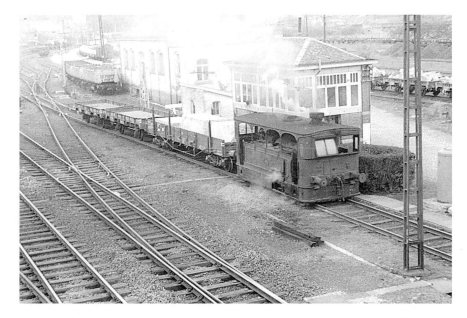

The standard gauge lines found transfers much easier. Here an SNCV locomotive shunts outgoing mineral traffic in the SNCB yard
(author

Appendix 5: Foreign railways and tramways in contact with the SNCV

a) Introduction.

Around the borders of Belgium, the SNCV inevitably made contact or near contact with a number of narrow gauge railways belonging to other countries. The Belgian side of the story is told in the appropriate places in the main text but some basic information on the contacts is given here. Of the provinces bordering on other countries:

* Antwerpen had links to the Netherlands
* Liége had links to Germany at Eupen
* Limburg had links into the Netherlands at Maastricht and Kessenich
* Luxembourg had links to France, at Corbion and Pussemange and to Luxembourg at Martelange
* Namur had links to France at Sorendal
* Vlaanderen networks had contacts with French lines in the southwest and with Dutch ones in the northeast.

b) Links with France:

Company:	*CF Economiques du Nord (CEN)*
situation:	Département du Nord
Belgian provinces:	Hainaut, Vlaanderen
links at:	(Bonsecours); Quiévrain; (Steenwerck)

The *CF Economiques du Nord (CEN)* was established in 1885 by the Baron Empain, whose companies had considerable

Junction with the CFD des Ardennes at Corbion. French train in foreground with a Corpet Louvet 2-6- 0T; SNCV tram on the left.   (Author's collection)

interests in SNCV concessions and, hence it was not entirely surprising that there were physical links. The CEN was formed to regularise a series of urban and rural tramway concessions around the town of Valenciennes, near the Belgian border. Two of the outlying routes, from Valenciennes to Bonsecours and via Blanc Misseron to Quiévrain reached or crossed the Belgian border.

The Valenciennes - Blanc Misseron - Quiévrain route (13.35km) was the first, reaching Quiévrain in March 1890 and

connecting with the SNCV's **Capital 35 (QUIÉVRAIN - ROISIN)**, then a detached line, in the forecourt of Quiévrain main line station. From November 1890 to 1911 the CEN also ran the Roisin branch as an SNCV concessionaire. The CEN line was electrified between 1911 (to Blanc Misseron) and on to Quiévrain in 1924. There was a physical connection but the service link was broken on the outbreak of war in 1939, French trains terminating at the frontier although tracks remained in place. The branch closed in 1960.

The Valenciennes - Bonsecours branch (18.33km) was opened to the frontier on 14 August 1892 as a steam-worked tramway, terminating in a balloon loop; there was no physical link. It was electrified in 1924 and closed in July 1966.

The SNCV's **Capital 75 (IEPER - STEEWERCK)** which crossed the French frontier was intended to link to an extension of the CEN's steam-worked Armentières - Halluin branch but it appears this never materialised. The section on French soil, from Nieukerke, was closed in 1932.

Company:	*CFD des Ardennes (CFDA):*
Situation	Departement des Ardennes
Belgian provinces:	Hainaut, Namur and Luxembourg
links at:	Bohan; Corbion; Petite Chapelle; Pussemange

The *Cie des Chemins de Fer Départementaux des Ardennes* was established in 1893 and between 1895 and 1909 built a system of some 342km in three stages. Its lines were largely separated from each other and initially were built to the unusual gauge of 800mm. This was at the request of the military with the intention of denying their speedy use to any invader but proved so much of a trial to the operator that early ones were soon regauged to metre and the final sections built to metre gauge from the start. Ironically, the German army, in 1914-18, simply replaced most of the useful lines with 60cm gauge field railways in any case and were just grateful for the ready-made trackbeds. The main lines and systems connecting into Belgium were:

* Le Tremblois - Petite Chapelle
* Monthermé - Sorendal - Bohan
* Nouzonville - Pussemange
* Sedan - Corbion.

The line from Le Tremblois was opened to Rocroi on 18 November 1895 and was originally 800mm gauge. On 19 September 1903 it was reopened on the metre gauge and, over the next two years, extended to Petite-Chapelle, in Namur province, where it met SNCV **Capitaux 97 (CHIMAY - CUL-des-SARTS - PETITE CHAPELLE and 109 (COUVIN - PETITE CHAPELLE - Le BRULY)**

The Monthermé line was metre gauge from the start and was opened eastward to Hautes-Rivières on 19 October 1901 and on to Sorendal on 1 May 1914, a total length of 19.400km. The final 5km link through to Belgium at Bohan in Namur province was not opened until 17 October 1938 and lasted less than a year, being closed on the outbreak of war. It connected to the SNCV **Capital 161 (GEDINNE - ALLE-s-SEMOIS)**

A line from Nouzonville to Gespunsart was opened, on the 800cm gauge, on 1 August 1896 but was converted to metre on 23 May 1903 and extended to the Belgian frontier at Pussemange (10.933km) on 1 May 1925. There it met the SNCV line from Bouillon **(CAPITAL 135 BOUILLON - CORBION - PUSSEMANGE)** which had the unusual feature of passing through a bight of French territory between Sugny and Corbion.

Lastly, the line from Sedan to Corbion (20.700km) was metre gauge from the start. It was opened throughout on 24 July 1910 and traffic was exchanged with the SNCV line from Bouillon mentioned above. The CFDA route was one of the first to be closed, on 30 June 1933.

In general the CFDA was a typical French secondaire, operating in hilly country with curves down to 50m radius and gradients of up to 30mm/m. It was operated mainly by standard Corpet Louvet 0-6-0T and 2-6-0T with a mixture of four-wheeled and bogie stock and was never very profitable. The remaining Belgian connections were not re-established after the 1939-45 war and the CFDA lines concerned were all closed in 1950.

c) Links with Germany

These arose through adjustment of national frontiers after the 1914-18 war. They involved the *Aachener Kleinbahn Gesellschaft* - The SNCV actually took over certain routes of this concern when frontiers changed after 1918 and the story is told in Chapter 10.

d) Links with Luxembourg

company	SA des CF Cantonaux du Grand-Duché (later state owned)
situation:	Luxembourg
Belgian Province	Luxembourg
Link at:	Martelange/Martelingen

The CF Cantonaux opened their 1000mm gauge light railway from Nordange/Nordlingen to Martelange in 1890. Nordange was a standard gauge junction and the line ran generally north-west to reach the Belgian border at the hill town of Martelange/Martelingen. The situation at Martelange was odd and not entirely clear. The Belgium - Luxembourg border actually ran down the Rombach road in the middle of the town and the CFC ended at a substantial station (Martelingen Rombach) on the Luxembourgische side. The SNCV, which arrived from Bastogne in 1906, had its own, fairly substantial, station a few hundred metres away, on the Belgian side of the border but there appears not to have been a direct physical link even when a second SNCV route came up from Arlon in 1911. There never was a through passenger service but it appears that eventually an indirect link was made through an industrial site and goods traffic was exchanged at times. The CF Cantonaux branch was eventually subsumed into a state-owned system and was closed to all traffic in 1952.

The German link was with lines of the Aachener Strassenbahnen, some of which were taken over after 1918. This is Aachen 2912 in SNCV service after 1945. (late G Desbarax)

e) Links with the Netherlands
(geographically, from west to east)

company: *Stoomtram Maatschappij Breskens -*
                          Maldeghem (SBM)
situation: Zeeland
Belgian province: West-Vlaanderen
links at: Retranchement (Grens); Sluis (St Anna ter
                        Muiden)

This company, based at Breskens, was founded in 1886. It was of metre gauge and opened a route from Breskens via Eede (Grens) to Maldegem in Belgium on 9 May 1887. other routes were: Breskens - Cadzand - Sluis; Cadzand - Oostburg; Draaiburg - Sluis. It also owned the sections in Netherlands of the SNCV Westkapelle - Sluis line (Capital 37; 1.8km) and of Knokke - Retranchement (Capital 7; 400m) which were operated by the SNCV. The SBM abandoned passenger traffic in 1948 and closed completely at the end of the 1949 sugar beet season.

Company: *Zeeusche Vlaamsshe Tramweg Mij (ZVTM)*
situation: Zeeland (Zeeuwsch-Vlaanderen)
Belgian provinces: Oost and West Vlaanderen
Links at: Veldzicht/Watervliet; Zelzaete; Roodesluis

Like the SBM, this concern operated in that odd enclave of the Netherlands known as Zeeusch-Vlaanderen and trapped between the river Escaut/Schelde and the Belgian provinces of Vlaanderen. It was set up on 20 June 1911 as a result of the fusion of two competing groups of entrepreneurs, with the intention of building a network of metre gauge tramways. The following year, the new concern also took over an existing line from Schoondijke to the Belgian frontier at Veldzicht (the *IJzendijksche Stoomtramweg Mij* see ch 6) and eventually linked to the SBM at Breskens and Schoondijke. Administrative headquarters was at Terneuzen on the banks of the Escaut and operating HQ at Drieschouwen. Between 1915 and 1919 it opened 10 routes with a total length of 108.157km. Two of these contacted Belgian territory, a line south from Sas van

Gent opened on 19 November 1915 and reaching Zelzaete/Zelzate, several kilometres inside Belgium and the line to Roodesluis on the Belgian border, opened 28 July 1916 and extended 5km to Moerbeke over an isolated SNCV branch which was handed to the ZVTM to operate. The reason for both these incursions was the agricultural traffic, in particular sugar beet to and from the Zelzaete and Moerbeke refineries, and they were always basically goods branches. Indeed the Zelzaete line was both owned and operated by the ZVTM.

In 1926-27 the ZVTM opened three further routes including a link to the neighbouring Stoomtram Breskens - Maldegem (qv) but none of these impinged on the SNCV. It started transferring traffic to road in the 1930s, was temporarily reprieved by the war and then closed its remaining lines to passengers between 1946 and 1949. The last vestiges disappeared after the 1949-50 sugar beet season.

Company: *Stoomtramweg Mij Antwerpen - Bergen-op-*
                        Zoom - Tholen (ABT)
Situation: Noord-Brabant Province
Belgian province: Antwerpen
link at: Zandvliet Grens

This comparatively simple company was formed in 1882 to build a 1067mm gauge tramway from Bergen-op-Zoom northwest to Tholen but soon also got involved with the SNCV which had built a line north from Antwerp to Zandvliet (Grens) on the same gauge in 1897, entrusting it to the *"Tramways du Nord d'Anvers"* (Capital 23, see p.87) The ABT accordingly built a branch south from Bergen-op-Zoom to meet the SNCV line and effectively went into partnership with the Belgian concessionaire, adding "Antwerp" to its company title to become ABT. The SNCV unusually allowed its concessionaire to provide stock of Dutch pattern and encouraged through working between Antwerp and Bergen. The SNCV connection was converted from 1067mm to 1000mm gauge after the 1914-18 war, the SNCV ending through services from August 1921.

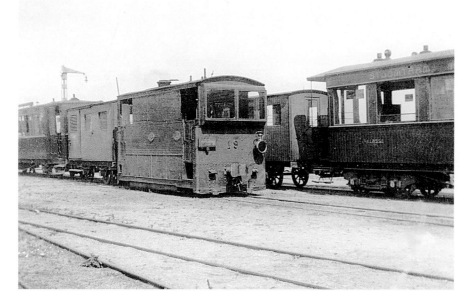

company:	De Zuid Nederlandsche Stoomtram Mij (ZNSM)
situation:	Noord-Brabant
Belgian province:	Antwerpen
links at:	Rijsbergen via Meersel (Dreef); Wuustwezel (Grens);

The ZNSM was a 1067mm gauge network with a complex early history involving English, Belgian and Dutch interests but by the 1890s had settled down to being a Dutch-Belgian company with lines centred on the town of Breda. One of these ran south-west to the Belgian frontier at Wuustwezel where, on 24 July 1890, it met and connected with SNCV Capital 22 from Antwerp. Through services were soon organised between Breda and Antwerp (Merksem), the ZNSM working in partnership with the SNCV concessionaire from 1891 - although the SNCV did have to provide special stock to suit the narrower loading gauge of the Dutch system. This arrangement survived reallocation of the Belgian concession to the AMDB in 1901 but was finally terminated from 3 September 1907. Thereafter passengers had to change trains but goods traffic was still worked through until the 1914-18 war. The other link was technically at Meersel (Dreef), on an extension of SNCV Capital 84 but in practice ran over Dutch territory to join the ZNSM Wuustwezel line at Rijsbergen. A specially formed SNCV subsidary, the Exploitatie van Buurtspoorwegen in Nederland, was set up to"own" this section of line which was independent of the ZNSM and operated by through trams of the AMDB and then the SNCV itself. It was opened on 1 September 1899 and lasted until 1937, except for the inevitable break during world war I.

company:	Vicinaux Hollandais/Hollandsche Buurtspoorwegen Mij (HB)
situation:	Noord Brabant
Belgian Province:	Antwerpen
Link at:	Poppel (Grens) - Esbeek (Grens)

This 1067mm gauge network was centred on the town of Tilburg, to the north north east of Turnhout to which it was also linked by a standard gauge railway. Officially termed the "Vicinaux Hollandais" it started as the Noord-Brabantsche Stoomtramweg Mij in 1880, became the HB/VH in late 1895 after various machinations and ran routes north from Tilburg and then east, to s'Hertogenbosch and south from Tilburg to the village of Esbeek. This latter was opened on 24 September 1907 and on 1 May 1909 was extended via Esbeek Grens to link with the newly built SNCV extension to Poppel (Grens) on the line from Turnhout to Poppel (Dorp). The Esbeek branch was closed to passengers on 15 September 1935, breaking the SNCV link, and the rest of the network followed in 1937-38.

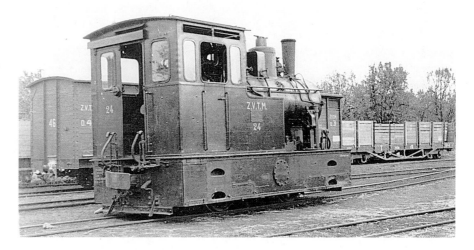

A rather indistinct view of a cross-border working arriving at Zoute from Retranchement. On the original one can just discern the plaques "Holland" and "Retranchement-Knokke"   *(collection Paul de Backer)*

company:	*Stoomtram "De Meijerij"*
Situation:	Noord Brabant
Belgian Province:	Antwerpen
link at:	Arendonk (Grens)

Like the HB, the Tramweg-Maatschappij "De Meijerij" was actually an amalgamation, on 7 January 1896, of two earlier companies. It ran three lines radiating from the industrial town of Eindhoven, north to 's Hertogenbosch, east to Helmond and south-west to the village of Reusel near the Belgian border. This was completed to Reusel (Grens) 30 June 1897, public service starting the following day. Here it met the SNCV Turnhout - Arendonk line, which had been opened in stages, the final portion to Arendonk (Grens) being constructed in 1894. There was apparently no direct passenger link but trams from Eindhoven and Turnhout provided connections to cross border travellers and through goods services worked from 1898 to at least 1914. The Dutch company went over to buses between 1930 and 1935, goods ceasing in 1937. The Belgian line withdrew to its original terminus at Arendonk Dorp following regauging after World War 1.

company:	*Centrale Limburgsche Spoorweg Maatschappij (CLS)*; from 1921 *Limburgsche Tramweg-Maatschappij (LTM)*
situation:	Limburg (Netherlands)
Belgian province:	Limburg
links at:	Kessenich (Grens)

This company was founded on 28 August 1912 with HQ at Roermond. It operated three metre gauge lines from Roermond, one being to Ittervoort (Grens), and linking at Kessenich with the SNCV line from Maaseik. This opened on 18 June 1915 but there was apparently no through passenger traffic. The CLS was taken over by the LTM in 1921 and the Ittervoort line closed early in 1935.

Transfer sidings at Sluis: on the left an SNCV wagon; on the right SBM vans. 1931
(the late KE Hartley)

Appendix 6: Brief Notes on other Urban Tram Systems in Belgium and their links to the SNCV.

We must confess to having thought long and hard about including this appendix at all. The histories of the individual non-SNCV urban tramways in Belgium are so convoluted and spread over such a long period that any attempt to summarise them risks being either inaccurate in detail or so broad as to be almost a caricature. On the whole however, it seemed worthwhile to try and at least present a broad picture of how they developed in relation to the SNCV. Those wanting detailed information will have to refer to the specialist publications in French and Dutch.

Six cities in the country developed their own urban transport systems during the last quarter of the 19th Century. Interestingly all appear to have started in the same way by importing the concept of what was known universally in Europe as the "Chemin de Fer Americain" - the conventional horse tramway, with balcony-ended four-wheeled cars pulled by one or two horses (or mules) and running on some form of grooved rail track laid in the street. Steam traction was hardly considered outside Bruxelles and early routes were short and built, if not at random, at least in a disjointed fashion where potential was perceived for traffic. Railway station to the town square (originally Grand' Place in French, Grote Markt in Flemish) was a common option for obvious reasons but choice depended eventually on the ideas of the individual entrepreneurs and the willingness of individual communes. By the end of the century, electrification was a viable option where the municipality permitted and most systems developed into a fairly coherent network under a single operator during the next twenty years or so. Then, of course, came the advent of motor buses and the eventual decline of the tramways although three cities - Bruxelles, Antwerpen and Charleroi - saw potential for developing metro systems of one kind or another in the last quarter of the 20th Century. Of these, Bruxelles outgrew its tramway origins (although trams survived as such), Charleroi was cut short by economic decline and only Antwerpen really succeeded in the logical conversion of its existing tramway system.

City: Antwerpen.
Dates: 1873 - present
Gauge: metre

Discussions started in 1871, for three horse tramway lines, from rue Anselmo to Bassin de Kattendijk; at Berchem; and at Borgerhout. The concession was granted to *Felix Neurenberg & Cie*, the Berchem line being opened on 25 May 1873 and the other two a few weeks later. All these had feeble traffic and were considered very expensive by the locals. The next serious attempt was by the *SA du Tramway du Sud d'Anvers*, opening a route in the south of the city on 20 June 1875 and followed during the next ten years by the *Sté des Tramways Nationaux, the SA des Tramways Maritimes d'Anvers, the Tramways du Nord d'Anvers, the Tramways d'Anvers* and several others. It would appear that up to the end of the century anarchy reigned, not much helped by the SNCV which, as recorded in chapter 7, was busy organising country routes with steam traction. Something

clearly had to be done and, with municipal approval, the various companies came together as the *Compangnie Générale des Tramways d'Anvers (CGTA)*, unifying the various routes under an authorisation of 11 September 1901. The company proceeded to relay all lines to a common (metre) gauge and started electrification of the busiest routes... at which point early conservationist organisations started protesting - "we don't want unsightly wires and poles in our streets". Serious negotiations ensued, eventually conceding the right to electrify the main routes providing that various responsibilities - notably provision of street lighting - were accepted by the tramways company.

With one exception, the changeover was complete by late 1903 and the Cie Générale then proceeded over the next few years to extend many of its existing routes. As related in chapter 7, it also agreed with the SNCV to operate various country lines, for which it formed the *SA "Les Vicinaux Anversois"*. The subsequent links are described in chapter 7 and need not be repeated here but it should be said that the system suffered severely during the 1914-18 war and was reorganised when the VA surrendered its SNCV concessions at the beginning of 1921. The Cie Générale continued to expand its system during the 1920s although it also acquired, and developed, a road-bus subsidiary. The parent company, like many other utilities, also diversified its operations, hiving off the tramways into a subsidiary company, *SA Les Tramways d'Anvers*, from 1 January 1927 and experimenting with trolleybus routes from 1929 onward.

The system in general survived World War II but its concession expired at the end of 1945 and a provisional *"Tramways d'Anvers et Agglomeration"* (Tramwegen van Antwerpen en Omstreken, or TAO), combining private and public interests, took over until 1962; it was notable for introducing a series of PCC cars as a first step toward modernisation. From 1 January 1963, however, a public-private partnership took over as the *Maatschappij voor het Intercommunaal Vervoer te Antwerpen (MIVA)*. This organisation started serious modernisation of the whole system, changing less economic routes to bus operation and starting to convert the rest into what was effectively a light metro with much underground (cut-and-cover) trackage; this has never been entirely finished. As at 1990 MIVA was running some 80km of tramroutes and 172km of bus routes.

City: Bruxelles:
Dates: 1874 - present
gauge: 1,435mm

As befits a capital city with an extensive hinterland, the story of Bruxelles trams is very complex and this account no doubt oversimplifies it! There was a plethora of horse bus lines from the early 1840s onward and from 1864 various companies started bidding for CF Americains - including examples of that, apparently characteristic, American variant the deraillable (lit: de railable). This employed light track and equally light cars which could be switched off the track to get round obstacles or extend a run where track could not be laid. They were more accurately railable omnibuses, having a fifth wheel for steering and with the front wheels fitted with special tyres which ran in the groove of the tramway-type track. (Even Rudyard Kipling commented on the American equivalent, one of his equine characters the ex tram horse Muldoon being proud of the particular skill..."On de Belt line we don't reckon no horse wuth his keep 'less he kin switch de car off de track, run her round on de cobbles an' dump her in ag'in ahead o' de truck what's blockin' him".

town lines in 1872-73.

d) The same pair then founded the *Sté du Tramway des Faubourgs d'Ixelles - Etterbeek* which was running two suburban lines by July 1874.

Charleroi: a typical tram train of the TEPC in the SNCV era. 4W motor and 4-w trailers at a turning circle   (author)

A company known until 1880 as the *Cie Genérale de Tramways* and afterward as the *Cie Genérale des CF Economiques* had a network of these at one time but, as we shall see, converted to proper tramways in the mid 1880s. Initially there appear to have been four successful tramway concessionaires.

a) In 1866 Frederic Nyst, of Liége tramways fame, applied for a line in the north east from Schaerbeek to Bois de la Cambre. He did not build it but in 1868 the concession - for a 90 year period - was transferred to one William Morris, of the English-owned Morris & Sheldon Company. The Cie Morris opened a first section, from the Bois to Porte de Namur on 1 May 1869 and soon completed it to Porte de Schaerbeek. It was extended to Eglise Sté Marie in 1870 and on to Rue Teniers the following year. At the same period he opened a second line from Place Stephanie to Uccle in the south. An interesting fact of all these early lines is that separate agreements had to be made with each individual commune traversed and the concession details often varied.

b) An existing bus operator, the *Cie Vaucamps*, joined the fray in 1972, opening lines in the centre and west between the Nord and Midi stations and around the districts of Anderlecht and Laeken. The routes, conceded in Spring 1872, were from Midi via Nord to Laeken; from Place Liedts to St Gilles; from the Eglise de Laeken to Anderlecht. This company, it is said, also had an English origin, Vaucamps being their local director.

c) Messrs Gustave and Julien Becquet put in for concessions over the boulevards and the Quartier Leopold in 1872, transferring them, once successful, to a Brazil-based company, the *Cie Bresilienne*, which opened three cross-

All are noted as having very light and defective trackwork which was causing many problems and were basically stadard gauge (deraillables were nominally of 1147mm gauge but were changed to standard when converted).

We now come to the second stage which was, to some extent, a rationalisation and effectively guided future development into two operating groups. In 1874 a rather mysterious character named Simon Philippart founded the SA *"Les Tramways Bruxellois"* by an amalgamation of the Vaucamps and Morris companies on 23 December 1874. At that time, they were running five tram lines:

Schaerbeek - Bois de la Cambre:	(6.638km) - Morris
Uccle - Place Stephanie	(3.998km) - Morris
Place Liedts - St Gilles	(4.521km) - Vaucamps
Laeken - Midi	(5.292km) - Vaucamps
Laeken - Anderlecht	(7.553km) - Vaucamps

They also had six bus lines but over the next few years most of these were passed to other operators.

After a lot of machinations, the TB also took over the other two operators, running the Ixelles - Etterbeek one briefly from 15.10.79 until its closure in 1882 and the Cie Bresilienne from 9 March 1880. They carried on with experiments in steam traction started by both Vaucamps and Bresilienne and from 1894 began electrifying the lines with most traffic.

By 1894 two other operators had appeared upon the scene. These were the *Cie des CF a Voie Etroite de Bruxelles a Ixelles-Boendael*, whose relationships with the SNCV have been related in chapter 8, and the short-lived *Cie des Tramways de l'Est de Bruxelles* which opened its standard gauge line to Evère cemetry in 1883; its subsequent fate is recorded in chapter 8.

In 1899 the TB eventually bought up the Ixelles-Boendael, being granted a long-term concession to expire in 1945. It was then running 17 lines (12 ex TB; 5 ex IB) with a total of 80 route kilometres. There was also our old friend the *Cie Générale des CF Economiques* which, during the 1890s and early 1900s, was busily engaged in converting its derailable network into standard gauge tramways. It had already rebuilt the lines to Etangs-Noirs and Place Stephanie into horse tramways in the early 1890s and it electrified its system centred on Bourse from 1904 on, as under:

- Gare Rogier 26.11.04
- Pl Communal, Jette 28.12.04
- Pl Stephanie 04.04.05
- Etangs Noirs 11.05.05
- Stn de Koekelborg 12.10.05 & 02.11.06
- Pl St.Josse 30.10.09 (2.075km)
- Rue d'Enghien ?

(via Porte de Ninove)

The Etangs Noirs lines appears to have been extended to Berchem from 19.04.07 (or thereabouts).

Matters remained fairly stable until the 1914-18 war but then the whole network suffered considerably from the demands of the occupier. Many horses were requisitioned, equipment was used for military purposes including the transport of wounded and maintenance was reduced to a minimum. After the war there was a long period of recuperation, fully normal service not being restored until 1925. Unlike other companies, the TB tried to develop its system, introducing bogie trams and even some trolleybuses. It was, inevitably, hard hit by World War II. As in other cities a public-private partnership was instituted in 1946, leading eventually to the formation of the *Societé des Transports Intercommunaux de Bruxelles (STIB)* which thenceforth ran the city's public transport. It continued to develop the tramway system, introducing a new series of bogie cars based on the PCC design and later developing articulated vehicles. By the time the SNCV finally closed its last Bruxelles area line in 1978 the plans for a city metro, supported by the trams, were well under way and have continued to develop since then.

City: Charleroi.
Dates: 1882-1974
Gauge: 1435mm then metre

The *SA des CF Vicinaux Belges (CFB)* was formed in Bruxelles in 1881 to operate trams and light railways throughout Belgium. At Charleroi it started running a horse tram from Place Buisset via the rue de College to rue de Marcinelle in 1882 and the following year added a second line, from Gare du Sud to rue de l'Ecluse. It then extended the Ecluse line to the suburb of Gilly, using steam traction on the outer portion. During the next three years, other steam-worked suburban lines were added, toward Montigny-s-Sambre and Couillet, steam traction being extended inward to the Gare du Sud. All these lines were standard gauge.

After the SNCV appeared on the scene (see chapter 9) with four metre gauge routes which were electrified in 1900, the city fathers decided matters should be rationalised. The CFB routes to Gilly and Montigny were to be metre gauged and electrified, being reconceded to the Liége-Seraing company from 28 September 1903. The latter reopened the Gare du Sud - Gilly line on 4 July 1904 and, to operate its new possessions, formed the *SA des Tramways Electriques du Pays de Charleroi et Extensions*

(TEPC). This, in turn, took over responsibility for existing SNCV routes on a concessionary basis in 1904. In 1911, it extended the Gilly line for about 2km and took over the Couillet route from the LS. After the war the SNCV and TEPC had a brief cooperative venture on a route between Charleroi - Gilly - Chateaulineau but in 1923 the SNCV took back its routes. This did not faze the TEPC which continued to develop its urban network to a maximum of nine routes and some 27 route-km in the 1930s. It also operated buses from 1932-on.

After World War 2, buses steadily took over from the trams, a situation acknowledged in 1962 by a change of name to *Sté des Transports Intercommunaux de Charleroi (STIC)*. The last tram ran on 30 June 1974 but this was not the end. The STIC was charged with development of a light metro system in conjunction with the SNCV. This was an ambitious plan which was badly affected by deindustrialisation and by 1991, when our story ends, was in considerable disarray.

City: Gent
dates: 1873 -
gauge metre

There had been horse buses in Gent since the 1850s but the first horse tram appears to have started in 1873, running from the Koornmarkt to the Zuidstatie/Gare du Sud and to the Antwerpen, Brugge and Kortrijk gates of the old city. The operator appears to have been the municipality and, from 1886 on, also worked SNCV Capital 8 to Zomergem. In 1887, as recorded in chapter 6, the *Liége - Seraing company* and the *Cie Generalé des Railways à Voie Etroite* (an LS subsidiary) took over all these concessions on 13 August and ran them until 1898 when they founded the *SA des Tramways Electriques de Gand*, more commonly known by its Flemish title *Electrische Tram van Gent (ETG)*. This concern agreed to operate seven urban routes plus the SNCV lines to Zomergem (extended to Ursel) and Merelbeke and to relay and electrify the system - in the meantime introducing battery electric cars on some routes. These were not very successful but overhead electrification was and by the eve of World War I the urban system had expanded to 32km

As elsewhere the war was a difficult period but the system expanded again during the 1920s, a need to increase capacity leading to that characteristic Gent vehicle the 6-wheeled tramcar. By 1931, just before the ETG gave up the outer end of the Gent - Zomergen - Ursel line, its total length had increased to some 45km and at its maximum, in 1933 it controlled 53km of track. Inevitably, however, the road bus also made an appearance, two routes being in operation by 1939.

Again as elsewhere, the war put a temporary hold on expansion of bus routes and for a short time afterward the ETG flourished. 1953, however, saw the end of its formal concessions from the SNCV and from 1961 it operated under a series of short-term agreements as the *Maatschappij voor het Intercommunaal Vervoer te Gent (MIVG)* - as in Antwerpen representing both public and private interests. In 1955, however, the ETG had finally surrendered its last SNCV lease, for route S, and for the first time the bus network overtook the rail one. Road transport, both private and public increased until the tramways became something of an impediment and a move to set up a light metro was met with a hostile recept Despite the introduction of PCC bogie ca the tram kilometrage was down to 25km bought out all private interests in the o

City: Liége
dates: 1871 - 1971
gauge: TULE: 1435mm; LS: metre

Liége was different, if only because it was home to two of the very few private light railway companies in Belgium, the *CF d'Ans - Oreye* which ran a suburban route and the *Liége - Seraing* which had a busy commuter tramway in the heart of the conglomeration. Various bus routes were early on the scene and as the surrounding area developed with industrialisation they did too. From 1864 bids were invited for a tramway south from the main line station of Guillemins to the Coronmeuse district and in November 1871 The *Liége Tramways Company Ltd* was formed to build (of course) a CF Americain; the title was English because the company was London-based, under the direction of one James Marmont. To meet traffic requirements the four-wheeled cars were double-deckers with open tops. Everyone got very excited - especially the local press - and the Coronmeuse line was duly opened on 20 January 1872. A second line followed in June and a suburban one to Herstal in 1875. Shortly afterward the Liége Twys Co metamorphosed into a locally registered "Tramways Liégeois" but alas tragedy struck a few months later when a fierce storm demolished the depot and wrecked most of the fleet. The company was generally execrated for its poor services but even so there was clearly a need for more transport as the city spread. Two new lines, from Place St Lambert to Haut-Pré and to Cornillon were built by "*Frederic Nyst & Cie*" during the early 1880s, utlising steam traction because of steep gradients. They were followed in 1887, more efficiently, by the afore-mentioned *Cie des Railways Economiques de Liége - Seraing* which built a steam-worked tramway from Guillemins to Seraing and on to Jemeppe.

Not to be outdone, the Tramways Liégeois converted their Coronmeuse - Herstal - Grand Puits line to the new fangled electric traction from 9 August 1893 and this was followed two years later by a new electric tram between Rue Sté Veronique and Cointe, initially allocated to yet another entrpreneur, one Paul Schmitz. There was some attempt at rationalisation, F Nyst & Cie disappearing into the maw of the *Tramway Est-Ouest de Liége* in 1898. There followed an orgy of extension and electrifcation by all the competing companies. The municipality made some efforts at unification, in particular supporting the Tramways Liégeois which became the *Tramways Communaux de Liégeois* in 1905. The various reseaux then developed more or less steadily - except for the war period - until 1927 when the TCL and the Est-Ouest company were amalgamated to form the *Tramways Unifies de Liége et Extensions (TULE)*, taking over the Schmitz concession two years later. This organisation was granted a concession to expire in 1960, at the same time as that of the only other major operator, the Liége - Seraing. At its maximum about 1930 the TULE had some 68km and the LS 21km of line.

The Cointe line, almost "au bout d'usure" was replaced by a trolleybus in 1930 and, from then on, new routes were either ̓uses ̓ ̓fter the 1939-45 war, road buses; the first of ̓ ̓e fleet in 1952. As elsewhere, the ending of ̓ions in 1960 was followed first by

Bruxelles: A (then modern) standard gauge bogie car of the STIB on mixed gauge track on the northern suburbs in 1974   (Author)

reorganisation of the RELSE and TULE and then by mergher and a period of public-private administration under the title *Societé des Transports Intercommunaux de la Region Liégeoise (STIL)* confirmed as a permanent body in 1964. The trams declined bit by bit, the old TULE routes transferring to the road from 31 August 1964 and the Liége-Seraing from November 1967. The trolleybuses followed, the last one running at the end of 1971.

City: Verviers
Dates: 1884 - 1969
gauge: metre

The Verviers network, for once, was blessedly simple but then Verviers was a fairly small town to have a tramway of its own. Although the railway reached it in 1843, it was not until the early 1880s that the municipality decided on provision of a CF Americain. The *Sté des Tramways Vervietois* was founded in November 1883 and the first two lines were opened on 1 July 1884, one from Verviers (Renoupré) to Ensival (5.878km) and the other from Verviers (Harmonie) to Dison (3.074km). Extensions, however, meant climbing steep gradients and the council was not over-happy about steam in the streets. It decided on electricity, the TV converting the existing lines from 13 March 1900 and opening a new one to Heusy on the same date. In the next few years further lines followed - from Dison up to Petit-Rechain in 1903; from Harmonie to Stembert and to Ma Campagne in 1907 and one from Verviers (place Verte) to Place Vieuxtemps the same year. Several other routes and extensions followed as the town developed, progress being interrupted only by the 1914-18 war with its troubles; the TV's relations with the SNCV are noted in Chapter 10 At its maximum just after World War II, the system covered 23.605km, mostly of double track. Alas, buses appeared in 1956 and steadily took over the main routes. The TV became the *Societé Vervietoise des Transports en Commun (SVTC)* in 1961 and the following year became the *Societé des Transports Intercommunaux de l'Agglomeration Vervietoise*. The remaining tram system closed at the end of 1969.

Appendix 7: trilingual dictionary of common terms

English	French	Flemish
authorised	autorisé	verleend
avenue	avenue	laan
battle zone	champ de bataille	slag veld
beach/bathingplace	plage	strand/badplaats
bow collector	archet	beugel
branch	troncon	aftakking
bridge(s)	pont(s)	brug(gen)
Capital	Capital	Kapitaal
closed	fermé	gesloten/buitendienst
closure	fermeture	afschaffing
company	societé	maatschappij
concessionary	concessionnaire	pachter
depot	depot	stelplaats/remise
district/commune	commune	gemeente
double track	double voie	dubbel spoor
electric tramcar	tram electrique	elektrische tram
extension	extension	uitbreiding
gate (of town)	porte	poort
goods/freight	marchandises	goederen
halt/stop	halte/arrêt	stilstand/halte
horse tram	tram à cheval	paardetram
junction	bifurcation	splitsing
light railway	CF vicinal	buurtspoorweg
main square	grand place	grote markt
network/system	réseau	net
occupied territory	zone occupée	bezette gebied
opened(for traffic)	ouverte	in gebruik genomen
operation	exploitation	dienst/uitbating
pantograph	pantograph	pantograaf
passenger	voyageur	reiziger
paved street	chaussée	steenweg
private company	societé anonyme (SA)	naamloze vennootschap (NV) or naamloze maatschappij(NM)
railcar (non-elect)	autorail	spoorauto
railway	chemin de fer	spoorweg (lijn)
river	fleuve	rivier
royal decree	arrête royal	koninklijk besluit
section (of line)	troncon	baanvak
single track	voie simple	enkel spoor
square (in town)	place	plein/plaats
station	gare	station
steam locomotive	locomotive a vapeur	stoom locomotief
street/road	rue	straat
terminus	terminus	eindpunt
town service	service urbain	stadsdienst
track	voie	spoor
trailer	remorque	bijwagen/aanhangwagen
tram-train	train	tramstel
trolley-pole	trolley	trolley
waiting room	salle d'attente	wachtzaal
war	guerre	oorlog
year	année	jaar

NOTES: Some of the Walloon French terms may differ from those used in France.

Appendix 8: glossary of French/Flemish place names

In French order

French	Flemish
Aeltre	Aalter
Aerschot	Aarschot
Alost	Aalst
Anvers	Antwerpen
Arlon	Aarlen
Assche	Asse
Ath	Aat
Audenarde	Oudenaarde
Bassenge	Bitsingen
Bastogne	Bastenaken
Beauvechain	Bevekom
Bourg-Leopold	Leopoldsburg
Braine-l. Alleud	Eigenbrakel
Braine-le-Comte	's Gravenbrakel
Bruges	Brugge
Bruxelles	Brussel
Coursel	Koersel
Courtrai	Kortrijk
Deynze	Deinze
Dixmude	Diksmuide
Enghien	Edingen
Furnes	Veurne
Gand	Gent
Gembloux	Gembloers
Grammont	Geraardsbergen
Grez-Doiceau	Graven
Gros Tilleul	Dikke Linde
Haecht	Haacht
Hainaut	Henegouwen
Hal	Halle
Herck-la-Ville	Herk-de-Stad
Heysel	Heizel
Heyst	Heist
Jodoigne	Geldenaken
Knocke	Knokke
l'Ecluse	Sluis
La Calamine	Kelmis
La Panne	De Panne
La Roue	Het Rad
Lanaeken	Lanaken
Le Coq	De Haan
Le Vert Chasseur	GroeneJager
Liége	Luik
Lierre	Lier
Lille (France)	Rijssel (Frankrijk)
Louvain	Leuven
Malines	Mechelen
Menin	Menen
Mons	Bergen
Mont St-Jean	St-Jansberg
Montaigu	Scherpenheuvel
Mouscron	Moeskroen
Namur	Namen
Neuve Eglise	Nieuwkerke
Nieuport	Nieuwpoort
Ostende	Oostende
Overyssche	Overijse
Petite Espinette	Klein Hut
Rebecq-Rognon	Roosbeek
Rhode-St-Genese	St-Genesius-Rode
Roulers	Roeselare
Schaerbeek	Schaarbeek
St-Croix	St-Kruis
St-Nicolas	St-Niklaas
St- Trond	St-Truiden
Swevezeele	Zwevezele
Tamise	Temse
Termonde	Dendermonde
Thielt	Tielt
Thielt Notre-Dame	OLV Tielt
Tirlemont	Tienen
Tongres	Tongeren
Tournai	Doornik
Tronchiennes	Drongen
Waremme	Borgworm
Warneton	Waasten
Wavre	Waver
Weert St-Georges	St-Joris-Weert
Wihogne	Nudorp
Winghe St-Georges	St-Joris-Winge
Ypres	Ieper

In Flemish order

Flemish	French
Aalst	Alost
Aalter	Aeltre
Aarlen	Arlon
Aarschot	Aerschot
Aat	Ath
Antwerpen	Anvers
Asse	Assche
Bastenaken	Bastogne
Bergen	Mons
Bevekom	Beauvechain
Bitsingen	Bassenge
Borgworm	Waremme
Brugge	Bruges
Brussel	Bruxelles
De Haan	Le Coq
De Panne	La Panne
Deinze	Deynze
Dendermonde	Termonde
Dikke Linde	Gros Tilleul
Diksmuide	Dixmude
Doornik	Tournai
Drongen	Tronchiennes
Edingen	Enghien
Eigenbrakel	Braine-rAlleud
Geldenaken	Jodoigne
Gembloers	Gembloux
Gent	Gand
Geraardsbergen	Grammont
Graven	Grez-Doiceau
Groene Jager	Le Vert Chasseur
Haacht	Haecht
Halle	Hal
Heist	Heyst
Heizel	Heysel
Henegouwen	Hainaut
Herk-de-Stad	Herck-la-Ville
Het Rad	La Roue
Ieper	Ypres
Kelmis	La Calamine
Klein Hut	Petite Espinette
Knokke	Knocke
Koersel	Coursel
Kortrijk	Courtrai
Lanaken	Lanaeken
Leopoldsburg	Bourg-Leopold
Leuven	Louvain
Lier	Lierre
Luik	Liége
Mechelen	Malines
Menen	Menin
Moeskroen	Mouscron
Namen	Namur
Nieuwkerke	Neuve Eglise
Nieuwpoort	Nieuport
Nudorp	Wihogne
OLV Tielt	Thielt Notre-Dame
Oostende	Ostende
Oudenaarde	Audenarde
Overijse	Overyssche
Rijssel (Frankrijk)	Lille (France)
Roeselare	Roulers
Roosebeek	Rebecq-Rognon
's Gravenbrakel	Braine-le-Comte
Schaarbeek	Schaerbeek
Scherpenheuvel	Montaigu
Sluis	l'Ecluse
St-Genesius-Rode	Rhode-St-Genese
St-Jansberg	Mont St-Jean
St-Joris-Weert	Weert-St-Georges
St-Joris-Winge	Winghe-St-Georges
St-Kruis	St-Croix
St-Niklaas	St-Nicolas
St-Truiden	St-Trond
Temse	Tamise
Tielt	Thielt
Tienen	Tirlemont
Tongeren	Tongres
Veurne	Furnes
Waasten	Warneton
Waver	Wavre
Zwevezele	Swevezeele

Select Bibliography (historical & geographic sources)

SNCV:

* Annual reports 1885-on
* Nos Vicinaux (house journal of the SNCV)
* Central records, including plans , photographs and general statistics
* SNCV Working Regulations
* SNCV Manuel du Mecanicien
* SNCV Cinquentieme Anniversaire 1884-1934. SNCV 1934
* Paper given by Leon Jacobs, Directeur General SNCV, to conference in 1937
* Series of regional pamphlets edited by SNCV 1946
* Les Vicinaux Pendant la Guerre (extrait de la Revue Genéralé , Belge No 14 - December 1946
* Avancez s.v.p. (cent ans d'histoire vicinale en Belgique. SNCV 1985
* Documentation on the proposed light metro system at Charleroi. 1984
* Connaisez Vous La Societé Nationale des Chemins de Fer Vicinaux, 1957
* Various published timetables including those for 1945 and Expo 58.

General sources

* Reports by Her Majesty's Representatives Abroad on Light Railways, with appendices, 1894
* Light Railways. JC Mackay, Crosby, Lockwood 1896
* Light Railways at Home & Abroad, WH Cole, London 1898
* Light Railways, their rise & decline. WJK Davies, Ian Allan, 1964
* Histoire des Tramways et Vicinaux Belges. J Demelle, Paullegrain. n/d
* 100 Years of the Belgian Vicinal 1885-1985. WJK Davies, LRTA 1985
* unpublished notes and reminiscences from the late Ingenieur Debot.

Some regional references:

* Les Chemins de Fer Vicinaux dans la Province de Brabant. Assn Ferroviaire des Cheminots de Charleroi, Blanchart et Cie, 2000.
* Aux Trams Citoyens......series of photo albums in progress
* De Buurtspoorwegen in de Provincie... Jos Neyens, author, 1977-on. - series of short histories on provincial systems
* Les Tramways au Pays de Liége. E Fellingue et al, GTF Liége, 1976-77
* Rollend materieel bij de Buurtspoorwegen 1885-91, J Block, Blanchart et Cie, Brussel, 1997
* De la Vapeur au GLT, R Van Vlaenderen, G Blanchart et Cie 1991
* Strassenbahnen im Aachener Dreilandereck, K Herberholz, ALBA 1980.

Periodicals

Modern Tramway - LRTA/Ian Allan
Presence du Tramway - AMUTRA
Voie Etroite - APPEVA
Chemins de Fer Regionaux et Urbains - FACS
La Vie du Rail
Rail et Traction
Tramway Touristique de l'Aisne - various guides and monographs

A view of Schepdaal museum in the 1960s, with preserved stock: The electric cars are: 9073 as rebuilt withclosed
ends; M19 in original condition; 9314 (Manage) as restored.   (AMUTRA)

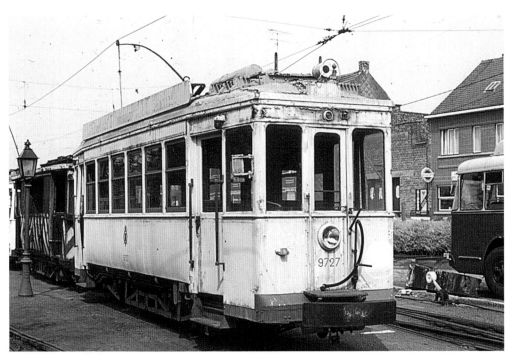

"Seneffe" type car 9727
awaiting restoration 1965 at
Schepdaal.   (WJK Davies)

*Type 11 standard gauge
locomotive 801 at Poulseur,
1965.   (WJK Davies)*

*Preserved Type 18 steam
locomotive at Blier, on the
Tramway Touristique de
l'Aisne in 1966.
    (W J K Davies)*

*Type 7 heavy goods locomotive
as preserved.   (AMUTRA)*

The classic view of a railcar and open trailers in front of the church at Han-s-Lesse (SA des Grottes de Han)

ART 159 shunts on the street track that was the former terminus at Han-sur-Lesse. (M R Taplin)

standard 4-wheeled railcar AR 193 as preserved with a typical reconstructed trailer. (AMUTRA)

S 10186, seen approaching Charleroi Sud in February 1975, is paired with 19724, created in 1974 as one of the de-motored post-war cars. *(M. R. Taplin)*

By 1983 the SJ cars were in service, rebuilt from S for pre-métro service, to supplement the new articulated trams. 9172 leaves the new tram station at Charleroi Sud. *(M. R. Taplin)*

BN 6151 accelerates up the ramp from Charleroi Sud to the pre-métro in May 1983. (M. R. Taplin)

The 1911 Wemmel depot in February 1975, with its usual stock of N cars, was also the terminus of line W from Brussel-Nord. (M. R. Taplin)

A typical suburban terminus in later years. Wemmel on the northern lines from Bruxelles (WJK Davies)

A typical view of a single N-class tramcar in suburban surroundings in Bruxelles. (WJK Davies)

Wooden bodied standard 9817 is at the Kortrijk (Courtrai) terminus of the latterly isolated line KM from Moeskroen (Mouscron). The car behind is 9752 on an LRTL special that ran on 21st April 1962 (John Laker)

On the evening of 28th September 1963, steel bodied standard 10332 pulling a trailer, is heading back to Place Rouppe in Brussels from Waterloo. The Mont St. Jean Waterloo Memorial is in the background. At this location the Wavre route joins the Waterloo route .(John Laker)

In April 1969 this coastal train of SO 9943 and trailer 19679 was waiting in the sand dunes at the former western terminus of the line at De Panne (the line is since extended to Adinkerke).

(M. R. Taplin)

On 16 July 1985 Oostende was the scene of Vicinal centenary celebrations, with freshly-painted baggage tram 9965 from Schepdael museum hauling a pair of restored A trailers. (R. N. H. Jones)

Also in the Oostende parade on 16 July 1985 was 9985, one of the 1932-33 wooden standards supplied by Ateliers de Braine-le-Compte, which still makes outings on the coastal line on special occasions. *(R. N. H. Jones)*

The coastal tramway serves the popular racecourse west of Oostende and meetings bring many extra passengers to the line. This BN tram, at Marie-Joseplein on a 2 barré short working between Westende and Oostende, was decorated with a racing theme to promote the course. (W. J. Wyse)

The ASVi museum group could originally run its preserved cars all the way from Anderlues to Thuin, until road widening destroyed much of the tramway alignment. In March 1985 two-axle tram 9888 of 1932 is seen with older hauled stock at Anderlues depot, having survived as a works car after its brothers were scrapped.
(R. N. H. Jones)

10498, seen at Anderlues in 1968, was one of the N cars built for Brussel–Leuven in the late 1950s, and rebuilt in the early 1960s as four-motor S cars for Charleroi.
(M. R. Taplin)

The retrieval of a PCC from Beograd (Belgrade) was a major achievement for the ASVi, permitting scenes such as this pairing of BN 6116 and PCC 101409 at Anderlues in July 1988.
(W. J. Wyse)

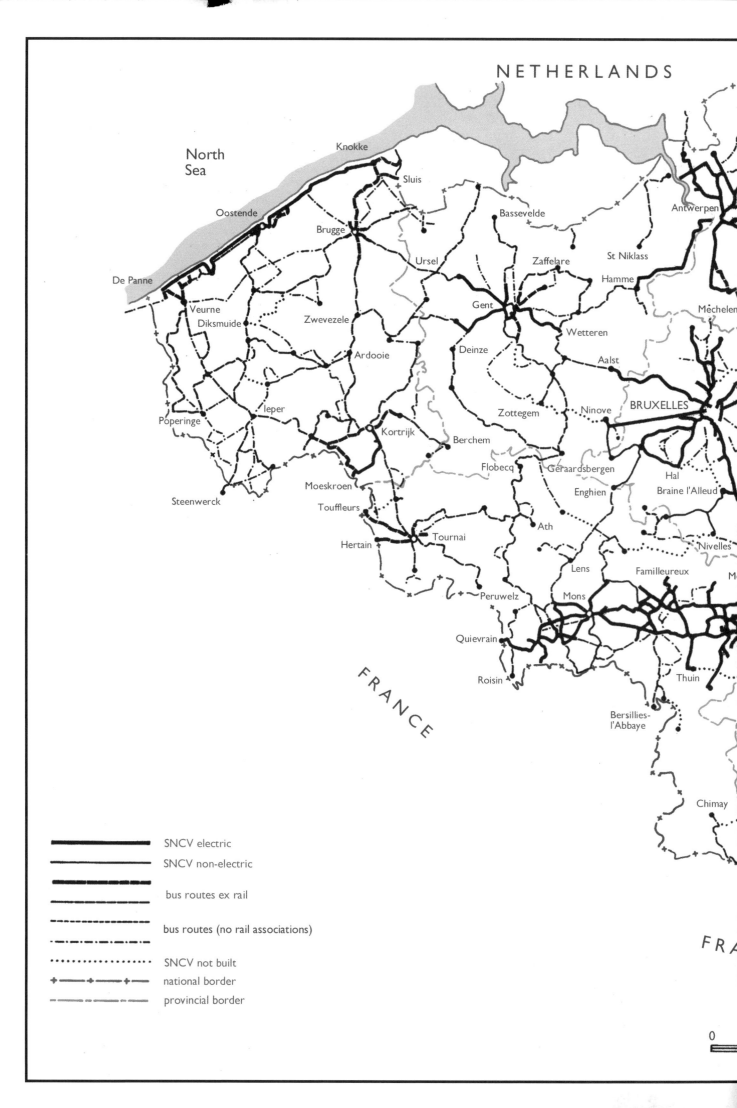

NETHERLANDS

North
Sea

Knokke

Sluis

Oostende

Bassevelde

Antwerpen

Brugge

Ursel

Zaffelare

St Niklass

De Panne

Hamme

Veurne

Mechelen

Diksmuide

Zwevezele

Gent

Wetteren

Ardooie

Deinze

Aalst

Ieper

Zottegem

Ninove

BRUXELLES

Poperinge

Kortrijk

Berchem

Flobecq

Geraardsbergen

Hal

Steenwerck

Moeskroen

Enghien

Braine l'Alleud

Touffleurs

Ath

Tournai

Nivelles

Hertain

Lens

Familleureux

Peruwelz

Mons

Quievrain

Roisin

Thuin

FRANCE

Bersillies-
l'Abbaye

Chimay

FRA

SNCV electric

SNCV non-electric

bus routes ex rail

bus routes (no rail associations)

SNCV not built

+ — + — + —   national border

provincial border

0